W9-BNK-486

Mentor in a Manual
Climbing the Academic Ladder to Tenure

Mentor in a Manual
Climbing the Academic Ladder to Tenure

A. Clay Schoenfeld
Robert Magnan

Second Edition

Magna Publications, Inc.
2718 Dryden Drive
Madison, WI   53704-3086

Mentor in a Manual: Climbing the Academic Ladder to Tenure
Clarence A. Schoenfeld, Robert Magnan
Second Edition

Cover design by Tamara L. Cook
Interior design by Darcy Kamps

Magna Publications
2718 Dryden Drive
Madison, WI 53704-3086
608/246-3580

Library of Congress Cataloging in Publication Data
Schoenfeld, Clay, 1918-
    Mentor in a manual : climbing the academic ladder to tenure / A. Clay Schoenfeld, Robert Magnan.—2nd ed.
      p.   cm.
    Includes bibliographical references and index.
    ISBN 0-912150-34-3 (hc) : $39.95.—ISBN 0-912150-35-1 (pb) : $31.95
    1. College teachers—Tenure—United States—Handbooks, manuals, etc.   I. Magnan, Robert. II. Title.
LB2335.7.S36 1994
378.1'22—DC20   94-38177
                                                                CIP

Published by Magna Publications, Inc., 2718 Dryden Drive, Madison, WI 53704-3086.
608/246-3580.

CONTENTS

FOREWORD

An American institution of higher education is not so much a set of buildings and grounds, or a hierarchy of administrators, or even a body of students as it is a community of individual scholars engaged in instruction, investigation, and interpretation in areas of their own academic expertise.

It is the perpetual task of each such community to recruit and nurture a steady flow of new members—and, yes, to screen out those who lack the necessary qualities of mind and heart.

As an issue of the Pew Higher Education Research Program's *Policy Perspectives* noted a few years ago: "The peer review process that lies at the heart of [academe] in this country has proven substantially more effective . . . than the programs of self-assessment existing in other professions."

For each newly appointed assistant professor, then, the path to ultimate acceptance as a full-fledged member of a community of scholars—to that award known as tenure—can be daunting. Yet navigating it successfully is essential not only to the personal and professional well-being of the individual aspirant, but to the recharging of an institution's batteries, and in a larger sense as an assurance to society as a whole that its colleges and universities are in a constant state of renewal and reinvigoration and responsibility to the greater community.

So, any sound, effective field manual or guidebook for new faculty can be an invaluable resource, indeed. That is the objective of this book and, on the whole, it succeeds admirably. Because our institutions of higher education are so disparate in their traditions, missions, and aspirations, not everything in this book can be universally applicable or even acceptable. But, to the extent that it is possible, this guide to climbing the academic ladder to tenure does its job tenaciously and with a minimum of cant.

I am particularly pleased that the authors not only present the essentials of acquiring a professorial state of mind but also deal in refreshing frankness with the pragmatic "politics" of assimilation into the basic unit of most institutions, the academic department.

Befitting the current national emphasis on strengthening undergraduate instruction, the authors offer three very strong chapters on the central role of a professor as teacher, outlining tested, student-focused strategies and tactics.

Solid chapters on research and on service sketch out the depth and breadth of a beginning professors's tripartite responsibilities.

To the extent that appearing periodically in appropriate journals is a measure of scholarly accomplishment, faculty seeking promotion to tenure will also find of special value the chapters related to getting published.

A final chapter treats in a definitive manner how a candidate for tenure might best present his or her credentials for that final peer review.

An Appendix—"What Do I Do if I Don't Make Tenure?"—deals sympathetically and helpfully with ways to turn a major disappointment into a challenge.

Yet this is no oversimplified "cookbook." It raises a new assistant professor's sights above the building blocks of career planning and professional development to the higher elevations of institutional ethos and public expectations.

I have known the senior author for some 40 years, so I can testify personally to his sensitivity and acumen in and about the halls of academe. As the editor of several newsletters and books for personnel in higher education, the junior author is alike most qualified. Their writing is eminently readable and practical, with wit and style.

If I had a son or daughter about to embark on a career in higher education, this is a book I would recommend strongly. In fact, I'd probably buy a copy for ceremonial presentation.

Allan W. Ostar, President Emeritus,
American Association of State Colleges and Universities

PREFACE

What **is** academic tenure, anyway, and **why**?

Tenure is intended to preserve and enhance an institution of higher education's excellence and its function in developing the human intellect. Tenure contributes to this objective by giving a strong measure of security and protection to faculty members; it frees them to teach, inquire, create, publish, and serve with less concern for the immediate popularity or acceptability of their efforts than would be the case if termination of employment were a constant possibility.

The granting of academic tenure represents a long-term commitment of institutional resources which requires proof of excellence in past performance and a forecast that an individual faculty member's intellectual vitality and contributions will continue to be of high quality for many years to come. There is no entitlement to tenure based upon a record that is merely competent and satisfactory for a prescribed period of time.

Most institutions grant tenure in part through an evaluation of the candidate by his or her colleagues—called "peer review"—not by arbitrary administrative decisions or through outside influence.

Academic tenure has evolved from the right of students to learn, untrammeled by constraints on professional teaching and research that may stem from internal or external political pressures, from the right of the public to an effective campus faculty quality-control mechanism, from the need of faculty for a level of economic security, and from the need of an institution for a striving, stable staff.

In the political and economic security it provides its recipients, academic tenure is somewhat analogous to seniority in a union labor force, to no-fire status in municipal, state, or federal civil service, or to a commission as a "regular" in the armed forces. But academic tenure is qualitatively different in that it cannot be earned by merely serving time, by passing a single exam, by attending a particular academy, or by taking an oath. It is the culmination of a dynamic process of trial and assessment.

Academic tenure has a tenuous basis at best in statutory civil law and has only limited protection in case law, but its inscription in institutional rules and regulations gives it powerful credibility. It is "policed", if that's the right word, by the academic community through the moral suasion of the American Association of University Professors and the practice of that society to "blacklist" institutions violating tenure principles, although the courts as well are increasingly willing to look at instances of an apparent breakdown in institutional due process.

The policing system has some holes. There's scarcely an issue of *The Chronicle of Higher Education*, but what you can read in its Faculty Notes section about reports that "five professors say their college violated their rights by dismissing them for 'insubordination,'" that "six professors have filed a $100,000 lawsuit charging they were forced out of their contracts by conservative political activists," that "faculty-union members have voted no confidence in the university president because he failed to address faculty evaluation concerns," or that "a state legislature is contemplating a law that would permit independent panels of experts from other institutions to handle grievances based on sex or race discrimination."

Academic tenure is not immutable. A professor can abrogate the "contract" through gross incompetence or moral turpitude, and an institution can void tenure under dire fiscal exigency. That such situations have been rare does not make them any less likely in the future.

Nor is tenure automatically transferable from one institution to another. It is campus-specific; indeed, on any particular campus, it is usually department- or division-specific.

To be sure, not everyone is a tenure fan. A 1986 Carnegie Foundation for the Advancement of Teaching national survey identified significant pockets of vocal campus disenchantment with the tenure system. More recently, a distinguished historian/provost emeritus has called for "a more humane and sensible system of tenure [before it] inflicts what may turn out to be fatal wounds on higher education."

Not long ago, the chair of the North Carolina University System Board of Governors called for a review of tenure principles and policies in all 16 System institutions. And an editorial in *The Wall Street Journal* fulminated that "the fact remains that the notion of jobs-for-life creates adverse performance incentives. Tenured performance tends toward the mean, with no pressure to innovate or do better." Writing in *The Chronicle of Higher Education* about "why scholars should give up the tenured status they hold so dear," a University of Michigan English professor pronounced that "departments that are fully or nearly 'tenured in' frequently experience intellectual arteriosclerosis." Early in 1994, Richard P. Chait, a university professor of higher education management, even came up with suggestions of how boards of trustees might create incentives for faculty to forsake a tenure policy that trustees see as "an outmoded, unnecessary, and counterproductive privilege of the professoriate".

Such reservations notwithstanding, academic tenure is among the most prized and honored of professional awards by both campus citizens and the public at large. It is the ultimate rite of passage from acolyte to academe, pursued with diligence by legions of assistant professors seeking promotion to associate professor and concomitant anointment as "tenured."

To the North Carolina System Board of Governors, James Peacock, Kenan professor of anthropology at the flagship University of North Carolina at Chapel Hill, delivered a defense of tenure that summarizes its strengths and its challenge:

> Tenure is not easy to get. It is not, as one journalist puts it, 'a smooth rail for the gravy train'. It is a long and challenging road. . . .Evaluation of the candidate for tenure is serious and thorough. Hours and days are

spent reading and reviewing research contributions. Teaching is reviewed extensively. . . .The basic reason tenure is bestowed is to preserve freedom for highly trained and capable people to do their best
work, to protect them from inappropriate political pressures. . . .Evalu-
ation does not cease with tenure. Tenured faculty are reviewed at
mandated intervals and also annually to determine what kind of raise,
if any, they will recieve. . . .Incontrovertibly, most faculty achieve more
recognition after tenure than before—locally and nationally, for research, teaching, and service.

In penultimate words from a specialist in higher education law,
Oscar Ruebhausen: "One compelling constant characterizes
higher education in America—the maintenance of academic freedom and a system of academic tenure as a means to assure such
freedom."

**How does an assistant professor earn tenure? Answering
that question is the mission of this book.**

Given the wide variance among institutions of higher education
in the United States, the authors have had to be something less
than utterly specific in trying to provide answers, but the advice
they offer should be applicable in most situations. Since both authors
have, "been through the wars," so to speak, and have conducted
extensive conversations on the subject with faculty and administrators of all ranks country-wide, what they say is at least as
concrete and practical as it is possible to render what is essentially
intangible.

Since the first edition of this book was written in 1991, the
literature of higher education research has been considerably en-
riched by the publication of several studies addressing directly the
ecology, so to speak, of new faculty members. Hence this second
edition is illuminated by frequent references to the works of such
scholars as Ann E. Austin, Robert Boice, Robert Diamond, Donald
K. Jarvis, Mary Deane Sorcinelli, and others representing the relatively new field of faculty development.

On a more personal level, this second edition profits from very
helpful assistance and/or review on the part of these colleagues
around the country:

Ira Baldwin, *University of Wisconsin-Madison*
James Bell, *Virginia Polytechnic Institute and State University*
Hallie Lou Blum, *George Washington University*
Scott Cutlip, *University of Georgia*

John Disinger, *Ohio State University*
Mavis Donahue, *University of Illinois at Chicago*
Ralph Frasca, *University of Northern Iowa*
William Feyerharm, *Kansas State University*
Laurie Golson, *independent textbook developer, Lake Bluff, IL*
Robert J. Griffin, *Marquette University*
William H. Haight Jr., *Michigan State University, retired*
John C. Hendee, *University of Idaho*
Virginia S. Hinshaw, *University of Wisconsin-Madison*
Susan M. Johnson, *Memphis State University*
John Knox, *University of Wisconsin-Madison*
Sally Sieloff Magnan, *University of Wisconsin-Madison*
Howard Mancing, *Purdue University*
Ann McElaney-Johnson, *Ripon College*
Robert F. Meier, *Iowa State University*
Dayle Molen, *California State University-Fresno*
Marjorie Moore, *College of St. Catherine*
Penny Morgan, *University of Idaho*
Robert M. O'Neil, *University of Virginia*
Allan W. Ostar, *American Association of State Colleges and Universities*
Jane Peters, *University of Kentucky*
Laurence M. Porter, *Michigan State University*
Carl Reidel, *University of Vermont*
Benjamin Rifkin, *University of Wisconsin-Madison*
Carolyn Saarni, *Sonoma State University*
Harland Samson, *University of Wisconsin-Madison*
Alan T. Seagren, *University of Nebraska*
Marie A. Wunsch, *University of Wisconsin System*
Donald Zillman, *University of Southern Maine*

But for any lapses in omission or commission, the authors take full responsibility.

ACS
RM

Madison, Wisconsin
August 1994

1 ACQUIRING A PROFESSIONAL FRAME OF MIND

You might expect we'd begin this manual with some practical tips on that bottom-line requirement—publishing in lieu of perishing. No, that comes later. Initially here we propose to confront you with a sort of philosophical issue: **Do you really understand what being a professor is all about? Are you sure you're deeply committed to pursuing a career in academia?** Only *you* can know deep in your heart whether you're a worthy candidate to enter the professoriate.

For a decade or so, on this campus or that, as student and perhaps as junior staff, you've been exposed to a process of socialization. That you have chosen to strive to join the elect *may* be an indication of your devotion to a life in higher education. But are you in fact of a suitable frame of mind?

A PITFALL AND A PRESCRIPTION

Most newly appointed assistant professors have a general idea what being a professor is all about, or at least what they think it entails. But since there's no West Point for professors, real training for the assignment comes from being in the assignment. So they learn from role models and from making their own mistakes.

The focus of assistant professor training is quite properly on what a professor does. Unfortunately in some cases that's where it tends to stop—just this side of what new faculty need to know each morning to get the day's job done. But you must go on from there to thinking and learning about what a professor is and should be.

Do you have a clear sense of yourself as an academic person with opportunities and responsibilities that are unique in American life? Or do you plod along day to day, working hard and developing essential skills, yet still missing a critical step: developing a feeling for how your growing confidence and competence relate to the essence of what a professor is meant to be?

An antidote: To gain a vision of yourself to be, to acquire a much richer image of yourself as a member of the professoriate, steep yourself in the literature of higher learning in America—classic histories and interpretations, chronicles of more recent developments, the current crop of somewhat acerbic commentators on the academic scene. (See "Suggested Readings" in Appendix B.)

And, of course, perform a weekly scan of *The Chronicle of Higher Education* and a periodic look at such national periodicals as *Change, Academe, AAHE Bulletin, Academic Leader, The Teaching Professor, The Journal of Higher Education,* and *Lingua Franca.*

WEIGHING THE PROFESSORIATE IN THE BALANCE

From your readings in the literature of higher education, you'll gain insights that will broaden your perspective. For one thing, you'll appreciate anew that while we're sometimes inclined to speak of America's "system" of higher education, there is in fact no system, unless a kaleidoscope can be said to constitute a system, so diverse are our colleges and universities in their traditions, circumstances, and aspirations. Nor are they, individually or collectively, so self-assured about the nature of their functions and policies as their promotional brochures might suggest.

So, diverse issues—pervasive, perennial, or passing—are constantly surfacing on the agenda of the professorate.

The point being that, as with any profession, the professoriate is neither so complete in all respects, without defect or omission, sound, nor so flawless that you need swallow it whole. Rather, make it your objective to search out those institutional attributes that are admirable, that command your respect, and give them your wholehearted support—and to identify those characteristics less than admirable and seek to help bring about constructive change.

To paraphrase Carl Schurz, 19th-century German immigrant become American educator/soldier/statesman: "My profession, right or wrong. When right, to be kept right. When wrong, to be set right."

In short, whenever, wherever you join, you will find the professoriate, like any calling, a mixed bag.

FORTUNATE ATTRIBUTES

The professoriate is at home in an enterprise unalterably dedicated as are few others to *the public weal*. In exchange for an outpouring of appropriations, higher education in America seeks to be a servant, not a master.

As individuals, professors represent scholarly attainment and love of learning. *Merit*, not *pull,* governs their promotions. Creativity and curiosity, not aggrandizement, motivate them.

The professoriate is devoted to *the life of the mind*, pledged to defend a climate in which free thought and unconstrained inquiry can flourish, to the benefit of students in particular and humanity in general.

To a degree the lay public doesn't appreciate, the professoriate on any particular campus is *a self-governing body*. Chief executive officers of institutions of higher education who haven't translated their thoughts into faculty thoughts and infused faculty sentiments into their own acts tend to be relatively powerless. No campus reform movement can sustain itself with which the tenor of the faculty isn't in sympathy.

No more rewarding *challenge* blesses any profession than to hold in its hands the young minds of the country—to fill, to shape, to stimulate, to teach—and in turn to be challenged. And no other profession gets such an automatic annual recharge of new enthusiasm with each fresh influx of bright, questioning students, undergraduate and graduate—a veritable fountain of youth.

The *intellectual resources* of the professoriate are tremendous. Like a seed whose germination requires only favorable soil and water, professors ask only for an environment that will foster the growth of their understanding and the application of their skills and insights—plus a living wage.

The professoriate is marked, as are few other callings, by *high standards* of initiative and honor. The academic life is a good life. The qualities it demands are fortitude, integrity, self-restraint, personal loyalty to others, compassion, and altruism.

The power and the glory of a college or university are in its faculty, and the most distinguished institutions are distinguished by the quality of the men and women they have been able to recruit and retain—able teachers working with eager students, probing investigators expanding our knowledge, outreach specialists carrying light and learning to every corner of a commonwealth, linking soil and seminar.

Speaking in more precise terms in 1994, C. Peter Magrath[1] of the National Association of State Universities and Land Grant Colleges said:

> Far more recognition needs to be given to the incredible success of American higher education, not as a mantra, but as a fact of life as measured in the research productivity and accomplishments of our universities, by our being an export industry generating $6 billion a year through the international students we attract, by our great contributions to America's economic and competitive strength, and by the sheer scope and volume of the efforts we have made to bring higher education to millions of Americans of all ages and circumstances.

A distinguished commission supported by four foundations may have said it all:

> As a group, and at their best, colleges and universities play a critical, and probably unique, role in establishing the quality of American life.

> Institutions of higher learning serve as one of the key storehouses of knowledge, understanding, and cultural values in our society, and they carry responsibility for developing new knowledge and providing the intellectual leadership needed for the rigorous examination of existing learning so that even better understanding may be achieved . . . . Teaching and research programs serve society in several ways. In providing education, they are society's servants. In continuously looking for new and better ways of doing things, they are society's critics. In addition, academic institutions also serve as a 'conscience' for society and as a stimulus for appropriate change.[2]

This is good company. You can spend your whole life in it with sure satisfaction.

The performance of public duty alone does not make a good life, of course; there is also the pursuit of private excellence. Both are to be found for the seeking in the academic life.

It gives much and takes more, enriching freely anyone prepared to give more than he or she can get, at least in terms of monetary rewards.

To paraphrase Stanford's professor of public service, John W. Gardner, a career in higher education isn't a mountain that has a summit. Nor is it a game that has a final score. A career in higher education is *an endless unfolding* and—if you wish it to be—an endless process of self-discovery, an endless and unpredictable dialogue between your own potentialities and the life situations in which you find yourself.

By "potentialities" Gardner means "not just intellectual gifts but the full range of your capacities for learning, teaching, sensing, wondering, investigating, serving, loving, inspiring."

All this is not to say the professoriate is a roundtable of intellectual collegiality. Like any profession, it has its flip side.

FLAWED CHARACTERISTICS

Some professors seemingly have an innate tendency toward *mental eccentricity and exhibitionism*. As higher education critic Carl Becker once remarked, "A professor is a person who thinks otherwise." All this is well and good provided it doesn't lead to an attitude of indifference to the fact that professors can't divorce themselves from their association with an institution. As a Yale Committee of Ten told their colleagues, "The public is bound to look upon you *as* the university," for good and ill.

Some professors, as well, have a bent toward *jousting with windmills*, "for an endless capacity for nonsense on stilts," as a recent *New York Times* editorial put it—too inclined to fight at the drop of a hat over fancied restrictions on their freedom or invasions of their privacy, meanwhile imposing on their students a level of restraint on speech and conduct the professors would never tolerate for themselves.[3,4]

No matter how liberal and progressive some professors may be as individuals, collectively they lean toward *conservatism*. It's been well said that it's easier to move a cemetery than a faculty curriculum committee. After trying to get fellow scholars excited about switching to research on consequences of global environmental change, Professor Richard A. Berk, UCLA sociology chair, recently complained they were "too slow-moving and timid." As former Modern Language Association executive director William D. Schaefer writes in *Education Without Compromise*, "The faculties of most colleges and universities have an extraordinary capacity to resist [curricular] change. [They] love to play at the margins, . . . making only minor cosmetic adjustments."[5]

In too many cases, *over-specialization* is a curse of the professoriate—to be consumed by highly differentiated subject matter, to be absorbed in departmental concerns, to place the interests of a divisional unit ruthlessly above the interests of the campus as a whole—all at the expense of a more inclusive frame of mind. In his recent book, *Killing the Spirit: Higher Education in America*, the noted American historian and emeritus provost of the University of California at Santa Cruz, Page Smith, criticizes over-specialization by summoning testimony: "As disciplines become increasingly technical, they tend to devolve into competing sub-groups scarcely able to communicate with each other." And "Members of a modern college faculty sometimes strike one, in an Emersonian phrase, as a collection of 'infinitely repellent particles.' "[6]

Witness the short, unhappy life, for example, of the American Association for the Advancement of the Humanities. Even with nearly 60,000 faculty members teaching humanities courses in colleges and universities, the AAAH was able to attract only 3,000 dues-paying members, and folded after just three years (1979-

1982) because, as its founder and chair admitted, "individual humanists have failed to develop a sense of their collective interest." In his *The Moral Collapse of the University*, Bruce Wilshire describes a "balkanized" university formed around disciplines who won't—indeed, can't—communicate with each other: "The only thing holding the university together is the central heating system."[7]

For an unwillingness to assume responsibility for *lack of attention to the teaching problems* in their fields, Ernest L. Boyer, president of the Carnegie Foundation for the Advancement of Teaching, has recently called on professors to redefine scholarship to include "the integration, application, and teaching" of knowledge as well as its "discovery"—and that the faculty reward system be reformed thereby. Schaefer admits that the humanists, for one group, "continue to stress the less important—dissemination in print, over the most important—dissemination in the classroom."

This denigration of professors as teachers has in recent years practically taken on the dimensions of a Greek chorus. In a biting assessment in 1993, a panel of college presidents and leading citizens chided faculty for neglecting undergraduate education:

> Among today's college graduates are too many whose intellectual depth and breadth are unimpressive, and too many who whose skills are inadequate in the face of the demands of contemporary life. . . . Much too frequently, American higher education now offers a smorgasbord of fanciful courses in a fragmented curriculum that affords as much credit for 'Introduction to Tennis' and for courses in pop culture as it does for 'Principles of English Composition,' history, or physics. . . . Colleges should tailor their programs—curriculum, schedules, support services, office hours—to meet the needs of the students they admit, not the convenience of staff and faculty.

In response, C. Peter Magrath, who we quoted so fulsomely a page or two ago, had to admit that "at times elements of higher education have acted arrogantly and unwisely. . . . as universities pursue glamorous, financially enticing research rewards and other opportunities, to the neglect of the undergraduate student as a learner."

Then there are some of what distinguished bacteriologist become university president E.B. Fred called *"pebble-pickers"* in research—those who become so immersed in details and methods that they identify those details and methods as productive scholarship in themselves, who mistake volume of data for true achievement. Smith concurs, stating that:

> The vast majority of so-called research turned out in the modern university is worthless. . . . It is dispiriting; it depresses the whole academic enterprise. . . . It robs the student. . .of the thoughtful and considerate attention of a teacher . . . unequivocally committed to teaching." In some instances, professors have even learned—in graduate school, no less—to fudge their data.[9]

Add the *"bean counters"* who try always to assess the degree to which things "count" toward salary raises and promotions. How does chairing a divisional committee count, compared with completing a research paper? Does it count to handle the local arrangements for a professional meeting? Does it count to offer to teach the course of an ill colleague? Faculty who are continually engaged in a utilitarian calculus for everything they do—who always ask, "What's in it for me?"—display the very antithesis of a professional orientation in which one does what one does because that's what professors do, not in order to impress a chair or a dean.

Collegiality is not necessarily a hallmark of professors. Despite a recent movement to encourage the "mentoring" of new hires by senior staff, three psychologists examining mentoring in actual practice have found that many departments continue to apply a form of social Darwinism which we could paraphrase as: "Let's throw the kids off the end of the pier and see whether they can swim or not. **We** didn't get any survival advice; why should **they**?"[10] As Schaefer confesses from his experience as a vice chancellor:

> Otherwise well-intentioned members of a campus personnel committee can reach tenure decisions without having seen, much less talked to, the candidate. If we were to begin feeding deep, deep upon their peerless eyes, trusting, at times, to our intuition in appraising an individual's worth, we might have to rely, or rely less frequently, on the printed word.

Besides ignoring their colleagues, there are some professors who not only *dodge the knife-and-fork circuit* but belittle those willing to act as ambassadors to the public—performing the essential and never-ending task of explaining the need of our institutions of higher education for "funds, freedom, and freshmen," to use the alliterative phrase of Professor Scott Cutlip, personification of university public relations.

The professoriate by and large acquiesces in the institutional struggle to raise ever more money for new programs, research, scholarships, named chairs, new buildings—a struggle that can force colleges and universities to *adapt to priorities* established by foundations, government agencies, corporations, and private donors. Far from living in an ivory tower, the professoriate is influenced too much rather than too little by the outside world, says President Emeritus Derek Bok of Harvard in his book, *Universities and the Future of America*, and it is "precisely this influence that accounts for failure of academia to respond better to urgent societal needs."[11]

Bok goes on to say that academic leaders are so burdened with fund-raising and other administrative duties they fail to convey a "compelling vision" of higher education. But even when they do, faculty fail to respond to those visions, says one of their own, Richard Chait, University of Maryland at College Park professor of higher education. The reason why, he says, is because "the majority of the faculty are deliberately and delightfully oblivious to the president's dreams," so immersed are they in their own *private worlds* of "courses, classes, research programs," and campus governance. "Presidential visions influence faculty work," he claims, "about as much as political party platforms shape the day-to-day decisions of government agencies."[12]

According to at least one critic, the professoriate is to blame for inventing and nurturing *a system of academic tenure* that has "inflicted what may turn out to be fatal wounds on higher education": the mandatory research criterion "does not result in any measurable benefit to anybody or anything"; the requisite "debilitating" promotion and tenure committee reviews "take literally uncounted faculty hours" and stress the nerves of candidates and families "filled with dread or resignation"; resulting decisions are often "highly questionable or blatantly unfair." Unsuccessful candidates are cast out in disgrace and with fractured self-esteem. Once safe in the tenure womb, associate professors can revert to a fetal position, never to be heard from again except for an occasional tremor, to paraphrase Smith.

Today the most serious flaw of the professoriate may be the safe harbor it can offer buccaneers who pledge allegiance only to an international guild of academic pirates or to the sources of their research money, who talk to their colleagues only en route to airports, meanwhile turning over their classes to teaching assistants who've never had so much as an hour of pedagogical training. It's these *peripatetic professors* who can leave open a campus door to a breed of amoral administrators who play fast and loose with the ethics of higher education. A recent result has been what national wire service education writer Anthony Flint calls "a crisis in public confidence—the ivory tower under siege," in consequence of a concatenation of flagrant abuses of public trust by personnel at some of America's most prestigious institutions.[13]

In his July 1991 inaugural address, University of Maryland System Chancellor Donald L. Langenberg told how things were going to be for higher education in the '90's:

> America's colleges and universities. . . .have rested for too long on our well-earned laurels. . . . Our self-satisfaction is exceeded only by our slowness to recognize that we have neglected the most central aspects of our enterprise, we have ignored our obligations to our most important clients. . . . We are coming to 'the end of sanctuary' for higher education, the end of a time in which American colleges and universities were sheltered from the cold winds that buffeted other institutions. Today, American higher education can be expected to be subjected to the same critical scrutiny and demands for accountability that all other institutions face.

Next door in Washington, DC, a newspaper commentary headlined "The Low State of Higher Ed," Robert J. Samuelson[14] exercised some of that critical scrutiny:

> Higher education is not a bastion of excellence. It is shot through with waste, lax academic standards, and mediocre teaching and educating. Higher education is bloated. Too many professors do too little teaching to too many ill-prepared students. . . . Professors are socialized to publish, to spend as little time in the classroom as possible. . . . Administrators created the mess and are its largest beneficiaries as empire builders.

ATTAINING AN EQUILIBRIUM

As you try to arrive at a personal assessment of what others see as the fortunate attributes or the flawed characteristics of the profession you are joining, be aware that the stance that you take may have a profound effect on how you conduct yourself in your calling.

For example, one commentator on this book used our own term of "pebble-picking" to degrade our "analysis of the ills of academia." He would have us, rather, "focus on power and money and away from education as part of a larger culture of academia as an institution with the same ossification and corruption as, say, IBM and General Motors." It's hard to see how such a person can be a happy campus camper.

On the other hand, another commentator said she was "sick and tired to see your carping criticisms that are both uncalled for and incorrect." For evidence, she cited a national survey by the UCLA Higher Education Research Institute that found "the professional goals noted as essential or very important by college and university faculty members to be headed by: 98.2%, 'be a good teacher,' and 80%, 'be a good colleague.'" A person with such a rose-tinted viewpoint could be in for an occasional disillusionment.

Manifestly, your own report card on higher education may come to reflect in some degree whom you talk to or how well you read the fine print. For example, one of the more caustic current critiques of academe is that of Julius Getman, *In the Company of Scholars: The Struggle for the Soul of Higher Education* (Austin: University of Texas Press, 1992). The author is a peripatetic professor of law who has taught at five universities, all in a vain attempt to escape his "sense of disappointment and alienation" with his perception of what higher education in America has become today. In the course of his highly personal reflections, Professor Getman rehearses a litany of campus issues: the pervasive conflict between teaching and research, threats to academic freedom, the impact of feminist activism, the struggle over multiculturalism, tensions between youth and age, the politics of promotion to tenure. Yet he cannot help but end on an upbeat note in his final words: "A salute to the love and affection that our best teachers and scholars inspire in their students and colleagues."

What, then, should be your own perspective on the site of your endeavors? Probably the soundest strategy is simply to be your own person, seeking your own equilibrium, and then let the chips fall where they may. That stance may or may not help you achieve tenure, but you'll retain your self-respect and strength of character. If you want our own assessment, for what it's worth, we believe the equities tilt on the side of the fortunate attributes of the professoriate and that a state of mind that sees the glass as half full is the healthier for a person striving for a lifelong campus career.

THE CONSUMMATE CANDIDATE

In your continuing socialization as a candidate for tenure, you are free as in few other professions to adopt or reject qualities of your calling, to mold your own vision of the professional you can be—provided you give your vision a 360-degree traverse.

You're not a castaway on an island. Put yourself in the context of higher education in general and of your institution in particular—rooted in the past, responding to the present, revealing the future. Appreciate your responsibilities for reinforcing such internal emphases as teaching and research, and understand your obligations to be in touch with the needs of the larger community through public service. Match the demands of today against the lessons of yesterday and the potentials of tomorrow. Seek both a diversity of culture and a "university" of thought.

Above all, see your institution as an integrated organism, with a spirit and a heart and a will that transcend the purposes of its separate parts and link it to the world, an institution that needs only a caring professoriate to enter new frontiers of educational excellence and public support as American life and American learning proceed together toward broader lands and fairer days.

Now if all that sounds to you like what they used to call "corny," so be it. Read on, please.

PREPARING TO BE A PROFESSIONAL

PERVASIVE ISSUES FACING THE PROFESSORIATE

Academicians like to make 'problems' out of problems. As Robert M. Hutchins, then chancellor of the University of Chicago, defined the distinction: "A real problem is a confusion about the aim and destiny of the institution. A 'problem' is a difficulty in the material order."

Put another way, a strategist asks, "Where should I go?" while a tactician asks, "How do I get there?" Hence government agencies speak of "goals" and "objectives."

An example: In 1862, the Congress of the United States made a monumental strategic, *what-where* decision, that higher education was not to be solely for the well-to-do or for those going into the learned professions but for "the industrial and agricultural classes" as well, and in the enabling Morrill Act allocated grants of public domain lands to each of the states to fund the establishment of (hence) land-grant colleges. The *how* was left up to the states. The result changed the face of higher learning in America.

Problems and 'problems' are still with us, and presenting them as dichotomies does not clarify. In fact, dichotomies tend to be mutually supporting or contradictory.

From your background reading, in your selection of role models, as you acquire a broader perspective, and as you cogitate about the dimensions of your chosen profession, you'll recognize that the professor you will become will have to grapple with a congeries—a "collection of things or parts mixed together"—of problems and 'problems,' of academic issues not limited to your discipline alone but endemic to higher education.

How better to prepare for the professoriate than to begin to confront some of those issues now?

We've compiled a list of questions and issues you may face as a newcomer to the professoriate. In researching what issues to pose here, we've drawn on the thoughts of: a professor of higher education in a large state university, the president of a foundation for the advancement of education, an emeritus president of an Ivy League university, the chair of social studies in a community college, a lawyer specializing in the ethics of higher education, an education writer for a premier daily newspaper, a professor and dean of a graduate school in a fine arts institute, a national campus trends survey conducted by a leading academic organization, current articles in a higher education weekly, a distinguished scientist, a recent recipient of an award for excellent teaching, a director of outreach for a midsize institution, a trustee, a West Coast historian/provost, a business executive, a congressional aide, and our own experience and observations. The resulting list is indeed a congeries; we've run all the questions together in the thought you may find it fun to try to decipher who phrased what.

Questions to ponder:

? How can adequate financial support be ensured in an era of uncertain economic conditions?

? If fiscal resources decline, how can we recruit and retain quality faculty, particularly in competitive disciplines?

? How can facilities renovation and renewal needs be met simultaneously with constructing new buildings?

? Can or should we address the growing enrollment differences between public and independent institutions?

? Can we maintain a desirable diversity among colleges and universities without perpetuating undesirable inequality and hierarchy? What is the public interest in private education?

? To what extent do administratively imposed measures of accountability and productivity represent a *bona fide* threat to cherished faculty autonomy?

? To what extent is the total quality management (TQM) concept applicable to higher education?

? How can the commitments of higher education to fairness and equality best be reconciled with requirements for efficiency, quality control, and value judgments?

? Is it morally permitted or required for colleges and universities to go beyond race-blind and gender-blind standards in encouraging the prospects of minorities and women? If so, which "quotas" are permissible and which are not?

? What should be the faculty role in achieving academic respectability and fiscal honesty in intercollegiate athletic programs?

? How are we in academe to recapture our moral and intellectual equilibrium from the academic fundamentalists and their schemes of orthodoxies?

? Can a more humane and sensible system of tenure be worked out? Or should the whole system be abandoned?

? What theories of human nature and the human mind will guide higher education in the future?

? Can we truly think critically and self-critically? To what end?

? How will we balance a sense of community and our heterogeneities?

? Can we correct historic injustices without unwittingly creating new ones?

? How can departments implement the recommendations of the Association of American Colleges that the undergraduate advising system undergo major reforms, as outlined in the 1991 report, "Liberal Learning and the Arts and Sciences Major"?

? How can institutions engage more closely the outside world and not succumb to its blandishments, its distractions, its corrupting entanglements?

? What should be the focus of undergraduate instruction—the liberal arts that cultivate a learning life, or professional courses that impart skills in how to earn a living? Whatever the decision, what are the relative merits of a required core curriculum versus a cafeteria of electives?

? How should the need to develop fully the talents of the most able students be weighed against the claims of less able and disadvantaged students for special support?

? What are a college's optimum strategies for preparing students for useful roles in the constituent community, as well as for roles in an increasingly global marketplace?

? Should the faculty reward system focus on the discovery of new knowledge or can it recognize as well the integrators and interpreters of knowledge? In that reward system, should an emphasis be on *equality* (treating everyone the same) or on *equity* (treating everyone fairly but differently)? How can newer fields of interdisciplinary study be accommodated among traditionally defined disciplines?

? What level of institutional resources is properly allocated to serving the needs of adult citizens in the community?

? What relationship should exist between the contributions of higher education to the economic well-being of the country and to its non-economic aims?

? Is there an optimum balance within the trilogy of teaching/research/ service? Who is to decide? What level of voice should be granted to faculty, students, alumni, trustees, administrators, governments?

? Why are our campuses slow to research and teach their own ethical behavior in the face of national press coverage of falsification of scientific research data, renewed racism on campus, expressions of bigotry by student publications, a seemingly endless chain of sanctions by the NCAA for major rule infractions, tuition and price-fixing, allegations of admissions quotas for targeted ethnic groups, actual or perceived abuse of institutional resources by presidents for personal gain, collusion on setting limits on financial aid, cavalier handling of federal research dollars, and so on? What is an individual professor to make of or do about all this?

? And perhaps the most compelling issue of all: What can you personally do to help stem the decline in public and governmental confidence that makes securing adequate resources one of higher education's major challenges today, in the eyes of college and university trustees.[15]

To this list you can undoubtedly add problems and 'problems' that have surfaced since these lines were composed—agenda-setting for the professoriate being a very dynamic process.

Whichever of these ideas seem the more relevant to you, begin confronting them now, as we've suggested. The more time you devote to profound academic issues, the more sure your professional sense of direction becomes.

On the other hand, if macro-issues appear intimidating at this stage of your career, you can identify micro-issues that will intrigue you.

PERSONAL ISSUES: RESEARCH

If we put research issues before issues of teaching and service, it's only because surveys have shown that faculty reward systems generally prize research over teaching and service.

? Should campus research emphasize investigating basic phenomena or applying research to solving practical problems? Or is this an unreal dichotomy? To what extent do federal and foundation funds skew the support of productive scholarship in the sciences, the social sciences, the humanities?

? Why is it that what Rachel Carson did for the environment, Ralph Nader for consumers, Michael Harrington for the poor, Betty Friedan for women, they did as independent critics, not as faculty? Why is it that the seminal work on the plight of blacks in America was written by a Swedish social scientist, not by an American professor?

? What truth is there to the traditional tenure threat, publish or perish? How are things changing—in word only, or in reward as well?

? How can faculty focus on *progress* in their research, not just *publication*? How can this be documented in tenure dossiers?

? Why do you publish your research results? To reach a few specialists? To share knowledge with a wider audience, to promote cross-disciplinary understanding? Do you choose prestigious journals or periodicals that provide for wider circulation but fewer 'prestige points'. Are there publications in your field that allow you the best of both worlds?

? Can a flood of "mediocre monographs for the sake of promotion" be dammed, or the profusion of journals for the same purpose be reduced to a readable number?

? With the emphasis that many departments place on publication credits, how can faculty who participate in collaborative research make sure they receive proper credit for their efforts?

? In working with senior colleagues, how do you benefit from their expertise, experience, and influence without letting your contributions be eclipsed?

? In working with graduate students and post-doc research assistants, how do you share credit without risking charges of exploitation?

? How do you produce the most articles out of your research without giving colleagues in your department or outside in your field the impression that you are overextended, more published than productive?

? Since journals often take many months to accept or reject submissions, how do you make the most of the few years before you come up for tenure? That is, how do you balance accepted publication ethics and practical concerns?

PERSONAL ISSUES: SERVICE

Issues of service generally receive the least attention in most departments, although the importance of service varies widely from discipline to discipline. Consider the remarks published recently by Ernest L. Boyer,[16] president of the Carnegie Foundation for the Advancement of Teaching:

> I'm concerned that . . . higher educations's historic commitment to service seems to have diminshed. I'm troubled that many now view the campus as a place where professors get tenured and students get credentialed. . . . And what I find most disturbing is the growing feeling

in this country that higher education is a *private* benefit, not a *public* good. . . .

The mission statement of almost every college and university in the country includes not just teaching and research, but service, too—a commitment that was never more needed than it is today.

? What are the rewards and risks in your department for new faculty who "connect with constituent communities?" Expressed more bluntly, how do your colleagues view specialists who can communicate and work with lay publics?

? What do you have to offer to people outside academia? How should you connect with these communitites?

? How can you benefit from your professional expertise and skills without risking the appearance of conflict of interest? What policies at your institution would apply to your situation?

? How can you document your service activities in order to derive the greatest benefit from them in terms of your tenure dossier?

PERSONAL ISSUES: TEACHING

Whatever else you're doing in academia, you'll be doing at least some teaching and, given the current focus on undergraduate teaching problems and opportunities, you won't be able to duck issues pertaining to college teaching.

Professor Peter Frederick[17] of Wabash College (IN) has compiled a list of challenging "questions for collegial conversations about teaching":

? What are the essential questions of your discipline? What are the irreducibly most significant basic facts, ideas, concepts, themes, and requisite skills your students must know? What in your course do they *have* to know, as distinct from what they can live without?

? What are your teaching goals? What's primary and what secondary? What do you want your students to know? to think? to be able to do? What knowledge, skills, and attitudes to have?

? What do you know about your students? Can you describe them? How do they learn? What kind of learning styles and cultural diversity exists in your class? What do your students already know about your course subject? How do you acknowledge their prior knowledge and experience?

? What do you know about yourself? your teaching style? What are your thoughts? How do you teach best? In what ways do you want to stretch yourself and expand your strategies as a teacher?

? Where are you in your course right now? What did you do last week? Yesterday? How did it go? What are your students learning? What are they having trouble with? How do you know?

? What about tomorrow's class? What are you going to do, and why? How can you connect your goals for tomorrow to what you know is already in your students' heads and hearts? How can you connect the epistemology of your field to a strategy for teaching the topic, text, or content for tomorrow's class?

? What does your class have to do with the departmental mission? the institutional mission? What kind of persons do you and your institution want your students, your graduates, to be? What does your course have to do with the kind of person/professional *you* want to be?

? Given all this, what are you going to do in class tomorrow, and why?

Academic issues, you see, are all around you for the confronting. It's the mark of the professional to face them head on.

THE SOCIOLOGY OF NEW FACULTY

Of all the issues facing you, the one most personal and pertinent at this stage of the game may well be, "Where am I in relation to the world of new faculty everywhere?"

Hence, of all the background reading you might do at this juncture, one resource we would recommend is *The New Faculty Member* (San Francisco: Jossey-Bass, 1992) by Robert Boice, professor of psychology and director of the Faculty Support Office at the State University of New York, Stony Brook. Boice has spent many years researching the life and times of new hires, and his book can be a compendium of consolation and inspiration for all such.

Wandering Lonely as a Cloud. In reading Boice, you will discover at the outset that new faculty he interviewed in depth at the midpoints in their first semester at four representative institutions "accentuated feelings of loneliness and of intellectual understimulation: Loneliness was new faculty's most salient complaint, one with clear precedence over the next most common types of concerns—of workloads and busyness."

So if you're feeling all alone, you aren't really.

In their loneliness, Boice finds that new faculty worry most about and work hardest at three common obstacles: teaching, writing, and collegiality. "New faculty," Boice writes, "often suppose that mastery of one of the three is difficult and that mastery of all of them is miraculous. My own observations of new faculty suggest that success at any one of the three activities rarely comes in isolation from success in the other two."

Hitting the Ground Running. In each cohort of the new faculty he studied, Boice found that some individuals stood out as exemplary. He calls them the "quick starters." From his examination of these quick starters, Boice has distilled four common attributes they share—each of them "a matter of mastering elementary things." Acquainting you with those four attributes here and now will serve as an admirable introduction to the substance of this guide.

Involvement. Quick starters proactively immerse themselves in the campus community. They ask colleagues for help and advice. They arrange collaborations for conducting research projects, for writing grant proposals, for coauthoring manuscripts for publication. They seek tips on teaching. They ask colleagues to guest lecture in their classes and they reciprocate. They get to know students, particularly laboratory assistants.

Regimen. Quick starters manage their time to include writing and social networking. They believe that the real challenge is task management. By limiting periods of involvement in such activities as class preparation, they find time, usually about an hour per weekday, for visits, phone calls, and memos. As their own displays of busyness drop away, they notice that then colleagues seek them out more readily.

Self-management. Quick starters have an instinct for what Boice calls "tacit knowledge"—knowledge so basic nobody would think to impart it—balance among chores, proactivity in establishing rapport, a spontaneous style of taking risks (for example, seeking communications with superstars in their disciplinary specialties).

Social Networking. Quick starters actively counter loneliness by seeking collegial involvement, if only in a faculty fitness club. As Boice writes, "they relax the usual proud autonomy so often characteristic of new faculty so that colleagues can assist as coteachers, as coauthors, and as mentors. It means, as the popular literature on excellence puts it, moving past independence to interdependence."

As you might guess, Boice, being a professor, has deduced from these data-driven attributes a theory of the basic skills of academic success. His **IRSS** theory, which runs as a red thread through his book, can serve well any new faculty member climbing the academic ladder to tenure.[18]

For much more on hitting the ground running, see Chapters 2 and 3.

AND NOW LET'S TALK
HARD-BALL DOLLARS AND SENSE

The moment you make tenure, society (in the guise of a state legislature or an institutional endowment fund) sets aside an interest-bearing annuity of some three-quarters to a million dollars with which to fund your annual salary and fringe benefits for a 35- to 40-year period of active duty plus another 10 to 15 years in retirement. That's no small change.

To qualify for society's investment on that scale in your academic career of a lifetime, you ought to be willing to make an appropriate financial investment of your own now:

- A professional library of books and serials.
- Computer hardware and software.
- Travel to conferences, and fees and accommodations there.
- Travel to and lodging at research sites.
- Summers spent working in laboratory, library, or field in lieu of vacation.

- Physical work space and facilities at home.
- A certain level of obligatory entertaining.
- Learned society dues.
- Frequent transportation to and from campus.
- Parking and/or shuttle bus fees.

And so on and on. The "laundry list" can be extensive—and shocking to an erstwhile graduate student used to a comparatively free ride.

"When my wife was starting on the tenure trail," the junior author (RM) recalls, "we had to get used to spending for association dues, journal subscriptions, travel, conference registration, and so forth—really tough after grad school years. But it's now a different game, with different rules and different rewards."

A not-so-minor reward is the fact that expenses that can be legitimately and directly attributable to the requirements of professional advancement are tax-deductible, provided you keep detailed records and use the long IRS form. For a savvy guide on the subject, consult *Tax Guide for College Teachers and Other College Personnel* (College Park MD: Academic Information Service, published annually).

But the massive payoff for your commitment of time, talent, energy, and money as a candidate for tenure is that massive lifetime annuity at the end of the rainbow.

And yet if your obsession with work is so overwhelming that you lose a slice of life and love in the bargain, it won't be worth it. As one commentator puts it, "By all means urge attention to family, significant others during the tenure process. I've seen quite a few lives torn apart during the tenure chase, partly because the assistant professor forgot to thank people."

AND SO, ON TO THE RACES

"All right," we can hear you saying, "enough of this frame-of-mind stuff. You may have helped raise my sights, but you haven't intimidated me. I'm still set on climbing the ladder to tenure and becoming all I can be as a professor. So let's get on with it."

OK, for starters, here's a once-over-lightly socialization guide for your next six years:[19]

YOUR FOUR LEARNING OBJECTIVES

1. Knowledge. Information, data, theories, concepts, facts. Answers the question: *"What should I know?"* May be achieved through many learning methods. Highly perishable in this age of information/research.

2. Skills. Abilities that can be developed and manifested in performance, not merely in potential. Answers the question: *"What should I be able to do?"* Includes technical, scientific, communication, information retrieval, analysis, and synthesis skills.

3. Insights. Ideas and thoughts derived internally from an ability to see and understand clearly the nature of things. A necessary part of making judgments, of "putting it all together," of "being aware" of wisdom, farsightedness. Answers the questions: *"What does this mean? What is important in this situation?"* Can't be taught directly, but can be induced by qualified mentors and by learning from mistakes.

4. Values. Convictions, fundamental beliefs, standards governing behavior. Includes attitudes toward professional hallmarks such as duty, integrity, loyalty, public service, objectivity. Answers the questions: *"What do I believe? Where and when do I draw the line?"* Values, like insights, can only be derived by *you* if they're to have any meaning.

OBITER DICTA

In preparing to be a professional, harken to these complimentary words of counsel from two senior professors, each of whom has served as a dean:

First. This is a generic manual, that is, one not unique to a specific institution. While what you will be reading summarizes the common wisdom, and general pitfalls relevant to the achievement of tenure, any assistant professor who actually thinks that any generic prescription might ensure him or her tenure is probably too naive to survive in academia. The generic suggestions herein may not apply in all situations. There are other items of required reading as well—department, college, and university tenure and promotion documents; the faculty handbook; the annual report of the faculty grievance committee; the texts of recent statements about tenure and promotion by deans and the provost—indigenous sources that address the specific decision, and decision-makers, on a particular candidate. The best use of this manual is probably as a 'text' for interactions between the assistant professor and his or her local mentor—a senior professor who is willing to work with and capable of advising that new colleague. We can't stress enough the value of a faculty mentor.

Second. Tenure decisions are much more than adding up teaching, research, and service points and how much each of these is measured and evaluated. The slavish reader could let this manual take the texture out of the process and smooth everything too much. The process is much rougher than the manual may suggest. The process is tough not just because the consequences are so important for the candidate; they are also important for the institution in all its divisions. That is one reason why tenure and promotion documents are vague. The actual decision involves more of a *gestalt* than just the sum total of individual costs and benefits on a curriculum vitae. Tenure is a single outcome that tries to capture a multiplicity of considerations.

This opening chapter has presented you with a lot of important questions. We hope that the rest of this manual will help you find at least a few answers—as well as provoke many other important questions.

NOTES

1. Peter C. Magrath, "Perspective," *NASULGC Newsline* Feb. 1994.

2. Commission on Colleges and Universities, *Pension and Retirement Policies in Colleges and Universities* (San Francisco: Jossey-Bass, 1990).

3. John Leo, "Our Misguided Thought Police," *U.S. News & World Report* 8 Apr. 1991: 25.

4. Robert G. Sands, L. Alayne Parson, and Josann Duane, "Faculty Monitoring Faculty in a Public University," *The Journal of Higher Education* Mar.–Apr. 1991: 174-193.

5. William D. Schaefer, *Education without Compromise: From Chaos to Coherence in Higher Education* (San Francisco: Jossey-Bass, 1990).

6. Page Smith, *Killing the Spirit: Higher Education in America* (New York: Viking, 1990).

7. Bruce Wilshire, *The Moral Collapse of the University: Professionalism, Purity, and Alienation* (Albany: State University of New York Press, 1990).

8. Wingspread Group on Higher Education, "An American Imperative: Higher Expectations for Higher Education" (Racine, WI: Johnson Foundation, 1993).

9. John H. Braxton, "The Influence of Graduate Department Quality on the Sanctioning of Scientific Misconduct," *The Journal of Higher Education* Jan.-Feb. 1991: 87-108.

10. Sands, Parson, and Duane 174-193.

11. Derek Bok, *Universities and the Future of America* (Durham, NC: Duke University Press, 1990).

12. Richard Chait, "Colleges Should not be Blinded by Vision, " *The Chronicle of Higher Education* 22 Sept. 1993: B2.

13. William W. May, ed., *Ethics and Higher Education* (New York: American Council on Education/Macmillan, 1990) 1.

14. Robert J. Samuelson, *The Washington Post National Weekly Edition* 7-13 Sept. 1993: 27.

15. Sandra L. Johnson and Joel W. Meyerson, "Top Concerns for 1993," *AGB Reports* Nov.-Dec. 1992: 18-22.

16. Ernest L. Boyer, "Creating the New American College", *The Chronicle of Higher Education* 9 Mar. 1994: A48.

17. Peter Frederick, "Questions for Collegial Conversations About Teaching," *The Department Advisor* Spring 1991: 5.

18. Robert Boice, *The New Faculty Member* (San Francisco: Jossey-Bass, 1992).

19. Roger H. Nye, *The Challenge of Command* (Wayne, NJ: Avery, 1986) 47-48.

2 GETTING TO KNOW YOUR TERRITORY

As he recalled in addresses to newly commissioned lieutenants, when former Joint Chiefs of Staff head General Colin Powell was himself a fresh "shavetail" being shuffled from Army post to post between wars, at each new station he was always at pains to locate promptly his first sergeant, the quartermaster, the medics, the PX, the pay officer, and the chaplain—in that order.

A newly hired assistant professor has different priorities, of course, invariably including the reference shelves of annual directories of grant-making agencies, the center for teaching support services, or the outreach office. But the principle's the same: as the traveling salesman sang in *The Music Man*, "You've got to know the territory!" And your No. 1 question is, "What do I have to do around here to get promoted?"

General Powell said something else pertinent: "There are no secrets to success. Don't waste time looking for them. Success is the result of perfection, hard work, learning from failure."[1]

There's no magic formula for making tenure, either. The whole process is both simple and complicated—involving something less and yet something much more than the contents of this manual.

Simple, because promotion-to-tenure is but the epitome of your professional career—translating Greek poems, chairing a curriculum committee, analyzing mysterious chemical substances, evaluating community development efforts, studying socioeconomic processes in Zambia, isolating a new germ plasm in corn, bringing history alive for a roomful of sophomores. Simple.

But the process is also made up of the stuff of which you'll read here. Complicated. Because it involves structures and persons beyond your control.

Yet if there are no recipes, there are clues to success, like getting to know your territory.

THE SACRED TRIAD

A representative American institution of higher education springs to a greater or lesser degree from three principal roots. First, the crown academy, with its focus on instructing an undergraduate elite in the classics as preparation for professional careers. Second, the German institute, with its emphasis on scientists tutoring selected graduate students in the discovery of new knowledge. And third, that peculiarly American invention, the land-grant university, with its emphasis on a utilitarian curriculum for an egalitarian citizenry, both on and off campus.

While a particular college or university may emphasize one departure or another today, each will engage to some degree in each function. In like manner, an individual professor will usually be asked to display in his or her career a certain level of talent at teaching, at research, and at service.

"Of course, those three labels—teaching, research, and service—can mean very little until you consider what they mean in specific contexts," a university chancellor[2] points out. For example, "educating freshman is very different from educating doctoral students, but both activities are called 'teaching;' likewise, outreach is very complicated in that it can refer to, say, technology transfer in a medical school or the development of new business management techniques for corporate executives."

William H. Graves, a University of North Carolina-Chapel Hill administrator,[3] has come up with novel wording to "recast the usual trichotomy of research/teaching/service" in such a way as to "defuse the false dichotomy between research and teaching" and to cease "confusing teaching with learning." He would substitute the single concept of "learning" as the unifying mission of a university, because "learning is what we do and understand."

Graves has a point, but until any such reform catches on, it's probably reasonable to continue to speak of a common teaching/research/service trivium.

For example, take this paraphrase of a typical *Chronicle of Higher Education* want ad:

MIDLAND UNIVERSITY COLLEGE OF LETTERS AND SCIENCE
ASSISTANT PROFESSOR OF BOTANY AND APPLIED ECOLOGY

Responsibilities: (1) Help develop courses for new master's program in biological conservation/sustainable development; teach standard intro botany courses; offer appropriate post-master's research seminar. (2) Advise undergraduate and graduate students; assist students with research design, prospectus writing, and thesis/dissertation studies. (3) Establish and maintain service to the University, community, and professional organizations. (4) Develop and maintain a record of scholarly productivity commensurate with the expectations of faculty at Midland; published research in support of this goal is expected.

As that Midland University ad suggests, at the outset you can assume that your institution, like most others, says it's engaged in three primary complementary activities—teaching, research, and service. But the extent to which your college or university emphasizes each of the three, and in what order, is up to you to discern. Or, better stated, which expectations apply to you in your particular niche in the big picture?

Don't even assume that all institutions seemingly in the same category have identical characteristics. For example, one land-grant university, occupying a "crown jewel" position in its state, can mingle a large extension apparatus with a strong liberal arts college and a graduate school/research establishment adept at competing for federal and foundation dollars, while in the state next door a second-class-citizen land-grant university can be relatively poverty-stricken in all three regards. Liberal arts colleges can be just as diverse.[4]

The various organizational echelons within an institution, befitting their particular missions, can vary widely in their adherence to any all-campus standard. For example, a school of business may have quite different priorities from a department of English or a college of life sciences. And yet all three can reflect markedly the stance dictated by the institution's traditions, current ethos, and future aspirations.

VARIATIONS ON A CENTRAL THEME

Oscar Ruebhausen[5] has characterized aptly the diversity among American institutions of postsecondary education and their faculties:

> The variability in roles, missions, and performances among the institutions of higher education is enormous. Some institutions are tied to public employment, others are not. Some faculties are represented by labor unions, others are not. Some institutions function on a merit-based system of faculty salaries, others do not. Some sustain a deep commitment to scholarship, while others see their primary mission as teaching. For some institutions, mobility of faculty is a constant consideration, for others it is less so. Some perform very well, others do not. Corresponding to these differences are important differences in the working conditions, aspirations, institutional and professional loyalties, and governance responsibilities of faculty.

Peter Seldin, professor of management at Pace University-Pleasantville (NY) and author of the book *How Administrators Can Improve Teaching* (San Francisco: Jossey-Bass, 1990), has visited over 200 colleges and universities of varying size, shape, and mission in his capacity as a consultant, and continues to be impressed by how totally different institutions can be, despite professed similarities in their pledge of allegiance to the triad. He notes: "At one institution the department chair may wield considerable power [in enforcing faculty adherence to institutional norms], at another the chair may be almost impotent. At one institution the faculty may be pressed to do extensive research and publication, while at another such involvement may be casually regarded. One institution may encourage and support faculty outreach, another not."

A colleague writes:

It's absolutely essential that a new hire ask these questions: What is the mission of the institution? Is the mission changing? Where has the school been and where is it going? Some traditionally teaching-oriented colleges now want their faculty to do research. (A former grad student of mine who is in her first year at East Tennessee State was told in her interview that professional presentations and publications were necessary for getting tenure.) On the other hand, traditionally research-oriented schools are now stressing teaching (for example, Stanford). What exactly are the expectations here?

FACULTY HETEROGENEITY

What's more, the individual faculty colleagues and administrators who will preside over your fate can be as varied as their institutions. By design or luck of the draw, some will be grindstone researchers, all but oblivious to any life outside their laboratories or carrels; some will take sheer delight in teaching both their specialties and introductory courses and in counseling undergraduate advisees, but will not have contributed much to the storehouse of knowledge since their dissertations; others will play public, institutional, and professional service roles with great zest, subordinating other duties; still others will manage to perform adequately, if not with distinction, in each area of the trinity of institutional missions.

Peer Traits. Some of your peers will take suggestions readily, others will revolt or sulk. Some will conform to all but the most ridiculous restrictions; others will revel in a maverick independence. Some will abhor even minor administrative chores; others will have their eye on the prize of an ever-higher administrative post. Some will be homesteaders; others will constantly seek offers to move. Some will happily share their insights; others will guard their privacy.

In like vein, some will be monastic, some gregarious, some cavalier. Some will sail through their careers with nary a distraction; some will be haunted by repeated tragedy; some will move in and out of alternating tranquility and travail.

The one thing all your judges will have in common: each will see it as his or her profound duty to academia to ensure that your career replicates and ratifies his or her own mode. The overwhelming biological desire of a species to reproduce itself is alive and well in academe today: no mutants need apply. Former UCLA Vice Chancellor William D. Schaefer describes the phenomenon thus:

"Having devoted their lives to a particular kind of study, . . . [professors] want to see their position filled by someone who will continue to do whatever it was they were doing—a perverse if understandable form of academic immortality."

One senior commentator states frankly:

> The academy tells us that tenure and promotion should be governed (if not determined totally) by universalistic rather than particularistic criteria—criteria summarized by, but not necessarily identical to, those mentioned in tenure and promotion documents. But we all know certain truths about the process:
>
> - Particularistic criteria are as important as universalistic criteria, at least in some cases.
> - Some disgruntled faculty seem quick these days to consult attorneys, or say they are going to.
> - Some tenured faculty even in good departments are generally fearful of denying tenure; they'd rather live with a less than adequate colleague than risk offending one with a negative vote.

A jaundiced opinion, perhaps, but not unique.

Peer Opinions. But don't take our word for it that all professors are not so many peas in a pod. Look at the results of a poll of professorial opinions reported by the Higher Education Research Institute at the University of California at Los Angeles:[7]

UCLA Higher Education Research Institute Professorial Attitudes Poll

Political views
37% said "liberal"
25% said "conservative"

Right to ban speakers
27% said "yes"
12% said "no"

Racial tensions
22% responded "yes"
11% responded "no"

Essential professional goal
98% included "be a good teacher"
58% included "engage in research"

Satisfactory aspect of job
82% included "autonomy and independence"

76% included "undergraduate teaching assignments"

Source of stress
84% listed "time pressures"
29% listed "subtle discrimination"

Attribute of institution
34% said "it's easy for students to see faculty"
10% said "faculty are rewarded for being good teachers"

Institutional priority
76% listed "promoting intellectual development of students"
45% listed "conducting basic and applied research"

Of course some of these responses may reflect as much the type of institution as the leanings of individual faculty, but the net lesson is clear: there's no peer uniformity out there.

A SETTING FOR THIS MANUAL

So diverse are the territories in which you may find yourself, we've decided to fabricate an institution to give a concrete shape to all the possible scenarios. This should help you better grasp the wide variety of tenure expectations and appreciate the practical politics of your professional path.

THE INSTITUTION

If our hypothetical institution were actually to be listed in a Higher Education Publications *HEP Directory*, its profile would look like this:

Midland University
P.O. Box 412, Midland, ST 53102   Con Dist 06
County: Pontiac   FICI #: 00398
Telephone 606/263-2331   Entity #: 1-38-700-6942-78
FAX 606/263-6299   Calendar System: Quarter
Established: 1881   (as a private normal school for teachers)
Annual Undergrad Tuition & Fees $2,907
Enrollment: 21,627   Coed
Affiliation or Control: Independent Non-Profit
Highest Offering: Doctorate
Program: Comprehensive
Accreditation: NH, ARCH, BUS, CYPSY, ENG, LIB, MBA, MT, MUS,
NSC, NUR, OT, SP, SW, TED
01 President
05 Vice President for Academic Affairs
Principal Divisions
Allied Health Professions
Architecture and Urban Planning
Business Administration
Education
Engineering and Applied Science
Fine Arts
Forestry and Environmental Studies
Graduate School/Research
Letters and Science
Library and Information Science
Outreach and Continuing Education
Social Welfare

THE COMMUNITY

Socioeconomics. With a population of 300,000-plus, the city of Midland is the metropolis of its heartland state—a transportation hub. Diversified mix of heavy industry, high-tech light industry, agribusiness, banking, and insurance. A relatively stable economy, yet with its vicissitudes. A growing gulf between the "haves" and the "have-nots": the former clustered around Burr Oaks Country Club (private) in a suburb, the latter in sub-standard housing literally on the other side of the Northwestern tracks. A reasonable array of cultural and recreational amenities, news media, churches, and service organizations. The only military-industrial complex is a small U.S. Air Force base on a prairie 10 miles to the south.

Town-Gown Relations. The Midland faculty used to be concentrated in College Heights near the campus but is now widely dispersed, although an enclave seems to be developing in Starlight Hills 12 miles westward. Community support for "its" university varies with the times, but in general would be rated comparatively solid. Midland alumni are well represented in the city power structure.

In no sense, however, is the university subservient to municipal interests, its increasing national stature giving it a prestige and independence much envied by the local community college and Baptist seminary.

Nonetheless, Midland University lives politically in the shadow of the sprawling state university 77 miles down the turnpike in Carthage, the state capital. State faculty steer clear of any entangling alliances, except when grant monies dictate a measure of collaboration.

An assistant president for university relations, a director of development, and an outreach dean work hard at cultivating Midland's publics. The graduate school/research dean has a part-time representative in Washington soliciting federal monies; a career development center under the chief academic officer (CAO) offers support services to faculty who seek them.

All told, the two Midlands are a microcosm of U.S. academia and its environs.

YOUR ALTER EGO

Your *alter ego* at Midland University is a new assistant professor in the Department of Botany and Applied Ecology in the College of Letters and Science. His full name is August Wilmot Campion. Growing up in the South, as he did, his boyhood nickname naturally was A.W., but in a later hitch in the Naval Reserve he acquired the appellation Bill, which he now prefers, although, because his middle name is that of a grandfather professor of linguistics and because it has a nice academic ring to it, he signs his research papers A. Wilmot. We'll refer to him as just plain Bill.

Bill comes highly credentialed from the Eugene Odum program at the University of Georgia plus a two-year post-doc assignment with the Chesapeake Bay Commission under a Midland botany Ph.D. One of his former Georgia professors is now the Dean of the Midland School of Forestry and Environmental Studies, a Georgia grad student peer has just joined the zoology department next door, and Bill's wife is a state native.

THE DEPARTMENT

Background, Development. The department traces its lineage to one of the original Midland chairs, that of natural history. It was one of the first to offer a Ph.D. (originally joint with zoology).

Stemming from its heavy teaching role in offering service courses to satisfy university science requirements and prerequisites for majors in related professional disciplines, the department is large, having a faculty of 31, and a healthy roster of graduate students supported by teaching assistantships. The number of undergraduate majors was limping until the addition of the "applied ecology" moniker in 1972, responding to student demands for programs "relevant" to the environmental era (and to the threat of the rise of environmental studies in what had been a conservative forestry school across campus).

The department's research stature jumped during WWII when its faculty participated in the national search for a penicillin mold that could be mass-produced. Combining his background in bacteriology with serendipity, Professor E. Ronald Pendarvis identified a mutant strain found on rotting melon rinds and cultivated it into a major source of the life-saving antibiotic. A grateful Department of Defense built the laboratory wing where Pendarvis still keeps office hours at the age of 87.

Based on that reputation, the department "took off" in the 1960s by staffing up to meet the almost bewildering requirements of modern botany in a university setting.

A Mason-Dixon Line. Today the department is less a department than a loose confederacy of two rival factions—the field or applied botany (taxonomy, dendrology, pathology, economic, agronomy, horticulture, and a revitalized ecology) and the laboratory or basic botany (genetics, molecular, morphology, cytology, histology, and bio-technology to include gene-splitting).

The two cultures are archrivals for funds, freshmen, and favors. The department chair position alternates between the two. At the moment it is a plant pathologist in her first year of a five-year term, so her proclivities are unknown and untested. The college dean does his best to help preserve civility by sponsoring departmental curriculum committees and so on. (Actually, from his perspective the department is no more split than a number of others in his domain.)

Bill's Challenge. Bill's assignment is to help beef up a new applied ecology master's program over the dead bodies of the more theory-minded botanists, a development that the dean of the college very much favors and that has a decent chance to rate support from state and federal environmental protection agencies and public conservation organizations.

Along with teaching his share of introductory courses, establishing a research program, attracting Ph.D. acolytes, and playing a service role, Bill is to design and offer a key course in "Biological Aspects of Environmental Impact Analysis" for graduate students.

All in all, Bill has his work cut out for him—as do you wherever you are.

TEACHING POINT

You'll recognize our Midland scenario as a common teaching technique—reducing a set of variables to a common denominator—and as a recommended essay-writing principle focusing on a representative situation or character.

In so doing, of course, we mask certain differences among the wide range of American institutions of higher education, from community colleges and teachers colleges, through church-related colleges, and on to private and public comprehensive universities.

For example, at not all institutions will you find Midland's generous use of teaching assistants (TAs). As one commentator recalls, "The university was very reluctant to fund TA-ships. As a result, faculty had to teach many basic courses because enrollments in graduate seminars were so low. I was in effect teaching at a college rather than a university."

Again, at not all universities will faculty enjoy free choice of residence:

> Church-related schools and some other four-year colleges may expect their faculty to live contiguous to the campus so as to be readily available to students. One friend of mine had to rent an apartment in a college town rather than commute from the home of her husband and children 40 miles away. Even so, she was considered unserious and disloyal, and did not receive tenure.

The point is, take all Midland data as "for instances" only. Under no (repeat *no*) circumstances assume that what's true at Midland necessarily applies at your institution. Midland mores are an example, not a prescription. On the other hand, they're a useful guide as you do considerable local reconnoitering to learn your own territory.

To help you further, we're about to suggest some essential elements of information to gather, and some available sources of that information.

Incidentally, the excerpts from Midland documents we'll present from time to time we didn't just dream up. They're actual quotations from the literature of real institutions—which we choose to use without attribution—to protect the innocent or the guilty, as the case may be.

IT'S CALLED "SOCIALIZATION"

In case you didn't realize it, as you get to know your territory the tenure-track regimen you're going through has a scientific name in a way. It's called "socialization," and it's increasingly the focus of studies on the part of higher education scholars.

Under the classic definition by cultural sociologist Robert Merton, socialization is "the process through which individuals acquire the values, attitudes, norms, knowledge, and skills needed to exist in a given society." Any campus is an organizational society of four dimensions—profession, discipline, institution, and locale, all framed by a larger influence of a national culture.

One of the latest socialization studies[8] emphasizes its role in determining successful initial and continuing performance of faculty. Researchers found that it is during the "ritual process of tenure and promotion" that institutional socialization comes into full sway, a stage that too many institutions fail to recognize can have certain inherent flaws.

To "improve the campus cultural system dramatically," the authors offer a variety of cost-effective interventions including:

- Creating incentives for senior faculty to work with junior faculty.
- Establishing orientation programs for new faculty.
- Instituting formal, yearly meetings on the part of tenure-track faculty with their department chairs and deans.
- Sharing as clearly as possible what one needs to know to achieve tenure.

With luck, you're on a campus practicing such enlightened socialization. If not, perhaps you could show this page—with discretion, of course—to someone empowered to act.

NOTES

1. Gen. Colin Powell, interview, "What's Next, General Powell?" *U.S. News & World Report* 18 Mar. 1991: 5.

2. David Ward, "Technology and the Changing Boundaries of Higher Education," *Educom Review* Jan-Feb. 1994: 23-27.

3. William H. Graves, "The Learning Society," *Educom Reivew* Jan-Feb. 1994: 8-9.

4. Charles Sykes and Brad Miner, eds., *National Review College Guide: America's 50 Top Liberal Arts Schools* (New York: Wolghemuth and Hyatt, 1991).

5. Oscar Rubenhausen, ed., *Pension and Retirement Policies in Colleges and Universities* (San Franscisco: Jossey-Bass, 1990) 282-283.

6. Peter Seldin, *How Administrators Can Improve Teaching* (San Francisco: Jossey-Bass, 1990).

7. Alexander Astin, *The American College Teacher: National Norms from the 1989-1990 HERI Faculty Survey* (Los Angeles: UCLA Graduate School of Education Higher Education Research Institute, 1991).

8. William G. Tierney, and Robert A. Rhoads. *Enhancing Promotion, Tenure, and Beyond: Faculty Socialization as a Cultural Process,* ASHE-ERIC Reports (Washington, DC: The George Washington University, 1994).

3 GRASPING GENERIC INSTITUTIONAL EXPECTATIONS

Contrasting life at "research-intensive" institutions vs. life at "teaching-intensive" institutions, a Carnegie Foundation for the Advancement of Teaching (CFAT) study of colleges and universities conferring the baccalaureate[1] makes it crystal-clear why it's so important that you learn what's expected of you at your institution.

For example:

At research institutions, the three most widely used indicators for tenure decisions are:

- Numbers of publications.
- Caliber of publications.
- Recommendations from outside scholars.

At teaching institutions, on the other hand, the indicators are:

- Student course evaluations taught.
- Service within the campus community.
- Number of publications.

Tenure-decision indicators least commonly used at research institutions are:

- Recommendations from current and former students.
- Observations of teaching by colleagues and/or administrators.
- Service within the campus community.

At teaching institutions the least common indicators are:

- Research grants received
- Recommendations from outside scholars
- Reputations of presses or journals publishing any books or articles

At research institutions, research salary outlay as a percent of educational and general salaries runs 20.8%; at teaching institutions, it's less than 1%. Considering hours per week to prepare for teaching, professors at high-intensity research institutions spend 8.4; at high-intensity teaching institutions that figure is 13.1. Mean hours per week spent on research runs 22 for researching professors and 9 for teaching professors. Mean enrollment in typical introductory undergraduate courses at research institutions is 82; at teaching institutions it's 29.

It's two different worlds out there.

In the mainstream of higher education, Midland University invests 14% of all salary funds on research salaries. Midland professors spend 11.5 hours a week on teaching prep and 15 on research, and enrollment in introductory courses runs 46.

Say the CFAT report writers:

> The type of performance needed for career success varies markedly, depending on where the institution fits on the research-intensive vs. teaching-intensive continuum. Where the institution is heavily oriented toward research, the professor must concentrate intently on impressing peers beyond the local campus with his or her scholarly creativity. Publishing in competitive outlets is therefore mandatory. It matters little what is happening in the classroom. In teaching-intensive institutions, what is happening in the classroom is all-important for career success. Scholarly creativity in the classroom is the prime objective. Impressing peers around the country can take a back seat.

Obviously the writers are describing polar positions; most colleges and universities fall in between the two extremes in one way or another. To discern where your institution fits, you have to ask some penetrating questions and develop solid answers.

ESSENTIAL ELEMENTS OF INFORMATION

The research literature on climbing the academic ladder to tenure is replete with the admonition that too many new hires fail to discern speedily enough the data they need to plot a sound course. As two researchers[2] quote one such candidate: "In the written evaluations provided each year, the neutrality of the language and the routine qualification of positive statements constitute far from constructive feedback. It's as if senior faculty tell you to go to your office, shut the door, and don't come out for six years."

While that may be in part true in places, it's equally true it's up to you to ferret out your own "feedback." You can do so if you pose the right questions that will lead you to elements of information essential to your career development.

HOW EQUITABLE IS MY P&T SYSTEM?

The caliber of the promotion and tenure (P&T)—the reward—system at your institution will have a marked effect on your progress, or at least on how you approach the task of climbing that academic ladder.

Robert W. Diamond[3] has developed a sort of "IQ test" you can use to evaluate the reward system you face:

- Does the institution's mission statement clearly identify its priorities and unique characteristics?
- Do administrators, faculty, and staff believe in and support the statement?
- Do individual units or departments have clearly articulated mission statements that identify their specific priorities?
- Do such statements mesh with and support the institutional statement?
- Do the members of the unit support the mission statement?
- Are units evaluated on how well they meet the specific goals as defined in their mission statements?

- Does the faculty reward system actively support the articulated mission statements of the institution and of the units in which faculty work?
- Do faculty understand the criteria by which they will be judged, and are they assisted in preparing the necessary documentation of their work?
- Is the faculty reward system sensitive to the differences among the disciplines, the strength of faculty, and the priorities of the department?
- Does the system allow individual faculty reward criteria to be modified based on assignment and individual strengths?
- Do faculty across departments or units consider the evaluation process fair?
- Does the system recognize the range of important activities performed by faculty in specific units?
- Are data provided to faculty throughout their careers to identify strengths and weaknesses? Is a formal procedure in place to provide assistance and support when needed?
- Do faculty who are assigned specific instructional or service projects receive guidance about how those activities will be evaluated?
- Are the priorities of the institution and department understood by new faculty? Are they clearly articulated at every point in the hiring and retention process?

Through his continuing "Changing Priorities in Higher Education" project, Diamond is working with deans, administrators, trustees, and faculty associations across the country to bring equity to faculty reward systems. With luck, your institution is taking a hard look at its P&T regimen.

A forthcoming book, *Scholarship Assessed*, by Ernest L. Boyer, president of the Carnegie Foundation for the Advancement of Teaching, will attempt to formulate national standards for the relative assessment of teaching, research, and service.

HOW LONG DO I HAVE TO MAKE TENURE?

While the testing or gauntlet period at some institutions is seven years, at Midland University it's six in which to either go up or go out, and that's the national norm.

If you're terminated at the end of your sixth year, you'll typically be granted a seventh, severance year of duty with pay.

However, as one reviewer points out, "You really have only four to five years in which to accumulate a tenure dossier, in that it takes time for work to be published, and the tenure process itself may take most of a year."

But don't panic. If they're on your side, evaluation committees will be understanding. If not, there may be greener pastures.

During your projected six years you pass through various stages of probationary status. At Midland your quarter-system schedule would look like this:

Annual Reviews

Submit Goals and Objectives Report	Aug. 1
Counseling session with department Chair	Aug and Sept
Submit Faculty Activities Report	April 1
Review session with Chair	May and June

Tenure Progress Review (second year)

Preliminary Screening Committee appointed	April 1
PSC Report to department Promotion and Tenure Committee	May 1
P&T Committee Report to Chair	May 15
Tenure Progress Report to candidate	June 1

Tenure Candidacy Review (fourth year)

PSC appointed	Aug. 15
PSC Report to P&T Committee	Nov. 1
P&T Report to Chair	Nov. 21
Chair's recommendation to Dean, copy to candidate	Dec. 1

Tenure and Promotion Review (sixth year)

PSC appointed	Aug. 15
Preparation of P&T packet	Oct. 15
PSC Report to P&T Committee	Nov. 1
P&T Committee vote and recommendation to Chair	Dec. 1
Chair letter of recommendation to Dean	Jan. 1
Review by College P&T Committee	Feb. 1
Dean's letter of recommendation to Vice President for Academic Affairs	March 1
Review by University P&T Committee	April 1
VPAA recommendation to President and Trustees	May 1
Trustee action	June 30

It's not unheard of that a particularly outstanding young assistant professor would be put up for promotion in his or her fourth or fifth year, the most likely circumstance being to forestall the raid of a star by a rival institution. And it's not without precedent that the promotion to tenure would come through. But by and large departments refrain from pushing an early promotion, for fear that if the appeal fails the candidate is stuck with a "blackball" on the record that might color future chances. So, don't expect your department to jump the gun.

Be sure to read the tea leaves carefully in any periodic counseling sessions and tenure progress reports. Unless you're blind, deaf, and dumb, from these sessions and reports you ought to be able to get a very clear perception of how you're doing.

For example, if your second-year progress report leaves a lot to be desired, either hitch up your bootstraps or start sending out résumés; in fact, if it's really bad you can be told you'll be terminated at the end of your third year. On the other hand, if your second-year report is glowing, while that doesn't mean you're "in," it does suggest that if you maintain your present pace, you have a favorable future—unless you start resting on your laurels.

While a favorable fourth-year report isn't a sure harbinger of promotion, it does mean you're definitely in the zone of consideration. But an unenthusiastic fourth-year report should strongly suggest that you get on your horse to other climes, even if your department chair doesn't so counsel openly.

That's because there's practically no way you're going to get promoted to tenure in the face of an unfavorable review at the departmental level. On the other hand, even the most ecstatic departmental recommendation can fail to pass muster at higher echelons. We discuss those hurdles a bit later.

WHEN DOES MY TENURE CLOCK TICK?

If you're starting out from scratch as an assistant professor with no prior service anywhere at the rank of instructor or above, your six-year clock starts from the date of your letter of appointment or thereabouts.

On the other hand, if you've had such prior service, it may or may not be included in your probationary period, depending on what's mutually agreed to at the time of your appointment. It's a judgment call on the part of both you and the institution. If you're bringing along an impressive record and prefer to spend as little more time as possible untenured, you may opt to count your prior service, particularly if it was at an institution with recognized standards. Your new department may concur, or it may prefer to give you and the department the maximum number of years in which to make sure you're a mutual match, in which case it will waive the prior service and put you on a fresh six-year track. Midland habitually prefers the latter option.

The one thing to double-check: make sure the department has the autonomy to render such a decision. At Midland only the dean of the college has the authority to decide when to start a tenure-track clock.

Once started, can you stop your clock temporarily? You can't of your own free will, but your institution can if it has such a policy. For instance, if you go on an approved research leave for a semester, your institution can say it'll stop your clock for the period. There are other circumstances, as well. Witness this exemplary statement in the Midland *Faculty Handbook* (II, A, 9):

> Ordinarily the probationary period will provide sufficient time for the faculty member to demonstrate his or her qualifications for tenure. On occasion, special circumstances may occur that would interfere significantly with the faculty member's opportunity to develop qualifications necessary for tenure in the ordinary time allowed. (The assumption of parental responsibilities or a major change in assigned job description might be two such circumstances.) Under such conditions the faculty member may request to be transferred temporarily from a regular-term appointment to an adjunct appointment for a specific term not to exceed two years, during which time the person's probationary term is suspended and no time toward tenure is accrued. When transferred back to a regular appointment, the faculty member will resume the probationary period at the point suspended.

Comments one colleague:

> The 'parental responsibility' element takes on heightened salience today. At the University of Illinois, the original 'stop the clock' policy came from a Chancellor's Committee on Women's Status, specifically to lengthen tenure periods for new parents (mothers being the primary candidates).

HOW TOUGH IS IT GOING TO BE TO MAKE TENURE?

The higher the academic ranking of your institution, the tougher it is to get promoted. For example, Harvard is extremely careful in its national and international search to fill tenured positions—with the president personally participating in every search and every appointment. It is determined to keep a numerical balance among the younger and older faculty members, with a rapid turnover of junior fellows competing for tenure. At UC-Berkeley, the elected Academic Senate plays a central role in ensuring high-quality additions to the tenured faculty, with common oversight of all departments and all professional schools and colleges. Similarly, at UW-Madison elected faculty divisional committees exercise practically immutable quality control over all promotions to tenure, irrespective of department, school, college, or extension.

Outside of the "top 10," screening processes and procedures may be not quite so rigid. For example, at 55-ranked Midland, the tenure hurdles are somewhat less rigorous.

But that doesn't mean it's going to be a snap at the Midlands of the country. For example, the Midland *Faculty Handbook* states (IV, B, 9):

> Superior intellectual attainment is the crucial qualification for tenure, promotion, and salary increases at Midland University. This standard of continuing performance is essential for faculty in a quality university dedicated to the discovery and transmission of knowledge.
>
> The University pledges to establish a climate that facilitates professional growth, stimulates cooperation and innovation, and promotes quality in all academic endeavors. But the ultimate responsibility for professional development and advancement rests with the individual faculty member.

For assistant professors at Midland, the batting average in making tenure is about .600. That's superior in baseball, but in academia it suggests pretty tough competition.

You should find out the batting average at your institution. Of course, the situation can vary significantly among campus units, depending on recruiting standards, departmental mentoring, and the vagaries of decision-making at higher echelons in response to changing institutional needs and external pressures.

Against profound pronouncements of rigid quality control at Midland, there is this interesting paragraph to be found in its *Faculty Handbook* (III, B, 2):

> In evaluating the candidate's qualifications within the areas of teaching, research or other creative work, and service to department/college/university/public service related to academic expertise, reasonable flexibility shall be exercised—balancing, where the case requires, heavier commitments and responsibilities in one area against lighter commitments and responsibilities in another. Each candidate is expected to engage in a program of work that is both sound and productive. As the University enters new fields of endeavor and places new emphasis on its continuing activities, instances will arise in which the proper work of faculty members may depart from established academic patterns. In such cases care must be taken to apply normal criteria with sufficient flexibility.
>
> Still, in all instances, superior intellectual attainment is the crucial qualification for promotion to tenured positions at Midland.

The lords giveth and the lords taketh away.

WHAT'S MY ULTIMATE MEASURING ROD?

A really essential element of information: What is the ultimate standard against which you'll be judged for promotion to tenure? Departmental? School/college? Institutional? National/professional? Constituency feedback? All or some of the above? The answer may lie under a rock.

Various tenure grievances and lawsuits over the past decade or two show that written "job descriptions" or "P&T guidelines" don't and can't cover every situation. Rather, faculty working toward tenure must contend with preconceptions, perceptions, personalities, and practical politics. While you keep your shoulder to the wheel, keep your ear to the ground. Detect comments about why tenure was granted to one applicant but not to another, about changes in procedures, about the nuances in departmental/institutional character you can find outlined in subsequent sections of this chapter.

WHO PROMOTES ME?

As we've suggested, promotion-to-tenure procedures can vary a good deal from campus to campus. As a guide to what to investigate at your institution, here's a rundown on the various Midland steeplechase barriers in ascending order of rank (but not necessarily of their crucial nature).

Department. As at most institutions, the botany department at Midland holds the primary fate of your *alter ego* Bill in its hands. After that series of annual reviews, in the penultimate year the chair appoints a Preliminary Screening Committee (PSC) to work with the candidate in developing a Promotion and Tenure Packet of documentation (which the young faculty member should have been assembling continuously throughout the probationary years). Theoretically any faculty member can serve on the PSC, but the chair usually opts to exclude untenured peers.

The PSC will send samples of the candidate's work to distinguished people in the candidate's field outside Midland, with a request for written appraisals. The panel can include persons the candidate suggests and persons the PSC selects independently. All responses—positive, lukewarm, or negative—enter the P&T packet for later appraisal by reviewing authorities, along with brief profiles of the respondents.

Once it's assembled all documentation, the PSC evaluates the case and prepares a report recommending for or against tenure. Voting in the PSC is by written ballot prepared and distributed by the department chair. All members must vote and a simple majority will prevail. The report then goes to the department P&T Committee, consisting of all tenured members of the department, which may or may not gather further documentation.

Voting in the P&T Committee is by secret ballot, with absentee ballots mailed to any faculty on leave. The department secretary and the chair of the P&T Committee tabulate all votes. A positive recommendation requires a simple majority. The committee chair then formulates a letter to the department chair, highlighting the candidate's strengths and weaknesses and recording the vote. Any dissenting faculty members can submit written demurs. These letters and the whole P&T Packet go forward to the chair.

The department chair, following critical review and assessment of the materials plus additional information he or she chooses to collect, prepares a letter of recommendation, positive or negative, for the dean of the college. (While the chair can overrule the P&T Committee, the chances of his or her decision carrying the day in such a case are remote, unless the dean has a like agenda.)

A commentator points out that so precise a departmental review as is in place at Midland may not exist at a small college:

> The faculty member on his or her own may have to go to the dean for input. At my institution, a third-year review has just been instituted. Until now, it was up to the assistant professor to figure things out. The dean is happy to meet at any time, but it's up to the assistant professor to initiate the conference—unless, of course, there are real problems in tow.

The College. Midland has no formal college procedure for the dean to consult with anyone. But he or she normally has a standing college P&T Committee of rotating tenured faculty members from various college departments, which in fact could include a member of the candidate's department. Such a member would normally bow out of the discussion, or at least out of the vote.

Depending on college tradition, the college P&T Committee makes either a detailed, routine, or perfunctory review of the P&T Packet in question, checking largely to see that the candidate's record does no damage to written and unwritten college standards of faculty quality. It then renders a report to the dean, who may or may not pay much attention to it. If, however, the dean would overrule the committee, he or she would have to document that decision to the Vice President for Academic Affairs when forwarding the P&T Packet.

Midland University's college-level protocol may or may not be representative. For example, as one commentator writes:

> In some institutions, a departmental P&T recommendation goes directly to a provost, bypassing any intermediate dean. In others, the departmental faculty has no role; the chair sends his or her recommendation to a college-wide committee. At some institutions every assistant professor must be formally considered for promotion every year, with the candidate formally presenting himself or herself before the committee.

What the drill is at your institution is a top item on your agenda of essential elements of information.

The President and Staff. While at Midland the President (CEO) technically is the sign-off official on any promotion-to-tenure recommendations going forward to the Trustees, in practice he or she delegates such decisions to the Vice President for Academic Affairs (CAO). Again at Midland there's no formal policy that the CAO consult anybody but his or her immediate staff, but habitually he or she employs a standing all-University P&T Committee consisting of appointed rotating tenured faculty members from each of the institution's principal divisions. In deference to faculty sentiments, Midland currently gives considerable weight to the P&T Packet review performed by the committee, and its subsequent recommendation. It's not unheard of that the all-University panel would reject the college decision, but if it were to do so, it could anticipate a vigorous appeal by the college dean and the department chair, assuming that the CAO goes along, the CAO reserving the right to be the ultimate arbiter. The CAO formulates a recommendation to the CEO, who would normally accept it and forward it to the Trustees, although he or she can, under duress, exercise independent judgment.

The Trustees. Technically, all promotions-to-tenure at Midland and other institutions are the prerogative of the governing board, but if the board were to go counter to the manifest desires of faculty and administrators with respect to the appointment and promotion of personnel, it would set off seismic reverberations on a scale of at least 7.0. Except for one circumstance: because promotion-to-tenure normally carries with it a substantial salary raise, in a day of fiscal constraints the board might have imposed a ceiling on the number of promotions-to-tenure in any given year, whereupon the President and his or her lieutenants would have to go back to the drawing-boards and perform triage on its list of recommended candidates—a grim assignment, indeed.

Midland has no written policy about what to do with any also-rans in such a situation, but the present CEO has made it known informally that any candidate denied tenure because of budgetary strictures would be reappointed until the money problems mellow—but as an assistant professor on indefinite hold—and the Trustees have unofficially concurred. Were the fiscal shortfall to continue indefinitely, nobody knows what would happen, except that there is this daunting sentence on the Trustee books:

> A chronic shortfall of income *vis-à-vis* expenditures might so jeopardize the University as to require the termination of faculty, even of tenured faculty, on the basis of fiscal-exigency decisions made by the President on the advice of the Committee on Faculty of the Faculty Assembly.

To ease any concerns that sentence may cause, let it be recorded there are few precedents for such draconian measures at any institution of Midland's comparable stature, but we suppose there's always a "first," in which case you can hope for an adequate alert as to when it's prudent to leave a sinking ship before it founders.

In your favor is the fact that, to stay afloat in the next 20 years, America's institutions of higher education will have to replace three-fourths of their faculty plus add staff to serve rising enrollments, so the odds are all in your favor—barring a total collapse of the system. The trick, of course, is to be at the right institution at the right time, but it has been ever thus.

People. Regardless of the organizational echelon involved in your promotion to tenure, in the final analysis it's people who are the key.

After all the student ratings are tabulated and assessed, after all the publications are counted and evaluated, after all the service records are weighed in the balance, after all the outside letters are read, the final decision is *qualitative,* not *quantitative*—arrived at by individual faculty personalities asking, "Does this person meet our standards?"

Despite what institutional documents may state precisely, there is inevitably a strong element of vagueness about those standards, stemming from the varied interpretations of faculty member to faculty member—relating to perceived importance of teaching, research, and outreach, and personal assessments of the potential of the candidate to "be a good colleague."

Individual recommendations of "up or out," in other words, are as gross as the ultimate decision itself. There can be no ambiguity about "tenure" or "not to tenure." Mixed evidence—decent research but nothing outstanding, excellent teaching, tough to work with on committees, offended my spouse at last year's Christmas party, connected big on a grant, midlevel outreach performance—must be reconciled at a general level by heterogenous evaluators.

So, while we can tell junior faculty they have to be excellent at research, teaching, and outreach, and have grant potential for future productivity, we cannot tell them (a) exactly how to do it, (b) if their voting colleagues will recognize excellence when confronted with it, or (c) that the same balancing act used by evaluators one year will be in effect the next.

Recognize, too, that, as one commentator points out, "some institutions are in greater flux than others, and some departments are in paradigm shifts. Look for indicators that 'uh-oh, the rules are changing.' "

How the rules can change in midstream at the hands of higher-ups is documented by Professors Robert Bing and Linda Dye[4] as they narrate what happened recently at an unnamed four-year, state-supported, multi-purpose institution:

> Each professorial candidate for promotion to tenure applied to an elected departmental committee of peers. The committee evaluated the candidates against four criteria defined in a negotiated all-campus policy: teaching, scholarly achievement, service to the college, service to the community. The departmental committee forwarded the names of the candidates meeting with favor to an elected, all-college faculty committee, which in turn endorsed the selections and forwarded them to the academic vice president and president. Substituting a criterion of publication in refereed journals, the administrators dropped the names of three candidates recommended by the all-college committee, inserted three names of their own choice, and took the revised list to the Board of Trustees, whereupon the Board approved the promotions without comment.

As the saying goes, if you need a guarantee, go to Sears or Chrysler.

Eternal Verities. On the other hand, it may be some solace to know that the criteria used by academic deans to evaluate the overall performance of faculty across the country have remained largely unchanged over the past decade, at least in liberal arts colleges. That's the net message from a recent study by Peter

Seldin[5] in which he surveyed 501 deans in 1993 and compared the results with those of a similar study in 1983.

Classroom teaching continues to be by far the most often reported "major factor." In rank order, other criteria today are: student advising, campus committee work, length of service in rank, research, publication, activity in professional societies, and public service. Criteria rank order for retention, promotion, and tenure would undoubtedly be somewhat different at comprehensive, doctoral, and research universities, of course.

The one criteria to show an appreciable change is "personal attributes," which dipped in importance. As a Texas dean wrote, " 'Fitting in' today means doing your fair share of teaching and research and doing it effectively. It's no big deal if a professor is from a different mold." A California dean agreed: "Diversity is the name of the game today."

One of our commentators takes issue with the truth of that report: "After watching a number of hiring and tenure decisions, I have to say the whole issue comes down to the faculty asking, 'Is he/she one of US?' That question encapsulates the good and the bad of the tenure process—'Is the candidate up to our standards of intellectual excellence?' *vs.* 'Is the candidate of the same socio-economic class as we are, and does he/she submit willingly to the dogmas we worship?' "

Perhaps at many an institution the truth lies somewhere in between.

WHAT'S WITH TEACHING HERE?

"If there is any one undoubted principle in higher education, it is this: instruction ranks every other consideration." John Bascom said that in the 1870s, and other college and university presidents have been saying it ever since. But on some campuses today an emphasis on undergraduate teaching consists largely of publicity brochure pieties and commencement oratory; in the classroom itself, devotion to effective teaching sits in the back row.

However—and it's a big however—you may very well have just joined the faculty of a growing number of institutions with a decent respect—and rewards—for good teaching. In that case, better shape up your instructional capabilities. Even if you're on a research-oriented campus, you could help energize there the powerful national trend toward what Ernest L. Boyer of the Carnegie Foundation for the Advancement of Teaching has called "the 1990s as the decade of undergraduate education."

Whether or not your institution subscribes, you can draw a personal azimuth from Page Smith's dictum in *Killing the Spirit:*

> There is no decent, adequate, respectable education . . . without personal involvement by a teacher with the needs or concerns, academic and personal, of his/her students; all the rest is 'instruction,' 'information transferral,' 'communication technique,' or some other impersonal or antiseptic phrase, but it is not teaching.[6]

Your Midland University *alter ego* got a pretty clear signal about the importance of teaching at that institution in the form of this memo from his Letters and Science Dean, E. Howard Harrier:

> I want it clearly understood by all College hands that I will brook no diminution in the devotion we all must give to undergraduate teaching and advising of high, consistent quality and quantity. If we allow the graduate school's definition of scholarly attainment to make its presence overwhelming in the work of the college teacher, it will fundamentally degrade the commitment of our undergraduate curriculum to the aims of general education. I pray each of you will reconsider the extraordinary emphasis currently placed on publication—an emphasis that can diminish the classroom experience of unsuspecting undergraduates.

Whether the Midland faculty reward system will actually reflect that memo is another question.

If you're under a Midland-type Dean Harrier, you can at least be sure you wouldn't get a memo like that unless the dean subscribed to the Smith dictum that the primacy of undergraduate instruction needs restoring in our institutions as a badge of professorial performance.

For more on teaching, see Chapters 5, 6, and 7.

WHAT'S MY TEACHING LOAD?

In the six years that Howard Mancing served as head of the department of foreign languages and literature at Purdue University, he conducted a large-scale recruiting program, hiring over 20 new faculty members. Virtually every candidate asked some variant of the same question—having nothing to do with salary, fringe benefits, or even what it's like to live among cornfields. No, the single universal query was, "What will my teaching load be¿"

It's a natural question. Your teaching load inevitably dictates the amount of other time you have to devote to research, service, and personal life. Right or wrong, too, a light teaching load has come to signify some form of peer accolade, sort of like a Distinguished Service Cross.

But if you look on teaching only as what you do when you aren't doing anything "significant," forget it. Particularly in this era of public insistence on improvement in undergraduate education, your teaching scorecard could turn out to be a crucial asset or liability.

Here's what the latest Midland University Faculty Development Committee Report has to say on the subject:

> Midland faculty members are expected to excel in teaching. They exhibit their command of the subject matter in classroom discussions and lectures, and they present material to their students in an objective, organized way that promotes the learning process. They outline the subject matter with logic and conviction, and awaken in students an awareness of the relationship of their subject to other classes, fields of knowledge, and cultures. They display concern and respect for their students, guiding and inspiring. They strive continuously to broaden and deepen their knowledge and understanding of their discipline, seek to improve the methods of teaching their subject, keep informed about new developments in their field, use appropriate instructional technologies, and prepare educational materials that are up-to-date and well-written. Their influence and reputation as teachers is demonstrated further by student and peer evaluation, by authoring textbooks, by lectures and publications on pedagogy, by the publication of such instructional materials as laboratory manuals and video-tapes, and by significant contributions to professional associations that seek to improve teaching.
>
> Excellence in academic advising serves to augment excellence in teaching, as faculty interact constructively with their advisees. Faculty are knowledgeable about scheduling and about curricular and extracurricular matters, keep informed of current policies and procedures, and aid students in making use of University resources to enhance their

educational and personal development. They assist students in learning to make intelligent decisions for themselves. They demonstrate excellence in advising by student and peer evaluation, advising awards, active participation in local and national advising conferences and seminars, by writing and presenting advising papers, and by preparing institutional advising guidelines.

That's quite a mouthful, but that's the growing standard in academia today at other than ultra research-intensive campuses; even there, zephyrs of change are blowing.

Want a standard reference for a teaching load? The American Association of University Professors decreed in 1968 that:

> Faculty members should spend no more than 12 hours a week per semester in the classroom. If there is an expectation of ongoing research, they should not be required to teach more than 9 hours per week. Institutions that require faculty members to publish for tenure and promotion should lower teaching loads, especially for junior faculty members.

At many institutions those loads would be considered excessive today. In the Midland department of botany and applied ecology, for example, the chair tries to limit each faculty member to a course a quarter, but current personnel shortages dictate that every third term each professor must teach two.

Whatever your teaching assignment, you'll just have to build the rest of your work load around it.

HOW WILL MY TEACHING BE EVALUATED?

You can get some clues to answers to that question from the results of a survey by Peter Seldin[7] of 501 academic deans at accredited four-year undergraduate liberal arts colleges around the country. In rank order, the percentage of those deans that "always use" the indicated sources of information in evaluating faculty teaching performance were:

- systematic student ratings—85.7
- evaluation by department chair—78.7
- evaluation by dean—67.9
- self-evaluation or report—56
- committee evaluation—48.6

- colleagues opinions—48.6
- classroom visits—33.4
- course syllabi and exams—29.1

Your evaluators may or may not conform to the average. For example, addressing the topic in one of her first memos to the faculty of the Midland department of botany and applied ecology, Chair Amanda Perkins wrote:

> On the advice of the department committee on instructional improvement, we will emphasize two objective means of measuring undergraduate teaching performance.
>
> The first is **classroom visitation.** Through a series of class visits, a duly appointed panel of peers will determine how proficient each of us is in practicing the teaching techniques that should mark undergraduate instruction. Admittedly, such a procedure may be somewhat alien to what some consider as academic freedom, yet so long as the panel confines itself to objectively assessing how effectively a subject is being taught, using standards long been refined by schools of education, the claim cannot be substantiated that inspection is any sort of damper on freedom to teach. Indeed, classroom inspection may be said to be an essential mechanism for protecting the other side of the academic-freedom coin—the freedom of students to learn, to learn from practitioners who are technically qualified.
>
> The second method we will use to measure teaching performance is **student ratings.** While some professors may have opposed this administrative technique on the grounds that it somehow invades their privacy without contributing anything valid to the measurement of professional proficiency, student evaluation sheets have been used too long on too many campuses and subjected to too many tests for them to be dismissed as dangerous or invalid. Undergraduate ratings of teachers have been shown to have a marked correlation with alumni assessments, and a negative correlation with the subject matter itself and with grades received. Such ratings are in fact relatively accurate guides to the effectiveness of teaching at the undergraduate level.
>
> Classroom visitations and student ratings can identify those qualities of effective teaching that must continue to mark this department:

- Define the major aims of your courses and keep them before your students.

- Develop adequate outlines for your course and revise them frequently.

- Discover early the extent to which your students have the basic skills and information to succeed in your courses work and adapt accordingly.

- Recommend an excellent basic textbook for each course or assemble a custom "text."

- Make certain that reference books and readings are readily available.

- Assign outside work in such a manner that it will challenge your students' interests and efforts.

- Afford your students adequate opportunities to raise questions on points about which they want additional information or explanations.

- Cultivate an interest in humorous incidents in your classes and make judicious use of humor in your teaching.

- Exhibit a genuine enthusiasm for the values and worth of your courses.

- Exhibit marked faith in the potential success of your students and show patience in dealing with individuals.

- Recognize the genuine value of a spirit of good will and friendliness in your classes.

- Experiment with teaching techniques and seek continually better methods of teaching, using your classroom visitation reports and student ratings as clues.

- Share with your students your own joy in learning, and present materials objectively, rather than seeking to impose personal opinions or prejudices.

The department committee and I are personally committed to placing the department of botany and applied ecology in a lead role in Midland University's renewed devotion to the improvement of undergraduate instruction. Please join us in this important mission.

With that memo in hand, your Midland *alter ego* Bill has no doubt about how his teaching is to be evaluated. If you have no such written guidance, ask. (See Chapter 4.)

Regardless of prescribed means of measuring teaching effectiveness, you can assume that your personal goal might well be to "knock 'em in the aisles," to warrant the accolade Willa Cather had a colleague pronounce in her profile of *The Professor's House:*

> I wish to pay my tribute to the lecturer's clarity. I have seldom listened to a lecture that explained so difficult a subject in such simple language. I'm left with the feeling that the most inexperienced student in this hall must have learned as much as I have today.

Tips from Student Evaluation Forms. We have before us three typical Student Evaluation of Instruction forms, one in use at a large public research university, one at a small comprehensive university, one at a college. Interestingly enough, the first questions on each are:

- How effective was the instructor in making clear the goals and objectives of this course?
- How clear were the goals, aims, and requirements of the course?
- How well organized was the instructor?

Since it's very likely that student ratings will come into play in evaluating your teaching, take those prime questions to heart and realize you can't neglect your classroom responsibilities by mounting the rostrum without careful preparation and organization—unless, that is, you want to be criticized by canny undergraduates. And pitch your presentation to those students, not to a faculty committee, just as you would pitch a research paper to peer reviewers, not to first year students. For more about "tailoring," see Chapter 10.

It Could Be the Company You Keep. After many interviews with entry-level faculty hires at two large universities over their first two years, psychology professor Robert Boice[8] has a bit of advice for you:

> Some tyro professors uniformly receive poor student teaching evaluations, don't seem to know what to do about it, rarely seek or get collegial help, feel isolated, say they have too little time for research.
>
> On the bright side, some beginners are off and running right away on their own as effective teachers, productive scholars, and happy campers.

Those who volunteer for a faculty development program find their
level of classroom comfort and time management improves.

You take it from there. In doing so, remember that you're not
alone. You have in your memory a kit of role models—the best sort
of company. Good teaching, you know, is like what a Supreme
Court Justice said about pornography: "You know what it is when
you see it." You've seen it as an undergraduate. Conjure up now
an incandescent image of one of your own excellent teachers.

Perhaps it is of a botany professor, striding up and down in the well
of an auditorium, saying again and again, "I want you to see this now,"
as she postponed the classification of angiosperms to open a door to the
marvelous evolution of the scientific method. Or a medieval historian
who clarified why the glorious days of Charlemagne were really not so
glorious. Maybe an instructor of English literature making the connection between Tennyson's "Ulysses" and you. Or a physics TA unrav-
eling the mysterious workings of the atom. It could be a Socratic
philosophy professor who never tired of asking the questions that ended
up blowing your mind, revealing you to him and to yourself. Perhaps a
Billy Graham type of economics professor who could construct a whole
sermon on state socialism out of a *U.S. vs. Schechter Poultry Company*
text. Or a poli sci professor reducing the whole of a course in American
government to a single question on a two-hour final exam: "Discuss
the U.S. Constitution as a conservative document."

These memories are now not to be dismissed. You can put
them to good use as teaching models.

WHAT'S PAR FOR THE RESEARCH COURSE?

When you cut through all the hype about the role of undergraduate
teaching and get down to hard cash, for professors everywhere the
payoff is spelled "research." That's the bottom-line conclusion of
a team of Pennsylvania State researchers based on a national survey
that compared the salaries of faculty members with how they
spend their time, to find that the more time a professor spends on
research, the higher his or her salary, by and large.

But surely, you say, this is a gross oversimplification that
applies only to research universities. Sorry—that's not what the
data indicate:

> This study substantiates the dominance of a research-oriented re-
> ward structure for most U.S. colleges and universities. Regardless of
> institutional type or mission and irrespective of field of study, faculty
> who spend more time on research and publishing and less time on
> teaching earn the most income. . . . Even schools traditionally struc-
> tured for teaching now follow the research model.[9]

Assuming you accept this writing on the wall, your next
question may well be, if I'm going to compete in this research/pub-
lishing game, what's par for the course?

According to U.S. Department of Educaton data garnered in a
1988 national faculty survey, each of the nation's estimated
489,000 full-time faculty members produced an average of two
refereed-journal articles and 0.6 scholarly books, chapters in edited
volumes, monographs, or textbooks during the previous two years.
Professors at research universities averaged twice as many publications; those at two-year colleges published far fewer.

If each professor were the sole author of each publication, those
efforts would add up to nearly a million refereed-journal articles
and 300,000 books, chapters, monographs, and texts over two
years!

Education Department data did not include the thousands of
book reviews, articles in general-interest publications, technical
reports, extension manuals, and conference presentations also
produced by faculty.

So it's a researching/publishing world you're in. What's the
score for your particular department/institution? Learning the
answer to that question is a key aspect of learning your territory.
The Midland University expectation: an average of 1.5 published
professional papers per year.

If you want to set your quantitative sights very high, how
about picking as a role model Sander Gillman, professor of human
studies at Cornell University and of the history of psychiatry at
Cornell Medical College? In 1993 alone, Gillman was the author
or editor of five books to add to 37 books written or edited since
he began publishing in 1971—42 works in all, not counting four
more in progress. And he's only 49.[10]

Or for a qualitative target, how about Bert Vogelstein, professor of oncology at the Johns Hopkins University Medical School?

In 1993 he had the title, "Hottest Scientist of the Year," bestowed upon him by *Science Watch*, a newsletter published by the Institute for Scientific Information. Professor Vogelstein was co-author on 16 frequently cited or "hot" papers that year, far outstripping his closest competitors. Nor was that a flash in the pan. A paper that he and his colleagues published in 1991 in *Science* about the role of p53 mutations in human cancers has been cited in no less than 697 other scientific publications.[11]

The character of your publications can be a factor as well. By the time the senior author (ACS) came up for tenure in the UW-Madison School of Journalism in 1959, he had written and published one scholarly book, one disciplinary text, two professional monographs, 32 professional papers, and 70 semi-popular articles, and had edited four serial publications. That was considered an acceptable record in his field at the time, but since none of the works represented hard-core, quantitative research, they wouldn't count for much today, at least not at Madison.

The Midland Graduate School/Research dean has just issued guidelines to the all-University P&T Committee under which it's to evaluate the research/publishing of tenure candidates. They read like this:

> Research, scholarship, and artistry are the vehicles by which Midland University, through its faculty, contributes to the discovery of new knowledge. This is a primary mission of the University. Research and scholarly activity enhance undergraduate, graduate, and outreach teaching by ensuring the currency of the information being transmitted and by exposing students to the excitement of learning at the cutting edge of new knowledge.
>
> In evaluating research productivity, quality as well as quantity should be considered. The primary guardian and arbiter of research quality is the peer review system. Therefore it is essential that faculty at all levels submit their intellectual products for rigorous review by peers. Such review is most often accomplished by submitting manuscripts to quality professional journals and research proposals to review panels for outside funding agencies. A record of peer acceptance establishes the academic and professional credentials of the faculty member; provides credibility to his or her non-refereed publications, presentations, and

teaching; and is the academic foundation for the titles of Associate Professor and Professor.

Because faculty members in the University vary considerably in their research and scholarship interests, flexibility must be maintained in evaluating the quantity and quality of production. In all cases, however, reviewers should look for evidence that the faculty member/candidate has established a program or direction of research and produced scholarly works that make a significant contribution to the field.

Neither superior teaching nor extensive outreach can replace a lack of evidence of an active mind at work at Midland University.

Your own institution may or may not be quite that arbitrary. To be on the safe side, get going on a sustained regimen of publishing.

For what it's worth, after studying the impact of departmental research and teaching climates on undergraduate growth and satisfaction, two scholars[12] at SUNY-Albany have concluded that "students in exclusively research-oriented departments report more growth than those in exclusively teaching-oriented departments," but that those departments that exhibit "a combination of strong research and strong teaching" make the most "significant contributions to undergraduate intellectual growth."

As a corollary, J. Fredericks Volkwein and David A. Carbone suggest that you can't generalize about the role of teaching on any particular campus because departments in that institution can differ so markedly in their teaching and research climates and their impact on the academic integration and intellectual growth of undergraduate majors.

When they do generalize from academic departments to a university as a whole, the authors "suspect that a vigorous campus research culture by itself is necessarily neither beneficial or harmful to students," but they go on to "hypothesize that the most powerful undergraduate learning environments may occur in research universities that also attend to the undergraduate program."

For more on research, see Chapters 8, 10, and 11.

DOES SERVICE REALLY COUNT?

The "service" component of the triad may be the most difficult for an assistant professor to grasp. As a graduate student, he or she has been abundantly familiar with the teaching and research activities of professors, but their service roles can have been largely invisible.

Yet the answer to the question posed in our heading is, "Definitely yes."

For the flavor of what service can connote to a P&T Committee, here is what the Midland College of Letters and Science "Promotion-to-Tenure Criteria" document has to say:

- While service contributions cannot be the sole basis for promotion to tenure, every faculty member is expected to be involved.
- Since the faculty plays a vital role in the administration of the University at all levels and in the formulation of policies, scholars are expected to participate effectively and imaginatively in faculty government and, in the case of assistant professors, particularly in departmental affairs.
- Faculty should seize opportunities to utilize their professional expertise to disseminate information to help improve the knowledge and skills of lay clientele or the environment in which they live and work.
- Service in and for technical, professional, scholarly, or arts societies and organizations related to the candidate's academic expertise is a required mark of the faculty member's local, state-wide, regional, national, or international academic citizenship.

At the outset, it's important to find out what *counts* as service, even in terms of institutional service. For instance, one commentator reports that, at a small liberal arts college, "service on faculty-appointed or -elected committees counts for more than service on president- or dean-appointed committees, and much more than voluntary work—for P&T, that is."

A tactical question: Do you spread yourself over the service continuum or do you concentrate on one or two activities? A possible answer: Try to develop quick visibility in (a) a role in faculty governance, say on a departmental committee, (b) an outreach or consulting activity, and (c) a professional association chore.

Consider service activities that could be mutually supporting. For example, our Midland botany professor could volunteer for membership on the department's public service committee, render counsel to a local prairie restoration project, and get appointed to the State Endangered Species Commission.

Note: To count as "service" for promotion to tenure, your extra-campus activities must be related directly to your academic expertise. Teaching a Sunday School class, leading a scout troop, or chairing a parents-and-teachers committee doesn't qualify (unless you're in a school of education). On the other hand, were your department chair's child one of your troopers and were to go home glowing about your camping-trip prowess, it couldn't hurt!

In recalling that "higher education and the larger purposes of American society have been—from the very first—inextricably intertwined," Ernest L. Boyer[13] has recently complained that "higher education's historic commitment to service seems to have diminished," and has called on faculty members individually and collectively to honor the "service" expressed "in the mission statement of almost every college and university in the country," although he acknowledges that "faculty members who spend too much time engaged in service projects can often jeopardize their careers."

In summary, does service really count? To answer that question pragmatically, answer this question: "As an assistant professor, can I afford to leave in the lurch the colleagues who will be voting on my case?" Without faculty at all ranks performing service chores, important institutional tasks don't get done. A large department may be able to afford a few brilliant researchers who don't pull their weight in other areas, or one or two "teacher only and nothing else" types, but most department members cherish well-balanced colleagues adept at the full range of expectations.

DOES A ONE-OR-TWO-OUT-OF-THREE RULE-OF-THUMB APPLY?

It's the conventional wisdom in some circles that any devotion to the sacred triad is observed more in the breach than in the application in some situations.

For example, the Midland University College of Letters and Science guidelines for promotion-to-tenure state unequivocally:

> Each faculty member, regardless of funding source, is expected to perform over the full range of responsibilities: teaching, research, and service. Performance in each of these areas will be given due weight when reviewing individual faculty members for salary adjustments, promotion in rank, and tenure.

Across campus in the Midland School of Architecture and Urban Planning, however, the guidelines equivocate:

> Evaluation of a faculty member for promotion and/or tenure shall be based on criteria related to the individual's appointment responsibilities and activities, domestic and/or international, in the following four areas: (1) teaching, (2) research, scholarship, or artistic activities, (3) outreach or professional practice, and (4) service. To be promoted and/or tenured, a faculty member must exhibit a strong sense of professional ethics.
>
> "Competence" means performance of tasks and responsibilities in an appropriate and proficient fashion as opposed to inept, unacceptable performance. "Excellence" refers to performance that exceeds what is expected or required.

Why the difference in nuance between the two guidelines? One befits the mission of a comprehensive college, the other that of a professional school. Make it a priority to determine which sort of guideline applies to you in your situation in your institution.

AM I IN ANY KIND OF SPECIAL SITUATION?

There are several types of tenure-track appointments that can present special problems—and opportunities.

Extension. There are two general forms of extension (or outreach) appointments.

If you're in a land-grant university (there's one in every state, founded under the 1862 Morrill Act), your appointment might be in whole or in part in the Cooperative Extension Service of a college of agriculture as an assistant professor of extension in one of the college's departments ("cooperative" because the enabling 1914 Smith-Lever Act called for tripartite funding—federal, state, and county). In such a case the institutional expectations will be unique. You will teach largely in non-degree situations—on-campus short courses and off-campus institutes and workshops—or in one-on-one consultations. Your research activities will be applied, constituency-oriented, problem-focused, synthetic. Your service role will be on college and university committees and in state and national organizations (any extension teaching and research work not counting for you as conventional public service).

If your tenure-track hurdles are within your department and college, colleagues and administrators sympathetic to the extension mission will understand your career contributions. But if your university employs any form of all-campus quality control, some faculty members on a review panel may find it hard to understand why, for example, a wildlife management extension professor should be given productive-scholarship credit for an extension bulletin on how to build and install back-yard bird houses in lieu of a paper in an appropriate scholarly journal on the changing ecology of the mallard *(Anas platyrhynchos platyrhynchos)* in the Mississippi Flyway.

As departments and divisional units go more and more to outside evaluations for promotion to tenure, the plight of the extension faculty member darkens. While outside assessments apply well to judging quality of research in a subspecialty of a decentralized discipline, and for determining the extent to which the candidate is making a reputation as a scholar, outside evaluations don't fit neatly the extension mission. Extension is local, usually visible only to immediate clients, and seldom to extension specialists in other climes who are potential letter-writers. To the extent that extension faculty A has an out-of-state "name," his or her status may rise among researcher evaluators but fall among extension evaluators who see the candidate neglecting the home garden plot.

Some institutions also maintain general or urban extension divisions, with faculty distinct from "residence" faculty. If your appointment is in such a configuration, your tenure-track problems will be much the same as those of an ag co-op professor, except that your mission will appear even less distinct to any all-campus P&T committee. General outreach faculty are not protected by the massive historic and funding traditions enjoyed by ag extension faculty in what is generally recognized as the finest lay education enterprise in the world.

But take heart. In any institution with tenure-track extension or outreach appointments, qualified extension faculty should get promoted—even in a climate of orthodox teaching, research, and service.

Split Appointment. If your appointment is joint in two departments, you will in effect have to run two tenure-track races. If the two departments are in the same school or college, you will at least report to only one dean; but if your departments are in different colleges, you'll be subject to two expectations. If joint appointments are common at your institution, P&T committees will be understanding; but if split appointments are irregular, you face a tougher hurdle. The best protection: make sure your appointment is not a 50-50 split but more like 60-40, so that one department feels particularly responsible for you and takes the initiative in helping forward your tenure-track progress.

Interdisciplinary Studies. To the delight of some faculty and the consternation of others, the 1960s saw the emergence on campuses nationwide of such interdisciplinary programs as women's studies, environmental studies, and various forms of ethnic and geographic studies. If your appointment is in such a department, particularly one so new it has no established track record of promotional criteria, you could have problems.

For one thing, universities tend to be more atomistic than holistic in their approach to knowledge, so interdisciplinary programs do not exist under a particularly benign reward system; thus assistant professors in cobbled-together programs live dangerously.

Secondly, faced with a threat to their ordained territories, established departments can muster awesome retaliatory power. The scalps of some of yesterday's interdisciplinary programs are dangling from the belts of defensive disciplines.

Finally, fiscal shortfalls can starve out campus configurations lacking fixed budget lines and well-cultivated constituencies, especially in the absence of nurturing government and foundation grants. The best defense: try to wangle a joint appointment in an orthodox department so that you look more respectable to suspicious deans and provosts—and break your back to amass an extra-impressive CV.

Professional School. An appointment in a professional department, school, or college can present problems, since some such units tend to be "schizo" about their proper stance, and hence can be ambivalent about their expectations for new hires—skills vs. scholarship, in other words.

A common internal dichotomy in a professional unit, for example, pits theory-and-methodology researchers against practitioners, as between oncologists and internists in a medical school.

Mature professional units in effect tend to employ two tenure tracks—one for avowed researchers and one for applied faculty. In such a situation your one essential question is, "Do the unit and I agree what track I'm on?"

The real trouble can arise when a professional unit is in transition, with the two camps vying for ascendancy, tugged one way or another by changing divisional agendas. Internal tensions can then reach flash-point proportions, with new hires—and students—caught in the cross-fire.

In a school of mass communication, for example, an assistant professor with a brand new Ph.D. from the Excelsior School of Communication, who can quote sociologists Melvin L. DeFleur and Sandra Ball-Rokeach *ad infinitum* on "theories of mass communications" yet who has had not one day of practical experience in a newspaper newsroom, can wind up assigned to teach "Reporting and Newswriting 101" to unsuspecting sophomores.

Similarly, an experienced senior TV investigative reporter turned assistant professor without a Ph.D. can do a polished job on that teaching assignment, yet find his or her track to tenure blocked in a professional unit seeking to raise its scholarly credentials.

Timing can be everything. The senior author (ACS), who doesn't have a Ph.D., could not now be appointed an assistant professor in a journalism school that welcomed him with open arms in 1953 as a young M.A. with an impressive professional portfolio and promoted him without hesitation in 1959, that school today being heavily oriented to research as a survival strategy in its research university.

A colleague of ours emphasizes strongly that the two-track tenure system "is not always honored" in a professional school:

The Ph.D. becomes the union card that allows you to remain a faculty member. An alternative to rejection for tenure for lack of a Ph.D. may be to enroll in a doctoral program. I know of at least two cases where the dean said there would be no tenure without a Ph.D. One person, who already had two M.A.s, finally got the Ph.D. The other did not, but found a teaching post at an institution more appreciative of his professional experience.

Even though a botany department is not normally thought of as a professional unit, your *alter ego* Bill at Midland is feeling the effects of tension between researchers and practitioners as that department seeks to fashion an applied-ecology thrust. Fortunately, Bill seems to have his own tenure track well defined.

The ABD Situation. Some departments in some institutions will appoint as a tenure-track assistant professor a person who has completed all his or her terminal-degree course work but who has yet to finish a Ph.D. thesis (hence ABD—**a**ll **b**ut **d**issertation). Such a person is obviously in a double bind—trying to meet degree and tenure requirements simultaneously.

Institutions hiring ABDs may adjust the term of appointment. For example, it was the experience of one commentator that at his state university:

> If you were appointed ABD and you completed the degree in one year, you could be reappointed for two years, then again for three years. If reappointed a third time, then you received tenure. If you completed the degree in two years, you could be twice reappointed for two years each time.
>
> Retirement benefits and departmental voting rights began only after you received the degree or after the two years of service, whichever came first. Promotion to associate before the probationary period ended carried tenure.
>
> When I came in, my dissertation sat on the end of my dining-room table for two years. I taught as many as four different preparations from 8 a.m. till 5 p.m., all over campus. That alone took 50 hours a week.

In other words, entering academia as an ABD is to live dangerously.

WHAT'S THE STATUS OF MY POSITION?

First, why the vacancy? Did somebody retire, leaving a slot the dean didn't recapture? Or is it a new position?

If the latter, you'll want to consult the department budget to see whether you're a firm line-item or funded temporarily on "soft money" from college discretionary funds or a grant.

You can't change the facts in any case, but they'll give you a clue to how your colleagues view the situation in terms of its longevity—and yours.

WHY ME?

If you can find them, there's nothing like consulting the minutes of the search-and-screen committee that recommended you—for determining your department's expectations for you *vis-à-vis* the attributes of your former competitors.

Your Midland *alter ego* Bill found those minutes that pertained to him. Out of an invitation-and-application list of 16, the committee had picked a "wish list" of six and proposed to interview all of them, but the dean would allocate travel funds for only four.

One was a generalist with two years of superior teaching at a fine four-year college in Iowa but no research publications worthy of the Midland name. A second was a combination geneticist/pathologist, one of the last of James Crow's grad students at the University of Wisconsin-Madison, with his name already on a multiple-inventor patent for a potential cure for oak wilt. A third was a taxonomist from Cal Tech with extensive Peace Corps experience in South American rain forests and a strong desire to energize campus concern for their fate. The fourth, of course, was Bill.

The minutes reveal a heated all-department debate between the two botany camps, the one side promoting the UW-Madison candidate, the other Bill with his experience as both a TA and RA under Eugene Odum at Georgia and his potential for the proposed new master's program in applied ecology. It's a wonder the Cal Tech candidate hadn't won out as a compromise. The vote had been close, and wounds there were, assuaged only by a sudden appearance at the decisive faculty meeting by Emeritus Professor Pendarvis, pleading for "civility," plus covert word from the college dean that he would "make things up" with new instrumentation for the lab people.

That reading, of course, gave Bill a pretty clear indication of how the land lies at Midland. Either he makes peace somehow with the malcontents, meanwhile driving ahead to fulfill his potential for the ecology faction, or he's in trouble.

If you at your institution can't find any revealing faculty meeting minutes, perhaps a mentor can answer the question, "Why me?"

WILL I FACE DISCRIMINATION?

It would be nice to be able to give a resounding "No!" to that question, but the fact remains that, while the situation is improving generally, discrimination on the basis of gender and race continues to haunt academe.

Gender discrimination. "When and where gender discrimination exists, it is often subtle and endemic," says Nancy Hensel[14] in a recent monograph on the subject. Hensel goes on to explicate the results of her study:

> Because academia has long been dominated by men, the male perspective generally prevails in policy development, performance evaluation, and interpersonal interactions. Student evaluations indicate that women's classroom performance is often evaluated more critically than men's. Research by women or about women is frequently undervalued by male colleagues. Initial salary differentials between men and women increase in favor of men as faculty progress through the ranks. Women take longer than men to achieve promotion and tenure, largely because of women's greater child care responsibilities. Each of these issues can lead to a cumulative disadvantage for the new female professor.

What can be done? Bernice Resnick Sandler[15] suggests these "success and survival strategies for women faculty members":

> Be active and energetic on your own behalf. Develop a strategy that will guide your progress over the next five years. Seek information, advice, and assistance, particularly about promotion-and-tenure criteria at your institution. Keep careful records of your activities. Develop your own networks. Above all, don't turn and run, withdraw into apathy or bitterness, or revolt but rather "try to help bring about change in whatever small measures you can."

That last is just what a cadre of women did at Stanford as 1994 began. Stung by the fact that 43% of Stanford departments had no tenured women faculty and almost 40% of the departments hiring new faculty in the preceding five years did not hire a woman, five women members of the Stanford Faculty Senate got that body to pass a resolution demanding that the administration increase the percentage of women faculty, ensure salary equity, create a culture of faculty support for its junior women members, and help faculty to combine work and family.

Changing institutional policies to better integrate work and family issues is the agenda recommended by Hensel for women faculty members. The agenda includes:

- Examining the hiring process to ensure that women are hired into positions for which they are clearly qualified.
- Supplying mentors and networks to support their scholarship.
- Developing collaborative arrangements with local employers in order to locate suitable employment for spouses.
- Providing support for dual-career couples.
- Instituting maternity and family leave.
- Reducing teaching loads.
- Adjusting tenure track demands for new parents.

Men can benefit, too, because, as Hensel points out, "faculty men in dual-career relationships can no longer expect the career and family support offered by traditional wives."

In cases of discrimination duress, women faculty members have a friend in court in the Legal Advocacy Fund of the American Association of University Women.[16]

Race Discrimination. While affirmative action has opened the campus door to new African American faculty in recent years, multiple voices attest they continue to face a form of double jeopardy.

"Minority faculty are hired with the assumption that they will serve as educator, counselor, mentor, and guardian for minority students," in addition to facing the normal teaching/research/service hurdles for promotion and tenure. So wrote Ed Wiley[17] in *Black Issues in Higher Education.*

"Some faculty of color see themselves as 'do-alls' and their colleagues as 'do-littles,' " Wiley said. He quoted a professor of literature: "I was hired to teach African American and women's literature, but there was also the expectation that a Black professor would be all things to all people, especially when it comes to representing the race."

Those words were echoed recently by an assistant professor of African American Studies:[18]

> The Black professor is often called upon to serve as mentor and counselor to African American students in an environment that is oftentimes hostile to them. The consequences of these multifaceted role expectations by students are compounded by the existence of similar demands placed upon Blacks by colleagues and administrators. If we consider the fact that Blacks often also have the same expectations to meet at home, it is abundantly clear that in many cases something has to give.

Stories of blatant discrimination are not often documented, but can occur where there are few people of color, Alison Konrad[19] has found:

> Faculty of color go all semester without getting the computer they need, the secretary will not answer phone calls for them like done of other faculty, and the president insists they work on projects that only senior faculty should be working on—loaded up with token memberships on multiple committees.

Says Konrad to new black faculty:

> It matters a great deal how well you are integrated in your department. Do you eat with your colleagues, discuss research with them? Also, how well are you integrated in your school, which affects your ability to get grants? Then the question is, how well are you tied in to the national network—how are you linked with faculty at other institutions in your discipline? And you can try to reach out to your dean and senior faculty members.

Wiley calls on black faculty to ask their administrations to "take a new look at faculty roles." At least this can be said; on most campuses, instances of gross racism affecting new black professors are being dealt with promptly under the 1991 Civil Rights Act (PL 102-166). Take heart!

Blacks aren't the only ones, of course, who can face racial discrimination. For example, a job search recently underway at a private Midwestern university screened out all Asian American candidates because "we don't want anyone who can't speak English."[20]

Double Jeopardy. Some 500 had been expected, but more than 2,000 black women in academe assembled at the Massachusetts Institute of Technology in January 1994 to voice both pride and pain—pride in the strides they have made in the past decade, pain in the double jeopardy they continue to face as both African American and female.

They spoke of the "double-bind" of racism and sexism and of the burdens of serving as mentors to black female students when black women professors are so few on any particular campus. They spoke of the "public humiliation" heaped upon two black female scholars, Anita Hill and Lani Guinier.

MIT's president, Charles M. Vest, characterized the landmark conference in saying, "I can't help but think that this conference is a major step in making the invisible visible."[21]

"It's Not Easy Being Green" (Kermit the Frog). As we've seen, Bill faced some negative attitudes in his new department. But he's a man, white, and American. As we've just discussed, some faculty come into situations where they must contend with more than the usual political difficulties. If you're a woman, a member of an ethnic minority group, or a foreigner, the ladder to tenure may be somewhat more slippery.

Why were you hired? (There's probably more than one right answer.) Because you have special talents and experiences? Then work to develop those talents and build on those experiences. Because you represent an underrepresented population? If you were hired for that reason, why? To bring different perspectives to your new department? Then you're likely free to be yourself. To meet some quota or other pressures to "diversify"? Then you may need to exercise a little extra judgment.

That doesn't mean to sell out, to deny your differences—not at all. But you should be particularly sensitive to your situation, to your environment. Some of your new colleagues may initially resent you or even be apprehensive. Be sensitive to potential conflicts. Don't try to avoid them; just weigh the consequences carefully.

Remember: much of the progress made through affirmative action has been at the lower levels. "Glass ceilings" and other such barriers exist in academia as they do anywhere in society where people have difficulty adjusting to differences. Don't be suspicious of every colleague and every word and action, yet don't be naive and idealistic.

Sometimes you may feel it's a no-win situation: you're damned if you do and damned if you don't. If you volunteer for committees, for example, some of your colleagues may consider you overly aggressive or too eager to please, but if you don't, then you're lazy or aloof or lukewarm in your commitment. Also, as a former colleague pointed out, the dilemma is "especially bad for female assistant professors who collaborate with male *heavy hitters*" because it's easy to undervalue the contributions of the junior collaborator. And if a woman or a minority associates with other women or minorities, this can be viewed as "ghettoization." As Kermit the Frog laments, "It's not easy being green."

Make the most of who you are and what you have to offer, so your new colleagues accept you as an individual. In other words, make it harder for anyone to simply label you in terms of your differences. Network with people who can better understand any particular obstacles you might face in your situation. But don't assume anything about "friends" or "foes"—as you wouldn't want your new colleagues to make assumptions about you.

If you're any type or shade of "Kermit the Frog Green," you may profit from the "10 guerrilla tactics to getting tenure" prescribed by Suzanne Rose, associate professor of psychology and women's studies director at the University of Missouri-St. Louis.[22] Her suggestions presage much of what you'll find in more detail in coming chapters:

1. Initiate a professional network with prominent people in your field so that at tenure time you'll have some evaluators to suggest.

2. Cultivate a campus network, both inside and outside your department.

3. Promote your own work by circulating reprints and getting mentioned in the campus faculty newsletter.

4. Be sure your teaching is at least acceptable; if not, consult your campus faculty development center.

5. Ration your service activities. Accept any high-profile committee assignments.

6. React to any negative annual evaluations immediately. State your case explicitly in the file.

7. Keep a private, detailed record of any discrimination or harassment you've experienced. It may come in handy.

8. Conduct a frank, personal third-year review. If your annual evaluations have been negative, start looking for another job.

9. If you're turned down for tenure, consider filing a grievance. Or, you may find a better fit elsewhere. (See Appendix A.)

10. Remember: you are not your job. Your worth as a person should not rest on your department's evaluation of you.

To some of you, these suggestions may seem a trifle cynical, to others, eminently sound. You'll just have to divine your own approach to any circumstances of "being green."

COULD I FACE ANY UNAVOIDABLE ENVIRONMENTAL HAZARDS?

Unfortunately the answer is "Yes." At least three come to mind.

We've already discussed one: A major institutional budgetary shortfall that would force the board of governors to put a cap on the number of slots open to new associate professors in any given year. While they could all be promoted without any salary raises, that would put faculty pay scales out of whack for 40 years.

Of course, looking on the bright side, the opposite could happen: a generous benefactor comes out of the alumni woodwork to endow accelerated promotions for outstanding young faculty.

Another type of crunch is a pile-up of eligible tenure candidates at the departmental level. It happened frequently in the 1950s, producing professional scrambles and personal vendettas. It could happen again as colleges and universities face massive faculty retirements between 1990 and 2010.

At the college level of review, you might run up against—let's face it—some sort of unofficial quota system, for good or ill. A dean can be under heavy pressure to reflect in his or her recommendations for tenure a campus drive for affirmative action, multicultural diversity, pluralism, political correctness, or some such thing—or a faculty backlash against claimed "diminution in faculty quality." You personally may or may not benefit from the tension. That's just the way it can be, sorry to say.[23]

There isn't much you can do about such hazards except build the most impressive CV you can—and keep your fingers crossed.

WHAT'S THE NATURE OF MY COMPETITION?

In any climb up the ladder to tenure, the success of any one candidate at one time and place will depend at least to some degree on the caliber of the competition. Thanks to a recent review[24] of the research literature on junior faculty, you can glean some insights on the generic attributes of the recruits with which you share a common quest.

First, who exactly are these candidates? Well, they've chosen to go against any trend of entering the private sector but rather to seek a career in academe, so they're highly purposeful and motivated. They include a significantly higher proportion of women than did earlier generations. Because of a longer average time period to earn a Ph.D., they're older and more mature than their predecessors. They come from increasingly diverse Ph.D. programs in diverse institutions with diverse doctoral socialization processes, so they may experience "culture shock" in their first appointment. And more of them than ever before are part of dual-career couples, each member of which may be struggling independently to juggle career and personal affairs.

Second, how do they seem to be handling their careers? New faculty increasingly find themselves initially in temporary contract positions. Once they secure tenure-track appointments, they face many pressures, especially in the form of the imperative to publish. They work long and hard, but differently than their senior colleagues, spending more time on teaching and research and less in service roles, meanwhile perceiving severe time constraints.

While they're generally satisfied with their choice of an academic career, they're often disenchanted with their choice of a particular institution. They're overwhelmed by teaching duties, run hard just to keep in place, and feel unaided in the undertaking, although those who seek faculty development program assistance tend to become more comfortable. They see department chairs as expecting them to "hit the ground running" and senior colleagues providing little collegiality.

You'll recognize, of course, that all of the above are generalities, but they give you a frame of reference for assessing your local compatriots—and perhaps hold up a mirror to your own "condition of servitude."

Finally, what might cause some to drop away? Surveying 60 faculty members newly hired in a six-year period who subsequently left campus before making tenure, two scholars of higher education[25] have identified some key reasons for the defaults.

A majority of the respondents cited problems in what might be called a "personal dimension"—cost of living, housing, spouse employment, aging parents, social isolation, children's education, standard of living, and alienation in the community.

The next most cited reasons clustered in a "professional interpersonal" domain—departmental support and relations, lack of professionalism on the part of colleagues, intellectual isolation, lack of mentoring—with women listing these factors twice as often as men.

Then there were "organizational" reasons—perceived lack of competence of administrators, poor working conditions, inadequate salaries, and limited research and travel support.

In this case, the data are derived from a single institution, but they can give you a clue to the types of hazards that may haunt some of your peers—or you.

WHAT ARE THE HIDDEN DUES?

Are there any campus or community organizations I or my spouse are expected to join? At what cost? What is my expected "community chest" contribution level? Does my department maintain a "slush fund," "coffee kitty," or "social budget" to which I'm supposed to donate? How much a month? Is there an expected periodic campus foundation tariff? A campus research fund to which I'm required to turn over all or a percentage of any royalties I might earn on writings or patents? If I run up mileage while representing the institution around its constituency, will I be reimbursed or not? For off-campus meals and motels?

As time goes on, you'll undoubtedly think of other questions about hiddden dues. Don't hesitate to ask. Start with your department office factotum. He or she will know the answers or whom to consult. Don't rely on "locker-room experts"; go to the campus specialists.

WHAT ABOUT LOGISTICAL SUPPORT?

Again, you undoubtedly checked into the broad outlines of this matter before coming on board. Indeed, some of its aspects may have tilted your decision.

Now's the time to pin down the details on such key matters as library resources, book and journal purchase funds, laboratory space and equipment, office space and equipment, long-distance phoning, fax access, instrumentation, computers, secretarial service, TAs/RAs, travel funds, leaves, instructional aids, in-house research funds, workshops and seminars on how better to meet your triad of responsibilities—the gamut of material that can make all the difference between smooth sailing and stormy weather in your navigation toward tenure.

But don't expect to get everything on a platter. As we suggested in Chapter 1, you've got to make your own fiscal investment in your career. If that means your spouse finds at least a part-time job and your children don't keep up with the Jones kids, so be it. The sacrifices are for six years, not a lifetime.

Incidentally, don't kid yourself that you can't be productive unless you get a sabbatical from teaching. Robert Boice[26] compared the writing output of new hires before, during, and after a semester or two of research leave and found "no general increase in outputs during or after their release time, despite the universal goal of using it to increase productivity." From his results, Boice doesn't conclude that faculty shouldn't seek release but rather that release time can be futile in the absence of vital "goals, supports, learning task management, and accountablility as parts of release-time programs."

WHAT ARE COMMON ROUGH SPOTS AND SAND TRAPS?

To stay on the fairway to tenure, it may help you to know why some professors don't shoot par. Faculty have identified these hazards:

- Personal problems.
- Faculty departmental quarrels.
- Alcohol.
- Being unprepared to follow when the discipline or specialty takes a new twist.
- Complexities of grantsmanship or academic politics that can be a prerequisite to success for even the most creative scholar.
- Inability to understand the institution's definition of a "good" or productive faculty member, particularly if that definition is "fuzzy" or changes.
- Gross methods used by reviewers to measure excellence in teaching, research, and service—relying on impressions and gossip rather than taking time to read and evaluate solid data.

Some of these hazards you can avoid with skill; others are endemic to the game. Talk to your caddie.

WHAT ABOUT PERSONAL-SUPPORT MECHANISMS?

- A professor is concerned because he knows the chair can smell liquor on his breath during daytime chats in the hall, but he can't shake the addiction.
- Another is at her wits' end because she's just received what she considers to be a grossly unfair reprimand from a superior.
- Still another is having such serious marital difficulties that it's affecting his ability to stay on track.

Farfetched? Not at all. It could happen to you. So it's natural that you'd inquire into personal-support mechanisms on your campus, should the need ever arise. At some institutions, faculty with personal problems have to muddle through a maze of counseling, employee relations, or other kinds of agencies before finding help. At others, a single one-stop resource is at hand.

At Midland, for instance, there's a central Employee Assistance Center that provides direction for any faculty, academic staff, or classified personnel who are struggling with personal, professional, behavioral, or medical problems.

Says its director:

> We provide an opportunity for university people to sort out the things that are going on in their particular situations and to identify a broad range of options available for dealing with them. We tend not to do actual counseling, although we can get involved if we feel we can help within three or four meetings. What we emphasize is problem assessment and referral to the right resources at the university or in the city.

In turn, Midland has published a comprehensive employee assistance policy stating, among other things, that employees may use Center services during working hours and that all conversations, with a few exceptions covered by law, are strictly confidential.

You may find you're so fortunate as to have access to a like service. If not, you're obviously pretty much on your own—a significant negative institutional factor.

WHAT DO I DO IN THE SUMMER?

Assuming you're on a standard nine-month appointment, you'll have the summer off.

What do I do? The temptation will be great to augment your income by teaching in the summer session, but that might bite seriously into your research pace. With luck your dean will have access to some discretionary funds to provide summer salary research support to worthy young assistant professors.

A compromise would be to teach in a three-week summer session if your institution has such a calendar, and then use the remaining eight or nine weeks in laboratory or library. That, and taking a vacation—without which you and your family could go stir-crazy. There's always the possibility, too, of combining vacation travel with research, a professional association convention, or a teaching workshop.

WHAT ABOUT FUNDING?

What keys open the department or college cash box? Research proposals? Requisitions for instructional aids? Requests for travel funds? All of the above?

Can I live forever on intramural "bootlegged" time and money? Or will I be expected to generate extramural funding on my own? To what extent? How soon in my career? What support mechanisms are available to facilitate my search for grants? What's the going average of outside funding in my department per faculty member?

Such are key questions for which you should seek answers early on.

To the question whether you're expected to attract some of your own funding, if the answer is yes, make no little plans. Sure, in terms of the size of an initial grant, you'll probably have to think small, but start contemplating already something much larger in scope—say, an institute, a center, a consortium, even a semi-independent named chair. Such devices seem to multiply on campuses these days like wire coat hangers in closets. Some are complexes of offices, some even buildings, others nothing but letterheads. Whatever, they appear to have a certain appeal to funding agencies. Scan, for instance, any academic newsletter and see how many academics cited are chairs, directors, or affiliates of those institutes and centers. It's almost as if in some circles the conventional department were becoming passé.

For example, the senior author (ACS) had a lot better luck attracting outside funding once he fabricated an inter-college Center for Environmental Communication and Education Studies than he did operating under a school rubric.

While such entrepreneurial efforts may usually wait upon your making tenure, there's nothing wrong with your reach exceeding your grasp—at least in your mind's eye.

One reviewer of this manual (a social science department chair at a state university) has this slant on the funding picture today:

> One reason grant getting is important these days is that state support is getting more iffy than in the past. A grant-getter is an important asset to a department, particularly when at least some indirect costs from grants are funneled to the department. Departments

now seem to be considering new areas of specialization depending, at least in part, on funding opportunities. A question: What's the sense in continuing to specialize in X that can no longer be supported when Y has funding? Another question: Does the tenure candidate work in X or Y? Wherein lies the future?

For more on attracting research funding, see Chapter 8.

WHAT ABOUT STRESS?

If you've been reading the research literature on higher education lately, you know that some of your colleagues have specialized in studying campuses as highly stressful workplaces. And from your own experience you know that assistant professors, under the gun to publish or perish in a very concentrated period of time, are particularly prone to suffer the effects of tension, much of it self-induced.

To get on top of the problem, Walter H. Gmelch[27] in his new book recommends that you first identify what exactly is bothering you—your "stress traps" as he calls them. From her review of all the research literature, Mary Deane Sorcinelli[28] says that, if you're like most tenure-track people, these are the "stress points" you'll contend with:

- Unrealistic expectations you've set for yourself.
- Not enough time in which to accomplish those goals.
- Inadequate feedback on how you're doing.
- Lack of collegiality on the part of your peers.
- Lack of resources essential to your tasks.
- Balancing work with life outside of work.

Deborah Olson's longitudinal study of a cohort of new hires at Indiana University-Bloomington[28] found all of these stress points in play—and more, and things didn't get any better over the first several years of appointment.

Just because such stressors are common doesn't necessarily mean you'll be a victim. But if you are, what do you do?

Gmelch prescribes:

- Take an active role in coping with stressors amenable to personal responsibility.

- Learn to endure the unavoidable.
- Get away from it all occasionally for an hour, a day, a week, or more.

His description of the "hardy professor" suggests there can be daylight at the end of the tunnel. The hardy professor sees problems as a challenge, has the ability to commit to the discipline and life's opportunities, and likes to believe he or she can affect the work environment. Several studies[30] confirm the idea that, despite the stress, faculty as a whole remain dedicated, resourceful, and resilient.

If it's any consolation to you, Gmelch reports that all members of an academic community share the stress syndrome—department chairs, upper-echelon administrators, librarians, cooperative extension personnel, and so on. Apparently stress is simply built into academia today, so you're not alone.

With luck you're at an institution trying to do something about endemic stress: giving faculty more control over their environment, offering supportive work and family policies, improving communication down and up, providing health insurance for mental illness and chemical dependency, and allowing more flexible scheduling of work hours.

It'll probably help to recognize that some stress is a good thing. As a French professor at Emory University wrote in the November/December 1993 *Lingua Franca*, "To be intellectually first-rate requires a kind of anxiety that does not necessarily allow for comfort." To paraphrase Robert Browning, "Our reach should exceed our grasp, or what's a heaven for?"

Probably your best antidote is simply to recognize that hundreds of thousands have been this way before and survived and flourished. That, and the relaxing thought that, after all, "90% of life is just showing up."

WHAT ABOUT WORK/FAMILY ISSUES?

Is the climate of your campus sympathetic to dual-career couples? Are there collaborative arrangements with local employers to locate suitable employment for spouses? What about family responsiveness policies—maternity and family leave, reduced teaching loads, and adjusted tenure-track demands for parents of young children? Are there mentors and networks to support scholarly development for assistant professors with dual responsibilities?[31]

IS MY INSTITUTION CENSURED?

You probably checked out long ago whether or not your institution is on the list of colleges and universities under censure by the American Association of University Professors. If you didn't, do so now.

The AAUP censures institutions when it finds they've violated the association's standards of academic freedom and tenure, which have become widely accepted in academia.

For example, in January 1994 the trustees of the College of the Ozarks (AR) figured that running a college was a lot like running a business, and since companies don't grant tenure, why should colleges? So they voted premtorily to abolish tenure and substitute periodic contracts. The trustee action came in the wake of disbanding the College's faculty governing body.

When the story broke in *The Chronicle of Higher Education* (January 26), bells went off in the Washington, DC offices of the AAUP leading to a full field investigation and likely "blacklisting" of Ozarks as a campus inimicable to professional health.

An institution can get off the AAUP list, but not without considerable remedial action. Joining and staying on the faculty of an institution on the AAUP's blacklist can be hazardous to your academic health.

HOW DO I KEEP FROM GETTING FIRED?

A brochure with approximately this title was issued in 1991 by *Changing Times Magazine*. Although aiming primarily at the business world and hence bordering on the patently "political," the editors nonetheless make some points not irrelevant to any campus scene:

- Develop your contacts, your networking with peers, superiors, staff, and off-campus influentials.
- Know your institution's mission and adapt.
- Think—and act—positively; be cooperative, don't be a crank.
- Don't assume your competence is a given.

- Keep your CV up-to-date and handy so you can argue your case.
- Practice communicating orally and in writing more cogently.
- Go back to school in workshops or on your own.
- And the clincher: make yourself too valuable to lose.

Perhaps more pertinent to the campus scene are "the problems with faculty most commonly voiced by department chairs" in a national survey by Robert Boice.[32] You'll naturally want to avoid these causes of an impending "pink slip"—listed in rank order:

1. Inactivity as scholars.

2. Shirking committees and student advising.

3. Opposition to department functioning.

4. Social isolation from colleagues.

5. Unfriendliness toward chair.

6. Source of student complaints.

7. Explosive with colleagues and students.

8. Suspicious or paranoid behavior.

Alan T. Seagren[33] has identified similar causes of failing faculty: dissatisfaction with work roles or assignments, lack or loss of enthusiasm, performing minimal duties, and negative attitude.

An astute chair can spot such signs that new faculty aren't performing up to expectations, Seagren says. Enough said.

WHAT IS THE "CULTURE" OF MY INSTITUTION?

In the words of Peter Seldin, prolific professor of management, academic culture is the unspoken language that tells you what's important, what's unimportant, and how you're expected to do things at your institution—the amalgam of beliefs, mythology, values, and tones that sets your institution apart. It's a term that describes rather than evaluates, concerned with perceptions rather than opinions.[34]

Why is it important to understand your academic culture? Because you must be comfortable in a culture to succeed in it.

Can a member of a college or university get an accurate picture of its culture? Yes. But as an insider trying to learn about your culture you must do three things:

1. Ignore your institution's promotional literature—it's probably written by a fugitive from a Madison Avenue PR agency.

2. Disregard your own prior assumptions, biases, and beliefs.

3. Mentally record only what you see and hear. And first impressions can be valid.

Seldin lists the following 10 characteristics as some of the definable elements of an academic culture:

1. *Individual Autonomy.* What degree of responsibility, independence, and opportunity do you actually have?

2. *Structure.* To what degree are rules and regulations used to control faculty, students, administrators, and staff?

3. *Support.* How much warmth and helpfulness does the administration exhibit to subordinates? Faculty to students?

4. *Identity.* To what degree do faculty and students identify with the entire institution? With your department?

5. *Quality of Personnel.* How much confidence do administrators, faculty, and students display in each other's integrity and competence?

6. *Cooperation.* How effectively do people throughout the campus work together toward shared goals? What about people in your department?

7. *Decision-Making Process.* How much genuine consultation and collaboration exist in formulating functions and policies? At the top level? In your department?

8. *Risk Tolerance.* How much are you encouraged to be professionally adventuresome and innovative?

9. *Communication Pattern.* How well does complete, accurate, and meaningful information flow upward, downward, and across the institution? Within your department?

10. *Sense of Community.* To what degree do members of the college or university feel a sense of oneness, a tone of genuine caring and sharing for each other? In your department?

If you keep your mouth shut and your eyes and ears open, you should be able to get a pretty good reading on this continuum of institutional characteristics fairly quickly. Members of site-visit teams and accreditation panels do it all the time in a week or so.

Don't expect to be utterly content with everything you sense. There is no perfect campus culture. On the other hand, if most of what you perceive is alien to your personal criteria, start sending out résumés right away.

SOUND SOURCES OF INFORMATION

So far we've been talking about elements of information essential to you in plotting a career development course. Here we're going to suggest some reputable—and not so reputable—sources where you can find that information.

YOUR LETTER OF APPOINTMENT

Although it was her first one, the letter Prof. Amanda L. Perkins wrote to your alter ego Bill at Midland University was explicit and helpful, perhaps because in her newness as botany chair she consulted an excellent *Chairperson's Manual* compiled by Kay U. Kerr of Colorado State University's Office of Instructional Services.[35]

If your own letter of appointment is more cryptic than clear, you might want to consider referring to that guide for clues to matters to be discussed.

With an award-winning record in faculty recruitment and retention, CSU Professor Stephen D. Roper, chair of anatomy and neurobiology, has these useful talking points:

A newly hired faculty member deserves a clear explanation of what is expected over the next few years. Detail the department's career criteria. The letter should include at a minimum the expectations regarding (1) teaching obligations (such as courses, number of students, when taught, and performance standards), (2) research activities (whether extramural grants are expected, whether the faculty member is to obtain salary support from grants, what level of productivity is anticipated), and (3) service activities (major committee assignments and so on). The letters I send to newly hired faculty members encompass our expectations for the first one to three years. These documents are quite comprehensive and typically run two to three pages in length.

The transition from Ph.D. graduate to new faculty member is a major change. Whereas to this point the individual may have been protected and nurtured, that has now ceased. That is why in our departmental letters of appointment we name a specific mentor or advocate for each new faculty member.

Protect the new hire from an overburdensome teaching/service load in the first year. The first year is a critical germination time to set roots at our University. All my faculty concur in understanding the need to assume slightly greater teaching loads in order to ease the new faculty member's load, and this policy is explained in the appointment letter.

Provide appropriate resources as start-up funds. Resources such as equipment, discretionary funds, and space should be communicated in writing and honored in full. Ideally a new faculty member should be provided with sustained research support—a safety net for one to three years as the new colleague pursues funding. The letter will so state. It will also suggest that the new hire initially team up with a more experienced faculty member and submit a joint funding proposal, and point out likely journals, funding agencies, and campus aids in writing grants and preparing papers.

Point out how a faculty member can obtain national visibility. My letters of appointment speak to interdisciplinary collaboration and joint projects across the state and nation, offer travel support and encouragement to attend and present papers at national meetings, and suggest how to attract invitations for talks at other institutions.

The career of the spouse may be a consideration. In these days of "dinks" (double income, no kids) and "diks" (double income, kids), the career of the spouse or significant other may become a factor in retaining the new faculty member. My letters of appointment offer such assistance as the department might render.

As we say, if your own letter of appointment falls short of CSU's standard, try to figure out ways to obtain information and support. Don't just let uncertainties ride. Matters you don't clear up in the first month or so can fester indefinitely.

DEPARTMENTAL MEETINGS AND MINUTES

Your Midland alter ego was dreading his first department faculty meeting even before he reported in: "I won't know anybody and nobody will know me." The meeting turned out not to be scheduled until mid-September, to allow everybody to get their feet on the ground.

He had arrived early, in mid-August, at the "request" of the department chair so he could attend "orientation" sessions for new hires, sponsored by the Midland Center for Faculty Development. (They turned out to be worthwhile: no "This is the blackboard and this is a pointer" stuff.)

As the rest of the department began to filter in, Chair Perkins stepped to the fore, having read that Colorado State University handbook, and followed its prescription to the letter:

> *Monitoring the new faculty member's interaction with other faculty.* This is a delicate situation, requiring interpersonal communication skills. The department head can help by taking extra pains to introduce the new faculty member to other faculty, describing backgrounds and areas of possible mutual interest. Interactions outside the department with departmental faculty and persons from other areas of the university can be encouraged, even arranged. Setting up coffee sessions or lunches among small groups of faculty, including the new member, is a prime example. Every new faculty member needs to feel wanted and needed.

With luck, your own arrival will be as hospitable, so that by the time of the first faculty meeting you won't face it with utter fear and trembling. Even so, it will probably be best to follow that well-known adage that new assistant professors are to be seen and not heard; unless, of course, you're asked to respond to a direct question, in which case take strategic evasive action without appearing to be totally dumb. Whatever you do, don't say, "Well, at Excelsior they did thus and so;" your new colleagues couldn't care less.

Keeping in the background has the advantage that it gives your undivided attention to the flow of the meeting. The agenda items themselves as well as the perfunctory or profound discussions they prompt will be the beginnings of your primer for learning your territory.

At Midland, departmental faculty meetings are habitually held on Friday afternoons after all classes are out. (Spouses just have to get used to late Friday dinners at least once a month.) Regardless of the state of the meeting, promptly at 5:30 Chair Perkins calls a pause in the day's occupation for what is euphemistically known as "the children's hour." Professor R. Hammond Louvre, the connoisseur, breaks out wine and everybody relaxes. (It's technically illegal to consume intoxicating beverages on Midland property, but nobody has ever questioned the department tradition.) Needless to say, the department meeting breaks up a bit later on a more convivial note than when it began. The ceremony may be the one device that keeps the two botany "camps" from shedding each other's blood on occasion. (The conundrum: if a new Midland botany hire is a teetotaler, or Jewish and observing the Sabbath, what does he or she do?)

Don't draw the conclusion that all the Midland protocols we cite apply universally. For example, as one commentator writes,

> At small colleges, committee work is done at the campus level, not departmental. Faculty committees are composed of faculty across the disciplines who are voted in by the entire faculty. Yet much of what you say about departmental committees and meetings is equally applicable to such all-college committees.
>
> Incidentally, your advice to a new hire to be seen and not heard in such meetings is excellent. It takes a while to know the whole faculty, and you really need to recognize the different camps before you stick your neck out.

Regardless of what sort of department faculty meeting climate you find at your institution, look forward to those meetings and the clues they're bound to offer about institutional expectations.

One strategic decision may confront you at that first meeting: the chair may call for volunteers to serve on a new department faculty committee. Do you raise your hand? Some colleagues will frown on such an unseemly display of "pushiness"; others will applaud your willingness to assume the burdens of department citizenship. It's a judgment call. On balance, we'd say, "Go for it," particularly if the committee assignment has some relevance to your background and professional interests. The meek don't usually inherit the academic earth.

Besides paying rapt attention to the pronouncements and nuances at faculty meetings, you may want to go into department files and read the minutes of faculty meetings in years past—again, to get a feeling for your new territory. You may find some minutes so sparse they merely record who made what motion and whether it carried or failed, while others will have recorded every blow-by-blow of discussion to the extent the ultimate decision is practically buried in verbiage.

Nonetheless, past faculty meeting minutes can be well worth scanning.

COLLEGE/DIVISION GUIDELINES

Your college or division will likely have some sort of a criteria-for-promotion-to-tenure document. Because it has to apply to a wide range of departments, it will speak in broad generalities, but they can be helpful to an extent in giving you a sense of college priorities.

But you have to be conscious of the fine print. The Midland School of Forestry and Environmental Studies guidelines, for example, state explicitly that "school procedures and criteria are specific for faculty in the School, but they do not supersede University criteria"—and then later go on to say that a candidate for tenure in the School need demonstrate excellence in only one of the three of the triad, while University policy clearly states that all Midland faculty are expected to "perform over the full range of University responsibilities." To an assistant professor of forestry, it would represent "a puzzlement."

You may find the same sort of discrepancies in the literature of your institution.

CAMPUS POLICY STATEMENTS

The Midland Faculty Handbook (II) devotes much of its space on promotion-to-tenure to specifying the policies and procedures to be followed by all principal divisions. These rules you can use to anticipate the major steps in the process—or to appeal a mishandled review of your record.

Statements issued by such administrators as the Dean of the Graduate School/Research tend to be more explicit and thus enlightening, as we've seen in the delineation of Midland's research expectations.

One caution: make sure any administrative statement you consult at your institution is current. Outdated policy documents tend to have an extended half-life in departmental files.

ANNUAL FACULTY ACTIVITIES REPORT FORM

You can tell a lot about institutional expectations from the form of that form. For example, we're looking at a community college form; it has space for "Instructional Activities," for "College Service," and for "Discipline-Related Public Service and Outreach," but none for "Research." A land-grant college of agriculture form in hand starts out with space for "Extension Activities." A liberal arts and science college form in a research university starts out with space for "Research or Artistic Activities," while a four-year academy form starts out with space for "Teaching." All those variations tell you something.

Because it calls for all the data you ought to be keeping track of in detail, we reproduce the Midland University annual faculty activities report form here (as adapted by the department of botany and applied ecology):

Current Personal Data
Full name
    University address and phone number
    Midland address and phone number
      Marital status
      Name of spouse, if any
        Names and birth dates of any children
    All degrees earned, dates, and institution awarding
      Area of research specialization
    Rank at Midland, with date of appointment to present rank
    Length and dates of faculty and/or professional service

Instructional Activities
    Regular course offerings, by number, title, credit hours, number of students, number of labs

Spring term

Summer

Fall term

Winter term

Non-regular scheduled course offerings, by number, title, credit hours, number of students

Spring term

Summer

Fall term

Winter term

Continuing education and extension teaching (short courses, workshops, etc.)

Guest lecture activities (lectures given in colleagues' courses)

Student Advising and Counseling

Number of undergraduates for whom you are the assigned advisor

Graduate students (name, degree sought, schedule; if degree was completed, give date and full citation for thesis or dissertation)

Major professor

Co-Major professor

Member, Steering Committee (other than those listed above)

Chair or Reader on thesis, exams, etc.

Research Completed or Underway

Grant-supported research (source, subject, amount, duration; list any graduate research assistants supported by each grant.)

Research proposals pending

School research (unsupported, bootlegged; state title, time spent)

Publications (provide full bibliographical citation; DO NOT use "with Jones" or "Jones et al."; detail any publications that were reported "in press" last year.)

Papers presented (give date, title, and location)

(NOTE: Textbooks, reports, newsletters, circulars, and similar publications are normally considered evidence of teaching ability or public service and will be considered creative work only when they present new ideas or incorporate original scholarly research or performance.)

Public Service

Funded service (include consulting activities)

Government agencies (federal, state, local)

Industrial and commercial groups, etc.

Unfunded service to government agencies, public interest groups, etc.

Professional Development

    Activities in professional organizations (offices held; service as chair, participant, or consultant)

    Professional society memberships

    Other professional activities

        Editorial activity (journal, responsibility)

        Other (books, symposia, etc.)

        Reviewer (journal, number of manuscripts; agency, number of proposals; other)

        Participation in workshops, symposia, etc. (name, date, place)

    Further education/retraining undertaken (leaves, workshops, etc.)

    Foreign travel (when, where, purpose)

    Noteworthy achievements (awards, licenses, inventions, citations, etc.)

Administrative and Service Responsibilities (including committee work)

    Departmental-level

    College-level

    University-wide (include Research Foundation)

Statement for Annual Departmental Report Summarizing Significant Accomplishments During Reporting Period (limit to one or two brief paragraphs)

Future Plans, Ambitions, and Potential Contributions for Your Own Professional Development and Enhancement of the Department's Programs (not more than one page)

Any Pertinent Information You Feel Is Not Elicited by the Form (again, be brief).

Your own institution's faculty activities report form may vary in degree but not in kind. If by some odd chance your institution does not require an annual report, use the Midland form as a guide against the day when you'll have to document your promotion-to-tenure qualifications.

GOALS AND OBJECTIVES REPORT

You may or may not have to file an annual goals and objectives report, as do Midland faculty members. Even if none is required, drafting one for your own guidance is a constructive practice.

Unlike its annual Faculty Activities Report, Midland has no prescribed form for the goals and objectives document. Here's what the chair of the department of botany and applied ecology has written in a memo to her faculty:

> Each faculty member shall submit to the chair an annual statement of long-term goals and objectives for the coming year. These should cover research, teaching, and service activities. Outline professional development plans, being as specific as possible. Indicate how the chair and the department can facilitate the achievement of your objective. The report becomes the basis for your annual counseling session with the chair.

By formulating your own goals and objectives document, you can in effect subtly prescribe for review a set of expectations.

COUNSELING SESSIONS

Remember, if you were at Midland you would meet with your department chair in August or September to discuss those goals and objectives. Department tradition holds this to be a formative session in which you and the chair arrive at an agreement on your activities for the coming year. Since you're not tenured, the chair will also counsel you on how your goals and objectives are likely to affect progress toward tenure.

In April or May you would meet with the chair again to review accomplishments and productivity during the past year. This meeting occurs after the chair has made preliminary performance evaluations and salary adjustment determinations, but prior to actually submitting salary recommendations to the dean of the college. The chair will identify strengths and weaknesses in your record and suggest ways to effect improvement, particularly in terms of progressing toward tenure. The chair prepares a written summary of the review and gives you a copy to which you may respond. All documents then go in your personnel file.

As you can see, such semi-annual counseling and review sessions are extremely valuable to you, not only in terms of grasping departmental expectations but also in actually getting a sense of how you're coming along, at least in the eyes of your chair.

Not all counseling sessions need be scheduled, and the trick is to recognize an opportunity when it walks up and shakes your hand.

If a senior member of your search-and-screen committee spots you one noon hour brown-bagging in the faculty lounge, sits down at your table, and asks, "Well, how's the course going?" he may be simply making conversation and you can reply, "Fine, how's yours?" On the other hand, if there's a certain intensity in the air, you might think, "I wonder what he's heard?" and say, "I'm glad you asked. I'd like your advice about what I think I'm discovering about my teaching goals, the way students learn, and how the two mesh with the content of that course I'm assigned this term."[36]

And then see what happens.

If your institution doesn't formally schedule counseling sessions, you might try manufacturing the process with grace.

As good an excuse as any would be to seek the counsel of your department chair when you get back your first set of student evaluations after they've been through the department numbers-cruncher. You won't know whether to dance a jig or cry like a baby, because the summary will likely include a combination of a single numerical rating and a set of narrative student comments. Reconciling the two components can be the neatest trick of the week, a task of interpretation for which a seasoned professor is well-suited.

Midland uses a local modification of IDEA (Instructional Development and Effectiveness Assessment), a 38-item diagnostic form available from Kansas State University's Center for Faculty Evaluation and Development under the direction of William E. Cashin, who has a 1989-90 data base of student ratings from 17,939 classes in 105 varied North American institutions.[37]

Your Midland *alter ego*, not without some trepidation, brought Chair Perkins a set of evaluations to look at from his second-term second-level course, Botany 335—"Morphology of Flowering Plants." The chair had already observed that Bill was enthusiastic, full of energy, and always seemed to have students hanging around his office. So obviously he was popular, but his ratings didn't particularly reflect that. From her experience, Perkins spotted the problem: Bill was rigorous. Despite his accessibility and ability to impart excitement to a not-too-thrilling subject matter, the students complained about his toughness.

That didn't bother the chair one bit, and she promptly advised Bill to maintain his standards, that students would come to respect him for it, that an "A" from Bill would take on a prized cachet around the department, and that his student ratings would go up accordingly. Perkins was also quick to point out that Bill's numerical rating was not out of line with that of other botany instructors in the IDEA data base.

That's how Peter Frederick of Wabash College (IN) recommends handling student evaluations.[38]

PERIODIC PROGRAM REVIEW REPORT

Sometime during your probationary period your department will in all likelihood be subject to a periodic program review. You'll be well served if you view the process as an opportunity for you and your department to "take stock," and the resulting report can be helpful in discerning institutional expectations, individually and collectively.

There are two types of program reviews—internal self-study and external evaluation. Midland University uses the former every four years, the latter every seven.

To initiate the internal evaluation, the department chair appoints a committee of faculty members prior to the beginning of the fall term. The chair is not a member of the committee but serves as a resource. The committee must finish its report and submit it to the Vice President for Academic Affairs Office by March 1. The chair responds to the report, indicating those points with which he or she agrees or disagrees and emphasizing the aspects of the report that the University should particularly note. The dean of the college and the graduate dean also respond to the report. The report goes to a University internal review committee composed of faculty and administrators from other major units. That committee reviews the report to determine whether any proposed plans are supported by data.

The VPAA Office summarizes the report and proposes plans for the department for the next four years. A meeting to review the summary and plans then takes place among the VPAA, the graduate dean, the college dean, the department chair, and the chair of the department's self-evaluation committee, out of which will come (hopefully) a consensus report that will serve as a collective and individual guide.

Every seven years each Midland department is subjected to an academic program review by an external site-visit team of invited colleagues from representative institutions. The department gets to nominate some team members; the VPAA picks the rest and names the chair.

John B. Bennett, provost and vice president for academic affairs at Quinnipiac College (CT), offers a thoughtful outline of what a site-visit team should look for and at, and hence how an assistant professor should tailor his or her career:

- Mission. How does the department stand historically/ currently and directly/indirectly to what the institution as a whole is widely known or knowable for being and doing?
- Demand for Services. What is the current level of demand for the services of the department in teaching, research, and service, to include trendlines, patterns, and projections?
- Societal Need. What are the societal needs—geographic, demographic, political—to which the department should be responding as the ultimate rationale for claiming societal resources, and how well is the department addressing those needs?
- Program Cost. Is the department cost-effective in terms of such factors as faculty-student ratios, cost of instruction per student credit hour, indirect costs, contributions to other programs, revenue generated by externally funded research projects or by outreach activities, size of faculty in relation to its teaching/research/service track record, and proportion in each faculty rank—in comparison with in-house departments and with peer programs elsewhere?
- Program Quality. What is the department's "Nielsen rating" with respect to conventional measures of faculty caliber, relationships among departmental members, trends regarding faculty turnover, assessments of student potential and achievement, evidence of learning actually achieved in the department on the part of both students and professors, coherence of the curriculum as the nexus wherein faculty strengths and expertise are hooked to student needs, adequacy of such material requirements as instructional and research technology, and physical plant, library resources, and outreach logistics, and faculty involvement in program planning and execution?[39]

Talk of evaluation or review will probably elicit from some faculty colleagues certain recitations of its manifold threats to traditional ways of doing things, or of malevolent administrative designs, as well as complaints about yet more burdens upon limited time and energy, Bennett points out. But he encourages assistant professors to participate with good will and reap the rewards of learning from what's working well and also from what's not. As he concludes, "Periodic self-study is the price of the self-regulated profession."[40]

ACCOUNTABILITY AND OUTCOMES ASSESSMENT

Responding to a rising drumbeat of dissatisfaction with the quality of undergraduate teaching at Midland University, the Midland Board of Trustees mandated that the University have an accountability program in place by Jan. 1, 1992.

The resulting "Midland Accountability and Outcomes Assessment Plans and Procedures" calls for an annual evaluation of both University-wide and department-based educational outcomes, involving these elements:

- Undergraduate goals and objectives developed with external constituencies such as professional organizations, parents, employers of graduates, and alumni, indicating what students are expected to gain from their education.
- Assessment methods that evaluated how well the undergraduates have learned what the goals and objectives state they will learn—through standardized tests, observational data, reports of employers, alumni self-reports, capstone seminar evaluations, and other methods.
- Dissemination procedures to inform constituencies of how well Midland students meet the established goals and objectives. Departmental assessment procedures results become a part of the four- and seven-year reviews.
- Use of the results to review curricula and revise them if necessary, and to counsel individual faculty members. A newly appointed Faculty Council Committee on Instructional Development serves as the official institutional monitoring instrument.

Your institution may not have so formal a curriculum and instruction development program as Midland, but read the writing on the wall: it says that on too many campuses undergraduate teaching has been weighed in the public balance and found wanting—and that assistant professors might well review their career priorities accordingly if they're to fit into what may be called "a new day—the '90s as the decade of undergraduate education."

TENURE REVIEW REPORTS

Unless they're couched in the opaque language characteristic of all too many faculty-composed documents, your tenure review assessments could be just what they're intended to be—your very best guide to departmental expectations.

If the assessments cast aspersions on your student evaluation ratings, head for the campus instructional services center right away and sit in on lectures and seminars conducted by colleagues known for their teaching effectiveness. If the assessments make astringent comments on a worrisome pace of productive-scholarship, get on the stick. If they note a lack of service activity, look around for assignments with visibility. If you score low on interpersonal relations with colleagues, you might read Dale Carnegie's venerable *How to Win Friends and Influence People*.

On the other hand, if your tenure review reports rate at least a B+ in such regards, keep on keeping on with renewed vigor and confidence.

YOUR MONITORING COMMITTEE

You may be in a department where the crucial help/hurdle is a monitoring committee, charged with at once mentoring and evaluating your progress.

A dean reviewing a draft of this manual asked us to include this comment:

> Such committees, if they're in place, deserve a scope of treatment. There are some serious ongoing debates as to whether such committee meetings should be open or closed, and what the committee's responsibilities are to the assistant professor they're tracking. For example, on my campus a recent failure to promote an assistant professor to tenure rested on his inappropriate use of statistical methods in his research. That error should have been noted by his monitoring committee the

very first year of his appointment. Who is at fault? The aspiring assistant professor or the monitoring committee?

My admonition to an assistant professor would be: "Use such a departmental committee if one is in place, but don't depend on it!"

What a sad commentary, but that's the way it can be.

YOUR MENTOR

When Odysseus took off for the wars, he consigned his young son to the care of the fatherly Mentor, and so the term has come down to us implying advice, protection, and caring.

Lately "mentoring" has become a "buzz word" in higher education as a variety of programs have come into use, particularly to help promote the advancement of minority group members and women.

Three educational psychology professors[41] recently looked systematically at how faculty at a public, research-oriented university in the Midwest actually envision and practice mentoring among themselves.

They found that faculty mentoring faculty is not common. When it occurs, it's mutually negotiated, primarily between persons of the same sex and between assistant and full professors.

Another result of the study demonstrated that mentoring is a complex, multi-dimensional activity. There appear to be four distinct types of mentors—friend, career guide, information source, intellectual guide (although multiple attributes can sometimes be combined in a single individual).

The researchers concluded that if you go looking for a mentor, know the type you're seeking; and faculty members willing to serve as mentors should acknowledge the kind of help they're willing and able to offer.

More recently, Robert Boice[42] has done a good deal of work on the mentoring phenomenon, experimenting with varying types of mentoring relationships—volunteer or assigned pairs within the same department, interdisciplinary pairs, committee configurations, and so on. His conclusions are that effective mentoring can be stymied by a reluctance on the part of the assistant professor to seek counsel, for fear of revealing his or her weaknesses, and a reluctance on the part of senior faculty to intrude on the autonomy of new hires.

Given a will to ask for help and a will to give it, any mentoring pattern can succeed, and succeed better by far than an absence of mentoring.

You'll recall that at Midland your *alter ego* Bill was assigned a mentor in his letter of appointment from his department chair. You may or may not be in that situation.

There's no question that a willing mentor can be of enormous assistance in leading you through institutional and interpersonal minefields. If you're faced with identifying one, here's a tip: Why not try to recruit the chair of the department search-and-screen committee that recruited you? After all, he or she already has a big stake in your success, as do all committee members. If you don't perform with distinction, it's a reflection on their judgment. So the chances are that chair will be happy to offer valuable "advice, protection, caring." Lean on him or her.

COLLEGIAL TRACK RECORDS

The information can be hard to come by unless a friendly department secretary can help. But if you can get your hands on the records of what happened over the past five years or so to previous untenured faculty members in the department, they're a gold mine of clues to institutional expectations.

There are personnel files for those fairly new associate professors in the department; whether they're open to your inspection, you'll have to determine. If you can review them, they'll tell you exactly how such and such an associate professor made it. (It won't do much good to look up the records of senior staff, because criteria for promotion and evaluation procedures are under relatively constant change.)

The records of assistant professors who tried and failed may or may not exist or be available, but, they can be an even more valuable guide to both generic institutional expectations and practical departmental politics.

If such a tactic strikes you as too much like snooping, forget it—or suggest it to a less scrupulous probationary peer. Let your conscience be your guide on this one. It's good to remember, however, Santayana's warning that those who are ignorant of history are condemned to repeat it.

UNION MANUALS

If you're at an institution with a faculty union or a facsimile of one, you may find its manuals a font of information about the P&T process, and particularly about grievance procedures should a candidate falter along the line.[43]

It's practically certain that your institution has a formal grievance procedure, since recent court decisions make such mandatory. It will likely provide that a faculty member denied tenure can file a grievance if he or she believes that the negative decision was based on an "improper evaluation."

As defined by Midland University rules (University Faculty 2224-6-07), there are two categories of "improper evaluations": (1) decisions made without adequate consideration of the pertinent facts by the individual(s) making the decision, or (2) decisions based on reasons that infringe on a constitutional right of the faculty member.

At Midland, the process for filing complaints alleging improper evaluation is codified:

> *Appeal for Reconsideration.* Where the negative decision was initiated at the department level, the faculty member may appeal in writing to the chair within 14 days of the decision, identifying how the evaluation was improperly handled. If the chair concurs, he or she asks the dean of the college that the denial be reversed. If the reconsideration is negative, the faculty member may file a grievance with the college.
>
> *College Grievance Review.* The appeal to the college must be presented in writing within 14 days of the negative department decision. The complaint is referred to the college Faculty Grievance Committee for investigation. Results of that investigation will be reported to the dean, who will inform the complainant.
>
> *University Grievance Review.* Complaints alleging improper evaluation must be submitted in writing to the Vice President for Academic Affairs and thence to the faculty members of the Committee on Academic Freedom and Responsibility within 30 days of notification of an unfavorable college review. The burden of going forward and the burden

of establishing proof is on the complainant (who may retain appropriate legal counsel).

Theoretically, a complainant disappointed with an ultimate faculty/administration decision could carry his or her appeal on to the board of governors and then to the courts, but the hazards of becoming known in academic circles as a "litigator" are measurable, like wearing a scarlet letter, and many courts have been chary about entering into debates on academic merit.

As Midland faculty rules go on to prescribe:

> Investigations of complaints alleging improper evaluation shall consider only whether the individual(s) making the decision(s) followed the appropriate procedures, considered the important evidence to a fair determination, and acted in a responsible manner. Neither College nor University grievance committees may substitute their judgment on the merits of the individual's performance for that of the academic unit concerned.

That last is a "sticky wicket," as they say. A faculty union grievance board may have quite a different opinion of "fair determination" or "responsible manner" than will the University's attorney.

In at least one state, the legislature is contemplating a law that would permit independent panels of experts from other institutions to handle tenure-denial grievances based on sex or race discrimination. Passage of such a statute would create quite a precedent, which would please neither faculty unions nor institution administrators.

Hopefully, you'll never be involved on either side of a grievance dispute, but it does no harm to brief yourself on institutional and union points of view and procedures. It's all a part of knowing the territory.

YOUR PROBATIONARY PEERS

You've had enough experience with grad student peers to know it's questionable whether to list peers under "sound" sources of information.

Some of your new faculty peers are going to be rocks of counsel and support, others frail reeds, still others will be all strengths in between. If there's any territory you've got to discern with precision, it's this one.

At Midland, Bill was in the company of seven untenured botany department members, at least one at each stage of the six-year marathon run. He discovered that several loved to tell exaggerated "war stories" about the grueling nature of tenure review sessions, that a couple of others were so close-mouthed as to be of no practical help at all, and the balance were good folk who could be relied on to pass on practical tips and rumors.

If you could know from the gun with whom you'd be spending a career together in warm companionship and fruitful professional association, and which peers would fold their tents and silently slip away, it would be priceless prescience—but of course you can't know any such thing.

It's little comfort that your probationary peers initially have the same reservations about you!

THE GRAPEVINE

We're even less sure about listing the office grapevine as a "sound" information source. Some of the gossip you pick up can be right on the money, and some can be off by a country mile. The trouble is, you don't know which is which when you hear it.

The senior author's spouse knew he was getting promoted to tenure before he did (she picked up the word at a faculty wives' tea), but her guesstimate at the size of the concomitant salary raise turned out to be very wide of the mark. As (ACS) recalls:

> My very best grapevine was the janitor, or 'maintenance engineer.' Because I was a lark, I got to the office just as he was leaving his night shift, and we would fire up the coffee-maker—and gossip. Because we had a mutual love of duck hunting, we also shared a marsh shore blind on an occasional weekend. Whether he was just reading wastebasket detritus or actually perusing files, I never knew nor asked, but his sense of what was happening or about to happen in the department was encyclopedic. His most valuable advice to me was advance warning that the department capital budget was about to undergo an emergency freeze, which gave me time to process a requisition for a new mag-card typewriter (an early version of a word processor) before the blow fell.

That sort of grapevine is rare. Most of the over-the-transom stuff you hear you might as well forget and certainly not pass on.

But if you take that advice, you'll miss out on a lot of department camaraderie!

A department chair who reviewed this manuscript confides:

> I wish I could do a better job of getting junior faculty to (1) hear as much gossip as possible, and (2) contribute to that gossip as little as possible. For some assistant professors with a strong sense of powerlessness, gossip seems to be a means of protecting themselves from surprises— a new course preparation next year, an office change to a different floor, a shift in secretarial assignments, and so on. Yet participation in a grapevine network can be debilitating and lead to mild paranoia.

CAMPUS MEDIA

There are three types of "news" media you'll want to pay attention to—with varying degrees of interest and confidence.

First, there'll be a steady stream of memos from higher-ups. Department memos are "must" reading because they may announce a change in policy or at least a departure in procedures.

A typical departmental memo might read: "I want to remind each of you to lock your doors whenever you leave your offices. I realize this can be inconvenient, but many times a quick trip to the mailbox can turn into a long wait for an elevator, or a hall conversation with a colleague can become extended. We try to ensure a secure building for you, and you can help by eliminating the open invitation an unlocked door can pose. Thank you."

This may seem like "Mickey Mouse" stuff, but complying can protect your computer or purse from a roving thief.

College memos are of indifferent caliber, assuming they're even grammatical; some will be relevant to you, others not. Even so, you dismiss them at your own risk. Front-office communiqués will typically start out with "It has come to the attention of the Vice President for Administration that . . ." Again, while most will be of only tangential importance, it's hazardous to toss them without at least a scan.

Second, there'll be a periodic all-campus house organ, giving you insight into the way the President (HEP position #01) views his or her—and your—world. It's not easy to write and edit such a publication. The chief PR officer has to phrase each sentence in such a way that it pleases or at least satisfies a varied audience— administrators, faculty, students, boards of governors, legislators, alumni, donors, and so on. For example, if a story downplays the significance of a racial disturbance on Greek Row, it can calm old sorority members while dismaying the dean of students and the faculty chaperones who were on the spot. You'll just have to learn to separate the wheat from the chaff.

Third, the campus student newspaper. Some are very good at investigating, reporting, and interpreting institutional issues, particularly those with an undergraduate angle; others are average; still others are flack sheets for either renegade student cabals or the President's Office itself. Again, you'll have to sift and winnow.

Whatever you do, don't ignore these campus media; no matter how dull or how slanted, they're a window on what somebody is thinking and doing. Sooner or later an item in one or another will be of vital import to you and your career, perhaps in the form of a practical "political" tip.

A FINAL EXAM

As a test of how well you're getting to know your territory and acquiring a sense of its promotion-and-tenure criteria, we want you to fill out a simple survey instrument used in a national study to plumb attitudes of campus personnel toward the pervasive issue of teaching vs. research:

Using the following scale, indicate your perception of the relative importance of research and undergraduate teaching:

teaching				**equal**			**research**	
4	**3**	**2**	**1**	**0**	**1**	**2**	**3**	**4**

A. In relation to each other
   a. To you personally
   b. To the majority of faculty in your department
   c. To your dean
   d. To the campus Office of Academic Affairs

B. Your perception of:
   a. The direction that you think your university is going
   b. The direction that you think your university should go
   c. The direction that you think you should go based on your interests

Within the past couple of years, that "exam" has been taken by 23,302 faculty, department heads, deans, and administrators at 33 public and 14 private research I, research II, doctoral-granting I, and doctoral granting II universities from all regions of the United States.

The results, as reported by three Syracuse University scholars,[44] may surprise you. The majority of the respondents were in agreement that an appropriate balance between research and undergraduate teaching should exist, but that it doesn't now.

While faculty personally felt that "the relative importance of research and undergraduate teaching should favor teaching in the future," they reported that their universities put "greater emphasis on research than on teaching" through a current faculty reward system that "places a premium on the quantity of scholarly work produced," and that the closer a person is to campus central administration, the more that individual is biased toward research.

Actually, administrators themselves in their responses tended to tilt toward the teaching end of the spectrum, perhaps because they are reflecting, the surveyers speculate, "the attitudes expressed in the national media and various national reports, as well as by pressure from students and their parents calling for a renewed emphasis on undergraduate teaching in America's universities."

All of which suggests to the researchers that "there is considerable inconsistency" on the part of various cohorts of academic personnel between, "the direction they see the university going and the direction they think it ought to go."

For the junior faculty member trying to climb the academic ladder to tenure, the moral of this exercise is crystal clear: You can't spend too much time or consult too many sources in trying to divine the going values of key individuals and the general culture of your institution *vis-a-vis* the teaching-research-service triad.

A BALANCING ACT

Because our forthcoming chapters on teaching are longer than our chapters on research and on service, one reviewer of the manuscript accused us of "overemphasizing teaching and trivializing research" and, by implication, service as well.

We don't mean it to be taken that way. "Balance" among the three is the desideratum, at least at many institutions. Again, it pays to know your territory.

The same reviewer has a constructive approach to the issue:

> A proper view of the "balance" issue is to place it in a career-span context. The probation period is a time for a new professor to prove to him/herself and the world that she/he can make significant contributions to a scholarly guild. This is the time to take advantage of every bit of "nurturing" and released time that your department is willing to provide.
>
> Professors' desires to be stellar teachers and do awesome research are wonderful, but can't they be given less emphasis for the short five-year (from arrival on campus to submitting your papers) probationary period? What makes for "balance" within a department is that different folks are in different phases of focus on teaching, research, and service.
>
> The crucial thing that needs to happen during the pre-tenure period is to make a transition from being somebody's graduate student to being a scholar in one's own right. This challenge requires carving out one's own scholarship turf or, as one of my professors once described it to me many years ago, "finding your own dead horse to flay."
>
> Also, on my campus people are sometimes denied tenure for lack of "programmatic" research, meaning that they flit from one related research question to the next. (Of course, this is at times a "code" for "We don't like your dialect.") Many assistant professors don't have the luxury of waiting around to analyze the feedback from one study before planning the next. (Which is why lots of biologists choose for subjects animals that have a short gestation period and life cycle.)
>
> Emphasis on a five-year research plan/program is essential.

You may be confused at this point: it's not easy to enter a new culture and to get a solid sense of what your new colleagues expect from you—especially as there is rarely any consensus. But it's worth the effort, because you likely don't have time and energy to waste in your climb toward tenure.

OBITER DICTUM

While we're on the subject of adjusting to the culture of our campus, it might be well to sound this note of caution:

"Getting on" is the great American aspiration. The way to get on is to be safe, to be sound, to be agreeable, to be inoffensive, to have no views on important matters not sanctioned by the majority, by your superiors, or by your group. We are convinced that, by knowing the right prople, wearing the right clothes, saying the right things, and thinking the right thoughts, we shall all get on. . . .

The most insidious, the most paralyzing danger you will face is the danger of corruption. Time will corrupt you. Your friends, your wives or husbands, your business or professional associates will corrupt you; your social, political, and financial ambitions will corrupt you. The worst thing about life is that it is demoralizing. Believe me, you are closer to the truth now than you will ever be again. . . .

Do not let "practical" men tell you that you should surrender your ideals because they are impractical. Do not be reconciled to dishonesty, indecency, and brutality because gentlemanly ways have been discovered for being dishonest, indecent, and brutal. As time passes, resist the corruption that comes with it. Take your stand now, before time has corrupted you.

That's President Robert Maynard Hutchins, talking to University of Chicago new hires in 1935.[45]

NOTES

1. Carnegie Foundation for the Advancement of Teaching, *Identifying Comparable Institutions* (Washington DC: John Minter Associates, 1990).

2. Deborah Olsen and Mary Deane Sorcinelli, "The Pretenure Years," *Developing New and Junior Faculty,* New Directions for Teaching and Learning, eds. Mary Deane Sorcinelli and Ann E. Austin. No. 50 (San Francisco: Jossey-Bass, 1992) 15-37.

3. Robert W. Diamond, "How to Change the Faculty Reward System," *Trusteeship* Sept.-Oct. 1993: 17-21.

4. Robert Bing and Linda Dye, "Hierarchical Decision-Making," *Academe* July-Aug. 1992: 16-18.

5. Peter Seldin, "How Colleges Evaluate Professors," *AAHE Bulletin* Oct. 1993: 6-8, 12.

6. Page Smith, *Killing the Spirit: Higher Education in America* (New York: Viking, 1990).

7. Seldin 6-8, 12.

8. Robert Boice, "New Faculty as Teachers," *The Journal of Higher Education* Mar.-Apr. 1991: 150-193.

9. James S. Fairweather, coordinator, *Teaching, Research, and Faculty Rewards* (University Park, PA: National Center on Postsecondary Teaching, Learning, and Assessment, 1993).

10. Liz McMillan, "Trollope of the Academy," *The Chronicle of Higher Education* 10 Nov. 1993: A10.

11. Footnotes, *The Chronicle of Higher Education* 14 Feb. 1994: A8.

12. J. Fredricks Volkwein and David A. Carbone, "The Impact of Departmental Reseach and Teaching Climates on Undergraduate Growth and Satisfaction," *The Journal of Higher Education* Mar.-Apr. 1994: 147-167.

13. Ernest L. Boyer, "Creating the New American College," *The Chronicle of Higher Education* 9 Mar. 1994: A48.

14. Nancy Hensel, *Realizing Gender Equity in Higher Education*, ASHE-ERIC Higher Education Report No. 2 (Washington, DC: The George Washington University School of Education and Human Development, 1991).

15. Bernice Resnick Sandler, *Success and Survival Strategies for Women Faculty Members* (Washington, DC: Association of American Colleges, 1992).

16. Elinor L. Horwitz and Kathryn Brandel, "The Struggle Continues," *AAUW Outlook*, Spring 1992.

17. Ed Wiley, III, "Ability to Manage Students and Collegial Expectations Key to Faculty Success," *Black Issues in Higher Education* 17 Dec. 1992: 3-6.

18. Adrianne R. Andrews, quoted in Joy James and Ruth Farmer, *Spirit, Space, and Survival* (New York: Routledge, 1993).

19. Alison Konrad, quoted in Ed Wiley III, "New Faculty Roles," *Black Issues in Higher Education* 26 Mar. 1992: 11-13.

20. John Knox, personal correspondence, 22 Dec. 1993.

21. Courtney Leatherman, "Black Women in Academe," *The Chronicle of Higher Education* 20 Jan. 1994: A17, 19.

22. Suzanne Rose, "10 Tips to Tenure," *Women in Higher Education* Feb. 1992: 4.

23. Carla Jimenez, "Legal Issues: Unlawful Discrimination," *The Department Chair* Fall 1990: 10-11.

24. Martin J. Finklestein and Mark W. LaCelle-Peterson, "New and Junior Faculty: A Review of the Literature," *Developing New and Junior Faculty,* New Directions for Teaching and Learning, eds. Mary Deane Sorcinelli and Ann E. Austin. No. 50 (San Francisco: Jossey-Bass, 1992) 5-14.

25. Linda K. Johnsrud and Christine D. Atwater, "Scaffolding the Ivory Tower," *CUPA Journal Spring 1993: 1-14.*

26. Robert Boice, *The New Faculty Member* (San Francisco: Jossey-Bass, 1992).

27. Walter Gmelch, *Coping with Faculty Stress* (Newbury Park, CA: Sage, 1993).

28. Mary Deane Sorcinelli, "New and Junior Faculty Stress: Research and Response," *Developing New and Junior Faculty,* New

Directions for Teaching and Learning, eds. Mary Deane Sorcinelli and Ann E. Austin. No. 50 (San Francisco: Jossey-Bass, 1992) 15-37.

29. Deborah Olsen, "Work Satisfaction and Stress in the First and Third Year of Academic Appointment," *Journal of Higher Education* July-Aug. 1993: 463-468.

30. H.R. Bowen and J. H. Schuster, *American Professors: A National Resource Imperiled* (New York: Oxford University Press, 1986).

31. Nancy Hensel, *Realizing Gender Equality in Higher Education* (Washington DC: George Washington University Educational Resource Information Center Clearinghouse on Higher Education, 1991).

32. Robert Boice, quoted in "Chair-Faculty Relations," *Academic Leader* July 1992: 1-2.

33. Alan T. Seagren, John W. Creswell, and Daniel W. Wheeler, *The Department Chair*, ASHE-ERIC Higher Education Reports (Washington, DC: George Washington University, 1994).

34. Peter Seldin, "Personal and Professional," *The Chronicle of Higher Education* 8 May 1991: A 15-17.

35. Kay U. Kerr, *Chairperson's Manual* (Fort Collins: Colorado State University Office of Instructional Services, 1989).

36. Peter Frederick, "Changing Collegial Conversation," *The Department Advisor* Spring 1991: 1-5.

37. William E. Cashin and Ronald G. Downey, *Instructional Development and Effectiveness Assessment* (Manhattan, KS: Kansas State University Center for Faculty Evaluation and Development, 1991).

38. Frederick 1-5.

39. John B. Bennett, "Organizing a Site Visit," *The Department Advisor* Jan. 1991: 1-3.

40. John B. Bennett, "Academic Program Evaluation," *The Department Advisor* Spring 1991: 5-8.

41. Robert G. Sands, L. Alayne Parson, and Josann Duane, "Faculty Mentoring Faculty in a Public University," *The Journal of Higher Education* Mar.-Apr. 1991: 174-193.

42. Robert Boice, "Lessons Learned about Mentoring," *Developing New and Junior Faculty,* New Directions for Teaching and Learning, eds. Mary Deane Sorcinelli and Ann E. Austin. No. 50 (San Francisco: Jossey-Bass, 1992) 51-62.

43. Charles Anderson, "Academic Bargaining Successfully: Some ABCs" (Washington, DC: American Council on Education, 1991).

44. Peter Gray, Robert Froh, and Robert Diamond, *A National Study of Research Universities on the Balance Between Research and Undergraduate Teaching* (Syracuse, NY: Syracuse University Center for Instructional Development, 1992).

45. Milton Mayer, *Robert Maynard Hutchins: A Memoir* (Berkeley: University of California Press, 1994).

4 APPRECIATING THE PRACTICAL POLITICS OF GETTING PROMOTED

In their little handbook on *Getting Tenure* (Newbury Park CA: Sage, 1993), authors Marcia Lynn Whicker, Jennie Jacobs Kronenfeld, and Ruth Ann Strickland open up with a frank discussion of "You and Tenure Politics." We concur it's a respectable and unavoidable topic.

Let's get one thing straight from the start: we aren't using the term "politics" here in any invidious sense of back-room influence-peddling or crafty back-slapping and unseemly publicity-grabbing. We're using the term in the best Websterian sense of "the total complex of relations between persons in society."

Oh, we suppose if we wanted to sound academic, we could title this section "The Interpersonal Relationships, Acclimatization Processes, and Acculturation Procedures Attendant to Achieving Promotion to Tenure in Colleges and Universities Today." But that would be both coy and inaccurate. Because we aren't talking here about any arcane theories; we're talking gut-pragmatic.

While grasping fundamental institutional expectations is basic to making it in academia, it would be naive not to acknowledge there's a very human side to the success equation as well. And that's what we're going to outline now.

We say "outline" because, if institutional expectations differ widely from campus to campus, that's even more the case for the kaleidoscopic variations in cultures, mores, ethos, and accepted codes of conduct among institutions of higher education, irrespective of size, mission, location, and wherewithal.

So all we can do here is tick off the questions to which we believe you should seek answers specific to your situation in your particular institution. When we can with any assurance, we'll suggest likely approaches and even solutions, but you must take them with a grain of salt, given the lack of uniformity—institution to institution and department to department.

The situation is analogous to asking a question of a horticulturist, "What's the best variety of tomato to plant?" The answer can only be a bundle of questions: "In what type, fertility, and permeability of soil? In what growing zone, with what amount of garden-plot sunlight? For what purpose—table use, salads, canning, ketchup, or sauce? For what preferred texture, size, and taste? Early fruitage, medium, or late? (Yes, a tomato is a fruit, not a vegetable, he or she will remind you.) Resistant to what diseases? With chemical or natural fertilizer and pest controls?"

And so it is with coming to appreciate the practical politics of getting promoted in your department at your institution.

TWO TYPES OF POLITICAL SUBJECTS

In general, there are two broad types of political subjects, situations, or problems: those for which your principal challenge is to understand the going standards or requirements and to adapt, and those for which you have to make a decision how best to weigh your personal code of ethics against the seeming demands of institutional constraints. The line between the two types may be more apparent than real, so in the dichotomy you're about to see, feel free to switch a topic from one to the other as your sensibilities dictate. After all, it's your institutional environment to be mastered, and your promotion that's at stake.

LEARNING AND ADAPTING

As we've just said, one broad type of political subject, situation, or problem encompasses those areas in which your task is to appreciate standards or requirements to which you can readily adapt with insight and aplomb.

Department Dynamics. You report into the office of your new department, walk up to the first desk and say, "Good morning. I'm So-and-So." A sassy receptionist in jeans grudgingly looks up from her screen to reply, "So¿"

Or a professional but obviously bemused receptionist says, "Good morning, sir! And what can we do for you¿"

Or a serge-jacketed receptionist breaks into smile, stands with hand extended, and says, "Good morning, Dr. So-and-So! We've all been anxious to meet you! Before I take you in to see Dr. Miles, may I get you a cup of coffee¿"

In any case, you've just had your first brush with the character, the culture, the style of your department. Later in the day you get another silent briefing.

A "get-acquainted" faculty meeting has been called for 3:45. At 4:10 various professors are still straggling in. "Let's get the show on the road!" booms a voice from the head of the table. From off at a flank the chair says, "Oh, now, Frank, let's give everybody another 10 minutes. I really don't have much anyway." Desultory conversation continues.

Or: At 3:42 everybody is seated and ready. Promptly at 3:44 the chair enters the room with a flourish, stills the animated chatter with a rap on a glass, and says, "Welcome once again, people! Glad to see you're all on time as usual. As you can see from your copy of the agenda, we've got a good deal to go over, so let's get down to business. Ms. Jones, my secretary, will continue the practice of taking copious notes which will be in your boxes by noon tomorrow. First off. . . ."

Our fictitious scenarios may be a trifle exaggerated for effect, but they make the point that each campus department has a unique way of doing things. So from Day One, deliberately reconnoiter the dynamics of your new department, the better to be at home there.

Key Objectives. All your initial efforts to understand the dynamics of your department should be directed at determining:

- What is expected of the department by the divisional CEO.
- What is expected of you by the department.
- The strengths and weaknesses of your compatriots.
- Other key people whose willing support is necessary to you and your department.

Key Questions. By whatever means are available and acceptable, try to obtain a clear understanding of the answers to such questions as these:

- What's the real power structure of the department?
- Who are the informal leaders in the department? What is the source of their power as informal leaders? Are the informal leaders positive or negative forces in terms of my meeting my responsibilities? In other words, who are strategic sources of support? of sabotage?
- Can I assume that my responsibilities, as outlined in my letter of appointment, are consonant with the understanding of the faculty members who will ultimately evaluate me?
- How do my assigned responsibilities fit in with the responsibilities of the department? the college?
- What specific functions am I personally responsible for on my own?
- What standards must I meet in my first year? the second? beyond?
- What policies and standard operating procedures exist to assist me?
- What are the formal norms I'm expected to comply with? Are these formal norms apt to be productive on my terms?
- What informal norms am I expected to follow? Which are likely to be productive? counterproductive?
- What are the strengths and weaknesses of department support staff personnel? of my graduate students, particularly any TAs or RAs? of my undergraduates, particularly my advisees?

- Who are the key people who support activities promoting the department mission? What are their positive and negative attributes?
- What are the strengths and weaknesses of the department in terms of each required function—teaching, research, service?

Such are essential questions driving your analysis of your new department. Getting a fix on the dynamics, the culture, the style, the character of your new surroundings and its denizens can be as intriguing as it is fundamental to the development of a personal azimuth, a career path.

On a small campus, identifying key people goes much beyond the department to the whole campus, a fact that, as one commentator notes, "will be quite obvious at your first college faculty meeting."

These pithy comments on "the human dimension" come from a senior professor who's been in six departments at four institutions:

> Tolstoy begins *Anna Karenina* with the observation that all happy families are happy in the same way, but all unhappy families are unhappy in different ways. So with academic departments. There is something in the chemistry of departments that makes them miserable or nurturing. I don't think it's possible to get a good sense of this as an outsider, but one can surely feel it as an insider.
>
> How does the tenure candidate fit in? You can't read it in a book. It goes beyond personal politics, I think, although sometimes that's the dimension blamed. It relates more to the mix that a person finds him- or herself in. Is there a good 'fit' there?

Disciplinary Ethos. Whatever your discipline, it's essential to sense the ethos of your calling—its content, traditions, culture. For example, here's the way Carla Howery of the American Sociological Association staff characterizes her discipline:[1]

> One thing we have going for us as sociologists: We're very comfortable measuring squishy things like marital happiness or alienation or urban decay, so we don't just stamp our foot and say, "It can't be done. . . ."

Sociologists are also comfortable flipping from one method to another, good at understanding the limits of national norms across institution-specific data. We understand the problems of generalization; we're more savvy here than, say, faculty in the humanities.

But sociologists are terrible about reaching consensus. They never want to reach consensus. People in sociology feed on differentness.

Sociology has a "young" or "horizontal" curriculum. That is, one department's offerings bear little similarity to others'; there's a strong sense of "to each his own." Sociologists have a very strong commitment to that idea; even within departments it's very hard for a faculty to reach consensus about common goals.

It's an interesting challenge for sociology. It helps that at least we know who we are.

If you're a budding sociologist, see how helpful that frank assessment is? If you're in another discipline, try to piece together a like analysis, the better to have a sense of "home."

Beware of "Terrorists."   Above all, in sensing the dynamics of your department, you'll want to avoid allying yourself with what M.B.A. Chair Thomas J. Hawk[2] of Frostburg (MD) State University calls "department terrorists" or "jungle fighters." Most departments have one, larger departments may have several, he says, and you can spot them at department faculty meetings as they engage in such drive-by-shooting tactics as these:

They want to be the center of attention by taking up an inordinate amount of time, whether or not their contributions are relevant to the topic under discussion. They often oppose completion of an issue by delaying closure as long as possible, complicating the issue to make it less workable, asking for unacceptable exceptions or provisions, and distorting or withholding information. To discuss the issues in a devious way outside of the meeting context. They prey on the suspicions, fears, limitations, and weaknesses of others in the department.

Writing with some feeling on the subject, Hawk warns junior faculty to be "keenly alert to the verbal and nonverbal signals of any departmental terrorists."

Department Suicide? "In a worst-case scenario, you really ought to include here a section on possible department melt-down or blow-up," writes one commentator. To identify signs that your department might be coming apart at the seams, Ronald F. Abler[3] has offered these "five steps to oblivion" for a department, any three of which will "normally place a program on the endangered list" and "even four should kill it."

1. Elect and re-elect a weak chair who can't lead the faculty to consensus or articulate the program's significance to administrators.

2. Lose several of your most productive colleagues, and don't replace them with individuals of comparable accomplishment and prestige.

3. Eschew undergraduate education and majors that are clearly beneath your program's dignity, assigning your largest courses to your worst instructors or marginal grad students, and making sure advising is slipshod and callous.

4. Forego participation in campus governance, which is well known as a complete waste of time; besides, a quality program with thoughtful scholars never needs friends in key campus positions anyway.

5. Glory in bitter ideological and personal vendettas, and never, ever fail to denounce your opponent(s) to your dean and provost.

On the off chance that you wind up in a department bent on self-destruction, you really only have two recourses: ride out the storm or bail out gracefully. It's a judgment call.

But, you say, I'd never be caught in such a department; I'd have spotted the warning signs during my job interview. Maybe, maybe not. Faculty recruiting practices often lack "truth, trust, and honesty," according to a survey of journalism/mass communication professors[4]. The professors were asked to rate a list of 23 specific hiring concepts as to (a) their perceived importance, and (b) whether or not the concept was well-practiced. Eighteen of the 23 practices were considered to be at least 50% important, yet of those 18, a full 11 rated less than 50% as being in fact well-performed by recruiting departments. For example, while the concept, "Administrators should clearly explain guidelines for gaining tenure," was judged to be 93.1% important, it was judged to be practiced only 41.7% of the time during interviews.

Remember that the first time you yourself are put on a faculty search committee!

Personal Development Plan. When it comes to the pragmatic politics of getting promoted, few practices can be so effective as to put in writing your own professional development plan, to include a five- or six-year timetable—with the advice and counsel of your seniors, peers, and other trusted people (who will be impressed by your self-reliance and diligence).

In other words, don't wait for somebody to order your career path. Then, about every six months, update the program based on your learning and development.

Suggested steps. Here are some thoughts as a guide to how you might go about developing a personal program:

- *Think in a quiet place*. Reflect about how you have performed in the past. Then visualize how you want to be able to perform in the future, given what you now know about the dynamics of your new department.
- *Identify your strengths and weaknesses* in such areas as these:
  - Beliefs, values, ethics.
  - Character traits.
  - Knowledge of yourself, your subject matter, human nature, your position, your department.
  - Directional skills—problem-solving, planning, decision-making, goal-setting.
  - Implementing skills—communicating, coordinating, supervising, evaluating.
  - Motivating skills—teaching, counseling, applying principles of motivation.
  - Investigative skills—research, productive scholarship.
  - Service skills—chairing, cooperating, seeking challenging assignments, sensing lay needs.
  - Environmental factors—institutional, professional, community, personal.
- As you review your list of strengths and weaknesses, *think of at least one way you could improve in each area, and a way you can reinforce or better your strengths*. Write them down.

Seek feedback from valued counselors, regardless of rank. They will see things that you simply can't or don't see. If the feedback makes sense and feels right, accept and incorporate it.

- After you've identified weaknesses and ways to improve, *set a goal* for each weakness or desired improvement. For example, let's say that one desire is to improve your counseling skills. Establish the following objectives: learn about human needs, improve ability to apply principles of motivation, improve communication skills, improve listening skills, learn the ins and outs of undergraduate curriculum requirements.
- Once you've stated your goals, *develop plans to achieve goals.* Identify tasks that must be accomplished, put them in priority, and establish all the conditions necessary for each task. Write a simple plan to reach each goal. For example, if one of your goals is to improve your understanding of human nature, one of your plans might well be to sit in on lectures in an appropriate psychology course.
- *Evaluate.* For each goal, write out two or three ways of evaluating progress toward the goal. You are your own best evaluator if you're honest with yourself. Seek feedback, too, from informal raters. For example, you might take the "pop" quizzes in that psychology course you're attending.

*It's **Your** Job.* Your professional development program is the basis of a career path. While your reviewers have responsibilities to assist in your development, the real responsibility rests squarely on your own shoulders. If you have the necessary character traits—initiative, will, and self-discipline—such a program will be valuable in terms of both political substance and style.

The DEO. Almost all academic departments have a department executive officer (DEO), although he or she will commonly be known as director, head, or—most likely—chair. And most chairs identify one of their top priorities as helping new faculty succeed. As one such chair has put it: "When we recruit an individual, we are convinced that this person has the skills that will benefit our program. Our responsibility, once we hire, is to provide him or her with the resources and support to be successful."

You ought to start out by assuming that your own DEO subscribes to the roles assigned to him or her in support of junior faculty as described in a recent guide.[5] The DEO should be available:

- As a resource link, "matchmaking" between you and support mechanisms and individuals;
- As a mentor, helping you learn the territory and understand the nuances of campus politics;
- As a facilitator of mentor relationships with others in and beyond the department;
- As an institutional authority or representative, negotiating and defining what the institution expects of you;
- As an evaluator, helping you assess your own progress;
- As a faculty developer, detecting your needs and arranging counsel;
- As a model of balance in preventing burnout and alienation of family and friends.

That's a tall order, and not all chairs measure up, at least not in all regards and all the time. For example, Bill Campion at Midland found Chair Amanda Perkins to be very good in her roles as a "nurturer" but, being new to the job, not yet adept at helping Bill sort out conflicting views from his peers on the one hand and the campus administration on the other.

As you work out a relationship with your own chair, it'll help if you appreciate his or her position. A chair is very much a person in the middle. Indeed, chairs have been described by some as "middle managers"; although the term "manager" is repugnant to most academics, "middle" is apt. The campus administration sees the chair as its conduit for communicating rules, regulations, and policies to department faculty. The department faculty see the chair as their "ombudsperson" for communicating their needs and wants to the administration. As one chair has phrased it colloquially, "The stuff flows in both directions—and piles up on my desk!"

Chairs see themselves as scholars only temporarily serving as reluctant leaders among peers, with their own stressors. In the words of one chair: "How do I maintain a scholarly career while administering a department while staying married and being a parent and member of the community and getting enough sleep and alone time?"

His concerns are echoed by Russell Edgerton,[6] president of the American Association for Higher Education: "Every year, with little preparation, scores of faculty members across the country step into the position of chairing their department. The ambiguity of being both a faculty member and an administrator—not to mention scholar, teacher, advocate, counselor, and friend—makes the assignment a tough one."

Chairs are busy people. A decade ago, Allan Tucker[7] identified 28 roles. More recently, in national studies conducted by University of Nebraska professors of educational administration, DEOs reported having 97 different responsibilities![8] So the next time you feel your chair seems bemused or detached, remember why.

A former chair, now Dean of the University of Maine School of Law, Donald Zillman, offers this particular advice to untenured faculty:[9] "Don't assume that every move your DEO takes is directed at you. A vast variety of factors go into many decisions that might impact you. If you think you have been unfairly treated, don't sulk. Talk to the 'boss', who in most cases can explain that this is not a reflection on you at all. In the rare cases where it is, the discussion of expectations will be a useful one."

The DAO. Increasingly, colleges and universities are designating the head, chair, director, or dean of a unit as its departmental executive officer (DEO), and her or his adjutant as departmental administrative officer (DAO). Next to your department chair (DEO), hardly anybody can so help facilitate—or founder—your academic career as can your DAO—the keeper of the keys, the power around the power.

Who is he or she? An assistant or associate professor in training as department assistant chair, or a tired full professor put out to pasture? Maybe an administrative specialist with a limited-term or indefinite appointment in that relatively new campus ranking midway between faculty and employee? Or perhaps a senior "classified," "civil service," or some such designation of long-time servant? Whatever—a crucial component of your department's culture.

Understand a DAO's natural tendency to be defensive and sometimes rigid: faced with largely routine tasks, everybody's "gopher," punching a 9-to-5 clock in a Grand Central Station surrounded by doctorates working on and off in relative freedom in private offices on various interesting assignments.

Yet beneath that austere exterior can beat a heart of gold if you can but sense its beat.

Discover what the DAO does and doesn't do or causes to get done or not done: typing projects not related to teaching? Research proposals? Travel arrangements? Meeting scheduling? How much lead time does the DAO need or demand (depending in all likelihood on your position in the department pecking order)? What directions does the DAO want, resent, or appreciate?

How does the DAO react to your use of office equipment? Copy machines, faxes, files, and so on? Territorial or tolerant of interlopers? Does the DAO encourage and appreciate those who help themselves or does he or she want to exercise dominion? Does the DAO ride herd like an IRS agent on supplies and long-distance phone calls, or is there free access?

Be nice, be friendly, and respect the DAO's time constraints, the need to concentrate, to supervise underlings, and to answer first to the call of the chair. Remember the DAO on appropriate occasions—birthday, anniversary, Christmas, and so on.

A simple but essential requirement: complete every form the DAO gives you, properly and punctually.

Above all, acquire a sure feeling for the DAO's fundamental *gestalt*.

"Your comments on the importance of the DAO are right on!" writes a reviewer. "Most departments I know of have an administrative assistant who keeps the place afloat, knows everything, and isn't shy about getting the word out."

Professorial Technology. Not only does it behoove you to become a master of the modern technology that can support your teaching and your research, adapting to the electronic age can smooth your career path by lubricating interpersonal relations.

For example, if you're facile with a word processor/computer, you can relieve the department office by typing an occasional manuscript from notes, then revising at the keyboard on the fly or from notes on hard copy. Or you can compose a form cover letter, then customize on your own for each occasion in a matter of minutes.

Another simple but invaluable high-tech tool is a personal answering machine. Without one, if you have your own office phone and can't be in your office from 7 a.m. to midnight, then you're likely to frustrate colleagues and students alike and play a lot of phone tag. An answering machine may bother some callers to the point where they'll hang up on hearing your recorded voice, but most others will willingly leave messages—and greatly appreciate it if you get back to them promptly. (If opportunity knocks but once, how often can you expect it to ring in the absence of an answering machine?) If your department has voice mail—great! Check for messages early and often: It's the next best thing to being there.

The real value in becoming at home with gadgets is the subtle message it sends that you're up-to-date. Faint heart ne'er won fair promotion; when it comes to technological experimentation, fortune favors the bold.

Lights and Shadows. But the bold recognize there can be shadows as well as lights associated with any innovation. Take Internet, for example—the network clusters of large computers, linked through global phone lines, into which anyone with a computer, a modem, and an account can tap. "Internet Is Radically Changing Academic Life—For Better or Worse," read a headline in the Jan. 17-23, 1994, issue of *The Washington Post National Weekly Edition.* Any assistant professor ought to be cognizant of both those aspects of emerging information technology:

- By making all kinds of information available everywhere, the network has begun to level the playing field for new hires wherever they may be—at big universities with big libraries or at smaller institutions. But that could raise the research expectations that departmental tenure review committees hold for new hires—again, wherever they may be.
- The computer links encourage long-distance collaboration, allowing isolated scholars and academic newcomers to tap into the collective wisdom in their fields. But some senior faculty may see Internet as prompting scholars to ask for

help rather than carry on their own research, putting individual accomplishment into question.

- The appearance of electronic journals on Internet will speed scholarly communications, however, some senior faculty may view such journals as essentially low-quality, "publishing" papers rejected by more established, "hard copy" publications.
- Internet E-mail offers frequent, inexpensive communication with family, friends, and favored colleagues. But hours can be invested in reading and responding to often-inconsequential dispatches.
- Internet has the capacity to eliminate the need for expensive, time-consuming, cross-country professional committee meetings. However, will such electronic "meetings" really be as effective as face-to-face discourse in which one can see how another is reacting?

Weighing the advantages and disadvantages of Internet and other information technology innovations is simply a mandatory assignment for anybody on the tenure ladder today.

Whatever stance you adopt toward professorial technology today, it's well to remember, *Post* reporter Brooke A. Masters pointed out, that whatever Internet is today, it's a crude forerunner of what Internet will be tomorrow. Masters quoted a computer scientist to the effect that "we're still in the Jurassic stage, the climbing-out-of-the slime stage."

Professorial Conduct. It will come as no surprise to any reader of this manual that the personal conduct of any professor of any rank is constrained today by emerging criteria of what is acceptable and unacceptable in relations between the sexes, and particularly in regard to relations between faculty and students.

The Sexual Harassment Hazard. Sexual harassment, according to a new study,[10] is a constant threat on any campus because "the hierarchial nature of the relationship between learners and teachers in most educational institutions creates a delicate and fragile imbalance of power where students may be especially vulnerable." Your recognition of the hazard can help you alleviate the scourge.

You may think that sexual harassment has to involve overt sexual advances or requests for sexual favors. Not so. Any conduct that makes a working environment hostile can constitute sexual harassment. For example, not long ago a graduate assistant was found guilty on the latter count for displaying in his office a picture of a bikini-clad woman to two fellow grad assistants. The fact that the picture was a candid snapshot of his wife was not deemed a suitable defense.

And don't get the idea that male professors are the only harassers. Female faculty have been known to harass male students and female faculty may be harassed by male students.

You may think that sexual harassment is simply inappropriate behavior. Not so. It is illegal—a form of sexual discrimination under federal statutes. And, under the credo of the American Association of University Professors, it constitutes a failure of professional ethics and academic freedom.

Check out the latest edition of your campus faculty manual for explicit guidance.

The Consensual Relations Conundrum. To avoid any perception of sexual harassment, when it comes to the issue of consensual relations between faculty and student, increasingly the advice if not the regulation is: *don't*. Personal relations with undergrads have always been questionable. While it has sometimes been acceptable that professors and their grad students got together romantically, that is changing, particularly in a situation where the professor has evaluative or supervisory authority over the student, as in a course or with a TA. Even in a consensual arrangement the risk is great the relationship can turn sour, with the student charging harassment. Even when the charges are unsubstantiated. Faculty are very rarely able to defend themselves completely in such situations. In instances where faculty are demonstrably at fault, severe discipline is increasingly the rule.

While there may be no written guidelines covering personal relations with students at your institution, that *"don't"* advice is sound. As one reviewer of this book commented, "One is less likely to get into trouble playing around with a dean's spouse than with a student."

At Midland, stated university policy is unequivocal: "No faculty member shall have an amorous relationship with any student who is enrolled in a course being taught by the faculty member or whose academic work (including work as a teaching assistant) is being supervised by the faculty member." Extending such a rule to all students is prudent on today's contentious campus.

Work Hours. When E.B. Fred was president of the University of Wisconsin, after leaving his office very late, he would invariably take a stroll around campus "to see what professors are burning the midnight oil." (It apparently never occurred to him that what he was witnessing could be a janitor at work.)

You may have moved into a department of workaholics. Early in your career, show up some weeknight and some Saturday to determine whether department custom expects you to labor all hours.

On the other hand, you may have joined a department where it's *de rigueur* to appear to have your nose to the grindstone as few hours of the day as convenient (which will simply mean that you either go against the flow or do your necessary work at home).

Calendar Times. In like manner, it may be the custom in your new department never to take a vacation, certainly not over the Christmas break. Again, check it out personally. You may discover that nobody's there except a couple of grad students. Or you may find a hive of worker bees.

When he was yet a bacteriology professor, the legendary E.B. Fred walked into his laboratory one night, looked around, and asked one of the grad students present, "Where are all my colleagues and where are all your fellow grad students?" "Well, you see, Mr. Fred," the student replied, "It's Christmas Eve!"

As we've said in another context, if you don't take at least a couple of weeks off in summer you can become a very dull academic. You don't have to go long or far, and you can keep in touch readily via electronic mail if you've got the equipment.

Again, whatever your calendar time, relax, enjoy—and accomplish.

Committee Work. "Much of the activity at a university is committee-centered," writes Gerald M. Phillips, professor emeritus of speech communication at Pennsylvania State University, in a new guidebook for new faculty.[11]

In all likelihood your department will view committee work as a civic responsibility, one of the prices to be paid to keep the department micro-society functioning properly.

Some faculty members love to serve, some serve well but reluctantly, others have to be dragged kicking and screaming to the table.

So what do you do?

On the one hand, some departments will help protect your teaching/research time by understanding if you serve when called but don't volunteer, except perhaps for a project or ad hoc assignment down your alley, least of all for a standing committee that does anything but just stand, and for a long time. Indeed, if you were to jump enthusiastically into committee work, some colleagues might view it as misplaced puppy energy or a lust for power.

On the other hand, some departments tend to load tiresome burdens onto the rookies, in which case it may be impolitic to shirk your responsibility.

In any case, grin and bear committee work as another of the rites of passage, being ever mindful, however, that in terms of brownie points it's normally outranked by teaching and research.

Environmental Impingements. Housing, health care, schools, spousal employment, recreational and cultural opportunities, libraries, stores, family budget, competent tradespeople, commuting time—a gamut of concerns can impinge on your institutional duties, at times markedly—particularly if you're a stranger in a strange land.

The character of one department may be such that colleagues couldn't care less about such personal concerns and will expect you not to bring them with you in your briefcase to the office. Callous? You bet. But it's a fact of life in some certain situations.

On the other hand, the caring culture of some departments can be positively cloying.

An early tip-off as to what style you've inherited can be the conduct of the department CEO. If he or she asks nary a word about how you're personally settling in, you can assume the department expects you to be strictly professional in your habits. If he or she wants to know all the details of your adjustment, you may almost be tempted to invent a problem so that the department chair can fulfill his or her need to be "helpful."

Depending on your own personality, you may be more comfortable in one situation or the other, but they're not much amenable to change. It's another case of going along to get along.

Salutatory Titles. As a matter of fact, you can get a feeling for one important aspect of institutional style—how you address people—by consulting a *HEP Directory* before ever coming to a campus.

Take a look at the description of Midland University. Although Midland is an institution of some pretensions, there's not a "Dr." in the house—except, of course, in the School of Allied Health Professions. On the other hand, at Cobalt College across the state, practically everybody's a "Dr."

It's all a matter of style. If you're at an institution where nobody addresses anybody else as "Dr.", respect the custom, no matter how proud you are of your new Ph.D.: You're just "Mr." or "Ms." If, however, you're at an institution that advertises its roster of Ph.D.'s at every opportunity, emblazon yours on your office door.

All this may seem like the height of the inconsequential, but nothing is so diagnostic of campus status as its employment of salutatory titles. In fact, you can almost say that the more prestigious an American university today, the more it will frown on the use of the title "Dr." for any faculty member except an M.D. or D.D.S., while the more "wannabe" a campus the more it will encourage you to display the title—at home and abroad.

DECISION TIME

So far we've been talking about "political" issues that call largely for assimilating and adapting on your part. As we said earlier, there is a second broad type of political subject, situation, or problem, encompassing those areas in which you have to make a decision how best to weigh your personal lifestyle or code of conduct against seeming demands of instituional constraints.

Your "Personality". What's to be the proper demeanor? Do you come on strong, eager, and sell yourself? Or should you be the humble greenhorn? Should you be known for the campus and extra-campus contacts you cultivate, or should you be largely a department garden-tender?

To what extent do you vary your "personality" depending on the working relationships you want to develop with key constituencies—the chair, college and campus administrators, senior colleagues, junior peers, staff, employees, collateral faculty, undergrad students, grad students, the community?

Obviously you can't be exactly one being to all people, but will too chameleon-like a pose open you to charges of "always putting on an act"?

The personality you present to your chair may be the most crucial of all.

Some assistant professors tend to demand a good deal of administrative maintenance. They display a continual need to talk with the chair about their teaching load, office location and size, exceptions to travel-funds policy in the department, the relative importance of committee assignments, and so on.

That sort of person can either summon up the chair's good Samaritan instincts or exhaust him or her. We don't know whether it's better to be that kind of person or not.

Nor can we say with confidence that a chair will respond favorably to the assistant professor who is constrained to keep the chair apprised of absolutely everything going on in his or her career. Every paper accepted for presentation at a conference, how a chapter revision is going, a recent phone call from a potential granting agency, advising work with a student organization, and so on—each topic can extend into a half-hour conversation with the chair over lunch, in the hall, at a chance meeting in front of the building. While the chair may act pleased to hear of such accomplishments and will try to reinforce the faculty member's sense of self-worth, the chair may actually find such encounters needlessly time-consuming, not to mention confusing, since he or she has to try to keep every faculty member's agenda straight and current.

Probably the best tactic in the long run is simply to be yourself. That, and to hearken to these words from a department chair who reviewed this manual:

"In my book, among the best predictors of tenure potential is clear evidence—direct or indirect—of hard work."

Want a definition of what it can mean to work hard in an academic setting? Stanford English professor and Pulitzer-Prize-winning author Wallace Stegner[12] left us a telling assessment by a fictional assistant professor in his first year—Depression-ridden 1937:

> Ambition is a path, not a destination, and it's essentially the same for everyone. No matter what the goal is, the path leads through *Pilgrim's Progress* regions of motivation, hard work, persistence, stubbornness, and resilience under disappointment. Unconsidered, merely indulged, ambition becomes a vice; it can turn a man into a machine that knows nothing but how to run. Considered, it can be something else—pathway to the stars, maybe. I suspect that what makes hedonists so angry when they think about overachievers is that the overachievers, without drugs or orgies, have more fun.

Role Models. You should quickly and surely assess the professional activities and "political" stance of colleagues within the department—particularly not-too-senior colleagues. Your overt or covert choice of role model(s) will be something that your colleagues will be watching for as a measure of your own promise and compatibility.

It'll be advantageous for you if at least one of your role models is open to conversations about your problems and progress. Some idols have ears but they hear not.

Collegiality—"Getting Along". A college is not called a college for nothing. Its root is *collegium* and its mark *collegiality*. While collegiality may encompass the cordiality or camaraderie of a work team, it is much more—the ground rules for "getting along" unique to academe.

With luck and/or foresight you'll pick a role model who personifies collegiality—the glue that binds a faculty.

Quinnipiac College provost and distinguished author John B. Bennett[13] several years ago composed an important and powerful definition of collegiality you can use as your lodestar:

> Collegiality in the sense of getting along with colleagues is more than just foreswearing hostility and belligerence. First, collegiality involves the disposition to credit colleagues with a share of the power and authority residing in the *collegium*, a share roughly equal to the share one claims for oneself. And second, since higher education attracts people who might value their independence to the point of isolation,

collegiality involves no less the willingness of each person to seek the judgment of colleagues on work in progress. . . .

Accordingly, a minimal level of cooperation with colleagues, an appropriate respect for their contributions, and a willingness to explore with them one's own ideas and work as well as one's teaching triumphs and frustrations seem essential for the conduct and continuation of the profession. Without some minimum intellectual reciprocity, the *collegium* no longer exists. . . .

Properly understood, collegiality does not stifle dissent or eclipse individuality. Indeed, it is only in the truly collegial department and college that diverse individuality can flourish. And ultimately it is this ability of colleagues to "get along" that is the prerequisite for expressions of collegiality in governance and shared decision-making.

Susan A. Cole,[14] vice president for university administration and personnel at Rutgers, expresses much the same sentiments:

The academy functions at its best when its members act in a commonsense fashion on the basis of their understanding of the traditions, expectations, and standards of the profession. Further, in a litigious society, the academy must act affirmatively to preserve its collegiality and traditions of academic decision-making. At their truest and best, such traditions abjure personal harrassment, exploitation of students and junior colleagues, and discrimination based on impermissible grounds, and encourage the free expression of views and respect for one another as colleagues.

"Seasons" of Academic Life. As an assistant professor mounting the rungs of the academic ladder, meeting varying challenges and frustrations along the climb, it will help if you recognize your particular frame of mind at the moment, the better to react positively, as suggested by developmental psychologist, Lee Knefelkamp.[15]

Knefelkamp, chair of the department of adult and higher eduucation in Columbia University's Teachers College, posits that all professors over time move into and out of, in random order, what she calls seven "seasons" in "the ecology of academic life," each characterized by a controlling "virture, vulnerability, and essential gesture."

By sensing correctly your "internal dynamics" at any particular time, you will be in a better position to "find the right role at the right time to serve your campus community in the most effective way," Knefelkamp says, because "all adult life is a series of transitions, a series of changes, a series of coping with new demands and new roles."

In no chronological order, the seven stages are:

- Appreciation of the power of words, conversations, and ideas accompanied by both joy of interpersonal engagement and the recognition that knowledge is not truth.
- Discovery of what it means to be a faculty member, with its terror of the new and a passion to perform.
- Discovery of students, with all their individual differences and different learning styles, each one in a personal "season" of his or her own.
- Recognition of the public self beyond the classroom in the realms of publication, service, and administration.
- Confrontation with multiple and competing commitments—everyone in academia leading at least three or four lives—personal, disciplinary, campus, and community.
- Recognition of the need to move fluidly across roles and to stop out of any given one without feeling shame.
- Feelings of "marginality" in the face of changing intellectual fields and academic environments.
- Discovery of "courage in spite of," to give up notions of control and venture into uncharted territory of personal and professional development—"the most important season in our collective academic lives."

Each of us needs, says Knefelkamp, "an appreciation of this ecology of academic life based on an understanding of the nonlinear nature of faculty lives, ... and a commitment to the mutuality of those who make up the academic community and to the community itself" as we seek to help "fulfill the unique and historic missions for which our communities were founded."

Expectations to Socialize. Your Midland University *alter ego* Bill and his spouse had scarcely moved into their modest townhouse in a faculty housing development than they found in their mailbox an invitation to attend a "start of the quarter" brunch at the home of Chair Amanda Perkins.

"I wonder how much they expect us to socialize here?" was the spouse's natural concern.

The answer to such a question is very much institution- and department-specific. Some departments at some institutions expect their faculty members to mingle often and long in a variety of social settings. Other departments at other institutions expect a bare minimum of togetherness. Even within a department/college, an individual professor may be able to risk his or her own lifestyle. You'll just have to feel your way. Chances are you'll discover a round of potlucks among probationary peers, plus an occasional sit-down dinner with senior staff or new-found department colleagues. When in doubt, don't hesitate to seek guidance from the person you identify as a social arbiter—faculty member or spouse.

Whom you invite and to what may be as diagnostic of your social grace as how often you entertain. Social events can be a useful and effective form of campus networking, but if you become known from your guest lists as a "social climber," the approach can backfire on many campuses. Better to be inclusionary in your choice of house guests.

Without question, even a modest social life can put a dent in your family budget. Most colleagues will understand if you're sparing in issuing invitations. If you or your spouse are so fortunate as to be independently wealthy, don't flaunt it.

Whatever you do, don't sweat the socializing code you find. On most campuses, any days of measuring tenure credentials on the basis of drawing-room flair are long gone.

Dress Code. We have in hand a paragraph from the faculty guidebook at a Princeton-like academy, reading: "The school tie (presumably with elbow-patch jacket) is appropriate wear at all but the most informal (department picnic?) or formal (black-tie concert?) occasions."

On the other hand, in his novel *No Highway*, author Nevil Shute (Norway) has a research director say:

> An unusual man is apt to look unusual. Mr. Honey sometimes presented an untidy appearance in his manner and clothes. I don't favor that, but I should be sorry to see the laboratory staffed entirely by

correct young men in neat, conventional, civil service minds. We seek original thinkers with the untiring brain that pursues its object by day and by night. If the untiring brain refuses to attend to such matters as the neat arrangement of collar and tie, I do not greatly complain.

Those polar positions on dress codes may well suggest to you that, if socializing expectations are site-specific, dress codes are even more so.

Writing on "The F Word" (Fashion) in *Lingua Franca,*[16] after interviewing campus colleagues around the country, Valerie Steele has some delightful comments on the subject:

> Obviously, a university is not like a law firm, where the rules governing appropriate attire are both narrow and explicit . . . . Peter Baldwin, an assistant professor of history at UCLA, remarks that academics are "under no pressure to dress well." And Deborah Kaple, a lecturer in sociology at Princeton, observes that some academics regard it as "one of the perks" of the job that they "don't have to pay attention" to how they dress. But if everyone in academia is happily doing his or her own thing, why is it so often the same thing? . . .
>
> "Theoretically, anything goes," says Susan Kaiser, author of *The Social-Psychology of Clothing: Symbolic Appearances in Context* and associate professor at UC Davis, "but in practice, within a small-group context, such as a department, a subtle kind of negotiation goes on. We influence each other." . . .
>
> In academic circles, many professors say, clothing is perceived as "material" (not intellectual) and, therefore, "beneath contempt." There is a sharp division between "the life of the mind and that of the body." . . .
>
> Among leftists, fashion is also regarded as "bourgeois," and so they often "go out of their way to distance themselves" from it, observes Michael Solomon, editor of *The Psychology of Fashion* and chairman of the Department of Marketing in the business school of Rutgers University. Aging " '68 types" are often "aggressively informal," agrees Baldwin, and "deliberately dress down for class." But even conservative professors often look barely respectable. . . .
>
> In the modern American context, to wear jackets rather than suits is to adopt a lesser degree of informality compared, for example, with businessmen or, closer to home, college administrators. But to wear a sports jacket and tie imparts an impression of formality and authority.

As a result, there is something of a split between professors who wear ties and those who don't. Baldwin distinguishes between "the Harvard compulsion to cravats versus the California obligatory tieless look." . . .

Blue jeans are the operative garment . . . . How better to assert solidarity with the young than to dress like them? . . . A professor might be the oldest, most powerful, and least hip person in the classroom, but his anti-establishment clothing signified that he was a free spirit opposed to pernicious hierarchical distinctions between the teacher and the taught. . . .

The sweater, either alone or under a jacket, is another garment frequently worn by male academics. . . . The majority of professors seem to wear baggy, stretched-out sweaters in boring colors and cheap materials.

Women academics are "a disaster," insists one female professor in California, citing frumpy suits, sensible shoes, and outmoded haircuts. With their "asexual clothes and handbags [that] are satchels," with "no makeup or jewelry," laments one woman professor at an Ivy League university. The "subconscious message" of her collegial sisters is: "If I could, I'd be male."

Certainly, femininity is out. So is anything too conspicuous or body-revealing. Like most female professionals, the majority of women in academia tend to minimize any sartorial eroticism while maximizing status signifiers. "Most female faculty look like bankers and lawyers, even when the men are in polo shirts," is the succinct assessment of a UC San Diego scholar.

Yet upon closer inspection, women academics do not really look like bankers, lawyers, or business executives. Sad to say, they lack marketplace flair. Skirts, for example, tend to be significantly longer than those of most professional women: to mid-calf, when the fashionable length is slightly above the knee. The jacket (the female executive's badge of authority) is seen less often in academia, where professors tend to wear separates. . . .

Can a style of dress hurt one's professional career? True to form, most academics deny that it makes any difference whatsoever. But a few stories may indicate otherwise. . . .

Well, there you have it. At least you can say this for dress codes: they're easy to discern. Just look around your department.

Whether you opt to conform is up to you, in most situations, but your response will say something.

As Polonius said in *Hamlet*, "The apparel oft proclaims the man." (Presumably, if Shakespeare were writing today, he would say "person.")

The Town-and-Gown Minuet. In some campus communities the line between town and gown is quite distinct, with senior academics looking down their noses at their plebeian counterparts, and assistant professors viewed askance if they cross the border.

In other campus communities, faculty and citizens share a general camaraderie. Local professionals are invited to give guest lectures, and deans take turns as chairs of city service clubs.

Whatever dance card you inherit, don't let it get in the way of forming friendships with your immediate neighbors, with the parents of your children's pals, with church acquaintances, or with the like.

Twenty years from now you may discover that your warmest relationships are not intra- but extra-institutional, or you may be content with a closed campus circle.

Job Offer Etiquette. Some departments assume their assistant professors are constantly on the market, and may even take pride in their being so. Other departments will view any sign of wanderlust as evidence of disloyalty.

As a professor on probation, you owe it to your career to make yourself available, provided your job-hunting doesn't get in the way of your current responsibilities or rattle the chair's cage. (Given the academic grapevine, there's no way you can keep any perambulations secret, at least not for long.)

Without question, an attractive job offer from a competing institution can be compelling leverage, *but*—never threaten to leave without being prepared actually to go, if you're bluffing and your bluff is called.

The senior author (ACS) has an indelible memory of a probationary peer who took an offer letter to the dean's office in hopes of accelerating his pace toward promotion or at least of generating a healthy salary raise. When next seen, he blurted, in surprise and dismay, "I . . . I . . . I . . . I'm going to Excelsior!"

To this discussion of job offer etiquette, Dean Donald Zillman[17] of the University of Maine School of Law adds this "piece of hard but necessary advice" that he personally has discovered:

> You may need to move to raise your salary significantly. Raises are scarce these days and the burden is against the faculty member who argues, "I'm underpaid and I alone should get a salary adjustment." It's quite correct that you don't play games of bluff with offers from elsewhere. But to avoid a salary lock-in, movement or the willingness to move may be essential.

Your Leadership Style. From the perspective of professors as leaders in relation to their students, there are roughly three leadership styles they can adopt—depending on their personal backgrounds and proclivities, the level of the student, and the mores of the department.

A professor is using the authoritarian leadership style when he or she tells students what's to be done and how, without incorporating their interests or ideas. When using the *participative leadership style,* a professor involves students in determining what to do and how to do it, yet retains final decision-making authority. In the *delegative leadership style,* a professor delegates decision-making to a student or group of students, yet retains responsibility for the results of his or her students' decisions.

The style you would use for a particular situation would depend on your analysis of the situation and your judgment of who has the necessary information to solve the problem or to accomplish the task. Your creative thinking is a key to the correct choice of role. Your beliefs, values, character, and experience will influence how you think. The way you think will determine how you apply what you know and what you do.

A professor can use a quick, flexible mind if he or she is to stay with or ahead of the rapidly changing forces in faculty-student relations on campuses today. He or she must continually identify and foresee shifts in important actors and forces. As the situation changes, he or she can change the mix of actions and style. One mix of actions and one style may work one time and be ineffective the next. Only by exercising good judgment can you successfully meet the demands of complex, stressful, changing interpersonal and institutional environments.

Grad Student Advising. Studies have indicated that the quality of relationship between a graduate student and his or her major professor is a better predictor of success in doctoral programs than is the student's GRE or undergrad GPA. You'll naturally want to help your grad students succeed. To do so, it may help to refer to a "mentoring-empowered model" that "provides a developmental framework for graduate student advising," formulated by Professors Mary J. Selke and Terrence D. Wong.[18]

First, as they point out, effective grad student advising can take place only in a context that features accepting and relating to each other, establishing good communications, and founding a relationship on trust openness, acceptance, and mutual willingness to grow.

Within that context, as an advisor you'll seek to fulfill five distinct roles: teacher, encourager, role model, counselor, and sponsor/socializer. That last role, while ill-defined, may be crucial—from representing the student's interests in departmental affairs to helping him or her subtly integrate into the culture of the college.

While you'll of course want to respect a grad student's right to and need for autonomy, choice, and personal involvement in learning, there's no law that says you can't be a friend. (And you of course can hope that your own faculty mentor or mentors meet the Selke-Wong standards.)

Moonlighting. Some departments encourage their faculty members to earn outside income by accepting consulting fees or similar emoluments, assuming the work is related to your academic expertise and doesn't interfere with your salaried duties. Indeed, an active consulting life can be a badge of distinction. Sometimes your public service activities can lead to such arrangements.

Other departments frown on outside work, particularly if it's unrelated to your professional competence, on the theory that the institution has bought all your time or that outside work can involve tainted money. Some institutions require that you report minutely all outside income, from whom, and for what. Others want to know about it in very general terms. Others ask nothing. In rare cases you may be expected to contribute all or part of your profits to institutional coffers.

Reimbursed expenses or honoraria in lieu of expenses seldom qualify in departmental eyes as outside income. Nor does substituting extensively on your youngster's paper route. Subbing as a seasonal store clerk probably would qualify, along with a certain amount of opprobrium. Military reserve pay seldom is considered as reportable income, nor are you usually docked for the necessary armory or summer-camp time. A call to active duty would be a different matter, necessitating a leave without campus pay.

For some strange reason, patent and book royalties usually occupy a niche all by themselves, being considered a natural accompaniment of scholarship, even though the institution may have underwritten a good share of the production costs. When royalties bulk really large, some grateful professors donate a percentage to a campus fund.

In short, the ground rules respecting moonlighting are so many and varied that it behooves you to double-check before you venture out.

A gratuitous word of advice: don't build any outside income into your family budget; it's too ephemeral. Use it for extras.

Conformity Codes. As Emerson said, "A foolish consistency is the hobgoblin of little minds." Wherever they may be, most faculty members agree; it's a badge of the profession.

And yet each campus has distinct limits on the degree of inconsistency it tolerates, particularly in its untenured staff. Put another way, campuses vary in the size and scope of latitude they allow their faculty members before imposing quiet ostracism.

A crucial aspect of appreciating the practical politics of getting promoted in your department/institution is determining the conformity codes under which you find yourself—and complying or not as a situation dictates. So diverse are those situations that it's impossible to generalize about them and about your reaction. The one ground rule we can suggest is this:

Respect the bounds of peculiarity on your campus, yet maintain a personal code of conscience. When the two are in utter conflict, recognize it as decision time.

Political Action. Your Midland *alter ego* Bill had scarcely gotten his first quarter squared away when he found in his campus mailbox an invitation to join a campus "Save the Lagoon League." On inquiry, he finds the situation to be thus:

Where a small watershed empties into Lake Midland at the northern edge of the campus, a 20-acre "lagoon"—or "marsh," depending on your perspective—has existed since the glaciers. In spring its willow-lined margins are the haunts of both waterfowl and campus lovers. Now in its wisdom the campus planning commission has opted to convert the lagoon into a subterranean culvert and use the captured land for a faculty parking lot. Most campus administrators are delighted; some faculty and many students and alumni are distraught, as well as are the county lake management technicians.

Your *alter ego* recognizes immediately that in the conflict he has an ideal case study for the new department program in biological conservation/sustainable development, but should he personally get involved in the league? He can't plead that the matter is irrelevant to his scholarly interests; quite the contrary, it's perfect. But can he risk the public exposure his participation would inevitably bring to focus? If he were tenured he could let his conscience be his guide, but as an assistant professor he may have to be circumspect.

Given the "political correctness" imbroglio that has made colleges and universities the topic of a multi-media news blitz, you may well find yourself in a comparable situation. Do I or don't I? We won't presume to prescribe an answer other than to suggest that the one person you ultimately have to live with is yourself.

Networking. Some departments will openly encourage you to work formally and informally with colleagues both within and beyond your department, and there are real advantages to so doing.

For example, by discussing your projects with department colleagues, not only will they be alerted to your enterprise, you will benefit from their input, enthusiasm, and even nagging. By linking up with colleagues across campus, you gain outside perspectives and interdisciplinary approaches—both of them intelligent and unembedded in disciplinary constraints.

Extra-campus conferences can be an intellectual banquet, exposing you to an even wider range of thought and manner, and to a broader world of scholarship. To get away, offer to trade missed classes with a colleague. Such an exchange can carry bonus benefits: the colleague will know of your off-campus status, you and he or she will establish a working relationship, the substitute may be impressed by your class and your preparation, and the liaison can lead to team-teaching or research collaboration.

But not all departments are eager to share your talents outside, as your Midland University *alter ego* Bill was surprised to discover. His former Georgia professor, now dean of the Midland forestry and environmental studies school, invited him to chair a planning-and-evaluation committee for a student in their non-thesis master's degree program. Chair Amanda Perkins ruled, "Absolutely not!"

Her reasons were both profound and picayune. As Perkins explained, Midland had no mechanism for transferring such graduate advising work from forestry to student credit-hours mathematics in botany and, given current tight budget constraints, it was mandatory that botany not squander any of its scarce economic resources beyond Pendarvis Hall. Secondly, some of their colleagues would think it beneath the dignity of the botany department to be associated with "that forestry trade school."

So, before you engage in too many beyond-department forays, check out the situation, weather, and terrain.

Pressure Points. Anybody who has ever consulted an osteopath for a back ailment knows the doctor can usually find a pressure point or two that will relieve the distress after proper massaging. Just so with department dynamics.

Early on it was obvious to your Midland University *alter ego* that, for the good of both the new applied ecology program and his own career, he had somehow to make peace with his recalcitrant theoretical botany colleagues.

A little detective work revealed that there were both profound academic reasons and personality peculiarities for their opposition:

Although a botany master's program had traditionally been a 24-credit regimen, six credits of which were required thesis credits, the department/college committee structuring the new biological conservation/sustainable development program had opted for a pattern of 30 course credits with no mandatory thesis. That was like waving a red flag in front of a bull. How could botany's high standards be so defiled? (And wouldn't grad students flock away from lab programs into the new configuration?)

Bill set out to do some diplomatic fence-mending. At an early meeting of the program planning committee, he proposed a compromise: Why not retain the 30-credit regimen so that students would be exposed to a necessary range of materials, but let's include in the 30 a four-credit research-paper-in-lieu-of-thesis requirement, said paper to be done up in such a fashion as to meet learned journal or research proposal standards? That turned out to be a happy solution to the matter-of-principle conflict.

The personality problem was tougher to handle. The acting chair of the new program was simply not a very likable person, and he had compounded that debility by being of uncertain caliber: not only had he come into the department with 18 years as a dendrologist with the USDI National Park Service in lieu of a Ph.D., he also held a joint appointment with "that" forestry school across the way.

As a first step, Bill proposed that the acting chair of the program take over the grad student program planning and evaluating assignment (on forestry time) that Bill had been asked to assume by the Midland forestry school, thereupon relinquishing his acting chairship. While it would have been logical for Bill to become the applied botany program chair, such a move would have been premature. Rather, he proposed that the program be administered at least temporarily by a three-person committee—one card-carrying cytologist, one geneticist (who was actually a "closet ecologist"), and himself, with the geneticist serving as chair pro tem. It was hard to argue against that strategy, and indeed nobody did so with any conviction. Even the dendrologist was content. (The only dismayed person was the forestry dean.)

Whether the makeshift strategy could hold together indefinitely, Bill wasn't sure, but it was a better shot than continued cold war. At least at the first meeting of the triumvirate, everything went smoothly. So Bill had taken a significant step at finding a key pressure point and mending fences. Chair Perkins was understandably impressed with his adroit handling of what had been a messy situation.

You can be on the lookout for a similar role of osteopathic diplomacy wherever you are.

Conferencing. Without question, it's a sound political move to attend at least one conference a year in your field, particularly if you're invited to present a paper; and many departments will "pop" for the cost. The attendant prestige toward promotion is measurable—unless you acquire a reputation as a constant traveler.

An even sounder political decision is to host a conference on your own turf, provided you do it with savvy: Figure about an 18-month lead time in which to line up funding and program participants; get yourself an administrative assistant of some kind; assemble a broadly based planning committee, to include extra-campus as well as all-campus representatives of appropriate agencies and organizations; pick a general topic or theme with some local relevance; select keynote speakers and panel members having reputations for pithy remarks with news media "bite." The credibility you gain from chairing a hometown conference multiplies manyfold a trip or two.

(This demur from one reviewer: "I would *never* recommend that an assistant professor take on such a charge!")

Your Midland University *alter ego* Bill figured out that the best way to capitalize on that lagoon vs. parking lot business was to use it as a peg for a regional academic conference along the lines of his department's new biological conservation/sustainable development theme. For the conference kickoff he got a promised appearance by Gaylord Nelson, former U.S. Senator from nearby Wisconsin, "father" of Earth Day, now general counsel for the Wilderness Society, who had recently made headlines with the ethic, "When somebody destroys something made by man, he's called a vandal; when someone destroys something irreplaceable, something made by God, he's called a developer." For the principal presenters Bill picked emeritus professors John Cobb, Jr., and Herman Daly, authors of the current book *For the Common Good: Redirecting the Economy Toward Community, Environment, and Sustainable Future*. But to keep the agenda balanced, Bill invited as presenters, as well, two forceful Midland urban planners to promote the parking-lot option—and to save the seminar from the charge that it was "staged by environmentalists." The resulting conference should stimulate student, faculty, administration, and public thinking—and lend visibility to the department and its new M.A. program.

Keep your eyes open for a similar opportunity where you are.

Leadership and Character. If all that's transpired so far in this section on practical politics seems to you like gamesmanship beneath your dignity, depending on your personal likes and professional standards, you could be right.

But there's one crucial aspect of qualifying for promotion to tenure you can't duck, and that's the responsibility you bear for yourself and your chosen profession to demonstrate incontrovertible hallmarks of leadership and character:

Hallmarks of leadership:

- Know yourself and seek self-improvement.
- Be professionally proficient.
- Seek and take responsibility.
- Make sound and timely decisions.
- Set the example.
- Know your colleagues and students and look out for their well-being; keep them informed.
- Develop a sense of responsibility in your students: ensure that any task is understood and accomplished.
- Practice teamwork.

Hallmarks of character:

- Integrity: searching for and doing the morally right thing.
- Maturity.
- Will.
- Self-discipline.
- Flexibility.
- Confidence.
- Endurance.
- Decisiveness.
- Coolness under stress.
- Initiative.
- Justice.
- Empathy or compassion.
- Sense of humor.
- Creativity.
- Humility.
- Tact.

Now if all that sounds like a bunch of platitudes, so be it.

THE TEN COMMANDMENTS OF TENURE
We don't know of a better way to summarize what we've talked about so far in this guide and to presage coming chapters than to

borrow lock, stock, and barrel "the ten commandments of tenure" carved in stone by authors Whicker, Kronenfeld, and Strickland:[19]

1. Publish, publish, publish.
2. View tenure as a political process.
3. Find out the tenure norms.
4. Document everything.
5. Rely on your record, not on promises of protection.
6. Reinforce research with teaching and service.
7. Do not run your department or university until after tenure.
8. Be a good department citizen.
9. Manage your own professional image.
10. Develop a marketable record.

To those 10 let us add one more: "Take not counsel of your fears." Or, as Wallace Stegner, in his semi-autobiographical novel of academic life, *Crossing to Safety*, has a lead character tell her assistant professor spouse: "Have some confidence in yourself! You're a splendid teacher, everybody says so. If they demand publications, write some. Just take it for granted you're going to get promoted, and they won't have the nerve not to!"

A FINAL P&T CHECKLIST

As a capstone to your socialization, we suggest you locate a copy of the official form on which, five or six years from now—the fates willing—your recommendation for promotion to tenure will be initiated by your department and reviewed by higher echelons before being placed—again, the fates willing—before the board of governors.

If your institution has no such form, you may find it useful to check the following Midland University form, covered by a memo of transmittal from the college dean to the department chair.

Chances are this Midland form is very similar to the documentation you and your chair will be asked to produce and package. At any rate, it certainly contains sure clues to the type of information you should start collecting and cataloging from Day 1.

Consult it conscientiously—and confidently.

However, in doing so, recall what brought you in the first place to seek a career in academia. It certainly wasn't money alone. Wasn't it the stimulus that comes from being around bright people—colleagues and students? The opportunity to contribute, discover and share knowledge? The ideal of service? So don't try to reduce your assistant professorship to merely a quantitative quest for tenure, important as that may be. Your probationary term can be qualitatively richer than that. Live it professionally to the fullest.

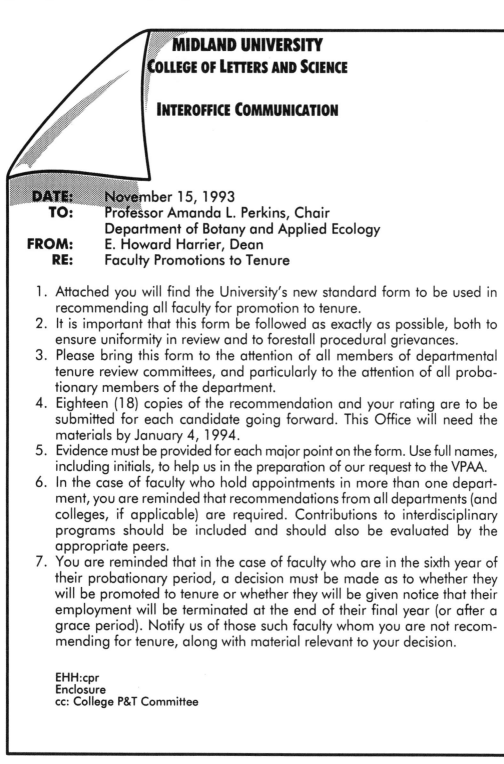

MIDLAND UNIVERSITY
COLLEGE OF LETTERS AND SCIENCE

INTEROFFICE COMMUNICATION

DATE: November 15, 1993
   TO: Professor Amanda L. Perkins, Chair
        Department of Botany and Applied Ecology
FROM: E. Howard Harrier, Dean
   RE: Faculty Promotions to Tenure

1. Attached you will find the University's new standard form to be used in recommending all faculty for promotion to tenure.
2. It is important that this form be followed as exactly as possible, both to ensure uniformity in review and to forestall procedural grievances.
3. Please bring this form to the attention of all members of departmental tenure review committees, and particularly to the attention of all probationary members of the department.
4. Eighteen (18) copies of the recommendation and your rating are to be submitted for each candidate going forward. This Office will need the materials by January 4, 1994.
5. Evidence must be provided for each major point on the form. Use full names, including initials, to help us in the preparation of our request to the VPAA.
6. In the case of faculty who hold appointments in more than one department, you are reminded that recommendations from all departments (and colleges, if applicable) are required. Contributions to interdisciplinary programs should be included and should also be evaluated by the appropriate peers.
7. You are reminded that in the case of faculty who are in the sixth year of their probationary period, a decision must be made as to whether they will be promoted to tenure or whether they will be given notice that their employment will be terminated at the end of their final year (or after a grace period). Notify us of those such faculty whom you are not recommending for tenure, along with material relevant to your decision.

EHH:cpr
Enclosure
cc: College P&T Committee

FORM FOR RECOMMENDING
PROMOTION OF FACULTY MEMBERS TO
TENURE AT MIDLAND UNIVERSITY

1. Name of Faculty Member, Current Rank, and Department.
   Append a current curriculum vitae.

2. Action Requested.
   Promotion to which rank, or tenure, or both.

3. Number of Years of Professional Experience.
   This figure should be a total of the number of years of experience in teaching, research, professional practice, and extension work. It should reflect the total number of years of professional service and should not be limited to the years of service at Midland.

4. Midland Personnel Record.
   Ranks held and date of appointment to each rank.

5. Present Responsibilities.
   Teaching. Describe responsibilities for teaching. Give the title, catalog number, and number of credit hours of courses taught during the last five years (by quarter). State approximate number of students in each class. If courses were team-taught, indicate percent of course taught by candidate.

   Research and Artistic Creativity. Describe responsibilities for research and artistic creativity.

   Extension and/or Professional Practice. Describe responsibilities for extension and/or professional practice.

   Student Advising. Does the candidate serve as academic advisor to undergraduate students or graduate students? How many of each?

   International Assignments. List international assignments on Midland projects during the last five years. Include project title, number of months served, and major accomplishments.

   Others. If contributions are made outside of the assigned categories shown above, describe the nature of these contributions.

6. Reasons for Promotion and/or Tenure (to be completed by chair)
   Identification of Area(s) of Excellence. The University's standards for promotion and tenure indicate that a faculty member must perform in: (1) teaching and advising; (2) research, scholarship, or artistic activities; or (3) extension and/or professional practice. *Identify the area(s) in which the candidate excels.*

   Teaching Performance. Give a thorough analysis of the faculty member's teaching capability and performance since the date of the most recent appointment. Indicate special qualifications by evaluating such items as: interest in students, advising skills, instructional methods, ability to stimulate student interest in subject, competence in subject matter. Submit evidence to support the analysis, including evaluations by students and peers.

   Performance in Research or Artistic Activities. List major publications since the date of the most recent appointment. Use documentation format appropriate to your discipline. Evaluate the publications in terms of the level of research ability reflected and their contribution to knowledge. Comment on the quality of journals in which the publications have appeared and the nature of their review process. List significant outside funding obtained. Appraise ability to attract, stimulate, and develop the research talents of graduate students. For multi-author publications, describe the shared contributions. Submit single copies of key publications separately so that they can be returned to the candidate following completion of the review.

Performance in Extension and/or Professional Practice (if applicable). Give a thorough analysis of the faculty member's extension and/or professional practice capability and performance since the date of the most recent appointment. List major accomplishments in professional practice. Evaluate the importance and quality of the individual's extension and/or professional practice in terms such as demonstrated expertise in the discipline; ability to instruct, inform, and assist the clientele; and the extent to which the individual displays leadership, initiative, and creativity in the application of the discipline.

Service Activities. The University's standards for promotion and tenure require that all candidates must have demonstrated excellence in at least one of the following: institutional service, professional service, or public service. Cite the ways in which the candidate has met this requirement. List departmental, college, and university committee memberships and evaluate contributions to each. Appraise relationship with colleagues in terms of cooperativeness, helpfulness, and willingness to assume share of responsibilities in the academic community.

National Professional Standing. Appraise national professional standing, such as memberships and offices held in professional associations, and professional awards and honors received.

Evaluation by Departmental Colleagues. If this recommendation is the outgrowth of consultation or action by special evaluation techniques, such as a committee on faculty promotions, please indicate.

Evaluation by Peers from Outside the University (to be solicited by the Chair or department review committee). The Chair or the committee shall solicit letters from qualified, impartial reviewers, with the understanding that, insofar as possible, access to them will be limited to persons involved in the promotion/tenure decision. Between three and six letters should be sought, with at least one of the reviewers being suggested by the candidate. A copy of the candidate's CV and other relevant materials should accompany the letter of request. The reviewers should be asked to be specific and to comment on particular aspects of the candidate's scholarly contributions and their impact on the field, as well as, where possible, to compare the candidate with others in the field at the same stage of their career. The Chair should assess the letters and should prepare a summary to be transmitted with the package, including an explanation of why those persons were selected in terms of their general qualifications in the field as well as their specific contributions to this review. To preserve confidentiality, the letters themselves should be transmitted with the package to the Dean and subsequently to the VPAA and will be retained in the Office of the VPAA. The essence of the letters should be shared with the candidate in a way that protects the anonymity of the evaluator.

NOTES

1. Carla Howery, interview with Barbara D. Wright, "Discipline-Based Assessment: The Case for Sociology," *AAHE Bulletin* Nov. 1991: 14-16.

2. Thomas J. Hawk, "Beware Department Terrorists," *The Department Chair* Fall 1992: 11.

3. Ronald F. Abler, "Five Steps to Oblivion," *AAG Newsletter* Sept. 1993: 4.

4. Roger Van Ommeron, Don Sneed, K. Tim Wulfemeyer, and Daniel Riffe, "Ethical Issues in Recruiting Faculty," *CUPA Journal* Fall 1991: 29-35.

5. Daniel W. Wheeler, "The Role of the Chairperson in Support of Junior Faculty," *Developing New and Junior Faculty*, eds. Mary Deane Sorcinelli and Ann E. Austin, New Directions in Teaching and Learning 50 (San Francisco: Jossey-Bass, 1992) 87-96.

6. Russell Edgerton, foreword, *The Academic Chairperson's Handbook*, by John W. Creswell, et al. (Lincoln: University of Nebraska Press, 1990) ix.

7. Allen Tucker, *Chairing the Academic Department* (New York: ACE-Macmillan, 1984) 7.

8. John W. Creswell et al., *The Academic Chairperson's Handbook* (Lincoln: University of Nebraska Press, 1990) 3.

9. Donald Zillman, letter to the authors, 18 Aug. 1993.

10. Robert O. Riggs, Patricia H. Murrell, and JoAnne C. Cutting, *Sexual Harassment in Higher Education*, ASHE-ERIC Higher Education Report 2 (Washington, DC: George Washington University School of Education and Human Development, 1993).

11. Gerald Phillips, *Surviving in the Academy* (Cresskill, NJ: Hampton Press, 1994).

12. Wallace Stegner, *Crossing to Safety* (New York: Random House, 1987).

13. John B. Bennett, "Collegiality as 'Getting Along,' " *AAHE Bulletin* Oct. 1991: 7-10.

14. Susan A. Cole, "Professional Ethics and the Role of the Academic Officer," *CUPA Journal* Fall 1991: 37-41.

15. Lee Knefelkamp, "Seasons of Academic Life," Conference for Community College Chairs and Deans, Phoenix AZ, 23-26 Feb. 1994.

16. Valerie Steele, "The F Word," *Lingua Franca* Apr. 1991: 17-20.

17. Donald Zillman, letter to the authors, 18 Aug. 1993.

18. Mary S. Selke and Terrence D. Wong, "The Mentoring-Empowerment Model: Professional Role Functions in Graduate Student Advisement," *NACADA Journal* Fall 1993: 21-26.

19. Marcia Lynne Wickler, Jennie Jacobs Kronenfeld, and Ruth Ann Strickland, *Getting Tenure* (Newbury Park, CA: Sage, 1993).

5 THE TEACHING CHALLENGE: PREPARING TO TEACH

In a sense this chapter and the next two may not seem necessary. For most faculty teaching is not a major concern along the path to tenure and promotion, for two reasons.

First, it's generally right there in your contract, inevitable. With research or service work there are choices: you choose whether or not to do it, how much, what kind, when. With teaching you usually receive your assignments: the experience is thrust upon you.

The second reason why teaching isn't usually an obstacle is that, at many institutions, only a horrible instructor would be denied tenure on the basis of teaching alone. Student evaluations may not matter much. Evaluations by colleagues may not be any more important: a study by John A. Centra several years ago indicated that 94% of faculty raters judged their colleagues' teaching as "very good" or "excellent."[1]

Fortunately for our students, that situation is changing as voices rise to demand better instruction. But that trend may make your upward path more difficult. If the decision-makers in your department and division want to promote teaching—or the "scholarship of dissemination," as Ernest Boyer promotes it in *Scholarship Reconsidered: Priorities of the Professoriate*—without relaxing expectations for (other) scholarship and service, you'll need to be more efficient in your efforts to teach better.

And you'll need to remember that many of your colleagues may not show much enthusiasm for teaching—or much appreciation for those who are enthusiastic about that activity. As Martin Anderson, author of *Impostors in the Temple*, puts it:[2]

> Teaching is an old and honorable profession. And yet many of today's professors view it with undisguised contempt. Indeed, they believe teaching to be beneath them. They regard their students as mere obstacles to their own intellectual hobbies and scholarly pursuits.

If you approach it in the right spirit, teaching provides intrinsic rewards and motivations. It can be a real joy to work with students, to help them develop, to challenge them to realize their potential, and sometimes to learn together with them.

As Northrop Frye expressed it in *Divisions on a Ground*,[3]

> A teacher who is not a scholar is soon going to be out of touch with his own subject, and a scholar who is not a teacher is soon going to be out of touch with the world.

But beware: as a colleague at Midland University warned Bill Campion, "Teaching can be like a black hole, drawing away your time and energy. And suddenly—you're up for tenure with your CV out of balance."

In Chapters 5, 6, and 7 we have two goals: to hit the essentials of good teaching and to suggest ways to maximize recognition of your efforts at tenure time. If you feel tempted to skip ahead to read only about building your dossier, we encourage you to at least skim the pages on the essentials of teaching.

REPRESENTATIVE STANDARDS

To begin our chapters on teaching, we're setting your sights high by quoting what a major university tells a candidate about its "standards to be applied in judging qualifications for tenure" in the area of "teaching and the development of teaching materials."

The "criteria" document developed by Midland states that "evaluation of teaching ability and performance takes into account the wide range of approaches to teaching." These include "lectures, discussion sections, seminars, institutes, workshops, media presentations, laboratory instruction, in-service training, media courses, correspondence courses, individual tutorials, advising and consulting, and consultative exchanges with client groups."

While no candidate is expected to be equally proficient in all teaching situations, "proficiency *must* be demonstrated in those teaching situations most appropriate to the candidate's teaching responsibilities."

Evidence used to evaluate teaching ability and performance will include:

- Surveys of student opinion.
- Assessment by colleagues, based on direct observation.
- Course outlines, bibliographies, scripts, program development, and other teaching materials.
- Assessment by teaching assistants, workshop participants, trainees.
- Record of student advising, consultations, and research supervision.
- Development of new courses and teaching materials.
- Client and peer evaluations of program presentations.
- Success of students: in your course, in later courses for which yours is a prerequisite, in careers based on majors in your field, and in high-profile areas—when they receive important fellowships, gain admission to prestigious graduate programs, present papers at conferences, and publish scholarly articles and books.

The guidelines conclude: "A balanced judgment of teaching ability *must* rely on more than one kind of evidence."

So, at this and comparable institutions at least, excellence in teaching is clearly essential for tenure.

At many research institutions new faculty may learn through experience that excellent teaching is considerably less important in practice than in principle. Even at liberal arts colleges, urban colleges, and two-year colleges—institutions where teaching has generally been held in higher esteem—there may be subtle shifts to stress productive scholarship. Once again, it's a question of knowing your territory—and realizing that not all expectations are in writing.

> The value placed on teaching in institutions of higher education is inversely related to the highest degree an institution offers. In our research, 96% of the deans in colleges offering no graduate study at all reported that teaching was the most important factor in tenure decisions, as did 91% of the deans in institutions that offer both bachelor's and master's degrees. Doctoral institutions...often conceal a very different set of priorities which guide internal decisions. Deans rated teaching as a secondary or tertiary factor in tenure decisions in slightly more than half (56%) of those universities.[4]

We must here again repeat the refrain of this manual: you've got to know your territory.

YOUR PERSPECTIVES ON TEACHING

AFTER 20 YEARS IN THE CLASSROOM . . .

New faculty may feel that they shouldn't have any problems teaching, since most have only recently emerged from the classroom experience as students and perhaps also served as graduate teaching assistants. This assumption is risky, for several reasons.

Faculty tend to teach as they themselves were taught; it's what they know and it has worked for them. But there are other approaches and techniques. And students aren't all the same. Most faculty are more intelligent than the average student. More important, they have a greater interest in the subject matter. And they're probably more comfortable in academic surroundings; after all, they've chosen to settle down there.

Approaches and techniques handed down from one generation of faculty to the next need to be examined and revised. Otherwise we could all just meet to talk in the marketplace, as they did in ancient Greece, or conduct all academic activities in Latin, as they did in medieval Europe, or just lecture from the podium as. . . .

SAME OLD SYSTEM

Many faculty stick with what they know. Some want to go beyond the tried and true, but they feel that educational research and pedagogy are a separate discipline, a *terra incognita* populated by such strangers as Dewey, Piaget, and Vygotsky. Not to worry: you don't need to be an expert in research on teaching and learning to try something a little different.

At an American Association for Higher Education conference a few years ago, one presenter was overheard telling another, "I don't know if this session will work, but we'll just try it." The candor, the honesty, and the enthusiasm were more inspiring than "canned" presentations that have proven "successful" over and over and over and. . . .

The lesson: don't always play it safe. Your students expose themselves to mistakes and failure constantly. You may be an expert in your field, but you can't know it all. You may be the one in charge in that classroom, but you can't make everything work out right.

Think of "teaching" as "facilitating." Your job is to make your students' environment conducive to learning and to provide activities that promote their development.

WHAT'S YOUR STORY?

What's your particular situation? Some beginning instructors are assigned established courses, complete with design and materials, while others may enjoy total autonomy, with the freedom and responsibility of creating their own courses. For most, the scenario is somewhere between those two extremes. So just move through the following sections and find what works for your particular situation.

CONCEPTUALIZING YOUR COURSE AND YOUR GOALS

Whether you're creating a new course from scratch (a challenge we'll cover later in this chapter) or, as is more likely, adapting an existing course to meet your particular objectives and perceived student needs, the process of course development is the same—and it can be scary. But you shouldn't feel overwhelmed, not if you examine each aspect carefully.

In preparing a course, the question "Why are you teaching?" is more fundamental than "What are you teaching?" The question "How do you want your students to change?" is more central to your purpose than "What do you want them to learn?"

Then you should ask yourself the following questions:

- Where are we beginning? Who are my students?
- How can I facilitate their learning?
- What are our circumstances? That is, class hours, time outside of class, classroom size and layout, resources.

For further guidance, you might try the more comprehensive, two-page worksheet for planning courses developed by Kathleen T. Brinko of Appalachian State University[5] or the Teaching Goals Inventory.[6]

GOALS: HOW DO YOU WANT YOUR STUDENTS TO CHANGE?

It's easy to think just about primary goals, the essentials of your field of study: students will learn this material, students will be able to solve these problems, and so forth. But there are other goals that may be secondary to your subject area but which are also very important, in a larger context. Many of these goals will likely be cognitive (knowledge and intellectual skills), while a few may be affective (attitudes, values, interests). Your particular goals might include critical thinking, better reading comprehension, verbal and writing skills, appreciation of the values and opinions of others, teamwork, research skills, understanding personal differences. . . .

Some teachers think of those goals as icing on the cake: if you make progress toward those goals, it's a bonus. A colleague likes to call those secondary goals "the mortar that holds all those bricks together." It's a question of attitude. Some instructors view secondary goals as a bonus or, worse, as a frill that detracts from the time and energy available to achieve the primary goals. For others the secondary goals suggest ways—often quite creative—of pursuing the primary goals.

Start with the basic question: What are you teaching? Then ask: Why? What is the value of what you intend to teach? How do you want your students to be different because of your course?

As some have put it, "Defend your course." Be specific. Make a list of general objectives: students will understand the causes of World War I, students will know the distinctive characteristics of species of mammals, students will be able to explain philosophical differences between Descartes and Pascal, students will write a program to sort records by any one of seven fields. These will be your primary goals.

Then consider what other goals would be worthwhile in your course. In a course for majors or minors, these goals could be closely related to the discipline. Just ask yourself, "What helped me succeed in my field? What do I wish I'd learned when I was studying that area of my discipline? What knowledge or skills are most useful to practitioners in this field?" In a general course for students with diverse interests, the secondary goals might be larger. With first-year students, for example, you might want to encourage intellectual curiosity, to help develop study skills, to promote cooperation.

YOUR STUDENTS:
WHERE ARE YOUR STARTING POINTS?

The next aspect of planning is often more difficult. Who are your students? An introductory class of beginners and visitors? A more advanced class? A class of senior majors? Grads and post-grads? Non-traditional and special students?

What knowledge, experience, and skills will your students bring to your course? Why are they taking your course? Don't make any unwarranted assumptions. Colleagues who've taught similar courses recently can be a source of valuable suggestions.

When Bill arrived to teach his first class, he found that a few of his students were older than he, two by several years. He was concerned, since a colleague had warned him about older students:

Because they're more experienced in the 'real world' they tend to
have higher standards, more definite expectations. Sometimes it's frustrating because they're more likely to focus on the bottom line, on
acquiring information and skills, and less on learning how to think.

But Bill had thought hard about his course goals; they were
solid and realistic, and he felt ready for any challenges.

Amanda Perkins, chair of the botany department, had also
helped prepare Bill for his students by providing him with some
demographics. So Bill knew that about 18% of students taking
courses in the department were part-time students and that about
20% of the full-time students were working part-time as well. He
also knew that Midland attracted some 22% of its undergraduates
from out-of-state and that MU recruiters were particularly successful in metropolitan areas around the Midwest and the East
Coast. Plus, Perkins had noted proudly, the campus had students
from a dozen foreign countries. Bill, a country boy from Georgia,
hoped he'd be able to reach all of his students, despite their
different backgrounds and situations.

The composition of your classes may well be similar. Statistics
from the U.S. Department of Education for fall 1993 show that
while 68.3% of first-year students were 18 years old or younger,
4.5% were 21 or older.[7] Some 39.4% of students beginning their
college studies in fall 1993 were planning on working to pay their
expenses, 5.6% with a full-time job.[8]

There were significantly more women than men enrolled as
undergrads in fall 1991—6,868,284 to 5,571,003.[9] In fall 1993,
79.6% of first-year students were "white," 10.0% were "African
American," 3.7% were "Asian American," 3.1% were "Mexican
American," 1.9% were "American Indian," and 1.2% were "Puerto
Rican."[10]

Students with disabilities constitute important minorities: in
fall 1986, according to figures published in 1993, 10.5% of college
students had disabilities, including vision (4.1%), hearing (2.7%),
speech (0.5%), learning disabilities (1.3%), and health-related disabilities (2.5%).[11] Some students have economic disabilities: 16.9%
of first-year students in fall 1993 estimated their parental income
as less than $20,000.[12] Finally, many students are first-generation
collegians: in fall 1993 42.7% reported that their fathers hadn't

attended college and 47.9% said the same of their mothers, while the percentages of students whose parents had no high school diploma were 11.0% (fathers) and 8.9% (mothers).[13]

These are just statistics, interesting numbers that provide merely a suggestion of the many differences among the more than 14 million students at our more than 3500 colleges and universities. Whatever the demographics may be for your classes, it's clear that the more you know about the backgrounds and abilities of your students, the more effective you'll be as their teacher.

FIRST LESSON: LEARN ABOUT YOUR STUDENTS

If possible, survey students at the start of the semester. Ask for a show of hands to a series of questions: Who's studied phantasmagoric parapsychology? Who knows the principles of pataphysical science? Who can explain the differences between widgets and doohickeys? Or pass out index cards and ask students to give their name, phone number, major, previous courses in the field, and additional relevant background.

Another approach is to give a diagnostic test, with questions that touch upon the various areas you intend to cover in your course. A simple diagnostic: ask for definitions of key terms to be used in your course and examples illustrating those terms. Of course, you should make clear to your students the purpose of the diagnostic test. Students can be easily overwhelmed by such tests as they begin the course.

Just as you want to have a good idea of who your students are, you should also be familiar with learning styles. This area of research has attracted a lot of attention in recent years. You can get a good introduction in *Learning Styles: Implications for Improving Educational Practices*, by Charles S. Claxton and Patricia H. Murrell (Washington DC: Association for the Study of Higher Education, 1987). Charles S. Schroeder provides an interesting perspective. He cites research using the Myers-Briggs Type Indicator that shows that "over 75 percent of faculty prefer the intuitive learning pattern, with the vast majority of these preferring the abstract reflective (IN) pattern," while only about "10% of the general population is IN, with about 50% of people being concrete active learners (ES)."[14] Simply put, half your students may have learning styles quite different from yours; if you teach the way you learn best, only one out of 10 may learn properly.

A colleague recommended that Bill skim *Learning Strategies and Learning Styles*, ed. Ronald R. Schmeck (New York: Plenum, 1988), for a general introduction, then read *The Learning-Style Inventory* by David A. Kolb (Boston: McBer, 1985) and use "The Kolb Model Modified for Classroom Activities," by Marilla D. Svinicki and N.M. Dixon (*College Teaching*, 1987, 35:4, pp. 141-146) for ideas on better shaping his teaching methods and assignments to his students.

Once you've developed an idea of who your students are and established where you want to take them through your course, you should consider what methods and materials will best suit that journey.

A recent guide that can take you from start to finish in planning, teaching, and evaluating a new class is *Charting Your Course: How to Prepare to Teach More Effectively*, by Richard Prégent (Madison, WI: Magna Publications, 1994).

HOW CAN I FACILITATE LEARNING? METHODS AND TECHNIQUES

LECTURE

> Our teachers never stop bawling into our ears, as though they were pouring water into a funnel, and our task is only to repeat what has been told to us. I should like the teacher to correct this practice, and right from the start, according to the capacity of the mind he has in hand, to begin putting it through its paces, making it taste things, choose them, and discern them by itself, sometimes clearing the way for it, sometimes letting it clear its own way.

These words come to us from 400 years ago, in the advice of Montaigne, who advocated a head that was "well-made" rather than "well-filled." To help make his point, Montaigne quoted Cicero: "The authority of those who teach is often an obstacle to those who want to learn."

Traditionally, instruction has often been in the form of a lecture, sometimes defined as "a process by which the notes of the lecturer are transferred to the notes of the students without passing through the mind of either." But a lecture doesn't need to be simply a mindless reading of material. And there are times when a lecture may be the most effective means of instruction—if done well.

Jim W. Corder, an English professor at Texas Christian University, has argued eloquently for the value of good lectures:[15]

> Arguments that lectures are pedagogically unsound are invalid because they are based only on bad lectures. . . . We often don't examine what makes a lecture good or differentiate the good from the bad, so we wind up opposing *all* lectures.

Corder points out two advantages to lectures:

> First, at their best, they dramatize the creation of knowledge. . . . Second, lectures can show the consequences of knowledge—show what comes of knowledge, how it can be used in ways not previously seen or guessed. Good lectures exemplify possibility. . . .
>
> To suppose that all or most classes should be arenas for active or experiential learning is as simplistic as to suppose that all or most classes should be lecture classes. No method is right for everyone in all circumstances.

If you decide that lecturing would be the most effective means of teaching a certain segment of your course, you should be attentive to the following aspects:

- *Structure*. If you decide to read your material (Is that really the most effective method?), pay attention to syntax and punctuation. Often a sentence that works great on the printed page can be too long, complex, or stilted. Listeners, unlike readers, can't stop and run through a sentence a second or third time. Be aware particularly of long sentences, dependent clauses, and comments within parentheses or dashes. Compensate orally for visual clues: pause after each paragraph, and bridge between sections with transition phrases, such as "Next we consider . . ." or "This brings us to . . ." Better yet, prepare an outline on a transparency to display with an overhead projector.

- *Volume*. Too low and your students may have to strain to hear you. Too high and they may develop headaches or tune you out. Increase volume to emphasize something important or to make your students more attentive. For larger classes, you may be able to get a cordless microphone from your instructional media center. Also, you may find it useful to warm up your voice before class, like an actor or singer.

- *Articulation*. Pronounce your words carefully, but without exaggeration or affectation. Your articulation should help convey your meaning, not distract from it.

- *Pace*. Moderation is the key: neither so rapidly that you and your students tire out, nor so slowly that you bore them. Although listeners tend to find lecturers who speak more rapidly to be more competent and persuasive, you should bear in mind that your goal is to teach, not to impress. Slow down when presenting or explaining difficult material. Speed up to underline changes in content or mood or to make your students more attentive.

- *Pauses*. Use short pauses to emphasize something, to mark a shift in direction, to gather your thoughts, or to allow students a moment to reflect or react, or to finish noting what you've just said. Avoid the tendency to fill pauses with meaningless sounds ("ah," "um," "OK")—and the mechanical "Any questions?" or "Do you understand?"

- *Pitch*. Vary your pitch naturally. Listeners may interpret a monotone as a sign that you lack interest or confidence. But avoid a repetitive pattern of pitch which doesn't fit the meaning of your words; leave that delivery to broadcast journalists reading unfamiliar, prepared scripts. Concentrate on the meaning of your words, not the sound of your voice.

- *Body*. Make sure that your students can easily see you, not just disembodied head and hands above a podium. Use movement: gestures and motion visually supplement the aural, but nervous fidgeting, repetitive and meaningless gestures, and constant activity are distracting, while any motion may undermine your efforts to explain complex material.

- *Face*. Relax and let your face naturally express how you feel about your material and teaching in general. Many instructors feel that they should be reserved, serious, formal, impersonal; students may interpret their facial expressions as signals of boredom, disinterest, or even hostility.
- *Focus*. Look at your students whenever possible; make eye contact with each. Look at your notes only when necessary. If you look at the ceiling, out the window, or at the clock, your students will do likewise.
- *Appearance*. Remember that your clothing, hair, and makeup convey an image. Many students (and your colleagues?) believe that grooming reflects attitude. Should you dress up? Should you go casual? It's your decision, of course—but it's wise to remember that you're likely not totally free to choose. (You may want to read one more time the passage in Chapter 4, "Dress Code.")

Most instructors are aware that students don't always follow every single word; in fact, they may get lost for considerable lengths of time. Students may experience four kinds of mental lapses during a lecture, according to Mary Budd Rowe, a chemistry professor:[16]

- *Short-Term Memory Overloads*. If new ideas come too fast, short-term memory—the mental buffer zone for temporary information storage—may overflow. Researchers estimate it takes between five and 10 seconds to transfer information from short-term to long-term memory.
- *Momentary Misunderstandings*. If a student doesn't immediately grasp an idea, confusion results. The student must make sense of the new idea, fit it into what he or she already knows and understands, or it can't move into long-term memory.
- *Translation Troubles*. When instructors use terms other than those used in the text or previous lectures, students may have difficulty making the necessary translation. They may struggle to integrate familiar and unfamiliar terms, to determine what they mean.

- *Sidetracks.* Something is said that leads the student into another train of thought, distracting him or her from the lecture.

Rowe recommends a two-minute pause every eight to 12 minutes, to let students review their notes with each other, fill in missing material, clarify unclear concepts, and briefly discuss what they're learning. Short breaks not only lessen the damage of mental lapses, she says, but they also seem to help prevent them.

Three other strategies are helpful in minimizing mental lapses. Keep your terminology as consistent as possible. If you need to introduce new terms, put them on the board, an overhead, or a handout, and define them. When presenting a new idea, moving to another phase, or changing direction, try to make contextual connections: "Now, in the case of XYZ—which, as you recall, is a variant form of ABC used for . . ."

Finally, a brief comment by Page Smith:[17]

> I must confess that my own attitude toward lecturing was deeply influenced by my experience in teaching Dante's *Divine Comedy* in a seminar. When I suggested to my students that they devise some modern hells for modern sins, two students in the seminar offered interesting hells for professors-who-neglected-their-students. They proposed that the professors be required to listen to lectures for all eternity. The only point of dispute between them was whether it would be worse torment for professors to have to listen to their own lectures or to those of an especially dull colleague. I have never been able to feel the same way about lecturing since.

DEMONSTRATION

Sometimes it may be most effective to provide a demonstration of a process, such as to solve a problem step by step. There are several essential points to keep in mind:

- Make sure that students can easily see the board, the overhead, or the lab table that you use for your demonstration. (An overhead is superior to the board, if only because you can face your students as you demonstrate.)

- Work through your demonstration at a pace that allows your students to follow, to take notes, to understand the process, and to formulate any questions.
- If you write on the board or an overhead, allow students time to copy your words of wisdom. Bear in mind that while you may have a 4' x 8' chalkboard or a series of transparencies with overlays, the students are limited to notebooks that are 8½ " x 11" or smaller. If you plan to fill large areas or multiple transparencies with your demonstration, you might want to mention this in advance, so they can plan better.

QUESTIONS

If you choose the route of show (demonstration) and tell (lecture), you should try to involve students through questions whenever possible. Sometimes instructors feel that they're allowing students plenty of opportunities to ask questions, while students feel quite differently.

It's not enough to end every few sentences with a quick "Any questions?" or "Do you understand?" before continuing. As a reviewer wrote in the margin of this manuscript,

> 'Do you understand?' is the *worst* question. Students are often embarrassed to say 'No.' They also know from experience (i.e., tests) that understanding isn't often a yes-no sort of process: they may understand enough to follow you, but not to use the information. If they say 'Yes,' can you be sure they understand as well as they should? If they say 'No,' you still don't know *what* they don't understand. If this question is a filler, silence is better. If you really want to know if students understand, ask questions that require them to demonstrate their knowledge or lack of it.

When you ask for questions, give your students time to reflect on what you've said. Scan their faces for signs that things may not be completely clear. And, if you've made several points, you might ask for questions about each, to break the material into more manageable chunks.

It's often more effective to ask a few review questions from time to time. Keep in mind the following techniques:

- Start with easier questions, then work up to the more difficult ones.
- Ask questions that are relevant and productive.
- Vary your question types and structures.
- Keep your tone exploratory, not threatening. Questions should be a way of assessing the results of the learning process, results that depend on the instructor as well as the students.
- Phrase your questions in as few words as possible.
- Give your students sufficient time. Instructors often feel uncomfortable with moments of silence, and research has shown that they often allow students too little time to answer questions. Try to simulate the reaction process: mentally repeat the question (as students might in order to absorb it), think about the answer (at their speed), then imagine phrasing the answer.
- Move out toward the class, among your students if possible.
- Call on a student by name—and avoid establishing patterns. (The laws of random probability shouldn't favor students who sit in front or students who get good grades, for example.)
- Repeat the question, but not every time and certainly not immediately.
- Offer some sort of a clue.
- If you allow adequate time for answers and there are none, reshape the question, but avoid changing it more than necessary. It can be very frustrating for a student to be close to offering a response, only to have the instructor substantially change the question.
- Answer the question yourself—but only as a last resort. This is an admission of failure, which easily undermines student participation.

Then, when your students answer your questions, there are a few points to keep in mind:

- Make sure the other students hear and understand the answer.
- Acknowledge the answer. Not just mechanically ("Yes," "OK," "Good," "Uh-huh"), but with at least a brief comment.

- Correct wrong answers. Encourage your students, but not by accepting answers indiscriminately.
- Bring your students into the answers. When you get a response, try returning it to your students: "What do you think about that?" This works best with responses that express opinions or value judgments, but it can also work for right-wrong answers.
- Build on the answers. Follow up an answer with a question or two. Don't aim all your follow-up questions at the student who gave the answer, or your questioning may be perceived as a punishment. Probe the class.

Lectures and demonstrations can be efficient ways of conveying material, but there are other methods that are often more effective—particularly since you want instruction to be more than merely a transmission of information or a display of skills.

What's really exciting is when both instructor and students learn, from the sharing and interaction of ideas, in a symbiotic relationship. As a colleague explains it, "It's by learning with a teacher that students develop their potential; it's by learning with students that teachers remain questioning and alive—and often how they come upon their best ideas for innovative research."

Lectures (a.k.a. "show and tell") tend to be just a one-way street, as E. Glassman observes:[18]

> I realized that when I lectured I was the one who learned the most. I was the one whose thinking skills were enhanced and whose creativity was stimulated. I played the active learning role: the students' was passive, often consisting of listening and trying to decipher what I was saying during the lecture.

Instructors may feel compelled to use teacher-centered methods such as lectures or demonstrations so they can cover more material. But they should carefully consider the following remarks by Jean MacGregor, associate director of the Washington Center for Improving the Quality of Undergraduate Education at Evergreen State College:[19]

> Learners are diverse individuals whose understanding of reality is shaped by their gender, race, class, age, and cultural experience. Therefore,

teaching is woefully inadequate if it is construed as an enterprise of "transmission" or "coverage." And learning is woefully limited if it is thought of as simply an exercise in "receiving" and "reflecting."

TOWARD MORE ACTIVE STUDENT INVOLVEMENT

There are many ways to involve your students more actively in their learning experiences. The choices depend on your particular circumstances, which include the subject, class dynamics, your personality, and logistics. Think of active learning experiences as expeditions into the wilderness. Choose an activity, prepare appropriately—then take a chance!

CLASS DISCUSSION

This is perhaps the most basic form of class participation. In fact, it's easy to be casual about discussions. But if you don't put energy and interest into them, why should your students?

You may be very familiar with class discussions, but we suggest you invest a few moments in reading "Leading Discussion in a Lecture Course: Some Maxims and an Exhortation," an excellent article by Margaret Morganroth Gullette, the former assistant director of the Derek Bok Center for Teaching and Learning at Harvard, in *Change: The Magazine of Higher Learning* (March/April 1992, pp. 32-39). Then, we suggest you read "Discussion Teaching Method," an article by William M. Welty, director of the Center for Faculty Development at Pace University, also in *Change* (July/August 1989, pp. 41-49). These two short articles are well worth the time spent reading them—and will save you time and energy.

To keep a discussion going, John H. Clarke, director of the Learning Cooperative at the University of Vermont in Burlington, offers the following suggestions:[20]

- Keep a visual record of student contributions: jot them on the board or a transparency.
- Use your record—to link contributions, to compare, to provide closure.
- Convert student questions to statements, then solicit other opinions.

- Convert student opinions to questions to involve reticent classmates.
- Turn questions of interpretation back to the group.
- Use student assertions to draw examples from others.
- Ask questions that encourage inference, prediction, analogy, or synthesis.
- If the discussion lags, convert the last student contribution to a new question or assertion.
- When a student makes an important contribution, label it with his or her name—the Jane Theory or the Mike Question—and use it as a pivot or anchor for further discussion.

Bear in mind, however, that some students may react adversely to this technique, as did one reader, who noted, "I personally find the idea of naming ideas . . . repugnant and in the worst tradition of Western culture claim-staking." As with any other technique, be sensitive to the reactions of your students.

When Bill used the board to record student contributions, he quickly became aware of some important factors in the dynamics of his classes. Although he'd anticipated problems in getting his students to participate, one problem surprised him—a handful of students tended to dominate the discussions, discouraging the others.

So, Bill changed his style slightly. First, after asking a question, he paused a little longer before calling on any student. Then, he chose one of the last students to raise a hand, although he realized he was risking frustrating the more eager students. He also tried to ask questions that allowed for several answers, so he could involve more than one student per question and encourage divergent thinking.

At times, though, some students simply spoke out. Then, rather than be overly strict about protocol, Bill simply acknowledged their contributions, then called on other students to comment. Occasionally after class, he sought out one of the more dominant participants and quietly asked him (they were usually males) or her to stay for a moment. He then thanked the student for being so interested and enthusiastic, but pointed out that it was important to have everyone in the class feel free to participate in discussions. One of the more dominant students got upset, but the others more or less graciously agreed to be less aggressive. Bill didn't really feel comfortable with that way of handling the problem, but he was relieved that the aggressive students generally allowed the others a chance. He resolved to talk with his colleagues about the problem and ask for suggestions. After all, he realized, what works in one situation may flop in another.

GROUP DISCUSSION OR PROBLEM-SOLVING

Although discussion involving your entire class can be effective, it's usually better to divide your students into smaller groups, with three to five in each. Depending on the subject and class composition and dynamics, you may decide to group students according to interests, abilities, or personalities.

Make sure that you set a time limit, clearly define your expectations, and indicate the sort of follow-up you want: you may wish to have each group report to the class or have each student write out as homework a summary of what happened in his or her group. Then move around among the groups to encourage participation of every student and to answer any procedural or factual questions that might arise. It may seem obvious, but if you expect group reports you should allow adequate time: nothing is more frustrating than to have a great discussion abruptly ended by the clock.

There's a growing effort nationally to involve students more actively in the learning process through collaborative and cooperative learning, which emphasize small work groups. Advocates maintain that students not only learn more in groups than individually, but also benefit emotionally.

You might want to check your faculty development office for *The Cooperative Learning and College Teaching Newsletter* (published by New Forums Press, Stillwater, OK). The editors also publish a *Directory of Cooperative Learning Practitioners in Higher Education*, which lists more than 1,400 CL practitioners in the U.S., Canada, and 16 other countries. If you're interested in exploring the advantages of discussion and group work, you might read *Classroom Communication: Collected Readings for Effective Discussion and Questioning,* edited by Maryellen Weimer and Rose Ann Neff (Madison, WI: Magna Publications, 1989).

Many instructors find small groups difficult. It's like a three-ring circus: you need to organize more flexibly, motivate the performers, set it all in motion, then step out of the spotlight and be everywhere at the same time. It may be useful to consult *Small Group Teaching: A Trouble-Shooting Guide* by Richard G. Tiberius (Toronto: Ontario Institute for Studies in Education, 1990).

But, as a colleague insists, many instructors find it easier to work with small groups than with whole classes— "less of a show, fewer machines to maneuver, less prep, at least after the first few times." But, she points out, "planning for small groups means preparing a smorgasbord of options, paths, and questions, which requires multi-analysis of materials." Whether you find it easier or more difficult, you owe it to your students—and to yourself—to explore the possibilities of small groups and cooperative learning.

DEBATE

This method may be most appropriate when there are two sides to an issue, but it can be valuable when there are several perspectives, since gray areas challenge critical thinking. This activity is generally best suited for smaller groups, where more students can get involved. You may want to keep track of the debate by listing on the board the points made by the parties. Once again, a follow-up can be valuable; you might ask students to take notes, then write up a summary or a position paper for homework.

ROLE PLAY

This sort of activity is often more difficult, since it requires a certain theatricality. It's also more difficult to involve a lot of students. But it can be a logical choice in foreign languages, for example, or an interesting change of pace in the social sciences, where students can act out attitudes, historical figures, literary characters, philosophers, and so on.

One instructor has a method of organizing role plays that allows her to maintain control but without intruding. She prepares slips of paper describing each role, assigns a few roles to begin, then hands out others one by one according to the flow of action. This "progressive playwriting" lets her shape the activity as it develops, by her choice of roles, and then stop it at any point, by not handing out any more roles.

SIMULATIONS AND CASES

This sort of "real-life story problem" activity can stimulate and challenge a class. It may be most effective at the end of a unit, as a review that requires students to apply the knowledge they've acquired. Although this activity can be done by an entire class, it's generally more effective in smaller groups. With simulations and cases, follow-up is crucial: What conclusion did each group reach? How? Make sure that the students understand that *outcome* may be less important and less informative than *process*.

If cases sound like an interesting possibility, you might start by reading *Teaching and the Case Method* by C. Roland Christensen and Abby J. Hansen (Boston MA: Harvard Business School, 1987).

WHAT ELSE?

There are other methods; your colleagues may have suggestions and there are shelves of journals and books that can provide more options. Cynthia Weston and P.A. Cranton provide a comprehensive and organized overview of the range of methods in their article, "Selecting Instructional Strategies" (*The Journal of Higher Education*, May/June 1986, pp. 259-288).

Just keep in mind your goals—both primary and secondary—and the abilities and dynamics of your class. And remember the words of that anonymous conference session participant: "I don't know if it'll work, but we'll just try it."

A FEW GUIDING PRINCIPLES

In the mid-1980s a team of educators developed "Seven Principles for Good Practice in Undergraduate Education,"[21] which have quickly become a classic touchstone. Quite simply, good teaching:

1. encourages student-faculty contact,

2. encourages cooperation among students,

3. encourages active learning,

4. gives prompt feedback,

5. emphasizes time on task,

6. communicates high expectations,

7. respects diverse talents and ways of learning.

You might consider posting a copy of these seven principles on your office wall, to help you keep them in mind as you prepare your courses or evaluate student assignments. If you wonder how you rate in terms of these seven principles, you might want to read "Inventories of Good Practice: The Next Step for the Seven Principles for Good Practice in Undergraduate Education" by Zelda F. Gamson and Susan J. Poulsen[22] or complete the Faculty Inventory (self-assessment instrument) in the collection of articles Gamson edited with Arthur W. Chickering, *Applying the Seven Principles for Good Practice in Undergraduate Education* (San Francisco: Jossey-Bass, 1991).

Thomas A. Angelo, director of the Academic Development Center at Boston College, has gone beyond the seven principles to create a list of 14 "research-based principles for improving higher learning," which he offers with implications and suggestions for applying those principles:[23]

1. *Active learning is more effective than passive learning.* Have your students teach or explain to classmates what they have just learned or paraphrase a central concept in a couple of sentences for a specific audience.

2. *Learning requires focused attention and awareness of the importance of what is to be learned.* You might list on the board the key points of a lesson, for example.

3. *Learning is more effective and efficient when learners have explicit, reasonable, positive goals, and when their goals fit well with the teacher's goals.* Have students each write down a few specific learning goals for your course, then discuss and compare their goals.

4. *To be remembered, new information must be meaningfully connected to prior knowledge, and it must first be remembered in order to be learned.* Use examples, illustrations, descriptions, drawings, images, metaphors, and analogies.

5. *Unlearning what is already known is often more difficult than learning new information.* Before beginning an area of new

material, find out what students know about it and can do with their knowledge. You may need to remove a few obstacles before you advance.

6. *Information organized in personally meaningful ways is more likely to be retained, learned, and used.* Show your students several useful and appropriate ways to organize a body of information.

7. *Learners need feedback, early and often, to learn well; to become independent, they need to learn how to give themselves feedback.* Ask your students to write out and give to you a brief comment about the "muddiest point" in a particular reading, assignment, or lecture. In the next class, clarify the "muddiest" areas. Also, find out what your students do with your comments on written work and tests, then guide them to use the feedback more effectively.

8. *The ways in which learners are assessed and evaluated powerfully affect the ways they study and learn.* Give your students sample items from your tests.

9. *Mastering a skill or body of knowledge takes great amounts of time and effort.* Provide a simple form on which your students can log the time they spend on work for your course outside the classroom. Then, help them determine how to use their time and effort more effectively.

10. *Learning to transfer, to apply previous knowledge and skills to new contexts, requires a great deal of practice.* Focus continually on connections between the general and the specific, between concepts or principles and examples.

11. *High expectations encourage high achievement.* Before beginning the course, find out what your students expect of themselves, explain what you expect of them, then discuss those expectations.

12. *To be most effective, teachers need to balance levels of intellectual challenge and instructional support.* Maintain high expectations—and help your students meet them.

13. *Motivation to learn is alterable; it can be positively or negatively affected by the task, the environment, the teacher, and the learner.* Show through abundant examples that what your students are learning is valuable and useful. Help them make connections between course goals and their own long-term goals.

14. *Interaction between teachers and learners is one of the most powerful factors in promoting learning; interaction among learners is another.* Show that you care: learn their names, work with their learning styles, and involve them in working together.

ASSESSING STUDENT CHANGE

When you consider your methods of facilitating learning, think also about your ways of assessing the results. Focus on the questions that serve as guidelines for your course: "How do you want your students to **change**?" "**What** do you want them to **learn**?" The next question is logical: "How can your students show you what they've learned and how they've changed?"

The primary traditional means of assessment is the exam. The best word of advice here, as in so many aspects of teaching: make sure it fits. Use exams only if they are carefully designed and appropriate to your goals. Supplement testing with other forms of assessment. Be sensitive to exam anxiety and its effects. To alleviate anxiety, Bill wrote out a series of sample final exam items and distributed copies to his students.

Finally, you may want to have your students grade you on your exam effort. You might simply attach a short evaluation form to the exam, asking such questions as:[24]

- Did the content you expected to see appear on this exam?
- Were the questions clear? List the number(s) of any question(s) that seemed unclear.
- Are you satisfied with your responses to most of the questions?

The evaluation should contain space for them to grade you and for additional comments.

Since many students are naturally reluctant to criticize, for fear of possible "grade retaliation," it's wise to have them separate their evaluation from their exam when they turn them in, to form two piles (with evaluations face down). When Bill followed this procedure for the first time, he noticed that several students, when turning in their evaluations, shuffled the others in the pile. Although he believes that their precaution was unnecessary, it seemed to reassure them, so he now makes a practice of periodically shuffling the stack of evaluations as students turn them in.

A good alternative to exams, in many disciplines: projects. Of course, there's the term paper, in a variety of forms—a comprehensive "thought piece," a detailed analysis, a research article. You might ask students to find, read, and analyze journal articles on a certain topic. You could have them create their own exam, a switch that lets them show how well they understand not only the material but also its relevance. Don't hesitate to experiment: just focus on your course goals and go with the creative flow!

If you have first-year students, you may want to consider some advice on assignments offered by Bette LaSere Erickson and Diane Weltner Strommer.[25] They caution against assigning term papers and projects as "especially ill-suited" for inexperienced students:

> They ask students who know little about a subject to identify topics of special interest prematurely and require in-depth study before students know what resources could or should be consulted . . . Attempts to provide the directions and guidance freshmen need turn into impossible tasks because we cannot supervise what are essentially independent study projects for twenty or thirty or more students. The most serious reservation about these assignments, however, is that they do nothing to encourage freshmen to study on a day-to-day basis.

Erickson and Strommer recommend the following alternatives:

- Shorter papers, four or five pages, less ambitious than the typical term paper or project.
- Assignments with focus, not simply general advice such as "Think about this for next time."
- Assignments that produce something tangible—a solution to a problem, a list.
- Outline, a paragraph, a newspaper clipping.

- Activities that promote understanding and thinking.
- A variety of assignments, to appeal to different learning styles.
- Frequent, short assignments to help your students keep up and study regularly. You don't need to grade all these assignments; focus on some in class discussions, skim through others to check for misunderstandings, and designate some as practice exams.

For many courses, particularly with smaller classes, you may want to assign homework. Although students may complain about frequent assignments, these can help motivate students to prepare regularly—an especially important consideration with first-year students or in required non-major courses. Assignments also lessen the weight of exams, reducing test anxiety. Major drawbacks: grading assignments can be time-consuming and exhausting, students also have a greater opportunity to avail themselves of resources that can distort your assessment of their learning (i.e., they may cheat).

GRADES

Finally, as the last aspect of assessment (but definitely not the bottom line): grades.

> Grade: "An inadequate report of an inaccurate judgment by a biased and variable judge of the extent to which a student has attained an undefined level of mastery of an unknown proportion of an indefinite material."[26]

That's a depressing thought, especially since most faculty are obligated to give grades of some sort.

Most faculty use either straight percentages or a curve. But here again, conventional methods are not necessarily sound. In their study of grading, Gerald S. Hanna and William E. Cashin reached the following conclusion:[27]

> Each of the common bases for assigning college grades—*percentage* and *class-curve* grading—has only limited meaning and lacks a sound rationale. Neither satisfies the major criteria for student grading systems. *Anchor measures* enable the advantages of norm-referenced grading

> to be achieved without introducing the evils of class-curve grading. . . .
> They, therefore, are recommended for use in assigning college grades.

An anchor measure may offer the most reliable basis for grading systems. An anchor measure is "a device with which one can judge or 'take bearings' of the status of a class." If several sections of the same course, all following the same syllabus and using the same text, take the same final exam, that exam can be used to reveal differences in achievement among the sections, allowing instructors to adjust grade distributions within each section accordingly.

But if there aren't any suitable data to allow you to anchor the grades for your students, what do you do?

Many instructors devise some sort of compromise between straight percentages and a curve. Some will anchor their system by comparing the scores of certain students whose grades in the course have been relatively stable. Of course, there's no such anchor for the first several grades or if there are few or no students whose grades offer reliable stability. The best alternative may be simply to give grades frequently, so the weight of the final grade is spread out, students have greater motivation throughout the term, and there are less likely to be surprises at the end.

Essay items are particularly tough to grade. How can you make that chore easier?

First, when you construct the essay question or topic, imagine what points you'd like the students to make in their essay and calculate the breakdown. Sure, it's simpler to just decide on five essays at 20% each. But then, when you have to grade them, you pay for that simplicity. If you consider the material to be covered on the test as consisting of a certain number of elements, you can weight these elements according to their importance and then construct questions or topics. It may violate expectations of symmetry to use items worth 13, 22, 18, 23, 16, and 8 points, but it makes grading easier.

It's also vital to explain to your students your grading criteria. Some students learned in high school to impress teachers with rhetoric, while others were successful in giving just the facts, however crudely organized and expressed. If you know what you want, you should be able to make your expectations clear to your students.

Bill likes to use a technique he learned as a teaching assistant at the University of Georgia. A few days before a big exam, Bill puts a sample item on a transparency. He then talks it through with his class, as if they were one collective student taking the exam. They all suggest points to be made, discuss the relative merits, then organize the elements of their answer. Bill then weaves the pieces together into a straightforward answer, choosing his words with care but not meticulously, occasionally "rewriting" himself. Then he changes hats, to play the role of the teacher, grading the elements as organized on the transparency. The students understand that what matters in their essays is substance, yet they gain a better appreciation for the way that the substance is organized and presented.

Finally, when you grade essays, you should consider establishing a curve. Some faculty avoid using curves, for various reasons—fear that they contribute to grade inflation (as if one instructor could have that great an impact on a problem that's been around for decades), that they suggest an "easy mark," that they seem too subjective.

But Bill, through his TA experiences, has decided that curving makes sense for assignments and tests. After grading the essays and calculating a percentage, he looks at the paper with the highest grade, any F or low D papers, and a paper receiving the median grade. If those grades seem appropriate for the particular students and for their performance, then Bill follows straight percentages. But if he feels that the top paper was better than the grade, that the bottom papers don't really deserve such a low grade, or that the median really should have been higher, he adjusts the grade profile slightly, by perhaps 3%-5%. He never gives his students lower grades than they earned; he simply admits that his test was perhaps too easy and he chalks it up as a learning experience.

Finally, keep a record of your grading behavior for each test or assignment. What elements did you expect in each essay? How detailed did you want the essays to be? How flexible were you? What alternative elements did you accept? In which areas were your students particularly weak? Such a record allows you to more knowledgeably and confidently deal with any students who might later come to you with questions about a grade. Of course, you also have a head start on constructing tests and assignments for the next time you teach that course.

Many instructors worry too much about giving grades. They fear gaining a reputation as Old Softie or Heart of Stone—or that student evaluations will hurt their chances at receiving tenure. Yes, some students may be obsessed with grades, but don't get caught up in their anxiety. Sure, the GPA is important, but your single course grade shouldn't make the difference between the ideal employment and just another job, between grad school and the cold, cruel world. Some students may not understand or accept it, but you're far more important in how you help your students develop than in what grades you give them. As for any concern about whether you should bend your principles in order to get better student evaluations, that's a question of knowing your territory—and your conscience.

CHOOSING MATERIALS

TEXT(S)

When choosing materials for your course, there are two extremes: choose a textbook or create your own materials. With the former you generally sacrifice freedom to pursue your specific goals with your particular students as you would like; but the latter decision may entail a great deal of time and effort, sometimes unnecessarily. Furthermore, remember that authors, reviewers, editors, and marketers have spent untold hours and dollars to create accurate and interesting products. Students often don't react as well to home-made materials simply because they lack professional touches.

The best strategy is often to choose one or several textbooks, then mix and match sections, supplementing with other materials. One word of caution: expense. Instructors eager to expose their students to an intellectual smorgasbord may forget that textbooks can be very costly. Sometimes a good alternative is to place certain materials on reserve, so students can read them at the library. But remember that many students have jobs or careers, difficult schedules, family responsibilities, and/or disabilities that might make reserve readings inconvenient or even impossible.

How do you choose a textbook? Glenn Ross Johnson, former director of the Center for Teaching Excellence at Texas A & M University, suggests that instructors consider the following criteria:[28]

- Authors: knowledgeable in the field?
- Reviews: favorable?
- Topic emphasis and sequence: appropriate and adaptable to your course objectives?
- Content: accurate and current, sufficient details, level appropriate to the background of your average student?
- Bias: free of national, racial, sexual, and other bias?
- Concepts, principles, generalizations: appropriate and clearly developed?
- Explanations: clear and succinct?
- Reading level: appropriate for your average student?
- Table of contents, preface, index, appendices: adequate and useful?
- Titles, headings, subheadings: helpful for visualizing the organization of the content?
- Summaries, review questions: appropriate, leading students to generalize, apply, evaluate, and think critically?
- Sources, bibliography: adequately documented, appropriate, current?
- Illustrations, graphs, tables, maps, charts: accurate, clear, appropriately located and labeled?
- Format, layout, type: clear and interesting?
- Price: reasonable for the use you intend?
- Construction: convenient size and weight, durable?
- Instructor's manual: supplemental materials, teaching aids, review and test questions, strategy suggestions?
- Supplemental materials: suitable for the text and your situation?
- Assessment: test items or other devices for evaluating learning and assigning grades?

In selecting your textbook(s), don't go with only what you know. Sure, maybe it was the greatest book in the world when you were taking that intro course a few (!?) short years ago. Times change—and fast. Ask your colleagues. Keep up with new publications through journals in your discipline and announcements in

The Chronicle of Higher Education. Request review copies of every relevant book that appears on the market. Take the time to skim every volume, making notes about coverage, quality, strengths, and weaknesses. Keep a file of reviews for each text.

A recent development has been the customized text. Instructors can compile readings from various sources, then have a photocopy service compile the readings and make them available to your students. Here again, though, you should pay attention to cost. The legal decision March 28, 1991, in *Basic Books v. Kinko's Graphics Corporation*, has made copy services very wary about reproducing any text, regardless of size, without paying royalties, which has made custom texts considerably more expensive. Also, unless there's a market for used copies of your custom text, it could actually cost your students even more than traditional textbooks. (Of course, your students will all want to keep their copies of your book forever, but some may be forced to be pragmatic.)

OTHER RESOURCES

A custom text may be too ambitious for new faculty. So you choose the best text available, then make "patches." These ancillary materials may consist of short readings, time lines, diagrams, specialized glossaries, guides for difficult readings, sample test questions—whatever might make the text fit your course better. Some you prepare before the term, some as you encounter needs throughout the term. And whatever you do, do it with care: make sure your materials are helpful, accurate, and clear. As Horace said of his poetry, "I have built a monument more lasting than bronze." Remember: your materials are not only for your students, but for the world—including those who will review your tenure dossier.

Consider human resources as well. It may be very beneficial to invite outsiders to your class.

- Invite guests who can make valuable contributions to your class, through their expertise or perspectives that differ from yours. You may want to present together: students can be stimulated and informed by a lively exchange between two experts—especially if they disagree.
- Prepare your guests with information about your course and your students.

- Prepare your students: tell them about your guest and encourage them to think of questions to ask.
- Use the contributions of the guest in subsequent classes: refer to them in discussions and relate them to new material.

Don't limit your consideration of instructional resources to the classroom. What outside resources could contribute to the learning experience? Would it be appropriate to take a field trip to a museum, a business or government facility, a movie, a lecture or other presentation, another class? Would it be useful to display student work outside the classroom in some way—publication, demonstration, exhibition?

Our students have been characterized as the "MTV Generation." Whatever the extent of truth in that statement, you should consider the dimensions of your classroom environment. When you present something, do you automatically put it on the board, even though you've prepared it thoroughly in advance? Do you tend to walk into class with five pounds of handouts?

If so, then you may want to add some pizzazz. Visit your campus instructional development center for some tips on using audiovisual materials. Sometimes it's really true that a picture is worth a thousand words—and it's certainly easier to prepare charts and diagrams in advance than to throw them up on the board in midsentence. If you use AV materials appropriately, you'll find that students understand better and pay closer attention.

But avoid overkill or misuse. Some instructors go wild with AV materials, building up a dangerous (and exhausting) dependency on colors and graphics. Don't depend on content to grab and hold their interest, but don't work so hard to interest them that you lose sight of your purpose. In short, aim at the ideal advocated by Horace — *utile et dulce*, mixing useful and enjoyable.

YOUR COURSE OUTLINE

ORGANIZATION/STRUCTURE/POLICIES

Once you've planned your course—what you want to do, why, and how—draw up an outline for your students. Pedagogically, this is a good idea, and in terms of your personnel dossier, it's essential.

Student evaluation forms virtually always contain questions about course organization, which can be helpful in preparing your outline.

- How effective was the instructor in making clear the goals and objectives of this course?
- How clear were the goals, aims, and requirements of this course?
- How well organized was the instructor?

Your course outline is your students' first impression of your organization. It should generally include the following items:

1. *Course Number and Title, Credits, Semester, Class Time and Location.*

2. *Your Name, Office Location, Office Hours, Office Phone.* You might choose to provide your home phone number as well. If so, however, it would be wise to indicate hours during which students may call you. For some it's a sign that you really accept calls at home. To others it sends a message that you don't want to be bothered at 3 a.m. (Students tend to have unusual schedules, and the questions that bother them most sometimes come at the worst times.)

3. *Course Description.* Give students, in just a few sentences, reassurance that they belong in your course or warning that this isn't what they expected. Descriptions in your institution's catalog may serve as a model. Make sure that your description matches the official description: students have the right to expect what's promised in the official course description.

You may also want to indicate your expectations of student level and background. Some faculty avoid specifics, for fear of scaring off students and risking cancellation of their course. Others believe that their courses should be open to all, regardless of level and background. Check with your department about policy and with your colleagues about practices.

4. *Course Goals.* Where are you going in the course? How will students be better because of a semester with you? They may already be enrolled in your course, but you still have to sell them, because they should share responsibility for their learning. Be as specific as you can for your subject matter, without burying your students with a comprehensive and detailed list.

5. Attendance Policy. Is attendance required? For every session or just for certain selected sessions? If you require attendance, how will you encourage students? Frequent written assignments to be collected? Pop quizzes? A grade for attendance? Will you excuse any absences?

6. Assignment Deadlines and Policy. How strictly will you enforce deadlines? Set policies that are practical and that you can adhere to fairly for all. And remember: it's easier to start out tough and loosen up than to start lenient and then have to clamp down.

7. Readings. Make sure that your students understand the difference between "required" and "recommended"—and make sure that you don't expect them to read materials that you only recommend. You should probably keep your recommendations brief, so as not to overwhelm your students, as some may feel obliged to read everything. If you want to suggest a large number of materials, it may be better to distribute a series of lists at intervals throughout the semester. Doing so can be particularly effective if you find that some students are weak in certain areas; it's easy to modify your recommendations to include background (remedial) readings.

8. Guidelines for Succeeding in This Course. Indicate that you intend to have lectures or discussions or group projects or written assignments or whatever. What preparation will you expect for each class? What will be your primary focus—general concepts? details? facts? analysis? How would you suggest that your students study? What should they do if they feel inadequately prepared for a particular unit of material?

9. Policy on Academic Integrity. Students are often fuzzy about what's allowed and what's not. You should cite the text of your institution's policy; if there isn't any, formulate your own. The policy should include plagiarism as well as in-class cheating.

Example: "Plagiarism: the deliberate use of any outside source without proper acknowledgment. 'Outside source' means any work, published or unpublished, by any person other than the student."

What's the institutional procedure when cheating or plagiarism is suspected? What are the penalties? Be prepared to enforce the policy and make sure that your students understand your position.

During the course, make it clear when you are allowing or encouraging cooperation and teamwork. If you let your students use their texts or notes for a test, make sure that they understand the rules of the game.

Try to anticipate ethical questions. For example, what if a student uses for your course an assignment submitted in a similar form for another course? Can students share notes or research? Remember: we don't all share the same assumptions about these matters.

Finally, understand that if you suspect dishonesty your reaction can lead to legal complications. Consider, for example, the case of Robert L. Wolke, emeritus professor of chemistry and founding director of the Office of Faculty Development at the University of Pittsburgh.[29]

When he suspected a student of cheating on an exam, Wolke suspended his grade, apprised him of the charges, got a written statement from the proctor, and notified the dean, following the prescribed university procedures. Wolke says that the student's father, a lawyer, phoned and wrote letters, requesting copies of all evidence and threatening to sue. The university attorney, concerned about legal complications and institutional liability, advised Wolke to drop the matter and give the student a suitable grade. Frustrated, Wolke sent the dean a retraction, together with the mathematical calculations to justify his suspicions. His report concluded that "there is still a perfectly good one in 29 trillion trillion chance" that the similarities in exam answers were a coincidence. Wolke then gave the student an A[+]. "The moral for students?" he asks rhetorically. "If you have a lawyer handy, go ahead and cheat like crazy. Universities are pushovers." The moral for faculty? Draw your own conclusions.

EVALUATION GUIDELINES

How will you know how well your students are learning? Class participation? Written assignments? Quizzes? Tests? Projects? Journals? Which activities do you intend to grade? How? How much will each activity or category count toward the final grade? If you give numerous homework assignments or a series of quizzes, will you drop a few of the lowest grades?

Since this aspect of a course is generally of paramount importance to students, you should be clear about what you expect of them. Make sure, however, that they—and you—understand and remember that learning is not simply a question of grades.

A final question here: What about extra credit? Students may not ask this question at the start of the term, but you should be prepared for it as the weeks pass. There are various advantages and disadvantages.

Advantages of Extra Credit

- It allows students the opportunity to explore specific areas in greater depth.
- It may promote more individual instructor-student relationships.
- It can increase motivation.
- It provides "grade insurance" for the weak and the worried, as well as for serious illness or other problems.

Disadvantages of Extra Credit

- It encourages students to confuse *quality* and *quantity*, which undermines their efforts.
- It may result in inflated, misleading grades. There's a difference between an A for A-level work and an A for B-level work supplemented by extra credit.
- It tends to shift students' attention from course content and class participation to extra credit projects.
- It adds to your work and it can be an administrative nightmare.

What's your concept of grades? A reward? If so, then extra credit makes sense. An indication of ability? Then extra credit would undermine the accuracy of those grades. A simplified and powerful form of feedback? You need to determine how extra credit supports what you're doing in your course.

If you decide to allow extra credit, here are a few recommendations:

- Maintain your focus. This is essential. Extra credit should be aimed at your course goals. Students can do additional problems or readings, with a report on each.
- Return extra credit work promptly, with feedback.

- Set a deadline for extra credit. Students should know their grade status and act to remedy any bad situation before the final week.
- Outline the ground rules. Some instructors refuse to allow extra credit to rescue a failing student or raise a D to a C.
- Establish standards. Is a mediocre effort better than none at all, especially as it probably reduces the time and energy spent on required work?
- Determine the weight of the task. Don't treat extra credit work subjectively, in terms of "brownie points" or a "halo effect." What will be the percentage impact on the final grade?
- Work with each student interested in extra credit, if possible, to set guidelines. The students will benefit more from their extra work, you'll build a better relationship with the individual students. . . . and you're also less likely to receive work done for another course or even by another student.

A MAP: YOUR SYLLABUS

The syllabus should serve as a map for your journey through the semester. It should provide enough detail to direct your students, but not so much that they feel overly programmed. Think of your role as that of a tour guide: you want your schedule to indicate the major sights and activities, but allow freedom to explore side roads according to the interests and needs of your clients, serendipity, fate, and human elements.

Your syllabus should indicate exams and major deadlines. You should outline the principal units of the course: what you intend to cover week by week, maybe even session by session. For further suggestions, consult the guide by Malcolm A. Lowther, Joan S. Stark, and Gretchen G. Martens, *Preparing Course Syllabi for Improved Communication* (Ann Arbor: NCRIPTAL, 1989).

Finally, consider the advice offered by Howard Altman, director of the Center for Faculty and Staff Development at the University of Louisville:[30]

> Since the course syllabus becomes a written legal covenant between the instructor and the students in the course, each syllabus should end with a caveat of the following sort: "The above schedule and procedures in this course are subject to change in the event of extenuating circumstances."

This caveat protects the instructor and department if changes in the syllabus need to be made once the course is underway.

Welcome to the '90s! On a more positive note, Mary McDonnell Harris of the Center for Teaching and Learning, University of North Dakota, recently explored ways to construct a syllabus that goes beyond guiding students, to motivate them.[31] Her 10 rules:

1. The syllabus conveys enthusiasm for the subject.

2. The syllabus conveys the intellectual challenge of the course.

3. The syllabus provides for personalization of content.

4. The syllabus conveys your respect for the ability of students.

5. Course goals are attainable and stated positively.

6. Grading policies convey the possibility of success.

7. The syllabus adequately specifies the assignments.

8. Assignments vary in type of required expertise.

9. You assess student learning frequently.

10. The syllabus conveys your desire to help students individually.

As McDonnell Harris concludes, "The potential of the commonplace course syllabus for generating excitement about learning is considerable if student engagement is considered more important than tests, dates, and policies."

Sample Syllabus: Bill Campion, BAE 311. Here's what Bill prepared for one of his courses:

**Botany and Applied Ecology 311:
Introduction to Applied Ecology
Spring 1992**

Instructor: A. Wilmot (Bill) Campion
435 Greene Hall/M W F 12:30-1:30/T R 9:00-10:00
637-8245(O) 624-7713(H . . . between 7 and 10pm please)
Lectures: MW 1:50-2:40 213 Mendel Hall
Lab/Quiz: F 1:50-2:40 Sites to be announced

Credits:

3 (an additional one-credit option is available to B&AE majors performing a course-related independent study project,

Prerequisites:

For B&AE majors—B&AE 101, 102

For non-majors—any introductory biological science course

Teaching Assistants:

To be selected and introduced

Course Description:

Botany 311 will introduce you to "the science of community"—"the study of the interrelationships of organisms and their environments"—and to the role of applied ecology in environmental management today. In a larger sense, this course will introduce you to a philosophical world view that says to us, "I am a part of my environment and my environment is a part of me."

Course Goals:

Botany 311 has two distinct yet compatible goals:

- to explain the technical tools and econo/social setting of the applied ecologist today;
- to elucidate the concept of "ecological awareness"—the realization that the community to which each of us belongs includes soil, water, air, plants, animals, and people—and the corollary concept, "ecological conscience"—a will and a way to protect the health, integrity, stability, and beauty of our humanity-land community.

Texts:

Odum, E. Laurence, *Introduction to Applied Ecology* (Garden City NY: Hill & Dale, 1991), $39.95, University Book Store.

Campion, A. Wilmot, "The Ecology of the Chesapeake Bay," Chesapeake Bay Commission Technical report #26 (Baltimore MD, 1990), $4, Speedo Copy Service.

Phloem, Ruth, "Identifying State Flora," Midland University B&AE Department Bulletin #16 (Midland ST, 1987), $4, Speedo Copy Service.

Materials and Equipment:

Standard field notebook, clipboard, hand magnifying glass, tweezers, field clothing (including waterproof footgear).

Recommended Readings:

Stamen, Charles, *Memoirs of a Field Ecologist* (Harper's Ferry WV: National Park Service Press, 1989).

Leopold, Aldo, *A Sand County Almanac* (New York: Ballantine, 1986).

Schoenfeld, Clay, *Everybody's Ecology*, 2nd edition (Cranbury NJ: A.S. Barnes & Co., 1989).

Hendee, John, *et al., Wilderness Management* (Washington DC: GPO, 1980).

Suggested Readings:

See attached bibliography.

Term Paper:

A lab report on your plant inventory of your assigned study plot on the Midland Lagoon littoral.

Exams:

Four pop quizzes during the quarter. (Typical question: "Briefly explain the substance and impact of Section 102(2)(C), 1969 National Environmental Policy Act.")

Two-hour essay/multiple-choice final. (Typical question: "The 1985 State Water Resources Management Act bans timber cutting within how many feet of the shoreline of all navigable waters? (a) 50, (b) 100, (c) 200, (d) 300, (e) none of the above.")

Attendance Policy:

I believe I'm reasonable, but I want to prepare you for the real world, so attendance is required, both for lectures and for lab/quiz sections. However, I understand absences can be inevitable. If you feel you have a valid excuse, come talk with me. You're allowed two unexcused absences; each additional absence will lower your course grade 1%.

If you miss a scheduled exam, you must arrange with me to make it up. If you have a legitimate excuse, there won't be any penalty. If you miss a pop quiz without an acceptable excuse, you'll receive a grade of 0 and the 1% penalty. If you turn in your term paper late without an acceptable excuse, you'll be penalized 1% for each day late.

Policy on Academic Integrity:

I'll enforce the policies laid down in Section IV, Subsection A, *The Midland University Student Handbook*.

My Expectations:

I grade on a modified curve for assignments and tests, but not for the final grade. Everybody who earns an A will get an A; everybody who goofs off will get a D or an F. I want all of you to succeed, and I'll meet you at least halfway.

Your Responsibilities:

To get the most out of this course, treat it as a professional experience. Be here on time for every class. Study the texts. Scan the recommended readings. Dip into your choice of suggested readings. Be a field team player. Take abundant notes. Understand not only *what* we're doing, but also *why*.

Postscript: This is my first year teaching at Midland. You'll have two chances to evaluate me, around week seven and at the end of the term. We're all in this together, to learn: that partnership is the essence of higher education.

Week 1 (1/14-1/18)

Reading: *Introduction to Applied Ecology*, chapters 1, 2, 3

M W: Introduction to B&AE 311, Applied Ecology: A Brief History

F: Discussion of history of applied ecology, assignment of study plots on Midland Lagoon and instructions for term paper

Week 2 (1/21-1/25)
> Reading: *Introduction to Applied Ecology*, chapters 4, 5
> M W: Applied Ecology: Econo/Social Setting
> F: Discussion of econo/social aspects of applied ecology

Week 3 (1/28-2/1)
> Reading: "Identifying State Flora"
> M W: Methods of Field Research
> F: Lab

. . .

Week 15 (4/29-5/3)
> M: Review, evaluation, term papers due
> W: Review (practice exam)
> F: Review (discussion of practice exam)
> Final Exam: T 5/7 3:00-5:00 (site to be announced)
> N.B. The above schedule is for guidance only and may change in the event of extenuating circumstances.

Fully Prepared and Ready to Go . . . With all that preparation, Bill felt ready to meet his students and eager to begin teaching. He hoped that Introduction to Applied Ecology would be a great experience for his students and for himself.

You should have a similar feeling of eager anticipation and confidence in your preparation. Now, on to the adventures of teaching!

NOTES

1. John A. Centra, "Evaluating College Teaching: Some Reflections," *Department Advisor* 5 Winter 1990: 1-5.

2. Martin Anderson, "What! Me Teach? I'm a Professor," *The Wall Street Journal* 8 Sept. 1992.

3. Northrop Frye, *Divisions on a Ground* (Toronto: Anansi, 1982) 150.

4. J. Richard McFerron, David M. Lynch, Lee H. Bowker, Ian A.C. Beckford, "The Importance of Teaching in Tenure Decisions," *The Department Chair* Winter 1992: 17.

5. Kathleen T. Brinko, "Visioning Your Course: Questions to Ask Yourself as You Design Your Course," *The Teaching Professor* Feb. 1991: 3-4.

6. K. Patricia Cross and Thomas A. Angelo, *Classroom Assessment Techniques: A Handbook for College Teachers*, 2nd ed. (San Francisco: Jossey-Bass, 1993).

7. American Council on Education and University of California at Los Angeles Higher Education Research Institute, "The American Freshman: National Norms for Fall 1993," *The Chronicle of Higher Education* 26 Jan. 1994: A30.

8. American Council on Education and University of California at Los Angeles Higher Education Research Institute, A31.

9. *Digest of Education Statistics 1993* (Washington DC: National Center for Education Statistics, 1993) 177.

10. American Council on Education and University of California at Los Angeles Higher Education Research Institute, A30.

11. *Digest of Education Statistics 1993*, 209.

12. *The Chronicle of Higher Education*, Almanac Issue, 25 Aug. 1993: 15.

13. American Council on Education and University of California at Los Angeles Higher Education Research Institute, A30.

14. Charles S. Schroeder, "New Students—New Learning Styles," *Change* Sept.-Oct. 1993: 24.

15. Jim W. Corder, "Traditional Lectures Still Have a Place in the Classroom," *The Chronicle of Higher Education* 12 June 1991: B2.

16. Mary Budd Rowe, "Getting Chemistry Off the Killer Course List," *Journal of Chemical Education* Nov. 1983: 954-956.

17. Page Smith, *Killing the Spirit: Higher Education in America* (New York: Viking, 1990) 214.

18. E. Glassman, "The Teacher as Leader," *Learning About Teaching*, John F. Noonan, ed. (San Francisco: Jossey-Bass, 1980).

19. Jean MacGregor, "Collaborative Learning: Shared Inquiry as a Process of Reform," *The Changing Face of College Teaching*, Marilla D. Svinicki, ed. (San Francisco: Jossey-Bass, 1990) 23.

20. John H. Clarke, "Designing Discussions as Group Inquiry," *College Teaching* Fall 1988: 140-143. Reprinted in Maryellen Weimer and Rose Ann Neff, eds., *Classroom Communication: Collected Readings for Effective Discussion and Questioning* (Madison WI: Magna Publications, 1989) 53-59.

21. Arthur W. Chickering and Zelda F. Gamson, "Seven Principles for Good Practice in Undergraduate Education," *AAHE Bulletin* 39:7 (1987): 3-7. Reprinted in Arthur W. Chickering and Zelda F. Gamson, eds., *Applying the Seven Principles for Good Practice in Undergraduate Education* (San Francisco: Jossey-Bass, 1991) 63-69.

22. Zelda F. Gamson and Susan J. Poulsen, "Inventories of Good Practice: The Next Step for the Seven Principles for Good Practice in Undergraduate Education," *AAHE Bulletin* 39:7, 1987: 7-8, 14.

23. Thomas Anthony Angelo, "A 'Teacher's Dozen': Fourteen General, Research-Based Principles for Improving Higher Learning in Our Classrooms," *AAHE Bulletin* Apr. 1993: 3-9, 13.

24. Miriam McMullen-Pastrick and Maryellen Gleason, "Examinations: Accentuating the Positive," *College Teaching* 34:4 (1986): 135-139.

25. Bette LaSere Erickson and Diane Weltner Strommer, *Teaching College Freshmen* (San Francisco: Jossey-Bass, 1991) 124.

26. P. Dressel, "Grades: One More Tilt at the Windmill," *Bulletin*, Memphis State University, Center for Study of Higher Education,

Dec. 1983, quoted in Ohmer Milton, Howard R. Pollio, and James A. Eison, *Making Sense of College Grades: Why the Grading System Does Not Work and What Can Be Done About It* (San Francisco: Jossey-Bass, 1986).

27. Gerald S. Hanna and William E. Cashin, "Improving College Grading," IDEA Paper No. 19 (Manhattan KS: Kansas State University Center for Faculty Evaluation and Development, 1988).

28. Glenn Ross Johnson, *First Steps to Excellence in College Teaching* (Madison WI: Magna Publications, 1990) 9-10.

29. Robert L. Wolke, "A Message to Students: 'If You Have a Lawyer Handy, Go Ahead and Cheat Like Crazy' " (Opinion), *The Chronicle of Higher Education* 15 May 1991: B2, and follow-up letters to the editor 12 June 1991: B3-B4, 26 June 1991: B3-B4, and 3 July 1991: B4.

30. Howard Altman, "Syllabus Shares 'What the Teacher Wants,' " *The Teaching Professor* May 1989: 2.

31. Mary McDonnell Harris, "Motivating with the Course Syllabus," *The National Teaching & Learning Forum* 3:1 (1993): 1-3.

6 THE TEACHING CHALLENGE: IN THE CLASSROOM

No matter how well they've prepared for their course, many instructors—both rookies and veterans—find the first meeting difficult. It's normal to have butterflies in your stomach, but the following suggestions may help you get them to fly in formation.

THOSE FIRST FEW MINUTES
- Use the entire hour productively. First impressions are crucial, so make sure you set the right tone.
- Take care of business. Provide the necessary administrative information, such as the procedures for adding or dropping courses and your school's policy on religious holidays. Take attendance.
- Introduce yourself and share your relevant experiences. You're there for a reason; let your students understand your background, and your interests (professional and other). Students naturally want to know who's going to lead them on this learning journey, so be yourself.

- Find out who your students are. You might pass around index cards and ask for names, phone numbers, major, background in the discipline, and reasons for taking the course. You may also ask each student to stand and give a short introductory spiel: name, major, hometown, campus residence, reason(s) for taking the course, expectations, or whatever. Students like to know who's taking the learning journey with them. This also encourages them to form networks from the start and to consider the various needs of their classmates, so they can better understand why you spend time on matters that they may consider to be of little value or interest to them personally.
- Plan at least one activity to get your students involved. It should entail something physical: have them stand and introduce themselves, ask for a show of hands (Who has the textbook already? Who's taking this course as an elective? Who took Intro to Xerology last term?), conduct a milling exercise (maybe a scavenger hunt: have each person find a student from a neighboring state, a junior, a chem major, a left-hander, and so on). Make them feel their presence in your class.
- Cover the appropriate resources. Many instructors will talk briefly about the texts and other materials, giving advice on using them, explaining strengths and weaknesses. If your course involves work at the library, a lab, the museum, the planetarium, or other facility, make sure that your students know where the facilities are located, their hours, procedures for using them, and how to get their questions answered or take a tour.
- Encourage questions from the start. Be specific—"Any questions about these three points?" "Is it clear how I expect you to prepare for each class?" Treat every question with consideration: the only stupid question is the one they don't ask. Make your students comfortable about asking questions.
- Assign some work. Some instructors like to give "diagnostic" homework, to find out how well their students are prepared and/or how they think, organize, and write. Some use the first assignment to get their students to go out and buy the texts, use the library or lab, or whatever.

According to your personality and teaching style, you may benefit from the following guidelines:

- Use prompts as necessary. We all have faults, both faculty and students. Remind yourself by placing one or more index cards on your desk or podium or as bookmarks: just a word or two—smile, be patient, eye contact, ask for questions, don't fidget, slow down, use gestures, move around—whatever might be useful.
- Think about humor. Some experts warn against using any humor, because it might offend some students or because it's not natural for certain instructors. Others advocate humor as a way to facilitate learning. Heed the Ancients: know yourself. And be sensitive to your students. Remember: you may be funny, but if your humor makes students uncomfortable, it's inappropriate.

CLASSROOM PROTOCOL

Before you enter the classroom, at the beginning of the term and before every class, you should think about the social dynamics of your microcosm—and whether you should establish policies and guidelines beyond the strictly academic. In brief, there are four basic questions:

- What can your students expect from you?
- What can you expect from your students?
- What can your students expect from each other?
- What does your institution expect of you?

WHAT CAN YOUR STUDENTS EXPECT FROM YOU?

They should expect you to guide their learning, to set relevant goals and reasonable expectations, to respect them as people, to maintain an atmosphere of respect and support, to be fair and open, to challenge and motivate them to develop their potential, and to be honest with them.

This means assigning work that focuses on course goals and neither insults their intelligence nor surpasses their abilities. And it means that you promptly return their written assignments and tests, with coherent and helpful feedback.

Think of yourself as a "facilitator" for your students. You're not responsible for their learning, but rather for making the environment conducive to learning and providing activities to involve them as actively as possible in learning. One instructor suggests keeping in mind the old line, "Not a sage on the stage, but a guide on the side."

Your students will also expect you to respect them, to maintain an appropriate learning environment. But just what does that mean?

Many campuses have adopted policies prohibiting faculty from creating a "hostile environment." Critics of such policies, which derive from wording used in federal guidelines, argue that the concept of "hostile environment" is at odds with academia, which must provide for a free exchange of ideas, however uncomfortable or offensive. Michael McDonald, a lawyer for the Center for Individual Rights, notes:

> The mission of a university, where the ideal is Socrates conducting an argument with all manner of speech needed to whatever end it leads, has been replaced with an amalgam of Alan Alda and Phil Donahue creating a non-offensive environment.[1]

It's an impossible conflict, at least in the mid-'90s. The best advice may simply be to be sensitive to all students, yet remember that the basic reason for them to be in your classroom is to learn—through you and from each other. Nobody should feel uncomfortable, alienated, or excluded because of comments or assumptions about ethnicity or gender or sexual orientation.

Estela M. Bensimon, Program Co-Director for the Research Program on Organizational Structures and Policies at the National Center on Postsecondary Teaching, Learning, and Assessment, raises the question, "What does it mean to be a culturally responsive faculty member?" Her answer is that a culturally responsive instructor has developed "a critical consciousness" about:

> ...the "invisible" cultural norms and paradigms that privilege some forms of knowledge as intellectual and scorn others as non-intellectual.
> ...the extent to which syllabi and other instructional materials integrate or exclude the experience of women, people of color, lesbian and gay persons, and others who are culturally different.

. . .ways in which syllabi and other instructional materials address race and racism, sex and sexism, class and classism, homosexuality and homophobia, and other forms of social and cultural marginalization. ... .

. . .the need to constantly question one's unexamined assumptions about race, gender, ethnicity, sexual orientation, and the stereotypes we form about those who are unlike us.

how to analyze the culture of the classroom (e.g., language, norms, values, interaction patterns, forms of power) and determine strategies of giving voice to students.[2]

Finally, although it's not something that your students might expect from you, you should also take precautions for their safety. If you teach evening classes or in remote locations, during your first meeting you should remind your students of potential dangers. Encourage them to form groups when leaving for home or parking lots. Many students often feel secure around campus, especially students from smaller communities. Don't encourage paranoia, but it may be wise to issue a regular reminder to take care. After all, one of your responsibilities is to help prepare your students for the real world—and it's all around us, even on campus.

On the Negative Side. . . Rita Rodabaugh, executive director of the Academy for the Art of Teaching at Florida International University, recently surveyed over 300 students, to arrive at the following list of top 10 teaching misbehaviors:[3]

A bad instructor:

1. Is partial to some students according to gender, race, age, or other factor.

2. Doesn't know the subject matter/gives incorrect information.

3. Grades unfairly or changes grading policy.

4. Tests unfairly, using trick questions and/or items on material not covered.

5. Embarrasses students and/or uses sarcasm and belittling comments.

6. Is underprepared for class.

7. Isn't adequately available to students outside of class.

8. Demands too much work.

9. Gives boring lectures.

10. Demands too little work, not challenging students.

Along similar lines, Larry M. Ludewig, a professor in social and behavioral sciences at Kilgore College (TX), surveyed students in various disciplines and established a list of the 10 instructor behaviors that students most feel "inhibit positive teacher/student relationships."[4] Students (the percentage is indicated in parentheses) are most bothered when instructors:

1. Assign work as though their class is the only one students have, or at least the most important one (45%).

2. Lecture too fast and fail to slow down when asked (40%).

3. Make students feel inferior when they ask a question (35%).

4. Are not specific on what exams will cover (34%).

5. Create "trick" questions (34%).

6. Deliver their lectures in a monotone manner (32%).

7. Give tests that don't correspond to lectures (28%).

8. Get behind and then cram their lectures into the remaining time (28%).

9. Assume students already have base knowledge for the course (26%).

10. Require a textbook and then fail to use it (25%).

So, that's basically what your students will likely expect you to do—and not to do—in general.

They also will have expectations specific to your course. To learn from the start about these expectations, Barbara K. Goza, a professor in behavioral sciences at California State Polytechnical University, uses what she calls the "Graffiti Needs Assessment."[5]

Goza takes 10 large pages of newsprint and writes one partial sentence at the top of each, such as the following:

- "My greatest concern this semester is. . . ."
- "In three years I will be . . . ."
- "The greatest challenge facing the world today is. . . ."
- "Personnel psychologists do. . . ."
- "Organizational research is. . . ."
- "I learn the most when. . . ."

Goza posts these pages on the classroom walls to start the first class, then allows her students 15 minutes to wander around writing completions for the sentences. Then, she collects and reads the student input, to answer key questions:

- Who is in this class and what are their goals?
- What and how should we study?
- Why should we study organizational and personnel psychology?

Goza posts the pages on the walls again, as a point of reference, when the class is discussing certain topics.

Whether you use a technique like the Graffiti Needs Assessment or simply distribute index cards and ask your students to jot down answers to a few essential questions, you can early and quickly gain an understanding of what your students expect of you and your course.

WHAT CAN YOU EXPECT FROM YOUR STUDENTS?

That's a tough question! Two expectations are vital:

- they should take responsibility for learning;
- they should respect each other and support the learning environment.

In recent years, many campuses have adopted speech codes, to ensure a learning environment in which all students feel comfortable. You should know what restrictions, if any, your institution places on expression, whether such restrictions apply to the classroom, and if you are expected to enforce the restrictions. Even if there are no restrictions placed on instructional settings, you may want to communicate the educational value of maintaining a balance between free expression and respect for others.

WHAT CAN YOUR STUDENTS
EXPECT FROM EACH OTHER?

You need to ensure a balance of enthusiasm and freedom with sensitivity and respect. This issue is of growing importance, as campus policies designed to protect the right of every student to an environment conducive to learning run up against the legal protection of the First Amendment. Your students probably don't expect you to have the wisdom of Solomon, but they have the right to assume that you'll be sensitive to their feelings and their expectations and that you'll supervise their environment.

As a result, unfortunately, you'll need to maintain discipline. A few guidelines for dealing with students who disrupt the environment:[6]

- Deal with them individually (not in groups), in person (not over the phone), outside of class (not during class).
- Keep it reasonable. If you or the student are emotional about the issue, suggest another meeting.
- Focus on behaviors that disrupt teaching and learning: anything else is basically a personality conflict, a "me vs. you" situation.
- Face challenging questions or statements honestly and openly. Fight the temptation to react defensively, to bluff, to rely on your authority. Don't pull rank.

WHAT DOES YOUR INSTITUTION EXPECT OF YOU?

This question is of rather recent origin. Traditionally, academic freedom has allowed instructors to teach as they choose, for better or for worse. Lately, however, campus administrators have entered the classroom with policies and states may soon follow with laws.

For example:

- In January 1994, the Iowa Board of Regents adopted a policy that requires instructors at the University of Iowa to notify their students about "unusual or unexpected class presentations or materials." The policy replaces one adopted in December 1993 that required warnings for "explicit representations of human sexual acts" in class.[7]
- In February 1994, the University of New Hampshire was working on a new code to fight verbal harassment after

suspending a professor in 1993 for making sexual references in his classroom that some students found "vulgar, degrading, and offensive." Meanwhile, some state legislators were sponsoring, with the support of the New Hampshire Civil Liberties Union, a bill to protect free speech rights on public campuses.[8]

- In January 1994, the Citizens' Alliance of Washington began collecting signatures to put on the state ballot an initiative that includes a section to prohibit the state's public colleges and universities from teaching or promoting homosexuality as "normal."[9] The group failed to gather enough signatures for its initiative by July.

Just a few examples of institutional and legal reactions to academic concerns. What does your institution expect of you? Again, you've got to know your territory—and keep up with the changes in climate.

NAVIGATING THE COURSE

With solid planning and a good first class, you should be well on your way to providing your students with a healthy and interesting learning environment.

You should prepare for every class. Some instructors simply reread their notes—which should never become dusty or worn out. Doing so is minimal preparation. For others, preparation may involve a complete set of plans, with visual aids and handouts, and a notation of approximate timing for every module. At minimum, you should reread the text or textbook section before you cover it in class. In addition, each term you should read at least one recent book or article for every unit of your course.

The key here is to not fall into a routine; it's vital to remain attuned to the effects of your preparation. If you stumble through class after class, if your students seem lost, if you regularly run on past the bell or end abruptly five minutes early, consider changing your approach to preparing your class.

The next piece of advice, intended for the meticulously organized and/or extremely nervous: follow your plans as a map, not a religion. They should remind you of where you want to go during a specific class and help you get there, but they should never be more important than the learning activities. If you feel like you're running the class with your lesson plans in one hand and a stopwatch in the other, maybe you should read this paragraph again.

Finally, back up to look at the forest from time to time. Students may become lost in details and lose track of the big picture, the greater meaning of what they're learning. Some instructors keep a journal of each class, briefly recording their impressions while they're still fresh, a practice which compels them to reflect on the progress of the class and provides an outlet for their emotions. Other instructors immediately revise their lesson plans and notes, to have a head start for the next time they teach that course.

No matter how busy you are, you and your teaching are worth a few minutes of thought. What went well? Why? What didn't go so well? Why not? How would you do it better? As a former colleague would say, "If you can't learn, you can't teach."

MOTIVATION

The spirit may be willing, but sometimes only the flesh seems to be in attendance. How do you keep students' interest alive and healthy? How do you get your students to do the work when they're distracted and overwhelmed by other responsibilities and pursuits?

From the start you should encourage appreciation of your subject. Students should understand the value of what they're doing: every lesson and assignment should have clear purposes, every "what" should be accompanied by "why." And as you explore details along your learning journey, make sure that your students don't lose track of the big picture.

You should also show your interest—not as a rah-rah cheerleader, but as an enthusiastic participant in the learning process. How do you feel about what you're teaching? Some faculty can teach intro courses for years and still feel the excitement of guiding their students through the early steps. They know that their subject has meaning and value, and that conviction and their love of the subject make them enthusiastic about bringing others into their "home" and making them feel welcome there. And that enthusiasm is often generally contagious.

OK, you point out, that may be fine for the classroom, where your presence inspires enthusiasm and motivates your students to ask questions, provide answers, and discuss. But what about outside the classroom? How can you motivate them to read and do other assignments?

The traditional, facile answer is to collect the written assignments and test them on the rest. Doing so is known as motivation by the letter, not by the spirit. At times this solution may be the best way, but there are certainly others.

When students turn in written assignments, they should receive more than just a grade or a check. Give them coherent and helpful, balanced feedback, noting at least one strong point and suggesting one area for improvement. And write on each assignment a brief note—to congratulate, to console, to put the grade into perspective, to suggest a few ways to improve, to invite a student to come talk with you. Such comments can motivate your students as well as guide their learning.

Sometimes students don't bother to read assigned material because the instructor tells them that it doesn't matter. Not in so many words, of course, but if you simply repeat the material in class or never refer to it in any way, students soon realize there's not much purpose in preparing. If your students seem unfamiliar with material from the readings, even if you're certain that a significant number didn't even look at the readings, don't repeat the material in class. Sure, it's easier for you to "cover the material" that way. But students who didn't read quickly learn that it doesn't matter and students who did read are punished with boredom for their efforts.

Don't just tell students *what* and *when* to read; tell them *why* and *how*. Why did you choose this reading? How does it fit into class activities? What do you plan to do with it? Discussion? Test? Integration into a later activity? How do you want them to read? For a general sense? With a focus on certain points? For a subtext?

If you plan to use a reading in class, do so. One instructor noticed that many of his students weren't doing the readings. So, in one class, he asked how many students had done the reading. (This question works better than "Who didn't do the reading?" because there's a certain inertia to overcome to raise a hand.) When some students didn't answer in the affirmative, he gave them handouts with the case studies that he'd planned for class, then asked them to leave and write commentaries on the cases. With the students who remained, he conducted an excellent discussion. And the students who hadn't prepared learned their lesson.[10]

One of Bill's colleagues suggested another tactic. She gives her students a quiz over the material before she leads a discussion of it. The quizzes don't need to be difficult or take much time: she merely covers the basic points of the reading, for a grade. Her students usually learn quickly that she's serious about the readings she asigns.

It's not enough just to get your students to read, of course. Glance at their books. Are the pages covered with highlighting? That could indicate problems: too many students simply scan the readings and mark things for later reference, without really trying to understand them or to grasp their place within the larger picture. Then, when they need to discuss or review the material, it may be almost like reading it for the first time. (Recently a professor at Yale University was quoted as blaming highlighting pens for "retarding the education of university students by distorting and cheapening the way many read.")

You might want to encourage your students to proceed by paragraphs or sections of several paragraphs. They read a chunk of material, then jot in the margin a few words to summarize that material — not to repeat the "what" but to note the "why." Why did the author write that passage? How does it relate to the preceding material and further the direction of the chapter?

In essence, your students are creating subheads for each paragraph or section. This exercise involves understanding, analysis, synthesis. When they need to discuss or review the readings, they have signposts that lead them through the material.

One of the best ways to encourage more thought when taking notes is to allow students to use those notes for tests. (Of course, you may have to use more thought in creating your tests!) To avoid simple regurgitation from pages upon pages of facts, you need to stress higher-level cognitive work, requiring application, analysis, synthesis, and evaluation.

Jules Janick, a professor at Purdue University, uses a novel approach. For the final exam he lets students prepare and use "crib sheets." The rules:

- Students may use both sides of a single 8½" x 11" sheet of paper.
- Notes must be handwritten—not typed—and signed. (No mass production!)
- Students must turn in their crib sheet with the exam.

His students learn to analyze, synthesize, and evaluate the course material. Then, if exam results are disappointing, Janick reads the cribs for insights into the reasons.[11]

A final suggestion: keep memorization to the necessary minimum. You should decide what your students should remember after their term with you, when they go off to other courses or their careers. Perhaps the best guidance in this matter is the comment by Montaigne that education should make people *capable* rather than merely *learned*, that a *well-made* head is better than a *well-filled* head.

PARTICIPATION

The best way to encourage participation is to plan interesting (irresistible) activities and truly appreciate whatever your students might contribute.

But how?

One instructor prepares questions on index cards, structured like those outlines you learned to do in fifth grade. He first lists the main points to be covered in the discussion. Then he classifies his questions. At the "Roman numeral" level he puts his easiest questions—facts. At the "capital letter" level are questions that go beyond recall, to require slightly more thought. Finally, at the "Arabic numeral" level within each section are the "why" questions and items requiring analysis, synthesis, and evaluation. A quick glance at his cards and he can choose questions appropriate to the level of his students during any given class period.

Sometimes he leaves the classroom in smiles, describing the discussion as "level three all the way!" Occasionally he only mutters, "We couldn't get out of level one." If the discussion wanders away from his prepared questions, he lets it go as long as the results are worthwhile. (As he puts it, "Better *their* direction enthusiastically than *my* direction pulling teeth!") Then, he simply works a transition into the next group of questions.

If you decide to encourage participation by grading it, consider the system used by Kevin Melvin, a professor at the University of Alabama. He explains at the start of the term that he intends to evaluate both the quality and the quantity of class participation. No grade will be lower than C- except in cases of excessive absences. He keeps an informal record throughout the term.

Then, the day before the last day of class, Melvin asks his students to rate the contributions of their classmates as high, medium, or low. He asks them to put about the same number of students in each category. For each student Melvin considers his grade and the median peer rating: if the peer rating is higher than his own grade, he averages the two; if the peer rating is lower, he uses his grade alone for participation. In classes ranging in size between 15 and 27 students, Melvin reports high correlation between the peer rating and his grade. The system may not work quite as well, he suspects, with very small or large classes.[12]

What if you get assigned to a large class, a sea of 50 or 100 or 200 faces?

- Plan activities. Set aside a certain period of time for questions, to focus attention. Answer as many questions as you can within that time, then move on. Don't spend too much time on one question unless it interests a lot of your students. If a student seems very attached to a question or very lost, offer to continue the discussion with him or her after class or during your office hours.

- Think "action." When you prepare lesson plans, try to find various ways to involve your students more actively. Some instructors use the "directed ellipsis." For example, rather than begin, "When Abraham Lincoln freed the slaves with the Emancipation Proclamation in 1863," you might pause and let students fill in the blanks: "When Abraham Lincoln freed the slaves with the . . . yes, the Emancipation Proclamation in . . . yes, that's right, 1863." (One instructor plays up the theatrical with a fine performance as "the Absent-Minded Professor.") This method takes more time than a straight delivery of the material, you need to be attentive to cuing your students, and sometimes you may feel like an auctioneer, wearily waiting for the right bid, but it's a good way to involve your students.

- Show that you appreciate input. Thank your students for questions as well as for answers. As a colleague once pointed out, you should be in control like a lion-tamer: be confident but on your toes. Sure, it's easier if you just keep those animals locked in their cages or whip them into submission, but the goal is to keep it exciting for lions and tamer alike.

- Work with what they give you. ("George brought up a good point after class yesterday. . . ." "Colleen suggested an interesting possibility in her essay. . . .") You can more actively elicit input from your students with a "comment box." Keep a box outside your office and bring it to every class. Encourage your students to contribute. Then, use the input in your presentations. (One instructor admits to dropping in one of his own on occasion, especially at the start of the term or during "dry spells.")

A good guide to the special conditions of bigger groups is *Teaching Large Classes Well* by Maryellen Weimer (San Francisco: Jossey-Bass, 1987).

PRESSURES, ANXIETY, AND CONFUSION

Students often suffer from pressures, anxiety, and confusion. The greatest pressures, highest level of anxiety, and most confusion usually come from tests. In addition to basing your course grade on several criteria—regular assignments, term projects, participation, and so forth—instead of tests alone, what can you do?

Through his work as a graduate student, Bill Campion has developed a method of dealing with "the big grades." He always returns tests and major graded assignments before class, as students arrive. He allows his students enough time to review their work, then puts up an overhead transparency with the basic numerical information. For example:

- mean grade: 81.3%
- median grade: 83%

- range of numerical grades for each letter grade and number of students receiving each letter grade:

92-100	A	6
89-91	A-/B+	4
82-88	B	8
79-81	B-/C+	5
70-78	C	6
60-69	D	2
0-59	F	1

He then asks if anyone has questions about the *material*. Students with questions about their *grades* must talk with Bill before or after class.

Since the focus in class is on the material, all the students benefit, substantively. Also, since every student knows how he or she fits into the class profile for each test or assignment, Bill rarely needs to deal with the matter of grades. (And he always files the grade distribution information along with a copy of the test or assignment, just in case questions arise later.)

You cannot protect your students against pressures and anxiety, but you can minimize their confusion

CHECKING ON YOUR PERFORMANCE

STUDENT FEEDBACK

You plan, you organize, you give your class blood, sweat, and tears. Then what?

If you wait for students to volunteer feedback, you may have a long wait—and the results are likely to be complaints, not compliments or constructive comments. Many instructors simply judge their teaching from student performance on assignments and tests, then expect the term-end evaluations to fill in the gaps and bring everything together.

It might be wise to try spot checks throughout the course. One example is the one-minute paper suggested by K. Patricia Cross and Thomas A. Angelo.[13] At the end of a given class period, perhaps a month or so into the term, you simply ask your students to answer the following questions, anonymously:

- What's the most important thing you learned during this class today?
- What question(s) remain(s) uppermost in your mind?

A colleague prefers two open-ended statements:

- What I value most in this class is. . . .
- I wish this class would. . . .

Bette LaSere Erickson and Diane Weltner Strommer recommend a somewhat more detailed evaluation form, the Class Reaction Survey in use at the University of Rhode Island.[14] They begin with a general assessment of that class period in terms of improvement needed—none, little, some, or considerable. Then the same four grades are used to assess the instructor in 10 areas, covering preparation, clarity, variety, use of examples and exercises. Finally, students grade the class—excellent, good, satisfactory, fair, or poor—and indicate why they rated it that high, as well as why they didn't rate it higher. The survey takes less than five minutes and, best of all, it's in plain English.

Three points to remember if you create a questionnaire:

- Establish a clear rating system. Some favor a five-point system, for symmetry (almost always, often, sometimes, occasionally, hardly ever), while others argue that such rating scales let student take the path of least resistance, the middle rating. Any more than seven points: too complicated. Fewer than four: not worth the effort.
- Make sure that every item is simple and straightforward. For example, rather than "Instructor presents material in an interesting manner, explains carefully, and answers questions sympathetically," it's better to divide the item into three, one for each instructional function.
- Vary the direction of the items, for greater reliability of results. For example, you're likely to get more accurate results if you put "Instructor speaks with expression" and "Instructor answers questions rarely or poorly" (mixing good and bad), rather than "Instructor speaks with expression" and "Instructor always answers questions well."

Another means of inviting student feedback involves more effort. Researchers at the University of Washington recently studied student reactions to course evaluation procedures.[15] They found that students preferred a method of class interview which allowed them to meet in small groups with a facilitator but no instructor, to discuss the class, to "generate their own categories of response," and to "check perceptions of teaching effectiveness with others in the class." The study also showed that students were more satisfied with evaluations at midterm than at term end and when the instructor provided an "extended reaction" to their evaluations.

This study suggests the following approach to student evaluations. Around the middle of the term, set aside some time to discuss the class. Divide your students into small groups, at random. Ask them to share their opinions and to take note of all feedback and suggestions, without identifying the contributors by name. Then leave, to return at the designated time and collect the notes. Consider them, then formulate some sort of response, to present to your students the following class if possible. (If you hold the discussion the last day of the week, you allow yourself a weekend to reflect.)

This approach to evaluations would take a little more time and energy, of course. But consider the conclusion of the University of Washington research team: "It is disturbing to find that students evaluated as least satisfying the predominant, traditional means of collecting student opinion about teaching effectiveness: the use of individual, standardized rating forms administered at the end of courses with limited instructor reaction."[16]

You may prefer a less structured approach to inviting feedback. Leslie Swetnam, an elementary education professor at Metropolitan State College of Denver, has found advantages to using what she calls an "interactive class journal" throughout the term. She uses a spiral notebook for each class; every day she puts the date on a page and passes the notebook around about midway through the period. Students are free to write any comments about the class, anonymously, with the emphasis on providing specific, constructive criticisms, compliments, or questions. After each class, she reads the comments. If she decides that any comment represents a general concern, she addresses that concern in the next class. If she wants to respond to the comment of an individual student, she pens her response in a contrasting color next to that comment, where the student in question can find it when the notebook circulates again. As Swetnam summarizes her results, "The class journal is one way to increase communication and improve our relationship with our students and make our teaching more effective"— as well as "a great way to document your effort to improve."[17]

SELF-MEASURES
Some instructors, especially with a little experience, can assess their teaching themselves, fairly objectively and without too much anguish. You don't necessarily need an elaborate procedure.

Richard B. Chase, a professor in the University of California business school, offers his personal money-back guarantee: he promises reimbursement of book expenses plus $250 toward class fees to any student who isn't satisfied with his course.[18] It's an interesting idea. Ask yourself at the end of every class, "How many of my students would be asking for their money back for this class session?"

VISITS
"O wad some Power the giftie gie us To see oursels as others see us!" What Robert Burns longed for can be yours. Invite a colleague from your department to visit one of your classes. Have him or her unobtrusively sit out of the way and observe everything—your techniques and behavior, the reactions of your students, the dynamics of the class as an ecosystem. Then meet for a few moments as soon afterward as possible, to discuss observations and interpretations. Bear in mind, of course, that what you'll gain is just one person's opinion, based on one class, but the experience might provide you with some valuable insights—and a valuable letter at tenure time.

Sometimes you may prefer to invite an instructor from another discipline, especially if no colleague in your own department seems an appropriate choice or if you would prefer an "outsider." In perspective, the "outsider" can experience your class as a student. For example, if you teach chemistry, you might find someone who teaches biology or zoology, maybe even someone in English or anthropology. An "outsider" is more sensitive to discipline-specific matters, such as concepts or vocabulary which might make it more difficult for your students to understand you.

You may be able to bring into your classroom a member from the instructional development staff. Their expertise may be the most effective way to get valuable analysis of your teaching and suggestions for improvement.

If an observer visits your class, what is he or she likely to expect? One of Bill's colleagues told him that she uses the following checklist when she evaluates an instructor:

- Careful planning.
- Start (on time? brisk?).
- Pace (fast enough to maintain interest, but not lose students).
- Variety, length, and sequencing of activities.
- Creativity.
- Humor.
- Contextualization of learning (how does this class fit into the larger context?).
- Participation (how many students? how substantial their output?).
- Learning checks (questions, exercises . . .).
- Style of dealing with questions.
- Style of dealing with challenges to authority.
- Ending (on time? "not with a whimper but a bang"?).

Still another option may be to have one of your classes videotaped. You can then view the video alone or with a colleague or member of the instructional development center. Looking at yourself objectively takes a certain amount of courage, but the benefits can be easily worth the effort.

What if you can't or don't want to get a visitor and your campus doesn't provide videotape services? You could use an audiotape recorder. Set it up where it won't be too conspicuous and where you can get good sound quality for the entire room. If you teach in a lecture hall, you'll probably need to set up at least one additional microphone to record student responses and questions.

What can you learn from an audiotape? Certainly not as much as from a video or a visit. But you can at least focus on your delivery—volume, tone, pace, pauses, annoying mannerisms. And an audiotape may be less obtrusive to students, less likely to affect class dynamics.

You can also learn a lot about the dynamics of your class environment. You might want to try the Cognitive Interaction Analysis System, developed by Glenn Ross Johnson at Texas A&M University,[19] or the assessment instrument developed by Ned A. Flanders when he was at the University of Minnesota.[20] Both systems help you track the verbal activities of your class, which may provide some valuable insights into the dynamics of your classroom interaction.

THEN WHAT?

Unless your assessments during the term reveal that your course is a disaster, it's probably wisest not to attempt any major changes, just a few tweaks here and there. A rider who thinks about changing horses in midstream should first consider adjusting the saddle and harness. After the term ends you can design plans for improvement.

Many inexperienced instructors take student input about their teaching far too personally, and often too seriously. If you're unsure about making changes in your organization, procedures, methods, or style, you might want to discuss the matter with an experienced colleague in the department or somebody at the center for faculty development.

Take note of all the comments, think about them, decide what fixes are feasible during the term, then set the others aside for the following term. A course is like a boat: instructor and students are working together, with the instructor providing guidance and the students pulling on the oars. The boat can feel shakier at the helm than on the benches.

THAT FINAL ASSESSMENT

STUDENT RATING FORMS

Your institution, division, or department will probably provide you with student evaluation forms. Whether they're required or not, use them. If there are no standard forms, create one. Make sure that your students understand how important the evaluations are, both for you and for future students. Evaluations should be anonymous. Assure your students that you'll read their evaluations only after turning in their course grades. Then leave the room while the students complete the forms.

You may also want to discuss the course in class. Students might be reluctant to criticize, particularly so close to grading time, but some may be eager to offer some valuable suggestions for improvement. Some may be more interested in venting their feelings—but that's also a worthwhile result, especially if you can handle the situation effectively and gracefully.

Read the evaluation forms after you've turned in your final grades and had a moment to relax. Set aside some quiet time, away from distractions: the evaluation forms should make you think and you should be ready to develop ideas. Take note of any comments or suggestions. Remember: your students aren't experts on teaching and they may have some biases, but their perceptions and opinions are very important.

Also keep in mind the words of consolation Chair Amanda Perkins offered Bill at the end of his first term at Midland: "Every prof gets a few comments that 'this was the worst course ever.' It's hard, but you just can't overreact to such criticisms. It's only natural for all of us, especially new faculty, to focus on the negative comments and forget the many positive reviews." She's right: you can't please all of the students all of the time. (But keep trying!)

When administering and reviewing student evaluations, be aware that research has identified certain factors that may undermine the validity of the results, including:[21]

- *Expressiveness.* Student ratings may be influenced more by style of presentation than by substance. But if you're attentive to making your classes interesting as well as informative, you shouldn't be concerned about this factor.
- *Student motivation.* Instructors tend to receive higher ratings in classes where students entered the course with an interest in the subject or were taking it as an elective.
- *Level of the course.* In general, the higher the level, the better the ratings.

- *Workload/difficulty*. Contrary to popular belief, students tend to give higher ratings in difficult courses where they have to work harder.
- *Purpose*. Ratings tend to be higher if the students know that they'll be used in personnel decisions.

Keep these factors in mind when you consider your ratings; you might also want to mention any relevant factors when you write up your assessment of the course for your records and your tenure dossier.

Finally, if your department doesn't use an adequate student evaluation procedure, you might suggest that your chair check into the Instructional Development Effectiveness Assessment (IDEA) forms (Kansas State University, Center for Faculty Evaluation and Development) and/or the Course/Instructor Evaluation Questionnaire (CIEQ), designed by Lawrence M. Aleamoni, a professor of educational psychology at the University of Arizona (Comprehensive Data Evaluation Services, Inc., Tucson).

SELF-EVALUATION

A relatively quick "checklist for developing instructional awareness" is proposed by Maryellen Weimer in *Improving College Teaching* (San Francisco: Jossey-Bass, 1990):

- What do you do with your hands? Gesture? Keep them in your pockets? Hold onto the podium? Play with the chalk? Hide them so students won't see them shake?
- Where do you stand or sit? Behind the podium? On the table?
- When do you move to a different location? Never? At regular 10-second intervals? When you change topics? When you need to write something on the board/overhead? When you answer a student's question? At what speed do you move? Do you talk and move at the same time?
- Where do you move? Back behind the podium? Out to the students? To the blackboard?
- Where do your eyes most often focus? On your notes? On the board/overhead? Out the window? On a spot on the

wall in the back of the room¿ On the students¿ Could you tell who was in class today without having taken roll¿

- What do you do between content segments¿ Say OK¿ Ask if there are any student questions¿ Erase the board¿ Move to a different location¿ Make a verbal transition¿
- When do you speak louder/softer¿ When the point is very important¿ When nobody seems to understand¿ When nobody seems to be listening¿
- When do you speak faster/slower¿ When you want to emphasize an important idea¿ When you're behind schedule¿ When you're having trouble understanding students' questions¿
- Do you laugh or smile in class¿ When¿ How often¿
- How do you use examples¿ How often¿ When¿
- How do you emphasize main points¿ Write them on the board/overhead¿ Repeat them¿ Ask the students if they understand them¿ Suggest ways to remember them¿
- What do you do when students are inattentive¿ Ignore them¿ Ask questions¿ Interject an anecdote¿ Point out the consequences of not paying attention¿ Move out toward them¿
- Do you encourage student participation¿ How¿ Grade it¿ Call on students by name¿ Wait for answers¿ Verbally recognize quality contributions¿ Correct student answers¿ How much class time is typically devoted to student talk¿
- How do you begin/end class¿ With a summary and conclusion¿ With a preview and a review¿ With a gasp and a groan¿ With a bang and a whimper¿

Being aware of your behavior in the classroom is only the first step, but it's fundamental to improving your teaching.

EFFECTIVE GUIDES

Perhaps the best quick guide to assessing your teaching is *How Am I Teaching¿*, edited by Maryellen Weimer, Joan L. Parrett, and Mary-Margaret Kerns (Madison WI: Magna Publications, 1988). It's a compilation of 12 forms for evaluating everything instructional, including:

- your classroom environment,
- your course materials,

- your attitudes,
- your classroom procedures,
- your teaching style and behavior,
- your stimulation of cognitive and affective gains,
- your relations with your students, and
- specific problems.

There are forms for you, your students, and peers. Everyone can provide you with input about your course; changes, of course, are up to you.

Faculty at Work: Self-Assessment Guide, by Robert T. Blackburn and Janet H. Lawrence (Ann Arbor: NCRIPTAL, 1991) should also help you evaluate your efforts and their effects.

Challenge yourself to make your teaching more effective. Consider again the example of the business professor who offers his students a money-back guarantee. Ask yourself at the end of the term, "How many of my students would be asking for a refund for this course? Why? What would have made the difference?" And then, because time is also a teacher, ask another question—"How will my students feel about this course in five years?" (That's a question often asked in tenure and promotion decisions.)

MOVING ON

INSTRUCTIONAL IMPROVEMENT PLAN

It's very likely that you'll find some negatives in your student evaluations and self-assessment. There may be sins of omission as well as commission, things you'd like to add, approaches you'd like to try. But it's only human to read the evaluations, do your self-assessment, sing and dance or rant and rave—and then take a break to charge up for the next term. Life goes on.

But you should take a little time to work up an instructional improvement plan. Simply list the content areas covered and the methods used, then make at least one suggestion for improving each area. This list will serve as the basis when you plan for that course again. If you're moving on to other courses the following term, consider areas of similarity in material or methods. What did you learn that might apply to your new courses?

WHO'S OUT THERE TO HELP ME?

One important thought to bear in mind, especially when reviewing your teaching: you may be alone in the classroom, but you're not alone in your efforts.

First, you can turn to colleagues in your department or related disciplines. Asking them for advice can be awkward, but it also may well be worth the effort. Why should students be the only ones in the educational enterprise to form study groups and support networks?

There are also, on most campuses, trained personnel. It may be a Center for Instructional Development, a Department of Curriculum and Instruction, a Center for Teaching Excellence, a Division of Instructional Support—but they're out there, ready and willing to help you.

Don't hesitate; don't wait for problems to develop. Some instructors conceive of instructional support in terms of urgent care. But those people aren't doctors and the facility isn't an emergency ward. It's better to think of your center as a facility for instructional wellness, a pedagogical health club where knowledgeable, experienced, committed, and usually very enthusiastic people will help you make the most of your efforts.

You can learn a lot from workshops and seminars on teaching your specific subject matter. But if there aren't any such activities in your discipline or related areas, consider attending workshops for graduate teachers in your discipline. Not only will you have an opportunity to learn some tricks, but as someone between a novice teaching assistant and an expert faculty facilitator, you may encourage by your presence a more open exchange of ideas.

Reach out beyond your campus. You may want to join an organization committed to teaching in your specific discipline. Or become a member of the Professional and Organizational Development Network in Higher Education—a.k.a. "The POD People." (For information, contact: David Graf, Manager of Administrative Services, POD Network, 15B Exhibit Hall South, Iowa State University, Ames IA 50011; phone 515-294-3808; fax 515-294-6024; email: j1dlg@isuvax.iastate.edu.)

BOTTOM LINE

What's good teaching? There are hundreds of books and thousands of articles out there—if you have the time and energy. (About a dozen are listed at the end of this chapter.)

As we suggested in Chapter 5, you might keep posted on your office wall a copy of the "Seven Principles for Good Practice in Undergraduate Education."

Good teaching:

- encourages student-faculty contact,
- encourages cooperation among students,
- encourages active learning,
- gives prompt feedback,
- emphasizes time on task,
- communicates high expectations, and
- respects diverse talents and ways of learning.

Although these principles can mean many things in practice, they provide excellent guidance. You should keep them in mind from the moment you begin planning your courses until you turn in your final grades.

ONE FINAL NOTE

The term is over, you've graded the last exam or paper and calculated final grades. Now what?

Many instructors post the grades, so eager (anxious?) students don't need to wait until the campus machinery processes and disperses them. However, you should be aware of recent concerns about privacy.

A federal court ruling in summer 1992 against Rutgers University, following a lawsuit filed by students, ordered the school to curtail its use of student Social Security numbers. One of the points in question was the use of SS numbers on classroom rosters and posted grade sheets.

Current interpretations of the Family Educational Rights and Privacy Act of 1974 (a.k.a. FERPA or the Buckley Amendment) would prohibit use of student names or SS numbers on posted grade sheets.[22] In fact, according to a FERPA public affairs officer, the use of the last several digits of the SS number is "sort of an iffy or gray area." Moreover, since faculty tend to use grade lists that are alphabetical, there are questions of privacy for students at the start and end of the alphabet.

How can you avoid legal questions? A FERPA Office representative suggests that you ask your students to each choose a password that you can then use on the posted grade sheet without jeopardizing any student privacy rights.

CREATING A NEW COURSE

STARTING FROM SCRATCH

If you have the opportunity to do something in an area that interests you, great! Maybe the department hired you specifically to open up a new area. If so, then you probably have some ideas about what you should offer in your course. Most likely, however, you'll have to identify and colonize a niche that doesn't overlap other courses excessively—or step on any toes.

POLITICS AND PRAGMATICS

You may want to consider this opportunity not only in terms of what you can bring to students but also in view of your situation in the department. (Few faculty actually enjoy the politics of academia, but wherever there are people there are politics.)

A former colleague was in the minority in her department: most of her colleagues were involved in areas of interests apart from hers—and sometimes in competition for department resources and personnel decisions. So she decided to create a course that bridged between her interests and the interests of the majority of her colleagues. The course was a hit with the students, it scored points with her colleagues—and it developed into a major career area that offers opportunities for teaching, publications, contacts, and service. Don't sell out for politics, but be aware of the politics in whatever you do.

Consider the merits of creating a course for a single credit. It's an easy way to test out a new offering—and you're less likely to step on toes, because a one-credit course generally won't draw students away from your colleagues' established courses.

You'll probably need to justify your proposal and parade your credentials before a jury of your peers, particularly as the outcry for better quality in higher education may rightly make deans and chairs skittish about any course that smacks of an ego trip, that might be motivated by selfish academic interests.

When you prepare your proposal for the review committee to consider, you should find the following headings a useful guide:

- Introduction
- Purpose of the Course
- Rationale
- Scope
- Content
- Objectives
- Relationship Within the Curriculum
- Summary
- List of Readings and Other Materials

CONCLUSION

Teaching can be a great challenge—especially if you set high expectations for yourself. But you don't have to face that challenge alone: work with your students, your colleagues, and those instructors out there who have faced the great challenge of teaching and put their experiences into hundreds of articles and books.

FURTHER GUIDANCE: IN THE CLASSROOM

As you teach, you'll find invaluable the following guides:

C. Roland Christensen, David A. Garvin, and Ann Sweet, eds., *Education for Judgment: The Artistry of Discussion Leadership* (Boston: Harvard Business School Press, 1991).

Barbara Gross Davis, *Tools for Teaching* (San Francisco: Jossey-Bass, 1993).

Kenneth Eble, *The Craft of Teaching: A Guide to Mastering the Professor's Art*, 2nd ed. (San Francisco: Jossey-Bass, 1988).

Stanford C. Ericksen, *The Essence of Good Teaching: Helping Students Learn and Remember What They Learn* (San Francisco: Jossey-Bass, 1984).

Kenneth A. Feldman and Michael B. Paulsen, eds., *Teaching and Learning in the College Classroom* (Needham Heights MA: Ginn Press, 1994).

L. Dee Fink, *The First Year of College Teaching* (San Francisco: Jossey-Bass, 1984).

Barbara S. Fuhrmann and Anthony F. Grasha, *A Practical Handbook for College Teachers* (Boston: Little, Brown, 1983).

Joseph Lowman, *Mastering the Techniques of Teaching* (San Francisco: Jossey-Bass, 1984).

Robert Magnan, ed., *147 Practical Tips for Teaching Professors* (Madison WI: Magna Publications, 1989).

Wilbert J. McKeachie, *Teaching Tips: Strategies, Research, and Theory for College and University Teachers*, 9th ed. (Lexington MA: D.C. Heath, 1994).

Chet Meyers and Thomas B. Jones, *Promoting Active Learning: Strategies for the College Classroom* (San Francisco: Jossey-Bass, 1993).

David Newble and Robert Cannon, *A Handbook for Teachers in Universities and Colleges: A Guide to Improving Teaching Methods* (New York: St. Martin's Press, 1989).

John C. Ory and Katherine E. Ryan, *Tips for Improving Testing and Grading* (Thousand Oaks CA: Sage Publications, 1993.

Maryellen Weimer and Rose Ann Neff, eds., *Teaching College: Collected Readings for the New Instructor* (Madison WI: Magna Publications, 1989).

NOTES

1. Courtney Leatherman, "Fighting Back: Professors Accused of Sexual Harassment Say Their Rights Have Been Breached," *The Chronicle of Higher Education* 16 Mar. 1994: A1.

2. Estela M. Bensimon, "The Development of Culturally Responsive Faculty," *Faculty as Teachers: Taking Stock of What We Know*, Maryellen Weimer, ed. (University Park PA: National Center for Teaching, Learning, and Assessment, 1993) 18-19.

3. Rita Rodabaugh, interview "Fairness," *The National Teaching & Learning Forum* 3:1 (1993): 5.

4. Larry M. Ludewig, "Student Perceptions of Instructor Behaviors," *The Teaching Professor* Apr. 1993: 1.

5. Barbara K. Goza, "Graffiti Needs Assessment: Involving Students in the First Class Session," *Journal of Management Education* 17:1 (Feb. 1993): 99-106.

6. Maryellen Weimer, "Tips for Productive Classroom Climates," *The Teaching Professor* Mar. 1990: 4.

7. " 'In' Box," *The Chronicle of Higher Education* 2 Feb. 1994: A15.

8. Courtney Leatherman, "U. of New Hampshire Wrestles with Issue of Sexual Harassment in Wake of Professor's Suspension," *The Chronicle of Higher Education* 12 Jan. 1994: A18.

9. Associated Press, "Professors to Be Silenced from Talking about Homosexuality" *Seattle Times* 27 Jan. 1994.

10. Adley M. Shulman, "When They Don't Do the Reading," *The Teaching Professor* Dec. 1989: 3.

11. Jules Janick, "Crib Sheets," *The Teaching Professor* June-July 1990: 2.

12. Kevin Melvin, "Rating Class Participation: The Prof/Peer Method," *Teaching of Psychology* Oct. 1988: 137-139.

13. K. Patricia Cross and Thomas A. Angelo, *Classroom Assessment Techniques: A Handbook for College Teachers*, 2nd ed. (San Francisco: Jossey-Bass, 1993).

14. Bette LaSere Erickson and Diane Weltner Strommer, *Teaching College Freshmen* (San Francisco: Jossey-Bass, 1991) 105.

15. Robert D. Abbott, Donald H. Wulff, Jody D. Nyquist, V.A. Ropp, and Carla W. Hess, "Satisfaction With Processes of Collecting Student Opinions About Instruction: The Student Perspective," *Journal of Educational Psychology* 83:2 (1990): 201-206.

16. Abbott *et al.* 205.

17. Leslie Swetnam, "Enhancing Instructor-Class Communication," *The Teaching Professor* Mar. 1994: 3-4.

18. Doris Green, "Prof Offers Money-Back Guarantee" (Bulletin Board), *Academic Leader* May 1991: 6.

19. Glenn Ross Johnson, *First Steps to Excellence in College Teaching* (Madison WI: Magna Publications, 1990) 33-43.

20. Ned A. Flanders, *Analyzing Teaching Behavior* (Reading MA: Addison-Wesley, 1970) 28-29.

21. William E. Cashin, "Student Ratings of Teaching: A Summary of the Research," IDEA Paper No. 20 (Manhattan KS: Kansas State University Center for Faculty Evaluation and Development, 1988).

22. Dennis Black, "Social Security Numbers: Must They Be Protected?" *Perspective: The Campus Legal Monthly* Oct. 1992: 4-5.

7 THE TEACHING CHALLENGE: OUTSIDE THE CLASSROOM

What else does a good instructor do outside the classroom? What else might a department and dean expect from faculty?

You may be expected to advise students or to get involved with student activities and organizations. You may be expected to expand your instructional activities into the campus community. Again, we repeat our refrain: you've got to know your territory.

WORKING WITH STUDENTS OUTSIDE THE CLASSROOM

YOUR OFFICE

Before we enter into these activities, it's essential to spend a few moments considering your primary campus workplace—your office. Faculty show great diversity in their office procedures. Some set generous office hours and respect the right of students to have access to an attentive instructor. Others neglect this duty and treat students as an inconvenience.

Set appropriate hours, announce them in class—and keep them. Nobody expects you to just sit there in your office waiting. If no students drop by, it's valuable time to prepare for your classes, read, write, maintain correspondence. But if a student comes by, drop everything and concentrate on that student's needs.

Since more and more students have responsibilities beyond their studies—jobs, family, campus and community extracurricular activities—faculty must remember that no schedule fits all. Maximize your availability: you might let students make appointments outside your regular hours, encourage them to call you at home (during certain hours), make sure they know where your campus mailbox is located, give them the department phone number so they can leave messages, set up an answering machine if you have an individual office phone.

Being available for your students isn't just the right thing to do. It also pays dividends when they do their term-end evaluations—which helps your tenure dossier. So if you feel like skipping out on your office hours, consider the odds: Is it likely that a student will come by? Is it likely that colleagues will notice the student waiting and perhaps grumbling? Is it likely that the student will complain or make a comment on your evaluation? Is it likely that the tenure jury of your peers will find you guilty of neglect?

For some faculty, the office is just four walls, a ceiling, a floor, and lots of books. For others, it's a home away from home. But it's always, unfortunately, a place of growing concern.

Although you may think of your office as your territory, remember that you share it with students and colleagues. You should feel comfortable there, but so should your vistors.

What impressions do visitors get from your office? Try to consider everything from their perspective. From time to time we receive difficult reminders of differences in perspective.

For example, several years ago, an instructor at the University of Texas-Austin was urged by his department chair to remove an AIDS awareness poster that some students and their parents had considered too sexually explicit. Although the instructor argued that it was "an informative poster that provides an opportunity for discussion on homosexuality, homophobia, and AIDS," he removed it.[1]

A graduate assistant in psychology at the University of Nebraska-Lincoln kept on his desk a 5" x 7" photograph of his wife in a bikini. Two fellow graduate assistants objected to the photograph. The two women demanded that it be removed, claiming that it violated UNL's sexual harassment policy because it created "a hostile work environment." His chair ordered the photo removed, as authorized by the assistant general counsel for UNL, who stated that department heads could use "reasonable judgment" in banning anything that interfered with "efficient operation" of their units. Regarding the specific incident, she said, "I have not seen the photograph, but feel no need to make any judgment concerning its content in order to respond to this matter."[2]

What is objectionable? What might create a hostile environment? Visit other offices in your department to gain a feel for the cultural climate. Try to view your office critically, from various perspectives. Some students might feel offended by a comic taped to your door, for example. Many might object if you smoke—or even if your office smells of smoke. Indications of political or religious choices might bother others.

It's a dilemma; there are no simple guidelines. On the one hand, you have your academic freedom, your constitutional right to free expression, and your duty not to shelter your students against reality. On the other hand, if students feel uncomfortable with the environment of your office and of your department, those negative feelings will undermine their educational experience.

When you meet with students, be attentive to what Iver Bogen, a psychology professor at the University of Minnesota-Duluth, calls "shadow messages"—subliminal statements.[3] Where is your desk in the office? Does it form a barrier? What do you have on your walls and on your desk? What is your reaction when students drop in—inviting or inconvenienced? Do you keep looking at your watch or out the window? As the song goes, "Every little movement has a meaning all its own."

ADVISING INDIVIDUAL STUDENTS

You may need to advise or counsel individual students, especially at smaller colleges, where it may be one of your major responsibilities. Although your department may not actively support faculty advising, you should take such activities very seriously.

In their book, *Teaching College Freshmen*, Bette LaSere Erickson and Diane Weltner Strommer emphasize this point:

> Providing accurate information is of major importance, since seemingly trivial errors can be costly to students, particularly freshmen who rely heavily on the adviser's authority.... If we do not provide accurate information we are unlikely to have an opportunity to do anything else, for students soon abandon an adviser who cannot give accurate answers to their questions.[4]

Advising is perhaps the campus service most maligned by undergraduates, even ahead of cafeteria meals and the health center. Why? Many students expect not only answers to their questions, but solutions to their problems. Act as a guide, not as a parent. Give them information and show them that you care—then leave the rest to them.

This behavior can be particularly difficult for female faculty, as students seem more likely to expect nurturing from them. Likewise, minority students may seek out a faculty member of the same race or ethnic origin, which imposes additional expectations. It's only natural to feel sympathetic and want to lend a hand. But the best advice is still to help the student help himself or herself.

Keep in mind that the world is getting more difficult for students in the '90s: they have more varied backgrounds and abilities, more academic requirements, more career choices, and more family and financial responsibilities. If students come to you, try to be sensitive to their reasons and needs—which they may have trouble expressing. Sometimes they may need a straight answer, just the facts. Or maybe an interpretation of policies or regulations. They may need help sorting out their lives—or even just someone to listen to them sorting things out.

You should be prepared for anything. It may make you uncomfortable, but sometimes students may need you to be more than just an instructor. A student may come to you with personal problems—substance abuse, sexual harassment or assault, depression—and you should be ready and willing to help. Keep information handy on campus counseling centers and support groups, including addresses and phone numbers. Centers and groups may be happy to provide you with brochures and other documentation for your students. Your campus may even provide counseling training for faculty.

Know your stuff. Be knowledgeable about current academic requirements, for your department, your division, and the institution as a whole. Some students like "one-stop shopping": they may ask you questions about virtually anything. Of course, nobody could reasonably expect you to know every campus policy and regulation. If you don't have an answer, offer to check into the matter. Then follow up, preferably by calling somebody in the know while the student is there in your office.

Legal Concerns. How important is it to be knowledgeable and to know how to get accurate and complete information? Very. Not only can incomplete or erroneous information hurt a student, it could get you an expensive lesson in the legal system.

In the words of Dennis Black, attorney, dean of students, and associate vice president for student services at the State University of New York at Buffalo:

> It's the easiest thing in the world: a student needs information or help, so you offer advice. The next thing you know, you're dragged into court. A scary scenario—but more and more part of academic life.
>
> Campus advisement is an important process, but when mishandled it can lead to thorny legal problems. . . . Within the past decade, there has been a rapid rise in the number of situations when students and universities take their advisement disputes into courts.[5]

You may be individually protected by agency law against legal liability. However, your actions could involve your department or your institution in a legal battle. Perhaps the best advice is common sense: know and respect the limits of your responsibilities as an advisor and fulfill those responsibilities as knowedgeably and scrupulously as you fulfill your instructional responsibilities.

The Business of Advising. Keep up to date with the "outside world." For students who major or minor in your field, you should be familiar with employment trends and career opportunities.

If your department has a graduate program, you may also have a chance to mentor grad students. Many faculty truly enjoy working with these "junior colleagues," but there are no roses without thorns.

As a colleague warned Bill, "You've got to be ready to work with the whole student. They're into their studies, they're intelligent, but they've got lives outside the classroom and library and lab—and there's lots of pressure on them to be cool and professional—especially around faculty." So, be attentive to "chinks in their armor" and help them make the most of their years in graduate school.

While a graduate student at the University of Georgia, Bill had worked closely with two professors. They'd discussed his projects and opportunities to turn his work into papers and articles. One had invited him to several professional conferences, where she introduced him to other faculty working in his field of interest. The other mentor had helped Bill earn a two-year post-doc assignment with the Chesapeake Bay Commission. And they both kept in touch with Bill, by mail and by phone, when he was applying for tenure-track positions. Bill appreciated all their efforts and hoped that he could be as helpful a mentor for budding botanists at Midland.

Many faculty dread advising: it takes time, energy, and patience—and may offer virtually no reward toward tenure. For a beginner it's particularly tough: there's a lot to learn about being a student on your campus. But some people claim that students may be shaped less by what you do in the classroom than by your activities outside. If advising is part of your job, you should consider it an important responsibility.

P.S. Advising isn't necessarily labor in obscurity. Colleagues are sure to take note of students hanging around your door and walking away, content or complaining. And every colleague carries a mental dossier with your name on it.

It may be useful to maintain a log or files to keep track of the students you advise: names, class level, major, dates of sessions, and any decisions. Don't trust your memory for details. If you keep track, you can advise students more effectively—and they'll appreciate the individual attention and effort. Of course, such records are also good documentation for your tenure dossier.

Letters and Legalities. One of your responsibilities or privileges will be to write letters of recommendation for your students. You should do so carefully—both to better help your students and to keep out of legal difficulties.

Consider, for example, the following case. In 1986 an instructor at Indiana University-Bloomington was asked to write a recommendation for a student who was applying for a teaching position. The instructor felt the student wasn't ready for a full-time position, however, and wrote that on the recommendation sheet.

The principal decided against hiring the student, then showed her the recommendation. The student sued the instructor and the university for defamation. A summary judgment (No. 36A 04-9009-CV-439) went against the student, as the court found no issues in dispute and the law on the side of the institution.

The student appealed the judgment. The state court of appeals sided with the school, in *Olsson v. Indiana University Board of Trustees*, 571 N.E. 2d 585 (1991). The student could not collect damages, it ruled, because:

- the instructor had shown no "malice or reckless disregard" for the truth,
- the instructor had not written the letter in "bad faith,"
- the letter had been seen only by the person for whom it was intended,
- the instructor was a supervisor of students, so evaluation was her responsibility, and
- others submitted negative evaluations of the student.

The court ruled that letters of recommendation, written in good faith and appropriately distributed to a limited audience, are protected against charges of defamation.[6]

Consider another case, from about 10 years ago. The chair of the orthopedic surgery department at the University of Nebraska was asked to complete an evaluation form for a former student who was applying for a job. The chair evaluated the student's academic performance as "well below average." When the applicant failed to get the job, he sued the school and chair for defamation of character. The lawsuit was dismissed on a technicality, but the student appealed. The appellate court ruled that there were grounds for a trial (*Burt v. Board of Regents of the University of Nebraska and Connolly*, 757 F.2d 242, 1985). However, when the student had no money to pursue his case, he dropped the lawsuit, so there was no decision on the question of defamation.

Nevertheless, the appellate court ruling suggests that faculty should be cautious in any evaluations or letters of reference.[7]

Dennis Black offers the following guidance:

> Honest letters of recommendation and evaluations have long been protected. While courts must remain open to defamation arguments, the truth remains an absolute defense. If an eveluator or letter writer takes care to ensure that comments are *accurate*, *appropriate*, and *defendable*, the law provides legal protection from dissatisfied students.[8]

You may want to read "Trends in Defamation Law: Let the Advisor Beware," an article by R.D. King in the *NACADA Journal* (Spring 1992). King offers the following advice to faculty and staff:

- Make sure that any information you communicate on students is based on facts and documentation that you can produce, if needed.
- Get the consent of the student before you communicate any information.

If a student sues you over a bad letter of recommendation, the odds are on your side. However, any lawsuit, no matter what the resolution, causes headaches.

In the case of evaluations and letters of reference, it may be best to rely on an old truism: if you can't say something good, don't say anything at all. If you do, proceed cautiously and weigh your words most carefully. As a colleague remarked recently, "In these times, good intentions are a poor motivation—and an even poorer defense."

PERSONAL RELATIONSHIPS

Finally, be careful about developing personal relationships with students you advise, whether undergraduate or graduate. In fact, it's safest to avoid close relationships with any student.

If you show an interest in a student, and that student is not similarly interested in you, you are open to charges of sexual harassment—and hundreds of students file charges of sexual harassment every year. If concern for your students is not enough to deter you, think about the likely effect of sexual harassment charges on your tenure candidacy.

What about if the feelings of interest are mutual? After all, romance can blossom anywhere. But faculty-student romances are increasingly dangerous. In recent years at least two dozen colleges and universities have established policies to limit or prohibit such consensual relationships.

Your institution may have such a policy. If so, you should read it and respect it scrupulously, in letter and in spirit. If no policy exists, at least heed the words of Eileen N. Wagner, a former professor and now a Virginia attorney "representing several plaintiffs in actions against colleges and universities":

> Fair or not, the fact is that teachers facing charges of sexual misconduct with students now bear a "strict liability" burden of proof. In other words, the blame automatically falls on the teacher, with little or no concern about the student's culpability. . . .
>
> Once a teacher student relationship turns sour, once the teacher is tempted to use pedagogical authority to influence the relationship's direction, once the student balks at the teacher's sexual demands, or, indeed, when the favored student flaunts the special status to less-favored students, there's trouble ahead. The Supreme Court has said that when such trouble develops, damages may be collected—and no limits on the amount have been set.[9]

You may agree with Kent Willis, executive director of the Virginia American Civil Liberties Union, that "the Constitution protects privacy and associational rights that allow consenting adults to explore and create their own relationships."[10] However, you are likely to face judgment in the media and among colleagues long before you could argue your case in court.

If you feel attracted to a student, fight the feeling. If a student expresses interest in you, discourage him or her; keep your relationship strictly professional. It's wisest to keep things cool and wait until that student receives his or her degree. To quote a popular advice columnist: "If it's real, it will last. If not, then it's not worth the risk."

What about friendships? What about meeting with students for soft drinks and conversations? Some faculty would find nothing wrong with such relationships. In fact, some of your senior colleagues may have occasionally developed solid, beneficial relationships with students. Unfortunately, times have changed: even casual socializing with students may seem questionable to your colleagues, who may suspect your motives or simply fear charges of favoritism or worse, with emotional and legal repercussions.

It may seem ironic that, as we discover the greater benefits to be gained when faculty mentor students, moral and legal concerns weigh against faculty-student relationships outside the classroom. Unfortunately, ironic or not, that's the situation.

The author of *Saints and Scamps: Ethics in Academia* and a professor of philosophy in the City University of New York graduate school, Steven M. Cahn observes, "During the years of undergraduate or graduate study the only appropriate relationship between teacher and student is professional. It is in everyone's interest to maintain these bounds."[11]

Peter J. Markie, a philosophy professor at the University of Missouri-Columbia, states in his essay, "Professors, Students, and Friendship":

> I conclude . . . that the activity of friendship, for all its intrinsic value, is morally out of bounds for professors where actual and potential students are concerned. Instead of trying to be good friends to our students, we can and should use our energies to be good teachers to them.[12]

Goodbye, Mr. Chips.

ADVISING STUDENT ORGANIZATIONS

You may also have the opportunity (perhaps thrust upon you) of advising a student organization. Remember high school? Remember the teachers who were in charge of the school paper, yearbook, debate team, pep squad, Spanish club? Some did it out of interest, some out of a sense of responsibility, and some because they had no choice. What's the situation in your department? Are you free to choose or do your colleagues expect you to get involved? If you're acting out of interest or departmental expectations, do it. Otherwise, leave that area of involvement to those who share the interest of the students.

It may well be that new faculty are expected to "pay their dues" by taking on a task that their established colleagues wish to avoid, as pledges in the campus fraternity. This is often a problem for female faculty in particular. In some departments advising student groups is considered a "pink collar" responsibility, a social service of secondary importance. If you find yourself under pressure to do more than your fair share of service, discuss the situation with an ally in the department. Sometimes that sort of discrimination is just viewed as "tradition." A few probing but tactful questions might put it to rest. If you accept every advising responsibility they hand you, you're not likely to have the time and energy to make tenure—and you'll be accepting second-class citizenship in your department.

If you become involved in any way in a student organization or special program, keep track of what you do—title, responsibilities, role in any particular activities. Later you'll need to sort these things out for your dossier and you won't want to forget anything. Remember: you get involved in student activities for the sake of the students, but evidence of your commitment to the students and the campus should be duly recorded—and rewarded. Of course the rewards vary from department to department and campus to campus. Again, you've got to know your territory.

KEEPING TRACK OF ALUMNI

When are your students no longer your students? After the term ends? After they graduate? Actually, your students may be a part of you—and you may be a part of them—for life. Good teachers should have a lasting impact on their students.

And you may well want to keep track of your "alumni" as they make their way through the world. Such relationships can help you remember what some faculty seem to forget—that students are people too. It can also be very rewarding to know that you're part of a success story. Share their stories with your colleagues, who may remember some of those students. Again, an enthusiastic and devoted instructor leaves a definite impression on his or her colleagues.

TAKING YOUR TEACHING OUT INTO THE WORLD

When it comes to teaching, it pays to think big. Too often good teaching gets little recognition because it's confined to the classroom and the office, documented only through student evaluations. You should also consider your teaching efforts in terms of scholarship and community service.

SCHOLARSHIP

Although scholarship and its importance to your tenure dossier are extensively covered in Chapters 8 and 10, they merit a few words in this chapter on teaching outside the classroom. Teaching and scholarship don't have to be adversarial pursuits: many "teaching professors" consider it a vital part of their vocation to contribute to the idea network through conferences, articles, and books.

Maybe a classroom experience might draw your attention to something interesting. Or maybe you can apply some aspect of your research to your courses. If your research has raised any questions in your mind, consider posing them in class, in the form of problem-solving and case studies. Have your students apply their knowledge of the field and of research methodology. Outline the problem and then let them approach it, providing guidance only as needed. Focus on the process, not the product: your students don't need to find answers, just the right questions.

But you may gain some interesting insights for your research activities—and you may want to present a paper or publish an article to share such classroom experiences with others teaching in your discipline. Remember: if you're putting a lot of thought and energy into your teaching, you're probably learning things of value and interest to others in your discipline.

A section in Chapter 10 will cover the matter of publishing in pedagogical periodicals. Such publications can provide an excellent forum for your classroom experiments—and be worth some points toward tenure.

Opportunities Outside. But what if your area of research and your courses don't match very well? A French professor specializing in Eustache Deschamps may not be able to share his research with an introductory language class, and a physics prof engaged in the study of quarks may not be able to bring that area of interest to her first-year students in a required general science course.

Check with colleagues who teach courses more relevant to your research interests. (Don't neglect extension courses or possibilities at nearby campuses.) Offer to visit their classes as a guest lecturer on a specific topic or, more generally, on research methodology and problem-solving.

"Aggregative Scholarship." You should consider also what has been termed "aggregative scholarship." As William T. Daly, a political science professor at Stockton State College of New Jersey, recently summarized and promoted this area of scholarship:[13]

> In most fields, knowledge advances in the form of a large number of highly specialized research findings which are only infrequently aggregated into sweeping paradigm shifts. Aggregative scholarship involves an ongoing attempt to aggregate and interpret these specialized research findings in search of interconnections, trends, and early indications of long-term significance. It also involves the attempt to present the results of this endeavor in ways that will be intelligible and interesting to non-specialists. . . .
>
> The advantages of this kind of aggregative scholarship as a bridge between scholarship and teaching are threefold. First, like research on pedagogy, it should impact directly and beneficially on undergraduate teaching. . . . Secondly, unlike research on pedagogy, the shift in standards necessary to legitimize aggregative scholarship would be a relatively small one. . . . Finally, aggregative research could help to make the economic case for higher education by making a direct contribution in two areas. . . identified as central to the rebuilding of the American economy—the strengthening of competence and morale among public school teachers and of the capacity for innovation in the American business community.

COMMUNITY SERVICE

Is your research of interest to local business or community groups? Maybe you could be of service to a high school teacher or counselor for career days. Be creative. And remember that such activities aren't necessarily one-way: you're bringing your skills and experience to others, but you may gain insights when you consider your work from their various perspectives.

John V. Moeser, a professor of urban studies and planning at Virginia Commonwealth University, recently explored the experience of "public teaching":[14]

> Public teaching takes many forms: a social scientist's article or commentary for a newspaper; a historian's speech to a group of citizens

about her research; a mathematician preparing media materials to be used by a local television station; an artist's instructional commentary to a congregation about an exhibit or piece of music; a geneticist talking about his research with a group of elementary school children; a business professor's interview with the local press about fluctuations in the stock market; a professor of medicine's testimony before a legislative committee about medical technology or medical ethics.

And Moeser summed up the benefits of these experiences:

> Public teaching is an activity which many faculty do willingly because of their love of teaching and the intrinsic rewards associated with it. The value of public teaching to the community is clear.... Both the teacher and the university as a whole benefit from public teaching. Teachers often become better teachers in the classroom as a result of their work outside the academy. The university gains greater recognition in the community.... The public relations value of public teaching is significant, an increasingly important consideration.

So, such "outteach" efforts can allow you different perspectives on your campus teaching, help educate people out in the community, and inform the local world about work being done at your institution. Maybe the tenure points for "Community Service" are disappointing, but that situation seems to be improving—especially as colleges and universities try to cope with growing image problems and as educational leaders such as Ernest Boyer encourage faculty to get involved in their communities.[15] (And the experience may inspire you to write and publish an article, which is more likely to result in points.)

Sometimes the results may be surprising. Take the case of Fred Hoyle, an astronomer at the University of Cambridge several decades ago. In 1950 he gave a public lecture about cosmology, in which he discussed the origins of the universe. To make one theory more interesting, he coined the term "big bang"—creating what has become a household term that the American Astronomical Society has been unable to supplant, despite a recent contest that elicited more than 13,000 entries.[16]

Once again, as in all your activities, document what you do.

These possibilities can open attractive opportunities, especially for faculty at smaller institutions, with more limited research facilities. And they can be alternative scholarship: presentations and articles on teaching can supplement other research, broaden your perspectives, encourage you to invest more energy and thought in your classroom activities, supplement student and collegial evaluations of your teaching, and give evidence of a greater range of interests.

Finally, you may want to find out what campus committees and/or publications are devoted to teaching. Consider serving on a committee and publishing articles based on those activities. A small investment of time and energy may help improve the quality of education and draw attention to the importance of that institutional mission—as well as providing you with some valuable attention among your colleagues.

Caution: "Extracurricular" teaching activities may take a lot of time and energy and carry little weight in your tenure decision. Depending on the climate of your department and division, you may have to put off some time-consuming yet undervalued opportunities until after tenure. As we stress throughout this manual, you've got to know your territory.

IN A NUTSHELL

If what you're doing to combine research and teaching or research and service is worth doing, it should be documented in your dossier and it may be worthy of a presentation or article.

DOCUMENTING YOUR TEACHING ACTIVITIES

INSTITUTIONAL CRITERIA

OK, this is the bottom line for most readers: How do you get proper credit for your teaching activities? It's also one of the hottest questions in higher education.

Leaders call for greater commitment to quality in education, but at many institutions the story remains the same. Several years ago at a major state university a new dean was appointed for the school of education. The chancellor reported being "absolutely delighted to attract such a well-known scholar who has continued to be a productive researcher along with his broad experience in university administration." But what about the teaching of this new dean of education? Not a word.

Even at institutions that traditionally stress the importance of teaching, candidates for tenure should document their instructional activities as completely and carefully as they document their scholarship and service. Remember: you can't trust your tenure to mission statements and the rhetoric of press releases. It's not what they say about the value of teaching; it's how they reward it.

It's essential to know what your department and division use as criteria for weighing the value of your teaching in tenure decisions. The possibilities include:

- Evaluation by chair
- Opinions of colleagues
- Systematic student evaluations
- Committee evaluation
- Informal student opinions
- Evaluation by dean
- Content of course syllabi and exams
- Popularity (i.e., enrollment in elective courses)
- Self-evaluation
- Teaching improvement activities
- Student performance on exams
- Ratings by colleagues (classroom visitations)
- Opinions of course alumni
- Long-term follow-up of students (performance in subsequent courses)
- Videotape of classroom teaching

These 15 criteria were used by John Centra in his survey of 453 department heads published a few years ago.[17] Respondents ranked the importance of these criteria in the order shown, reporting that only the first six were of *major* importance. How much has changed over time? How do your department, division, and institution compare? Once again, we repeat the refrain—you've got to know your territory.

When Bill arrived at Midland University, he checked the faculty handbook and learned that "documentation of teaching quality and effectiveness can include but is not restricted to":

- Evaluation by colleagues and department administrators, particularly if based on class visitations or the results of the

candidate's teaching in courses prerequisite to those taught by the evaluator.
- Evaluations by students.
- Exit interviews of graduating seniors by the department chair.
- Evidence of innovation: teaching techniques, content, materials, and evaluative procedures (tests).
- Development of new courses and programs.
- Publications and presentations pertaining to teaching.
- Invitations to consult or lecture on teaching.
- Opinions of graduates who have achieved notable professional success.
- Numbers and quality of graduate students attracted to the department because of the candidate's professional reputation, and the number of those guided through master's and doctoral degrees.
- Authorship of textbooks, audiovisual materials, software.

DOSSIER/PORTFOLIO

Traditionally the P&T dossier contains lists of presentations, publications, and work on campus and in the community, together with copies of all materials, as evidence of research and service activity. In recent years, however, faculty and academic associations have been promoting the importance of documenting teaching activity as well.

Your portfolio should contain evidence of the following general areas of your teaching activities:

- Subject area mastery.
- Curriculum development and innovation.
- Course design: goals, content, methods, assessment.
- Delivery of instruction: methods, skills, and materials.
- Assessment of instruction: assignments, tests, grading practices.
- Availability to students.
- Administrative requirements and expectations.

These areas are outlined in greater detail, with suggestions for appropriate documentation for each area, by William E. Cashin in "Defining and Evaluating College Teaching," IDEA Paper No. 21 (Manhattan KS: Kansas State University Center for Faculty Evaluation and

Development, 1989). You might also consult the references at the end
of this chapter.

Floyd Urbach, faculty development officer at Indiana University at South Bend, suggests documenting seven dimensions of
teaching:[18]

1. What you teach

   - content of each course
   - skills and performance abilities
   - attitudes and feelings
   - values and philosophies

2. How you teach

   - repertoire of teaching skills and models
   - specific instructional skills
   - use and/or preparation of instructional materials
   - preparation of materials for students

3. Changes in your teaching and course activities

   - evolution of change
   - innovations: successful and unsuccessful
   - additions to each course
   - deletions from each course

4. Rigor in your academic standards

   - standards for grades
   - efforts at improving test validity
   - congruence of testing with what you are teaching

5. Student impressions of your teaching and their learning

   - use of formative feedback
   - accommodation of individual students
   - end of course trends on selected data

6. Efforts at developing your teaching skills

   - participation in faculty development programs and confer-
     ences

- efforts to become more aware of your teaching
- research and publications related to teaching and learning

7. Assessments of your teaching by colleagues

- visitations (peers within your department and outside)
- administrative evaluations

Urbach notes:

> Each of the seven dimensions may be recorded through a variety of "artifacts"; your artifacts should trace the evolution of each course that you have taught. Each document should illustrate some significant and specific aspect of your development as a college teacher to create and preserve a "paper trail," or sometimes a media trail, which will chronicle significant events in your teaching career.[19]

So, what can you put into your teaching portfolio? Here are a few suggestions:

- Student evaluations. It's probably policy or hallowed tradition that your department put the evaluations into your file. If not, it's up to you. If the department doesn't provide a summary of each set of evaluations, you probably should do so yourself, including a copy of the course description and any other details that would help your colleagues better understand the evaluations.
- Evaluations by visitors—colleagues or instructional development staff.
- Self-assessments. Whether you've completed forms, maintained a journal, or simply written down your reactions to each course, these documents are evidence of your interest, commitment, and attitudes.
- Course outlines and syllabi. You may want to attach a commentary sheet, to explain what thoughts and considerations went into putting the course together. List and describe your goals, both primary and secondary. Your commentary should include your reading and other preparation, to show your professional development—How are you better for having taught the course?

- Ancillary materials you've prepared: handouts, review sheets, bibliographies, overhead transparencies, and so forth. You don't need to include everything, but you should give evidence of variety and depth. Again, a commentary sheet may be useful: Why did you decide to develop the materials? How did they facilitate learning? How would you grade them? What might you do differently?
- Documentation on activities outside the classroom. Did you organize a field trip, an exhibition of student projects, or any other "above and beyond" learning activities?
- Audio- and videotapes. You'll need to briefly outline the context of the segments recorded: course, level and background of your students, stage in the syllabus, preparation, type of activity. You should also describe your reactions— How would you judge the class or specific activities? What were the ups and the downs? What would you do differently? (When you put together your commentary, remember that your colleagues may not all review the tapes, unfortunately, so your comments should be able to stand on their own as evidence of your teaching.)
- Student projects. These might include exceptional term papers or essay exams, descriptions of special group activities, photographs of three-dimensional creations, videos of student debates or role-play or skits. Remember to attach a brief explanation of the instructional circumstances.
- Records of your advising activities. If you maintain a log or files, include these as evidence of your interest and commitment beyond the classroom.

Teaching portfolios are valuable not only as documentation but also as guides to improvement. When you develop your portfolio, you focus on what you consider important. Then you take note of your weaker areas and work to strengthen those areas.

Teaching portfolios have been in use on some campuses since the early '70s. With the AAHE promoting their value and the quality of undergraduate instruction attracting greater attention nationally, the use of teaching portfolios should rise considerably through the '90s.

HEART AND SOUL

Your academic career may emphasize research and publication, focus on discovering knowledge and advancing your discipline: these activities may be what most impress your colleagues and the dean. But teaching is traditionally the heart and soul of faculty activities. You should take your teaching responsibilities seriously, as opportunities to make a significant contribution to our future.

You may spend months, even years, to provide a small step for a few specialists in your field—or in those same months help your students to make giant strides. Whatever they become, you become a part of their success.

Be idealistic, but keep a grasp on reality. Know the value of good teaching in terms of tenure in your department and division. Many new faculty find it easy to become so committed to teaching, so devoted to their students, that they forget to wear their two other hats, research and service. They neglect their responsibility to present and publish and to otherwise serve the campus community—and they risk losing their chance to make an impact through teaching.

Higher education leaders and associations are progressively insistent that institutions recognize the importance of effective teaching, particularly for undergraduates. If you believe that your teaching responsibilities are vital to your professional life and if your department and division encourage and support more effective teaching, then you should promote your activities in your tenure dossier.

FURTHER GUIDANCE: OUTSIDE THE CLASSROOM

For your work outside the classroom, you should refer to the following sources:

Russell Edgerton, Pat Hutchings, and Kathleen Quinlan, *The Teaching Portfolio: Capturing the Scholarship in Teaching* (Washington DC: American Association for Higher Education, 1991).

Peter Seldin, *The Teaching Portfolio: A Practical Guide to Improved Performance and Promotion/Tenure Decisions* (Bolton MA: Anker Publishing, 1991).

NOTES

1. "Professor Removes AIDS-Awareness Poster" (In Brief), *The Chronicle of Higher Education* 8 Apr. 1992: A4.

2. Nat Hentoff, "Censors Go Overboard on Picture of Grad Student's Wife," *The Capital Times* (Madison, WI) 25 May 1993: 9A.

3. Iver Bogen, "Shadow Messages," *Instructional Development,* 7:4 (Instructional Development Service: University of Minnesota-Duluth).

4. Bette LaSere Erickson and Diane Weltner Strommer, *Teaching College Freshmen* (San Francisco: Jossey-Bass, 1991) 184-185.

5. Dennis Black, "Talk Is Cheap but Advice Has a Price," *Perspective: The Campus Legal Monthly* July 1989: 1.

6. Dennis Black, "Is a Bad Recommendation Defamation?" *Perspective: The Campus Legal Monthly* Nov. 1992: 5.

7. Dennis Black, "Just Ask!" *Perspective: The Campus Legal Monthly* Dec. 1989: 8.

8. Black, "Just Ask!" 8.

9. Eileen N. Wagner, "Fantasies of True Love in Academe," *The Chronicle of Higher Education* 26 May 1993: B1-B3. Quoted by Clay Schoenfeld in "Faculty/Student Consensual Relations: A Tough Issue," *Academic Leader* Sept. 1993: 2.

10. Kent Willis, quoted by Jean McNair, "Faculty-Student Sex Ban Backed," *Wisconsin State Journal* (Associated Press) 23 Apr. 1993.

11. Steven M. Cahn, *Saints and Scamps: Ethics in Academia* (Totowa NJ: Rowman and Littlefield, 1986) 36.

12. Peter J. Markie, "Professors, Students, and Friendship," *Morality, Responsibility, and the University: Studies in Academic Ethics*, Steven M. Cahn, ed. (Philadelphia: Temple University Press, 1990) 147.

13. William T. Daly, "Teaching and Scholarship: Adapting American Higher Education to Hard Times," *The Journal of Higher Education* Jan.-Feb. 1994: 51-53.

14. John V. Moeser, "Public Teaching," *VCU Teaching* (Virginia Commonwealth University) Winter 1993-94: 2-8.

15. Ernest L. Boyer, "Creating the New American College" (Point of View), *The Chronicle of Higher Education* 9 Mar. 1994: A48.

16. "Footnotes," *The Chronicle of Higher Education* 26 Jan. 1994: A8.

17. John A. Centra, "Evaluating College Teaching: Some Reflections," *Department Advisor* 5 (Winter 1990): 1-5.

18. Floyd Urbach, *Seven Dimensions for Documenting Teaching* (South Bend: Indiana University at South Bend Faculty Devolopment Office, 1992).

19. Floyd Urbach, "Developing a Teaching Portfolio," *College Teaching* 40:2 (Spring 1992): 71.

8 THE RESEARCH PARADIGM

Unless you're in a college devoted exclusively to teaching, you'll be expected to engage in research. Particularly at a prestigious research university, research is the *sine qua non* of the faculty role. Even in a "wannabe" institution, at least a modest level of research is a criterion for retention and promotion.

Why is research esteemed so highly in academia?

Academia is pre-eminently a place of learning. If it is to teach by example, a college or university must have faculty who themselves are exemplary learners. If it is to serve, it must constantly supply an expectant society—with everything from smart armaments and biotech zygotes to archeological digs and Zoroastrian prophesies—from a reservoir of knowledge that is constantly being renewed. If it is to be dynamic and inspiring, a college or university must be more than a repository of what others have said and discovered; it must continuously be pushing forward and outward its scholarly frontiers. Academia is an anachronism if it puts its graduates into the modern world with only the information of yesterday.

So to display intellectual curiosity, to investigate at the boundaries of your discipline, to advance those very boundaries, will be a key measure of your worth as a professor, of your being *of* as well as *at* your institution.

From a sheerly pragmatic point of view, research is important for you simply because it is at the heart of most faculty reward systems—and rightly so, most of your peers believe. They will cite four reasons why research should be the main criterion on which to base promotion and tenure:

- it carries the potential for international prestige
- it is the best indicator of the quality of a candidate's mind
- it is valuable to students and society
- it is easier to measure objectively than is teaching.

Donald K. Jarvis, author of *Junior Faculty Development*,[1] holds the first claim to be true, the second and third sometimes true, and the fourth "patently false." His reservations notwithstanding, research remains the name of the game on most campuses in most disciplines most of the time.

DECIPHERING THE CODES

You'll notice we've been using here only the generic term "research," but that term is actually a code word in wide campus usage, standing for a number of related yet distinct academic activities. It will be important that you readily decipher what exactly the term "research" implies in your department at your institution.

For example, in its January 1994 revised mission statement, the University of Minnesota identifies its "threefold mission" to be "research and discovery, teaching and learning, and outreach and public service." In turn, "research and discovery" is said to be "generating and preserving knowledge, understanding, and creativity by conducting high-quality *research, scholarship,* and *artistic activity* that benefit students, scholars, and communities across the state, the nation, and the world."

THE SEMANTIC AXIS

How is one to distinguish among "research, scholarship, and creativity?" Howard Mancing[2] offers this explanation:

> Scientific research often requires teams of investigators and enormous sums of external grant money; it is what much of the public and too many university administrators think of when they use the term *research*.
>
> Humanistic scholarship—the research engaged in by most professors of foreign languages and literatures—tends to be carried out by individuals whose major resources are time and books.
>
> Artistic creativity, of course, includes the literary, visual, musical, and theatrical works that are conceived, executed and performed for or presented to the public. . . . It is undoubtedly poets, sculptors, or actors who feel most uncomfortable when their work is described as research.

Midland University's "Criteria and Procedures in Promotion and Tenure Decisions" are a little more precise in deciphering the semantic code:

> In certain fields, such as art, architecture, dance, music, literature, and drama, distinguished achievement may be considered in addition to distinction in scholarly analysis involving the particular branch of creative endeavor. In evaluating artistic activity, an attempt should be made to define the candidate's merit in the light of such criteria as originality, scope, and depth of creative expression. It should be recognized that in the fine arts, distinguished performance, including conducting and directing, is evidence of a candidate's creativity.

Whatever the semantic differentials on your campus, you have to assume that in each regard the vector is the same—excellence.

THE PROCESS-PRODUCT AXIS

Just as it's valuable for you to decipher the semantic code on your campus, it will be even more important that you detect any crucial nuances among the terms "research," "scholarship," and "publication." Your task is made more difficult by the persistent logomachy that has grown up in recent years over their usage and implications.

Ernest Boyer[3] stimulated the debate in 1991 in his classic *Scholarship Reconsidered* with a plea that "scholarship" encompass the integration, application, and dissemination of knowledge as well as its discovery.

Julius Getman[4] followed with these definitions:

- publication: "academic writing that is essentially the restatement of other people's thinking";
- scholarship: "writing that introduces or challenges academic concepts, involving a debate within the academy, its concern with the organization, rationality, and persuasiveness of ideas";
- research: "the effort to discover something significant about the way the world works."

Getman even says that "a policy that promotes mere publication may actually reduce scholarship and discourage research."

Donald K. Jarvis[5] likewise holds to a distinction among publication, research, and scholarship, "even though the three terms are often used synonymously." He says "scholarship—broad knowledge of the field—is essential to good teaching, but a sound scholar may not be innovative or imaginative enough to be a good researcher; and, at least in the sciences, a number of excellent researchers either hate to write or do it poorly, and therefore are worse at publication than at research." And he adjures chairs to "clearly think through what they must have from each department candidate."

Besides deciphering that code, Mancing urges candidates for tenure to distinguish *process* from *product* in research, and he has some strong opinions on the subject:

> Professors who read to keep current with developments in their fields but do not add to existing knowledge in ways that are useful to others (generally by reading papers at scholarly meetings and publishing articles and books) are not doing research but merely maintaining their professional competence.
>
> Similarly, professors who generate grant or contract money for their universities and do not publish the results of work carried out with that support are not engaged in research.
>
> Research is not a *process* or an activity but a finished *product*. That is why publication (or, for artists, performance or showing) is crucial. The products of original research—the published books, articles, or short

stories, the concerts or exhibitions—become, in turn, teaching tools, and they extend an institution's teaching mission beyond the campus.

As you can see, it's tough to arrive at a working consensus out of all this "war of the words," and it would be a mistake for us to prescribe one, since the standards under the rubric "research" vary so widely from institution to institution and from discipline to discipline. You're on your own wherever you are!

THE "PURE" RESEARCH AXIS

However, to help you grasp your crucial research role, to set your sights high, we can suggest what a representative research university is likely to tell its applicants for tenure—a "pure" research standard widely applicable at other than liberal arts colleges and, in many cases, even there:

> You should have demonstrated the ability to conduct research that *reflects original scholarship* and *makes a contribution to knowledge.* Your competence may be manifest in one or more of these categories:
> - To conduct research with appropriate methodological techniques and vigor;
> - To conceptualize and theorize in an original way, with logical and mathematical formulation as appropriate;
> - To synthesize, criticize, and clarify extant knowledge and research;
> - To innovate in the collection or analysis of empirical data;
> - To relate research to the solution of practical problems of individuals, groups, organizations, or societies.

> Evidence of research performance and of your standing in a discipline includes:
> - Articles published or accepted for publication in scholarly or professional journals;
> - Scholarly books, monographs, chapters, bulletins, and so on;
> - Reviews and other evaluations of your publications or manuscripts;

- Citations of your work, if particularly frequent and laudatory or by distinguished scholars;
- Research awards, grants, and proposals;
- Evaluations by authorities, especially those from other major colleges and universities, in your field of specialization;
- Papers read at professional meetings, invited lectures at other colleges and universities and learned societies, invitations to participate in professional meetings, editorial positions with major journals, professional honors, awards, and consultations.

You will be expected to accompany your record of achievements and current projects with a succinct statement about your future research plans, say, over the next five years. Such standards will vary from institution to institution, of course, and from discipline to discipline, but you have to assume that the overriding criterion will be that you have achieved some level of national prominence in your field.

Does all this sound tough? It is. As Midland's guidelines make explicit:

> Attaining tenure at this institution is very difficult. Every effort is made to ensure that tenure is awarded only to already productive, hard-working faculty who give solid promise of the ability and attitude necessary for a productive *lifetime* career.

Tough as the research regimen may be, assistant professors make tenure all the time. You can, too. Your task begins with deciphering your campus research codes.

RESEARCH PREREQUISITES

INSTITUTIONAL CONTRIBUTIONS
In your quest for excellence as a productive scholar, you're not alone. Your college or university, to a greater or lesser degree, can provide a starting gate. If you didn't negotiate varieties of support before accepting your appointment, negotiate them early on.

Freedom. You have every right to expect your institution to:

- Employ a fair promotion system that ensures you a decent opportunity for steady advancement based on scholarly merit;
- Provide a climate of academic freedom—the privilege, derived from the very nature of democracy, to study, discuss, and write about facts and ideas without restrictions, other than those imposed by conscience and morality;
- Rely not upon regimentation but upon the free play of intellectual curiosity;
- Encourage professors to follow indications of truth wherever they may lead, with no thought but to gain a deeper insight into the order of the universe and its denizens;
- Remind the powers that be, in the words of a university president, Charles R. Van Hise, that "all human values are the legitimate field of sober inquiry," that "knowledge is ever incomplete, never reaching a final goal";
- Resist the siren blandishments of tainted private monies;
- Keep alive a sense of adventure, encourage imagination, and boldness of thinking, and revive enthusiasm when it flags.

You have every expectation as well that you'll be allocated clock and calendar freedom to engage in research—through considerate teaching loads, acceptable service chores, sabbaticals, summer subventions, and other means of releasing your time to pursue the most productive scholarship of which you are capable—all assuming your own time-management skills permit you always to salvage the unforgiving moment in your day.

Facilities. When he was a graduate school dean, E.B. Fred used to say all a good scientist needed was a coil of baling wire and a hank of string. That was in the 1930s. While it is true that even today a philosopher may make do with a loaf of bread and a jug of wine, for most scholars the trappings of research can be staggering—dedicated buildings, laboratories, libraries, equipment, instrumentation, computer software and hardware, research assistants, logistical and secretarial support, and so on. Colleges and universities with an expectation that their faculty produce new knowledge are constrained to provide the wherewithal, and you have every right to expect your share.

Does this mean, however, that without massive accoutrements there can be no research? Hardly. The scholar with less apparatus and fewer books can still perform that invaluable function of drawing to a magnetic mind the steel filings out of the dust of papers. The interrelationship of natural phenomena that may escape the molecular biologist peering into a high voltage electron microscope may strike an ecologist on a vacant lot. The formula hidden in the synchrotron radiation center of a physicist may become crystal-clear to a mathematician in an attic. Main currents in American thought undetected by a political scientist with a computer may be revealed by a professor of literature with personal insight.

The senior author of this manual (ACS), for example, drafted his first scholarly book on scratch paper by gaslight in a pyramidal tent while on an enforced "sabbatical" in Korea in 1952—although he polished the MS once he got back to a campus carrel. *The University and Its Publics* (New York: Harper & Brothers, 1954) won a publisher's prize, thanks in part to the perspective that tent provided.

Funds. Research costs money, and a campus is at pains to provide it. With luck your institution will have internal fluid funds you can tap in a variety of ways—released time, RAs, computer support, and so on. Your institution, too, may be of such repute that it regularly receives block grants from federal, state, and local government agencies, from philanthropic foundations and individuals, from business and industry, from regional compacts— some of which can come your way.

For example, in a national survey, department chairs reported to John W. Creswell[6] that they take the following types of actions to help junior faculty with their research agendas:

- Provide resources—start-up funds, travel money, RAs, equipment.
- Offer information about grant sources and publishing outlets.
- Adjust teaching loads and committee assignments.
- Act as a "promoter" for faculty becoming productive.
- Personally mentor faculty.

- Suggest research activities and goals and link faculty with research projects.
- Actively challenge, confront, or prod faculty, befitting the situation.

PERSONAL CONTRIBUTIONS

In the final analysis, however, the monkey is on your back to deliver. Let us repeat here that Midland University proviso, that tenure goes to hard-working faculty with ability and attitude that hold promise for a lifetime productive career.

Particularly, you'll be encouraged to attract some of your own support. While the institution will undoubtedly maintain reference directories of funding sources by discipline and topic, help in writing proposals, and a business office skilled in bookkeeping, your academic leaders know full well that it is not the dean or the president that lure the most research dollars but the creative mind of the individual professor or team of professors.

Now you can search for new grant sources using your own personal computer, thanks to a remarkable new computer program that makes the task easy and "The Chronicle Guide to Grants," updated every month by *The Chronicle of Higher Education* and *The Chronicle of Philanthropy*.

The next time you're working out the budget for a grant proposal, these guidelines might help:

- Don't pad the budget in anticipation of its being pared, which foundations seldom do. Rather, be sure the budget proposed isn't greater than the average grant size awarded by the funding body.
- Don't allow personnel salaries to approach 70% of the budget. Foundations prefer to fund programs, not personnel.
- Avoid hidden consultants' fees. Usually the only consultants you need are those who do independent evaluation at the beginning, middle, and end of a project to ensure expertise, impartiality, and accountability.
- Keep administrative overhead well below 40%—if possible. You might want to negotiate that your institution claim no administrative overhead.
- Minimize travel expenses, keeping them strictly in support of the project.[7]

NORMS OF CONDUCT

Academic freedom not being unbridled license, there are rules of the research game you are obligated to follow.

For example, any research involving human subjects will undoubtedly be constrained by policies promulgated by a campus human subjects research panel. Generally, such a panel requires that researchers give subjects enough information "for a reasonable person to make a decision" about whether to participate in a study or experiment. But now bioethicists have concluded that, while that standard may be acceptable legally, it is insufficient morally and that researchers consequently should be held to a "subjective standard" under which they must be sure that subjects understand fully that when they sign consent forms it really means they are authorizing a study or treatment or experiment, that they know what any risks are, and that they have an opportunity to say no. Increasingly, colleges and universities are holding social scientists, in addition to life scientists, to human subjects research norms. You'll want to check out the policy on your campus if you do any research involving human subjects.

Research involving animals is likewise subject to policies respecting the care and use of laboratory animals. The National Academy of Sciences issued revised guidelines in spring 1994. Your campus and you are expected to comply.

Recent news media attention focusing on incidents of campus scientists, funded with federal dollars, forming alliances with spin-off commercial ventures has campus research administrators reviewing their "conflict of interest" policies. What concerns them is the potential for divided loyalties and divided commitment to create troubling pressures on both individual researchers and their institutions. Here again, you'll want to learn the rules of your campus. For example, the University of Minnesota's tough new, comprehensive conflicts-of-interest policy runs to 94 pages of fine print. (See *Academic Leader*, June 1994)

Looking over your shoulder will be outside "police" such as the Office of Research Integrity in Washington, DC and the "watchdog" society of your discipline.

Not only should faculty be responsible for the ethical conduct of their own research, but three scholars[8] have recently proposed that those same faculty be responsible for educating their graduate students about the ethical standards and practices that should govern research, as well as assume individual and collective responsibility for the professional conduct of their colleagues, although they concede that "fear of retaliation for reporting wrongdoing is a key problem in the way that ethical problems are dealt with in universities."

NORMS OF RESEARCH

Quite apart from specific regulations governing specific situations, there are to be observed certain time-honored codes of scholarship, what Robert K. Merton and others have termed "the norms of science"—the rationale for the self-regulating autonomy that society generally grants the academic profession.

While such norms have never been carved in stone and indeed have been questioned as inapplicable to all disciplines, four have achieved a good deal of consensus:

Universalism. Research findings must be assessed on the basis of scientific merit rather than on such criteria as race, sex, nationality, class, geography, personal qualities, or political correctness. Scientific careers should be based on merit, not on extraneous factors.

Community. Research findings must be made public, because such findings are the property of the research community. However, the scholar should receive recognition by the scientific community for his or her contribution.

Disinterestedness. Research should not be conducted for the primary objective of receiving recognition from one's colleagues or gaining prestige and monetary rewards from the lay community. In other words, productive scholarship for the primary purpose of advancing knowledge is the motive of the professional scholar.

Organized skepticism. No knowledge claim or research finding should be accepted without an assessment based on empirical and logical criteria. Hence, professionals should hold a critical stance toward scholarly contributions, as in the peer review mechanism of scholarly journals.

The international community of scholars presumably rewards colleagues who adhere to these norms and sanctions those who deviate. While the norms may appear clear, application in particular cases can be murky, so when in doubt consult your department chair.

Or you can refer to Steve M. Cahn, Ed., *Morality, Responsibility, and the University* (Philadelphia: Temple University Press, 1991).

NORMS OF NEWS MEDIA RELATIONS

Be wary of that rarity, but nonetheless painful person, who occasionally shows up. Be on your guard against 'firsts,' 'seven-day wonders,' 'cure-alls,' and 'nature faking.' Watch out for the person trying to beat out his competitors by seeking a public announcement on the basis of half-baked data. Recognize the charlatan who's out only to gain the attention of his or her employer and the visibility that can help win awards.

You think that is a warning to scholars to be on guard against unscrupulous representatives of the news media? Guess again. That quote is from a recently published text, *Interpreting Public Issues,* by Robert J. Griffin, *et al* (Ames: Iowa State University Press, 1991) warning college and university journalism students to be wary of the occasional buccaneer in campus laboratory or library who is more willing to seek headlines than to advance scholarship.

How do you establish your *bona fides* as a reputable scholar with your peers and at the same time with an increasingly sophisticated press? By following these generic canons of news media relations (unless they're at variance with the standard operating procedures on your campus):

1. Make your first public announcement of a major research finding through a paper in a refereed journal or in an invited presentation to an appropriate learned society—thereby both sharing your scholarship initially with fellow scholars and acquiring the cachet of peer review.

2. Arrange with your campus news service in advance for simultaneous media release via a prepared account which you check for accuracy and which the news service then makes available to all local, regional, and national outlets at a single time.

3. If they're interested, arrange for collaborative release with the public information personnel of the funding agency and the learned society.

4. If you've generated friendly relations with a particular reporter, tip him or her off that such and such a release is forthcoming, offer to provide additional background information,

but don't violate the news service release date by giving your friend a "scoop."

5. Once the report of your finding is in the public domain, feel free to make yourself available to the news media or even to initiate clarifying reports for popular consumption.

How this protocol plays out in actual practice was well illustrated by the way the organizations involved handled the release of a big story in spring 1992—the announcement that scientists had seemed to confirm the "big bang" theory of how the universe was created, based on research funded by the National Aeronautical and Space Agency:

Professor George Smoot of the University of California, Berkeley, the team leader, touched off the announcement by reading a paper at a meeting of the American Physical Society in Washington, DC. NASA public relations personnel staged a follow-up press conference at which UC-Berkeley/APS/NASA press releases were distributed. The next day, team members appeared on all major TV network newscasts, which were then followed by news analysis features in upcoming Sunday newspapers and weekly newsmagazines.

By adhering to such a responsible strategy of media relations, scholars help the public learn what their tax dollars are buying and at the same time avoid any charges of self-aggrandizement.

MAKING PEACE WITH THE PEERAGE

Perhaps one of the most vexing problems for new recruits engaging in research in academe is achieving a state of intellectual equilibrium in the face of the beating that research is taking in both the public and the professional literature on higher education today, often focused on a charge that teaching and research are not only incompatible but mutually debilitating.

If it's any consolation, the debate is not new. It can be traced at least as far back as to the 1850s and John Henry Newman, who argued in a series of lectures published as *The Idea of the University* that research, like theology, had no place in the university, which was to be devoted to undergraduate and non-professional education. On the other hand, the social theorist Thorstein Veblen, whose ideas about the American university took shape at Chicago in the 1890s, asserted in 1918 in his *The Higher Learning in America* that, at most, "the work of teaching properly belongs in the university only because and so far as it incites and facilitates the university's main work of inquiry."

Scarcely a decade has gone by since but what somebody has said something like "the university's central function of undergraduate instruction has gone into partial eclipse" because of "the growth of the graduate school with its overweening demand for productive scholarship on the part of professors at the expense of an honest devotion to classroom performance."

SCHOLARS FOR THE NEGATIVE

But the 1990s have seen a dramatic rise in the scope and depth of the vitriol, to the great discomfort of assistant professors caught in the travail. It may have started when Page Smith, noted American historian and emeritus provost at the University of California, Santa Cruz, in his 1990 book, *Killing the Spirit: Higher Education in America,* took aim at a "highly questionable and blatantly unfair" faculty reward system that exalts the over-specialized, "worthless" research that "robs the student...of the thoughtful and considerate attention of a teacher . . . unequivocally devoted to teaching."

In 1991 came Ernest K. Boyer, president of the Carnegie Foundation for the Advancement of Teaching, in his landmark book, *Scholarship Reconsidered: Priorities of the Professoriate,* charging professors with being unwilling to assume responsibility for lack in attention to teaching problems in their fields, a call for them to redefine scholarship to include "the integration, application, and teaching" of knowledge as well as its "discovery" (read "research"), and a plea that campus administrators thereby reform the faculty reward system.

Then in 1992 came more denizens of academe taking up the cudgel:

- George H. Douglas, professor of English at the University of Illinois, who is mad as hell and not going to take any more the deflowering of college and university undergraduate education, in his book, *Education Without Impact: How Our Universities Are Failing the Young,* holding up for particular calumny the large land-grant research university, with its "Mandarin" professors of science ensconced in their disciplinary castles, the "Druid" professors of the humanities engaged in assaults on "the canon," its administrators concerned only with "department store productivity," its undergraduate students stuck on assorted "conveyor belt" curricula, with a common core of liberal understanding long since atrophied.

- University of California, San Diego Chancellor Richard C. Atkinson and his anthropology colleague Donald Turin, in the May/June *Change:* "The relative over-valuation of research has done more than separate undergraduates and faculty—it has estranged them. . . .The situation breeds cynicism, which students take with them upon leaving the university. . . .Public antipathy toward academe is not the naive hostility of the uneducated that universities should fear; it is the reprisal of their own graduates."

- Bryan Barnett, a Rutgers academic-program administrator, contending in a June 3, 1992 Chronicle of Higher Education "Point of View" essay headlined "Teaching and Research Are Incompatible" that "a genuinely independent reassessment of the undergraduate curriculum is desperately needed" but that such can be accomplished "only if teaching resources are not tied to a pre-existing research agenda determined by considerations, such as the availability of grant money, that are extraneous to students' needs."

- Roger Bowen, professor of government at Colby College, in an "Opinion" essay in the June 10, 1992 *Chronicle of Higher Education* confessing that "a college that no longer puts teaching first pays a high price for its exalted reputation" when it "demeans one of the most important qualities that defines a small liberal-arts college—a faculty committed primarily to teaching—by forcibly recasting its faculty in the image of those at large research institutions."

- Eight scholars[9] blame the problem on the graduate school itself, because "the on-the-job activities of new faculty members call for knowledge and skills not inherent to the standard Ph.D. program." They want those graduate schools "to better prepare college teachers, to educate the faculty of the future, to provide diverse voices in the academy, and to incorporate new forms of disciplinary integration, professorial practice, and pedagogical scholarship into graduate programs."

- And the unkindest cut of all—the anti-research lobby offering a bit of research on its side. Studying the ratings of all 3,000 students of all 200 faculty in all courses over a three-year span in a four-year residential institution, Bryant College in Smithfield, RI, three staff persons[10] report that publishing faculty rate lower student evaluations of their teaching effectiveness than do non-publishing faculty, and part-time faculty are at least as effective in the classroom as full-time faculty. Their conclusion: "Faculty who appear less concerned about the need to publish . . . may be devoting more time and attention to preparation for teaching and to instruction."

Nor has the calumny tapered off in the past few years. If anything, it has become more sophisticated. For example, in the January-February 1994 issue of the *Journal of Higher Education,* two distinguished higher education scholars at the universities of Stanford and Pennsylvania use some arcane mathematical analyses of departmental decision-making on class sizes and teaching loads to document that what they call an "academic ratchet" is driving up tuition and driving down the caliber of undergraduate education.

William F. Massey and Robert Zemsky explain the operation of the ratchet this way: When one member of a department wins a reduced teaching load because of a research grant, that teaching load becomes a new norm against which all members of the department measure their own required commitments to teaching. The net results are predictable:

First, there has been a "deconstructing" of the undergraduate curriculum over the last two decades that has meant fewer required courses and less of an ordered course sequence, leaving students at sea. Second, individual faculty members are loosening their institutional ties and undergraduate teaching responsibilities in order to pursue research, with its personal and financial rewards. Massey and Zemsky offer mathematical models to prove their point that "students are paying more for less."

SCHOLARS FOR THE AFFIRMATIVE

While they tend not to be so high-pitched, research has its voices in strong support.

- One of them, Robert A. McCaughey,[11] professor of history and dean of the faculty at Barnard College, uses research to hold that research and teaching can coexist. Surveying the scholarly activities of faculty members at two dozen selective liberal-arts colleges, he found that "the marriage of teaching and research is alive and well" because senior professors who were identified by external reviewers as being among the college's most active scholars were more likely to be ranked (by deans) as among the most effective teachers than were senior professors with little or no scholarly record. If faculty members in sufficient numbers are both effective teachers and productive scholars (on liberal-arts campuses), there would seem to be no inherent incompatibility in the teaching-research relationship.

- One of the more cogent defenders of the faith is Peter Balbert,[12] professor and chair, English, Trinity University:

    There is a legitimate professional need for excellent research from all faculty in the university . . . Publication is that privately undertaken and publicly submitted enterprise of an academic that in a major way further legitimizes his right to teach in front of a university classroom for the period of tenure. . . . The species of 'good teacher-no research' raises questions about that faculty member's real authority, engagement, and educational vision. . . . Put simply, the research imperative is not an arbitrary or digressive obligation, but an integral, ongoing call for renewal that all faculty must consider part of their inheritance. It requires all teacher-scholars to willingly test a basic aspect of their competency not only before their generally accepting, supportive students, but also in the more competitive crucible presided over by their vigorously judgmental peers.

- Perhaps somewhat surprisingly, as ringing a defense of the inextricable teamwork between teaching and research is offered by the senior editor of *Community College Week*. Writes Robert P. Pedersen:[13]

    To be actively engaged in the work of a discipline, to publish regularly, and to present at disciplinary conferences is not a sign of 'divided' loyalties. . . . Within the academic disciplines, good teaching is animated and informed by scholarship. As an active participant in scholarly research, an instructor is not only specially equipped to awaken students to the rich intellectual heritage conveyed through the academic disciplines, but to convey as well the dynamic nature of those disciplines. Through his or her own scholarly work, the faculty member comes to know first hand the debate by which every discipline continuously reassesses its assumptions, its methods, and its canon, and in the process avoids the real danger of disengagement from the dynamic nature of the disciplines. . . . Old stereotypes notwithstanding, an interest in research and publication is not antithetical to a concern for student learning or devotion to teaching, but reflects a love for a discipline that inspires teachers to share that discipline with generations of students.

- Perhaps somewhat facetiously, Milton Greenberg,[14] former provost and now professor of government at American University, says the whole argument is irrelevant because "we all know that, except for faculty members at a thin slice of elite institutions, the amount of research and publication is exaggerated!"

THE UPSHOT

What is an assistant professor to make of all this give-and-take?

One approach is to adopt the position of Timothy D. Johnson,[15] professor of psychology and associate dean of the College of Arts and Sciences at the University of North Carolina-Greensboro. He argues that the nature of the debate depends on the level of teaching and research: "There is a natural compatibility between cutting-edge research and the education of graduate students and advanced undergraduates. . . . There is much less compatibility between cutting-edge research and the kind of teaching required in a first-year introductory course." So, he argues, we need two kinds of teacher-scholars.

Johnson goes on to point out the debate depends, too, on individual proclivities:

Professional advancement in almost all the disciplines is best ensured by heavy investment in the scholarship of discovery, requiring a focus on one or a very few narrowly defined problems. Some people are quite content with this state of affairs, but others find the narrow focus encouraged by academic specialization to be limiting and confining. So, he says, an individual professor's type of scholarship should vary with the type of teaching a professor chooses.

Let's face it, an assistant professor may not be at liberty to choose!

What seems inescapable is the fact that whenever and wherever it occurs, the research *vs.* teaching debate is the stuff of the continual assessment and reassessment that always enliven and inspire American higher education, to keep it on its toes as it seeks to be both responsible for great academic traditions and responsive to changing public needs. It is your great privilege to become a part of that continual sifting and winnowing.

Undoubtedly you'll come across some peers who are natural-born teachers and who bridle at the requirement that they do research. And you'll meet other peers who fight the problem of teaching obligations eating into their research time. A healthy way to make peace with your peerage is to try to see that, in a very fundamental sense, teaching and research can be mutually supportive, even though they may be carried out by different actions under different forms of motivation. Your teaching can be kept creative by means of scholarship; your scholarship gains impetus from the instructional demands of your students. Which is precisely why campuses are home to both—and why you're doing what you're doing.

Perhaps Jaroslav Pelikan, author of *Scholarship and Its Survival,* has it about right. While he holds that teaching and research belong together, he recognizes that the combination "is not always for anyone, not at all for everyone, not in the same proportion for every university"—and, he might have added, not at all times in an individual professor's career.

In Midland University's department of botany and applied ecology, Assistant Professor A. Wilmot Campion is by no means immune from making personal peace with the teaching *vs.* research logorrhea. For what it's worth, his approach has gone something like this:

> The formal promotion-and-tenure guidelines and informal advice from my mentor make it perfectly clear that I'm certainly expected to produce a very good record of published research during my probationary period, along with laudable performance as undergraduate and

graduate teacher, and acceptable service as a campus and community citizen—all in keeping with departmental and institutional missions. I'm confident I can make the three responsibilities more mutually supportive than competitive. For example, my research can feed directly into my grad seminar as a role model, keep my survey course fresh, and lead to public service assignments. In turn, provocative classroom questions from students and from professionals in the field can stimulate my research, and service assignments in turn can feed back into both teaching and research. If I can pull off a fruitful balance among my three tasks, I believe that can be my best answer to any fancied dichotomy among the three. To use a good botanical term, I see the three as naturally "symbiotic."

TUNING UP FOR RESEARCH

Before launching any research effort, consider putting down on paper a tentative objective and scheme of maneuver. Such an exercise will markedly clarify your thoughts about your research question and the feasibility of answering it—research design, scope, needed evidence, and so on. A written plan will also give you a "talking paper" for bouncing your idea off colleagues.

A WORKING OUTLINE

Your schema might contain the following elements, looking ahead to the research grant proposal you'll probably be writing:

Title. A brief, clear, specific designation of the subject of the research, providing a concrete idea what the project is all about.

Content and Justification. You conduct research in either a theoretical or conceptual setting, as you know. Describe briefly the relationship of your area of inquiry to broad disciplinary issues. For example, a focused study of "damages" in civil libel is part of the larger context of First Amendment issues which intrigue mass communication scholars, just as a study of mass media political content may be in context of economic structure, of democratic political theory, or of the psychology of persuasion. Similarly, a study of the effect of "clean" fencerows on the gray and fox squirrel population in Michigan farmlands is an aspect of the larger issue of the ecology of the wild squirrel in a modern agricultural environment.

The justification for a piece of research is the knowledge it contributes to the context. The research may fill a gap in existing knowledge, draw out and test fresh inferences from existing theory, propose and test a new theoretical position, revise conventional wisdom, solve a significant practical problem.

In general, remember, research answers questions about relationships and yields information not previously known; research is not just a compilation of data.

Literature Review. Summarize and evaluate pertinent previous research. (Note *"pertinent"*; yours is not to compile an exhaustive disciplinary bibliography.)

Objective. Compose a clear, complete, and logically arranged statement of your specific objectives, featuring the major question(s) to be answered or hypotheses to be tested.

Procedure. Explain your design, your methods, and the data to be gathered—all of which must obviously relate to your objectives. Pay attention to these components: sources of evidence and how available; definitions of the concepts you're employing; any special problems of design and analysis you foresee and how you propose to assail them.

Calendar. Make a realistic estimate of the dates for completing the various phases of your project.

Cost. How much will your project cost? Who will pay for it?

Outline of Report. To the extent you can at this stage of the game, draft clear versions of the section headings in any eventuating report. Contemplate a minimum of four chapters: introduction, methods, findings, conclusions.

Expected Products. Papers to be submitted to refereed journals, improved procedures, applied policies.

Executive Summary. A once-over-lightly capsule statement.

Topics and their order in any such research plan can vary, of course, with the nature of your discipline and your specific subject matter. Don't let a format constrain you; after all, this is only a training exercise. But if you put your thoughts on paper, it will give you practice toward what may well be a necessity—writing a request to a funding source for a subvention.

A GRANT-GETTING STRATEGY

There's another reason for not getting too tied too fast to a particular research schema because in any granting agency there's a person who's just as interested as you are in funding a successful enterprise and who will actually help you formulate a proposal that will best meet your needs—and the goals of the agency.

Listen to these words from two scientific program staff officers at the National Institutes of Health:[16]

> Without a doubt, all scientists funded by the NIH are fully aware of the role of the Scientific Review Administrator in the review of the grant applications. ... However, few scientists are fully aware of the role of the Scientific Program Staff both before and after the review of their grant, ...how this important voice on the other end of the phone plays an invaluable role for the research scientist.

The voice on the other end of the phone, as a Scientific Program Officer, has far-reaching impact on NIH-funded science because it is the direct responsiblity of the Program staff to interest themselves in a scientist's research findings, their grant applications, and their grant problems. For this reason, it is of unquestionable benefit for a scientist interested in a grant award from an NIH Institute to contact the Scientific Program Staff.

Every such granting agency—be it government, foundation, or industry—has such a person. Leon Neuenschwander,[17] associate dean for research at the University of Idaho, has made a science of what he calls "playing the inside game" with the person "on the other end of the phone."

Neuenschwander has these "bottom line" precepts: "People give to people," and "Most grant proposals are funded before they're ever written." You may find valuable his six principles of "jump starting your grant-winning potential":

1. Employ interpersonal skills. Become genuinely interested in the organization and its people from whom you seek funds, particularly the person who can authorize check-writing.

2. Know human nature. People will find a way to help you if they believe it will be of value in meeting their goals.

3. Engage in networking. Establish a reputation in your area of expertise.

4. Inform, involve, respond. Make people feel important by asking their advice. Create a forum with like-minded scholars and respond quickly to their ideas.

5. Ignore myths about grants: "There's no money in my field."

6. Tailor your proposal to the specific needs of your sponsor without jeopardizing your own independence of action.

Using such a strategy, Neuenschwander changed a College of Forestry, Wildlife, and Range Science proposal success rate from 22% to 80% and an annual "take" in outside grants from $1.2 million to $4.5 million.

You may find his person-to-person approach equally effective.

DIFFERENT DISCIPLINARY CONCERNS

Generalizing about research is tough because of the inherent differences in viewpoint between the broad fields of the sciences on the one hand and the humanities on the other, with social studies falling somewhere in between, as Donald K. Jarvis[18] has so clearly delineated. The sciences progress primarily by each researcher studying a small part of the cutting edge of the discipline, often in collaboration with a team. Reports of research will be confirmed or superseded by other reports or perhaps even be rendered meaningless by a paradigm shift. On the other hand, in the humanities a small number of old classics is more likely to be valued than recent works, and the most damning judgment is to call a piece "ephemeral." For scientists, ephemerality is in a sense a norm.

A second difference is that specialization plays a much smaller role for humanists. The average scientist can be respected for good work within very narrow parameters, but practicing humanists are expected to compare and contrast widely disparate phenomena. They are expected to integrate more than analyze.

A third difference is that humanists tend not to be confident about the concept of progress in their disciplines, that being "the thinking of the human race." Is today's writing more moving than that of Homer or Shakespeare? Is modern criticism more illuminating than Aristotle? It is hard, however, to find scientists who disagree that their research is more advanced now than it was at almost any time past. After all, they've pretty much taken care of the issue of the origin of species, the cause of cystic fibrosis, and the ecology of the ladyslipper.

Given these gross distinctions, here we want to focus attention on some of the concerns assistant professors will face in particular disciplines.

IN ARTS AND LETTERS

As we've indicated, many arts and letters faculty don't really fit the laboratory or empirical investigation paradigm, so promotion-to-tenure criteria need to be adjusted accordingly.

Here's how one university lists such criteria:

> Faculty members who excel in artistic activities engage in creative work that is appropriate to their area of specialization and is respected by their colleagues and peers, both within and without the university. They disseminate the results of their work through means appropriate to their specialty, such as publications, lectures, performances, and exhibits; and by participation in appropriate technical, professional, and scholarly societies that reflect their artistic reputations. They are aware of new developments and strive to broaden and deepen their knowledge and understanding of their specialties and, where relevant, related fields.

That isn't exactly a specific road map, but it provides some guidance.

Actually, arts and letters faculty can have certain advantages:

First, at least in the case of the languages, society's new fixation on the global marketplace has vaulted foreign language departments into a prominence not enjoyed since the Sputnik era. Ditto for area studies consortia.

Second, the emergence of the National Endowment for the Humanities has given arts and letters a federal government cachet which, while it's nowhere near the scope of the NIH and the NSF, has at least demonstrated a public commitment institutions can't ignore.

Third, as Derek Bok, emeritus president of Harvard, has pointed out, the arts and letters fit a time-honored history of higher education—as the custodian of the preservation and enhancement of culture. This tradition explains "why most universities will struggle to maintain excellent programs in French literature" while allowing some plebeian pursuits to languish.

Fourth, many arts and letters departments have a natural constituency in the form of the lovers of art, dance, drama, music, and literature in their institution's patron community. In many cities across the country, the college or university is the prime purveyor of culture through exhibits, plays, concerts, and readings, and hence local aficionados of arts and letters display a very proprietary and potent interest in the health and long life of their professors.

So if you're an arts and letters assistant professor, you've got a lot going for you even in a research environment. But there's a flip side.

A university president once said, "It is not the purpose of a university to question carelessly or disturb recklessly the current traditions, customs, or morals."

But that was in 1904. Today his strictures are exactly what arts and letters professors are bidden to do by the very nature of their calling. As French professor and former Yale dean Georges May pointed out recently, "There are no ivory walls to our tower. The world outside the university is divided, and that division is reflected on campuses." Consequently, no campus activity can give an institution's president so many public relations headaches as a "lascivious" art exhibit, a "scandalous" play, a "heavy metal" concert, or a "politically unacceptable" poet.

Yes, you do live dangerously as an arts and letters professor—unless you're fortunate to be on a campus that extends you the same measure of academic freedom enjoyed by its biochemists.

But who ever said life should be fair?

It has only been in the last decade or so that institutions have recognized that all faculty, not just those in the "hard" sciences, need start-up funds for research. A new biochemist assistant professor might require hundreds of thousands to get a lab started, but a comp lit professor needs only a word processor, library acquisitions, and some travel money. But while the new comp lit faculty member's needs require less money, the biochemist is more likely to get the funds. Why? The biochemist will in all probability replenish the money someday out of grant overhead, but it's unlikely the comp lit professor can. So it behooves the humanist assistant professor to bargain hard before even signing on, because the chances may be slim of getting that computer later on.

IN THE SOCIAL SCIENCES

Basic vs. Applied. Research in the social sciences is often deeply involved in the ordering of public values and public goals—in education, in crime prevention, in health care, and so on. Some people like to say such a role is either too controversial or too nonacademic.

Unlike natural scientists, whose objectivity as scholars is not often questioned, social scientists are often criticized for displaying greater subjectivity and hence less scientific rigor. The critics claim that the tendency of social scientists to compromise objectivity is a natural byproduct of their goal of social reform, that the very desire to produce useful knowledge impairs the ability to approach research "scientifically."

Rather than seemingly being led astray through utilitarian investigations—instead of being willing to try to help reshape society—some social scientists feel safe only in studying it, eschewing any concern for the political or ideological environment. It is on unexamined concepts that these experts depend for their professional lives. Asked to render a pragmatic judgment on an issue, they march right up to the moment of decision and then turn and run. Yet the long-term value of social science research is likely to rest quite heavily on the ability of scholars to recognize and analyze the societal implications of their investigations, other scholars contend.

Some social scientists as well, adept at building theoretical models, tend to regard with some scorn the applied researches that constituent agencies seek. Preferring fundamental questions and gross problems universal in scope, they shun what they call "manhole counting" or "brush-fire fighting." Administrators are caught between their responsibilities to their supporting publics and their esteem for the new basic researchers they've fought so hard to recruit.

Stung by the charge that social science research has little practical value, other social scientists are willing to go into the streets with the aim of improving the utility of their product.

For example, the flames had scarcely died down from the Los Angeles riots before an emeritus professor of urban planning[19] on the spot at UCLA was challenging his younger colleagues in the social sciences to project their scholarly skills and resources into the arena of public debate, to "become engaged with moral issues" rather than worry so much about "compromising the conventions of objectivity."

At the same time in the spring of 1992, Harvard President Emeritus Derek Bok[20] was telling campus social scientists, "We must associate ourselves more prominently with solving the social problems that concern Americans the most" if institutions of higher education are to "regain public confidence."

Sociologist Theda Skocpol[21] thinks part of the problem is that, "for the most part, contemporary experts in the social sciences spend their time talking to—and for—one another, giving too little thought to building political coalitions and expanding electoral support" that are necessary to convert theories into public policy.

Cosmopolitan vs. Community. Those social scientists willing to perform research that "makes a difference now" increasingly are cosmopolitan rather than community-oriented. To professors contemplating advancing their careers on a world stage, local and state research has to some extent gone out of style. As one department chair recently put it, "The question is now, not how do you get colleagues out of their ivory towers, but how do you keep them at home?"

In short, in the social sciences a gulf is increasingly appearing between global, theory-oriented and generic, problem-oriented studies—a dichotomy that may make career-building difficult for new assistant professors. If you are one such, assess carefully the tilt in your department and its impact on the reward system you're operating under. Recognizing the problem may be at least part of the solution.

Interdisciplinary vs. Departmental. Whereas the social sciences today are an assortment of disciplines and sub-disciplines, once upon a time there was only "political economy." Yet today there continue to be scholars in the social sciences who see modern habits of thought and institutional configurations inadequate to address real-world problems that don't come packaged along departmental lines. However, coordinating the efforts of researchers from diverse fields runs hard up against the inertia of a departmentally based structure of promotions and rewards. Promising as interdisciplinary studies may be, grass-roots social science faculty and administrators tend to be biased against extra-departmental research that demands a reallocation of power and resources.[22]

Here again, junior faculty members must tread circumspectly. If you believe that individuals working within a disciplinary setting are handcuffed by narrow intellectual frameworks that militate against producing research attuned to contemporary social problems, check signals before you shove off all alone onto an interdisciplinary sea.

"No Study Is Immune to Criticism". Another pervasive problem for new social science researchers lies in the simple fact that the methods and results of their research can closely resemble conventional wisdom and hence be subject to popular trashing.

As higher education researcher Alexander Astin writes:[2]

> Finding flaws in any piece of social science research is like shooting fish in a barrel. Thus decision makers who want to undermine the results of a particular study can always find an expert to argue that the results can't be trusted because of deficiencies in the research method, the variables, or the sampling. No study is immune to criticism.

When faced with such flak, the scholar can seek out an honest and meaningful appraisal that would "try to assess whether, and by how much, the results may have been distorted by the defects, and what the odds were that the key findings and conclusions would be different if the defects could be remedied."

Young social science researchers can take heart from Astin's belief that in a non-adversarial climate, when studies are used objectively to inform planning and policy making, "social science research can improve our understanding of how institutions function, suggest alternatives to existing policies, and help administrators anticipate the likely consequences of alternative courses of action."

IN EXTENSION/CLINICAL

To what level of productive scholarship do you hold a young assistant professor with an extension appointment? Institutions have been wrestling with that question for years.

As a partial answer, some institutions have created extension divisions, outreach faculties, colleges of continuing education, or similar instrumentalities with more or less autonomous tenure criteria which do not include conventional research performance at all, in effect running the risk of housing what some might view as a sort of second-class citizenry.

Land-grant universities, on the other hand, habitually employ integrated departments, particularly in agriculture, in which the person with an extension appointment is a full-fledged member, cheek by jowl with regular teaching/research colleagues, subject technically to regular promotional criteria. In actual practice, however, such departments have come to recognize the peculiar nature of extension work and hence weigh the attainments of an extension appointee with custom scales.

In the words of one such document:

> Faculty with extension appointments have significant responsibilities to utilize their professional expertise to disseminate information outside of the traditional faculty-student interactions to help improve the knowledge and skills of their clientele or the environment in which their clientele live and work.

Or another:

> In evaluating the record of candidates with extension responsibilities, the evidence must show that the candidate's work has significantly contributed to the translation and dissemination of the results of scholarly inquiry in his or her discipline to the benefit of society, and that this work has extended the knowledge base of the university to the citizens of the state.

The fact that the chair of an integrated department himself or herself is paid in part with extension monies affords some assurance that the department will factor in specialized extension requirements in arriving at tenure decisions.

If you're one of those assistant professors with a partial or full extension appointment, make doubly sure that the criteria for

promotion against which you'll be measured are clearly stated—
and then hope that any resident professors in your institution's
quality-control structure understand and appreciate the outreach
mission.

A clinical assistant professor in a medical school is in much the
same boat as an extension assistant professor in a college of
agriculture—by what promotional criteria will he or she be measured? A solution: besides consulting all available sources of essential guidance, seek out a helpful mentor.

IN SCIENCE AND ENGINEERING

While the research paradigm fits neatly if you're an appointee in a
science or engineering department, you nonetheless have some
special research concerns that warrant attention.

Mushrooming Fields of Inquiry. While the humanities and
social sciences are by no means static fields of scholarship, at any
given moment they are probably not so explosive as the physical
and biological sciences and their engineering applications. For
example, rapidly growing, important areas of biology include neu-
roscience, cell biology, immunology, developmental biology,
biotechnology, sustainable agriculture, and biological aspects of
environmental impact remediation. Keeping an individual young
professor—and an institution—at the growing edge of such mushrooming fields of inquiry calls for more than ordinary alertness,
particularly when traditional department lines may work to stifle
the interdisciplinary teamwork that is often essential to progress
in research in areas of study that don't fit neatly into existing
organizational patterns.

If you're in a research area that transcends current configurations, you might start early to push for facilities that could bring
together groups with related research missions and provide a focal
point for coordinated investigations. Don't ever assume that a
dean or provost who dates from another generation is necessarily
on top of all the possibilities inherent in interdisciplinary configurations. And don't assume that he or she will necessarily defend
rigid campus walls and yesterday's programs when confronted
with documentation of emerging needs.

For example, *alter ego* Bill Campion in the Midland University
department of botany and applied ecology is at least as apt to find

willing research collaborators in Midland's School of Forestry and Environmental Studies as in his home department. But working out joint funding and facilities may take some fancy footwork in tune with Midland's current stance *vis-à-vis* interdisciplinary research programs in emerging fields of investigation.

All this exciting activity in science and engineering research may cause Bill and you to rethink your position on SCIENCE in capital letters. Do you believe that *knower* and *known* are separated, that *theories* are distinct from *facts* and *facts* from *values*? That subjectivity plays no part in the gathering of objective knowledge? That natural laws are inferred from experience, involving confirmation and verification—scientific empiricism? Or do you concede that sociological, historical, economic, and philosophical points of view impact on you and other researchers, that we cannot identify *science* with *truth*, for we think that both Newton's and Einstein's theories belong to science, but they cannot both be true, and they may be false?[24]

It is, indeed, a conundrum. Just so you realize that fact and to your own self be true.

Patenting Procedures. So you believe you may have a patentable idea. What do you do?

The first step is to determine whether the idea may in fact be patentable (as opposed to being a copyrightable piece of software or literary, musical, or artistic expression).

There are three types of patents: utility, design, and plant. Ordinarily you'll be concerned with the first, utility patents.

To be considered for a utility patent, an invention must be a machine, a process, a composition of matter, or a manufacture. Further, the invention must be useful, new, and non-obvious. And, of course, the person who seeks a patent must be the inventor; nobody but the inventor can apply for a patent.

Patent lawyers sometimes refer to a technical field as an "art." Let's say your contribution to an art seems to meet the basic tests we've just outlined. The next question: do you own this piece of what is called "intellectual property"?

The inventor must be the applicant for a patent but may be obligated to hand it over to someone else. Your college or university policy may state that all rights to a faculty member's discovery reside with the institution. If federal funds supported the research, the government reserves certain rights. Or a non-government funder of the research involved—industry or foundation—may have a contract reserving rights to any discovery. Also, one or more colleagues or graduate assistants may have a partial claim as joint inventors.

But if you or a group of joint inventors do in fact own an invention free and clear, what are your options?

- You can simply give it away to the world by publishing the idea and making no attempt to patent it. But then you lose control of its application.
- You can turn entrepreneur and attempt to commercialize the idea. But that takes forms of business acumen and amounts of venture capital ordinarily beyond the reach of scholars.
- For a share of any royalties to be earned, you can seek the services of your institution's in-house patent management office, or of one of the national corporations that make patent management their business.

A frequent question is this: if my idea is of such great potential value, do I risk losing it to the public domain via publication in a scholarly journal? And publication is vital. Unless you want to violate that sacred code of scientific conduct—the norm of commonality—you are absolutely obliged to share your concept with the world of scholarship. To do otherwise would seriously tar your reputation.

Fortunately, sharing an idea via publication need not mean allowing just anyone to commercialize it. By being prompt, you can both publish your research and seek a patent. Simultaneously with submitting your paper for publication, arrange to apply for a patent. In a normal time-frame, a patent application can be written by an attorney and filed before the journal article comes out. To preserve patent rights overseas, it's usually necessary to file a U.S. application before first public divulgation of the invention. The requirement is often inflexible. U.S. patent law is more generous: you have a one-year grace period after publication in which to file a patent application.

Now if all this sounds complicated and enervating, it is. Few subjects are so arcane as patent law and management. So the best advice we can give you is: see a good patent attorney as early as possible. Most campuses will have at least one in house or on call.

Research Record-Keeping. If only to buttress a patent claim, it behooves any scholar to follow commonsense rules of record-keeping. A researcher's success in obtaining and defending a patent may depend as much on how carefully he or she has kept a research notebook as on how original and patentable the discovery. And even if a patent isn't in the picture, meticulous record-keeping is simply good scholarly practice.

So you should follow these basic mechanics:

- Record all research in a bound notebook to demonstrate that pages have not been added, subtracted, or substituted.
- Leave no blank spaces on a finished page; draw an "X" through any unused portion to prevent adding later entries.
- Number and date every page; begin each day's work on a new page.
- Use pen, not pencil; use the same pen throughout the day.
- To correct an old entry, enter the correction on the current day's page, citing the earlier page and noting why the original record required change.
- To verify the legitimacy of data, have your notebooks witnessed on a regular basis by an impartial party, such as a colleague who can understand but is not participating in your work: have the reviewer sign off in writing. This is vital.

To the basic rules, add these refinements:

- Record events as they happen, not as they are recalled.
- Record what you are thinking as well as what you are doing; a researcher can spend months on experiments, but if her or his notebook fails to indicate awareness of eventual potential, that person may have a hard time later answering challenges to the prior ownership of the resulting discovery.
- Arrange with someone else to witness and archive the work of your graduate students or lab assistants.
- Archive your own work by having it photocopied, the copies stamped "received" with a date and locked in a department file cabinet not accessible to you.

- Lock your notebook up at the end of the day in a fireproof cabinet.
- Collect the notebooks of graduate students or temporary workers when their terms are up; they may keep photocopies.
- If you keep your research records on a computer, use a "time stamping" program that automatically dates all entries into the system and would detect any late entries into already complete work.

There is no precedent in patent case law where computer-based data have been used to establish priority of a claim; hence there's no proven substitute yet for a permanently bound, handwritten research notebook. And that notebook should be more than a repository of static data with no hint of your evolving thoughts that are driving the research.

Quite apart from anticipating a patent matter, keeping an articulate notebook provides a useful personal reference, helps maintain workplace continuity when a long-term project passes from one lab assistant to another, provides evidence of where your ideas came from, documents compliance with a research grant, and facilitates responding to any allegations of scientific fraud.

In the final analysis a professional notebook is the quintessential hallmark of the careful scholar.

(You can find a very good review of research notebook practices in *Writing the Laboratory Notebook* by Howard M. Kanare, American Chemical Society, 1985. The Society also offers a 1990 free pamphlet, "Electronic Record-Keeping: Cautions and Pitfalls." The Society address: 1155 16th Street, NW, Washington DC 20036.)

The University-Industry Relations Quandary. Whether corporate funds inspire or stifle the free flow of ideas in academe is a perennial topic of debate. Put more personally, should you participate in any short-term applied research alliances with industry?

Let's listen to some of the voices in contention as they sounded off in the July/August 1992 issue of *Academe*:

Two sociologists were vigorous in opposing campus-commerce partnership: "Partnerships between universities and corporations bring on intrusive focus on the bottom line," nudging a campus "closer to the model of a cost-effective business operation in which producing and disseminating knowledge is efficiently targeted to specific markets and clientele," and in which "traditional bodies like departments, faculty councils, and senates become less and less important in setting the university's real academic priorities."

But a political science professor said that, far from distracting higher education, business leaders are finding traditional liberal arts values to be very much in keeping with changing workforce needs. And a doctor concluded that business has been benign in "extending managerial habits to the administration of the natural sciences in universities."

The beat went on in the Sept. 16, 1992, issue of *The Chronicle of Higher Education* in a Colleen Cordes roundup headlined "Debate Flares Over Growing Pressures on Academe for Ties with Industry."

In telling testimony, the coordinator of a Campaign for Responsible Technology said:

> The dangers of academic research that focuses too narrowly on commercial values should be evident from the unintended consequences of agricultural research and extension at land grant universities. Strong industry support led to an agricultural revolution that produced a cornucopia of cheap food, but the aftermath also includes technologies that poison farmland, promote large businesses over family farms, and contribute to the decline of rural communities.

A Pennsylvania State professor said that in the face of blandishments from industry,

> universities will have to increase their vigilance on upholding the core values of openness in communicating research findings, the freedom of faculty members to study the fundamental questions that most interest them, the unbiased reporting of results, and the protection of independent or dissenting critiques of national policies.

A UCLA doctor argued that "extensive ties between medical researchers and drug companies already are compromising medical research at many universities because their interests are 100% profit."

But a Council of Graduate Schools spokesman said the presence of industrial influence on campus research was not the problem, but rather the absence of influence by other groups:

"The pressure from a wider range of interests—from environmentalists, for example—would help balance the pressure on colleges and universities to focus too exclusively on commercial relevance."

A 1993 survey found that many scientists oppose the politically popular notion of linking academic research more with industrial goals. In a random sample of its members, the American Association for the Advancement of Science reported that nearly two-thirds of the 1,766 scientists and engineers surveyed opposed the idea of closer links.

That attitude may have been capsuled by two management professors:[25]

> It is a mistake to push universities into becoming the research and development units of American corporations. Universities have other very important missions—educating new generations of scientists, providing space for the free exchange of ideas, and generating powerful new concepts.

The debate was brought into sharp focus in a January 1994 announcement by the U.S. Department of Commerce that universities would be banned from holding patents on any intellectual property generated under its Advanced Technology Program, which funds cooperative arrangements between industries and colleges. In other words, business holds the trump card.

Of course, all this discussion can be irrelevant to an individual assistant professor of science or engineering. If his or her dean is a devotee of, indeed a supplicant for, corporate dollars and industry-slanted research, then it'll be difficult to maintain a neutral stance. On the other hand, if he or she has some elbow room, maybe there can be worked out an entente in which corporate monies don't lay too heavy a hand on the direction and ultimate application of a research project. It happens all the time.

IN EVERY DISCIPLINE
Your Students. Unless you bore them with too minute a travelogue, sharing your research odyssey with your undergraduate students can be as refreshing for you as it is stimulating for them.

But that sensation can be eclipsed when you walk down the commencement aisle with your first Ph.D. recipient.

To a degree you probably never recognized when you were one of them, graduate students can just about make or break a researching professor, so you should take care in recruiting them and consideration in nurturing them.

Not only can grad students save you mountains of physical and mental labor, their insights while under your tutelage can raise the caliber of your productive scholarship. What's more, their future accomplishments and their proffered assessments of you will come into play when your P&T committee evaluates you.

You'll feel this subtle symbiosis markedly when you preside over your first Ph.D.'s orals. With its probing questions, the committee will be testing you quite as much as the candidate—even more so, you may think as you sweat out the experience.

Hence the time and attention you lavish on promising grad students, even though at times they may seem almost a distraction, can be rewarding in more ways than one.

The colleague who jokes, "A university would be a great place if it weren't for the students" is missing the whole point.

Your Research Proposals. The tender, loving care you devote to your students is equaled in importance only by the attention you bring to conceiving and writing research proposals.

While what we said about how to develop a research paper is directly relevant to developing a research proposal, there are some differences in degree between the two.

At the very outset, of course, you must satisfy yourself that your idea is sound. Face the fact that a proposal based on shoddy conceptualizations and procedures isn't going anywhere. As one foundation reviewer has complained, "The avalanche of utterly unintelligible thinking dumped out in research proposals each year is ghastly."

Assuming you've surmounted that evaluation, you can then turn to the task at hand.

To help you, Carolyn Saarni, professor of counseling in the Center for Teaching and Professional Development at Sonoma State University (CA), has put down some apt "Tips for Developing a Basic Research Grant Proposal":[26]

BEFORE YOU START TO WRITE

☐ Study successful proposals in your field, looking particularly for organization, buzz words, and strategies.

☐ Prepare to cite scholars who are likely to review your proposal.

☐ Run your idea past colleagues in your field to test its currency.

☐ As you scan articles in learned journals, check the acknowledgments to see who supported what sort of research.

☐ Face up to your status and/or credibility in your field. If you're relatively unpublished, it's probably wise to shoot for a relatively small grant yet one that will yield at least two publications and two conference presentations.

☐ When you attend society meetings, seek out the grant administrators there and ask them what's the cutting edge of methodology and topic these days.

SITTING DOWN IN FRONT OF YOUR COMPUTER

☐ Reassure yourself that your mind is indeed creative, original, and alert.

☐ Using the organizational format of successful research proposals, begin to sketch an outline, making sure you don't put "method" ideas under "objectives," and so on.

☐ When you're on top of your subject, go to the campus office that maintains directories of research-funding agencies and match your idea to the current thrusts of likely sponsors and to the size of their pocketbooks.

☐ Revise your tentative outline in the light of funding agency requirements.

☐ Now flesh out your outline into a draft proposal and circulate it for review among fellow professionals whose savvy you respect and whose time you can draw on.

☐ Revise your proposal to reflect reviewer comments, suggestions, and criticisms of value.

If you're confident you're sufficiently prepared to discuss your research plan coherently over the phone, call the staffs of your target funding agencies to "dry-run" your proposal.

FINAL PLANNING AND WRITING

☐ Assemble a file of "trimmings," such as vita revisions, probable appendices, recent relevant references, budget items, and so on.

☐ Back up with hard copy everything you enter into your computer.

☐ Remember whose approval you may have to have before you can formally submit your proposal: a campus committee for the protection of human (or animal) subjects? an office for sponsored programs? your department chair or college dean?

☐ Whether the funding agency wants one or not, make yourself a time-line to keep on track the sequential steps of your project.

☐ Write very clearly and explicitly. Your reviewers will be busy people, not mind-readers.

☐ Write and revise, write and revise, write and revise. If you submit your proposal simultaneously to several agencies, acknowledge the fact, probably on a "concurrent support" page.

MIND-SET

☐ Steel yourself for rejection.

☐ If that is indeed the outcome, take seriously but not personally the negative comments—and revise your proposal for another try.

☐   Show the criticisms and your revision to a colleague
     for his or her feedback.
☐   Be persistent and of good heart.

For a more detailed, lively discussion of "Writing the Winning Grant Proposal," see Judith Rudermann's chapter by that title in *Writing and Publishing for Academic Authors,* edited by Joseph M. Moxley Lanham MD: University Press of America, 1992.

To Be a Collaborator or Not to Be. That is a question new assistant professors often pose to themselves. The answer may lie partially in what's meant by "collaboration." For example, to his question, "How do you generate and develop research ideas?" Donald K. Jarvis[27] reports that the No.1 response by university scholars was "collegial exchange, personal contacts, professional meetings." So that type or level of collaboration is very much the norm.

A science policy administrator at the American Physical Society[28] has called on the National Science Fondation to go out of its way to cultivate collaborations among individuals and on the part of institutions "to help preserve U.S. strength in basic science."

A university chancellor[29] believes "team scholarship could help strengthen scholarly traditions" in the humanities, "giving departments greater responsibility for successfully delivering the university's products."

But the most definitive study of the status of faculty collaboration in the United States today[30] points out it's tough to generalize about the subject because of differences among the disciplines. Collaborative research has been around for a long time and may almost be considered the norm in "data" disciplines like physics and biochemistry, occasional in policy studies, and uncommon in the "word" disciplines like literature and history. Even within the disciplines, the extent of collaboration can vary; the more theoretical the pursuit, the less the odds favor teamwork.

In general, the study finds collaborative research more attractive and productive "in turbulent environments, rapidly changing technologies, and increasingly specialized knowledge." At its best, collaboration seems to promote "greater intellectual creativity, higher productivity, an atmosphere of mentoring and role modeling, and collegial appreciation."

But collaboration is not without its hazards, particularly for young assistant professors who have not yet established professional identities. For them, collaboration can present difficulties for promotion-and-tenure committees trying to assess individual merit. Even Nobel prize judges have foundered in trying to decide who did what when.

The issue most often comes to a head over joint authorship. Here again, the disciplines are all over the lot in their ground rules, the sciences tending to accept multiple authorships, the humanities not, the social studies in between. Nor does experience as a graduate student necessarily prepare one for the mores of collaboration. Lone hours in laboratory or library, or drudgery as a lackey under a hierarchical professor, are the antithesis of training in collegial teamwork.

All we can say is, you'll just have to perform a sort of "cost-benefit analysis." Access to research funds may depend on your becoming a junior member of a team. Can you then carve out of that liaison enough independence to produce at least one research paper of which you are the lead author? Solitary research may net you a sole-author paper, but will it gain you the collegiality of a peer review panel? Is the environment of your department and your institutional reward system favorable to collaborative relationships?

It's a judgment call. But then, that's life.

Your Program. New faculty in a research-oriented department have to know they're expected to:

- Develop a program of research wherein there is maturation in ideas and methods over time on a single topic or a small group of related topics, and
- Extend this research beyond that done for the dissertation.

In other words, a promotion-and-tenure committee will want to see growth beyond graduate school and a sense of direction that will carry a young assistant professor into associate professor years. Creating such a program requires a commitment to scholarship, hard work, and mentorship. The hard work and commitment are up to the candidate; the mentorship is a responsibility the department should assume, but you may have to seek it out.

Unfortunately, you may need to pass up some interesting research paths, to return to them after tenure. As one reviewer notes, "On my campus people sometimes are denied tenure for lack of 'programmatic' research, meaning that they flit from topic to topic, instead of marching from one research question to the next."

Looking ahead to your tenure review—which, after all, is a major consideration—be cognizant of the crucial need to turn your research program into published papers and, as another reviewer points out, "of the eventual need for letters from scholars of associate or full professor rank, exhibiting geographical distribution around the country or beyond, and the need to go out and meet such future writers of testimonials early in your career and to keep them aware of the fruits of your research program."

For full details on "A Bottom Line: Getting Published," see Chapter 10.

WHAT RESEARCH SAYS ABOUT RESEARCH

Since this is a chapter about researching, it's probably only fitting that we conclude it with a summary of what research says about research on the part of new faculty, so here we draw on the empirical studies of Boice, Diamond, Jarvis, and others:

The habit of researching and writing is best established early if it is to be established at all. First-employment positions seem to affect researchers' careers more than do the graduate schools they attended.

Research impetus is not usually a lone effort that happens spontaneously in private, but it rather is largely a product of "evocative environments" in a community of scholars. Ideas for research projects tend to emerge from personal conversations with other scholars or from the imagined dialogue that a scholar pursues through questioning and critical reading.

Most productive scholars in a variety of fields do their research in regularly scheduled spans that can range from interstices in the day to extended blocks of time.

Support mechanisms range from research funding, facilities and equipment, appropriate amounts of time for research, travel monies, and so on to mentoring—and the greatest of these is mentoring.

Traditional, voluntarily formed mentoring pairs don't work too well. They tend to fall into a professor/grad student pattern in which the senior member is reluctant to impose his or her insights for fear of encroaching on academic freedom and in which the junior member is reluctant to come forward with problems for fear of appearing inadequate. Arbitrarily paired mentors from the same department are successful, but not as much as pairs in which the mentor is from an entirely different department from the mentee, each partner then being more open. The best solution seems to be a committee of mentors in which give-and-take becomes so collegial that "the expectations and progress toward goals become so clear that the mentee will know the retention-tenure decision in advance."

Research has led to a four-element formula for research success on the part of new professors:

- *Involvement*, in which newcomers get immersed "in supportive and communicative networks with influential faculty, campus activities, and in developing a sense of trust in the campus."
- *Regimen*, a "cataloging" of progress "as a means of staying on schedule."
- *Solving the right problem*, such as learning to find blocks of undisturbed time for writing, and playing a role of department citizenship without becoming overburdened in committee work.
- *Social networking*, to the end that "those faculty who fare best strike a balance between teaching, research, and outreach. Balance is the single component to adjusting to life as a new faculty member that quick starters cite as pivotal in their successes."

These insights reflect a norm which you might well copy. On the other hand, there's no law that says you have to be a conformist.

A FINAL RESEARCH CHECKLIST

At Midland University, "documentation of research quality and quantity may include but is not restricted to:"

- A record of ongoing scholarly production in refereed journals, including information on the relative contributions of multiple authors and the rejection rates of the journals involved.
- Review papers written for professional journals if they reveal the scholarly knowledge and judgment of the reviewer. (Thoughtful synthesis when accompanied by the ideas of the synthesizer can and often does lead to the creation of new knowledge.)
- A record of success in obtaining research or performing-arts funds from competitive outside funding sources.
- A record of publication in monographs, proceedings of professional meetings, extension bulletins, and other non-refereed outlets.
- Presentation of research and other scholarly work at conferences of professional organizations, especially when the presentations are invited and the conferences are national or international in scope.
- Frequency of citation and critical appraisal of research, scholarly work, or artistic activity, especially when the appraisals are sought independently by evaluators.
- Recognition and awards received for research and scholarly contributions or artistic performance.
- Evidence of work in progress, including manuscripts, grant proposals, and draft scripts.
- Invitations to be visiting lecturer, scholar, scientist, or performer, if that invitation relates to research, scholarship, or the fine arts.
- Evidence of national or international reputation as a researcher and/or scholar.

NOTES

1. Donald K. Jarvis, *Junior Faculty Development* (New York: Modern Language Association of America, 1991).

2. Howard Mancing, "Teaching, Research, Service: The Concept of Faculty Workload," *Association of Departments of Foreign Languages Bulletin* Spring 1991: 44-55.

3. Ernest K. Boyer, *Scholarship Reconsidered: Priorities of the Professoriate* (Princeton, NJ: Carnegie Foundation for the Advancement of Teaching, 1991).

4. Julius Getman, *In the Company of Scholars: The Struggle for the Soul of Higher Education* (Austin, TX: University of Texas Press, 1992).

5. Donald K. Jarvis, *Junior Faculty Development* (New York: Modern Language Association of America, 1991).

6. John W. Creswell and Martha L. Brown, "How Chairpersons Enhance Faculty Research Careers," *The Department Chair* Winter 1992: 19-20.

7. William Vartorella, "If You're Seeking a Grant," *NAASS Newsletter* Apr. 1994: 3.

8. Judith P. Swazey, Karen Seashore Louis, and Melissa S. Anderson, "The Ethical Training of Graduate Students," *The Chronicle of Higher Education* 9 Mar. 1994: B1-2.

9. Laurie Richlin, ed., "Preparing Faculty for the New Conceptions of Scholarship," *New Directions for Teaching and Learning* 54 (San Francisco: Jossey-Bass, 1993).

10. Michael B. Patterson, Sidney P. Rollins, and Alan D. Olinsky, "Business Students' Rating of Faculty: An Analysis of the Entire Population of a College," *The Journal of Staff, Program, and Organizational Development* Spring 1992: 37-46.

11. Robert A. McCaughey, "Why Research and Teaching Can Coexist," *The Chronicle of Higher Education* 5 Aug. 1992: A36.

12. Peter Balbert, "From Rejection to 'Renuwel' to Renewal: Chairperson, Faculty, and the Research Imperative," *Innovative Higher Education* Winter 1991: 139-156.

13. Robert P. Pedersen, "Viewpoint," *Community College Week* 13 Apr. 1992: 4.

14. Milton Greenberg, "Accounting for Faculty Members' Time," *The Chronicle of Higher Education* 20 Oct. 1993: A68.

15. Timothy D. Johnson, "Teaching vs. Research: No Simple Debate," *Academic Leader* Jan. 1994: 3-4.

16. Stephen H. Koslow and Hilleary D. Everist, "The Other End of the Phone," *Professional Scholar* Oct. 1993: 6-7.

17. Leon Neuenschwander, "Jump Start Your Grant-Winning Potential," *Academic Leader* May 1992: 2-4.

18. Donald K. Jarvis, *Junior Faculty Development* (New York: Modern Language Association of America, 1991).

19. Peter Marris, "How Social Research Could Inform Debate Over Urban Problems," *The Chronicle of Higher Education* 20 May 1992: A40.

20. Derek Bok, quoted in Carolyn J. Mooney, "Personal and Professional," *The Chronicle of Higher Education* 8 Apr. 1992: A17.

21. Theda Skocpol, "The Narrow Vision of Today's Experts on Social Policy," *The Chronicle of Higher Education* 15 Apr. 1992: B1.

22. Mark Solovey, "Shattered Dreams and Unfulfilled Promises," MA thesis, University of Wisconsin-Madison, 1991.

23. Alexander W. Astin, "VMI Case Dramatizes Basic Issues in the Use of Educational Research," *The Chronicle of Higher Education* 24 July 1991: A 36.

24. Robert Donmoyer, Arthur L. White, and Michael H. Klapper, "The Knowledge and Pedagogical Base of Science Education: An Overview," *Teaching Education* Spring 1991: 11-16.

25. Richard Florida and Martin Keeney, "Universities Should Not Become Research Units for Corporations," *The Chronicle of Higher Education* 10 July 1991: B1, 3.

26. Carolyn Saarni, *Tips for Developing a Basic Research Grant Proposal* 1-3 (Rohnert Park, CA: Center for Teaching and Professional Development, Sonoma State University, May 1990).

27. Donald K. Jarvis, *Junior Faculty Development* (New York: Modern Language Association of America, 1991).

28. Francis Slakey, "Getting the Most from Our Investment in Academic Science," *The Chronicle of Higher Education* 14 July 1993: A36.

29. Donald N. Langenberg, "Team Scholarship Could Strengthen Scholarly Traditions," *The Chronicle of Higher Education* 2 Sept. 1992: A64.

30. Ann E. Austin and Roger C. Baldwin, *Faculty Collaboration*, ASHE-ERIC Higher Education Reports (Washington DC: The Georgetown University, 1991).

9 THE SERVICE SYNDROME

It is the rare American institution of higher education that doesn't list *service* in its triad of faculty missions (as if teaching and research weren't themselves services). But what the term encompasses for you as an assistant professor depends vastly on the character of your discipline, your department, the divisional "home" of your department, and your institution as a whole. In an English department in a bucolic liberal arts college, for example, "service" will have quite a different connotation from that in a school of communication in an urban university.

The literature of higher education is ambivalent about the importance of service, particularly for new faculty. Donald K. Jarvis,[1] for example, says that "all junior faculty members should have some, but not too much, experience in service assignments." But Susan Rava[2] proposes that, rather than picture teaching and research as "hierarchically superior" to service, "we look at them as a triangle." And the authors of a recent monograph on the subject, Sandra E. Elman and Sue Marx Smock,[3] hold that "all three functions constitute scholarly work."

Nor is there a consensus on just what the term "service" implies. Elman and Smock distinguish four categories:

- institutional service—work to maintain the institution, sometimes called "campus citizenship";
- disciplinary service—activities for the discipline, sometimes called "professional service";
- professional or community service—the scholarly use of one's expertise in areas other than traditional teaching and research, sometimes called "public service"; and
- private service—activities totally outside professional or institutional life, sometimes called "individual service."

Most of the institutional documents we've examined describing faculty tenure criteria, generally employ three categories or dimensions of service, although not necessarily in the same rank order. We'll use their terms here: *public service, institutional service,* and *professional service.*

To help you grasp your service role and to set your sights high, let's look at what a representative state university might tell its applicants for tenure.

REPRESENTATIVE STANDARDS

PUBLIC SERVICE

"The university of the people has the responsibility of taking the university—the professors, the books, the skills, the findings of research, the interpretations, the insights, the forums, the publications—to the people . . . to make all the resources of the university available beyond the college walls." So did Frank Graham characterize the dimensions of public service when he was president of the University of North Carolina.

Not all institutions share this massive commitment, of course, but all subscribe to the principle to one degree or another.

You can participate in various ways in carrying out your institution's obligation to serve the public at large. Your public service might include membership on committees and boards, preparation of popular articles and booklets, testifying at public hearings, speaking to or consulting with public bodies or clientele groups, participating in or organizing workshops and conferences, speaking to lay gatherings, and so on.

The outreach function, as public service is increasingly being called, has engendered "widespread interest and increasing resolve both within academe and without." Elman and Smock explain:

> During the last decade, requests for assistance from state legislatures, government agencies, business and industry, and others have elevated the university's service role to greater prominence. In difficult times, these groups seek the best minds to address society's formidable economic, political, and social policy challenges, and it is faculty who can and do respond. They respond by providing technical assistance, consultation, policy analysis; they do applied research; they teach outside the classroom. They respond by using their academic expertise to apply and disseminate knowledge.

For example, the Western Interstate Commission for Higher Education has recently called on public colleges and universities to formulate new outreach efforts to help solve their states' economic and social problems. In particular, the group advocates "campus-wide involvement" with public schools and teacher preparation, and calls on public institutions to view that role as a primary collaborative activity with other institutions, businesses, and government agencies. "Campus-wide involvement," of course, means "faculty," including junior professors.

But outreach is not alone the province of public institutions. In recent years an Options University Outreach Project, funded by foundations and based at Brown University, has been making small grants to develop speakers' bureaus on foreign-policy issues at private colleges and universities across the country. During a six-year period, some 1,500 college faculty members have given more than 5,000 talks to a wide range of community, professional, church, military, and business organizations on national security issues.

You'll find more about this important public service or outreach function—and your potential role in it—in a succeeding section.

INSTITUTIONAL SERVICE

The effective operation of any institution requires a high degree of faculty participation in faculty government, departmental and campus committees, advisory functions, administrative roles, and similar tasks. While a P&T committee will recognize that a heavier burden may and should fall on the shoulders of more senior and already tenured faculty, it will not excuse you for playing hookey. You're simply expected to accept an appropriate role in institutional service as your vital contribution to the functioning of your campus.

Jarvis offers three reasons why it's in your best interests to perform a decent amount of institutional service as an assistant professor. First, since you'll be expected to perform a good deal of such service as a senior faculty member, it's a good idea to find out early how it's best done. Second, because early professional habits tend to be continued, an early start will position you well later in your career as a model academic citizen. And third, the right amount of collegial service can combat the anomie and sense of isolation that plague many junior professors.

If you happen to be a woman or a member of an ethnic minority group, in many departments and divisions you may face a special problem. You may be invited to serve on many a committee, to represent the perspectives of your gender or race. Obviously you'll need to find tactful ways of dodging many of these "honors" or you'll burn out and fade away long before you can come up for tenure. Do whatever it takes to be "good citizen" in your department and division, but no more. And, assuming you have a choice, choose appointments to high-profile committees.

PROFESSIONAL SERVICE

As a professor you're a professional, with all that word implies in terms of relating to all other professionals engaged in your calling. Service to your profession or academic discipline can occur at local, state, national, or international levels.

Recognized activities typically include:

- service as an officer or member of a board, committee, or task force of a professional group;
- on-site program evaluation visits;

- reviewing research proposals or manuscripts;
- organizing or participating in professional meetings such as training institutes, workshops, conferences, and continuing professional education.

Peer judgment will distinguish your contributions that should be rated as *real* service from those activities that reflect mere membership.

Junior faculty are apt to approach professional service with a good deal of psychasthenia—an inability to resolve doubts. For years, as grad students and post-docs, they've spent hours in bull sessions and at beer bashes deconstructing and reconstructing their disciplines. But now that they're in at least a tentative position to do something about it all, they don't know whether to be heard or just be seen. While their senior peers probably won't take kindly to rash outbursts, the fact remains there isn't a discipline that can't profit from and won't welcome, at times, the rational input of young minds.

Particularly in the interstices among the disciplines, it has typically been new faces, unwed to old strictures, that have pioneered interdisciplinary advances in teaching, research, and service. While for a time they may live dangerously in hidebound departments, sooner or later these Balboas stand exuberant on peaks in Darien. Before the 1960s, whoever heard, for example, of environmental studies? It was iconoclastic junior faculty who helped bring the associated disciplines into a new configuration in conformity with national needs. Similar challenges await junior faculty in all the fields of professional service today. Just don't get too far out ahead of your field too soon in your career!

OUTREACH STRATEGY AND TACTICS

PHILOSOPHY

The embodiment of the concept of public service, outreach is fundamentally an institutional state of mind which views the campus not as a place but as an instrument. Translated into an operational philosophy, outreach asks faculty members individually and collectively to make themselves as available as possible to the whole of society, or at least to the constituency from which an institution draws its inspiration and support.

In actual practice, outreach leaders seek to identify public problems and public needs, to interpret those concerns to the campus, to focus institutional skills and resources upon them, and thence to translate campus insights into educational activities throughout a state or region.

As a corollary, the outreach function brings back to the campus those essential public impulses that enliven teaching and stimulate research. What is more, outreach helps to build those public appreciations that keep open the doors to free inquiry and broad educational opportunities, to reinforce the support of the constituency that nourishes the institution and to continue the acceptance of college and university as the highest order of free institutions of learning.

The outreach mission, in essence, is to bring campus and community into fruitful juxtaposition, thereby immeasurably enriching the lives of both. In so doing, an institution seeks to be both responsible for traditional academic standards and responsive to current public issues.

Manifestly, outreach has public relations overtones. As a pioneer outreach-oriented university president put it: "The purpose of extending an institution should be simply that of educational service. But utilizing the opportunity to carry out knowledge to the people will be a practical advantage to the growth of the institution along all other lines."

As has been said, a true American college or university should have "both open gates and cloistered libraries, both practical messengers and theoretical scholars." Hence has emerged this third function, a role in which the campus, freely and without perversion, lends its knowledge and skills to all the people in its communities and regions for the solution of everyday problems of living and for intellectual and spiritual enrichment of lives.

METHODS

Outreach methods are manifold. Perhaps not on your campus, but as a whole they may encompass specialized residential instruction, evening classes or colleges, short courses, field studies, staff experts on loan to government agencies or private industries, centers for continuing professional education, exhibits, radio and TV programs and stations, educational TV networks, off-campus undergraduate installations, area agents, touring orchestras and theater groups, correspondence study, lectures, concerts, newspaper and magazine columns, summer-school seminars, library services, film and other visual aid distribution, manuals and bulletins, demonstrations, formal consulting services, and a wide range of informal instructional liaisons with individuals, institutions, agencies, and groups.

In other words, in your public service responsibilities, you have a wide range of options.

ORGANIZATION

While you can, of course, perform public service duties independently, you will likely have on your campus an administrative officer charged with energizing and coordinating institutional outreach.

What that person will be called on your campus is anybody's guess: dean, director, coordinator, or even vice president of extension, outreach, continuing education, adult education, public service, or educational services. His or her unit will be variously called a division, center, office, bureau, university college, or some such.

For assorted reasons, not all of them logical, some forms of institutional outreach may not be under the domain of this instrumentality, such as the campus TV station or the evening college. As we've said, you've got to learn your own territory.

Almost certainly, if yours is a land-grant university with a cooperative extension service, that unit will be set up separately from other outreach configurations, befitting its charter in federal legislation "to aid in diffusing among the people of the United States useful and practical information on subjects relating to agriculture and home economics, and to encourage the application of the same."

Unless you hold part or all of an appointment in co-op extension, you normally will engage its clientele by invitation only, since deans of agriculture and home economics are zealous guardians of their turf.

A handful of institutions have attempted to arrive at some sort of organizational entente among "ag extension" and "general outreach," but with indifferent success, so disparate are the traditions and mechanics of the two entities. More than one president has stumbled at the chore, so it behooves you to step with caution.

This is not to say there's a shooting war on. Both organizations subscribe to the proposition that "the essential motivating force behind a university's work in all times and places when universities have flourished has been the connection between the scholar's activities and the burning issues of the day."[5]

GETTING DOWN TO YOUR SPECIFIC OPTIONS

Again, what service expectations hold for you will vary with the situation and the terrain.

This is a good time to check in with your *alter ego* Bill in the Midland University department of botany and applied ecology to see how he's handling the service syndrome.

Bill is uncertain about exactly what should be the scope and depth of his service role, particularly in his first couple of years on the Midland faculty, so he seeks counsel from his assigned mentor, who happens to be the senior plant ecologist in the department and the chair of Bill's search committee—Professor Donald R. Gray.

"Don," Bill said (it's an informal department), "I've read the Midland P&T guidelines on service expectations (see last pages of this chapter), but I still need advice on what my options are."

"I'm glad you've come to me, Bill," Don said, "because it's tricky balancing your civic service duties against your teaching and research obligations. What I'm going to do is tick off some of the service activities I've engaged in during the past 10 years so you can see how you can exploit your professional strengths in a service mode without getting in the way of your teaching and research, and in fact reinforcing them. But it's with the proviso that you take it slow your first couple of years. Do what comes naturally in terms of service, but save your heavy hitting for a while until you're on top of your research program and your new courses. OK?

"University service—

- I chaired the *department curriculum committee* that set up our new biological conservation/sustainable development master's.
- I was a member of the college *student life and interests committee.*
- I served on an all-university *ROTC program evaluation panel.*
- I substituted for Amanda Perkins' predecessor as acting department chair one summer when she went to China.
- I advised the president on university *arboretum management.*
- I represented the department on an interdisciplinary Ph.D. team.
- I advised the *botany student group* observing the 20th anniversary of E-Day.

"Disciplinary service—

- I served on a state public school *science teaching advisory commission.*
- I held a *contributing editorship* on Plant Ecology.
- I was president of the regional *plant ecology society.*
- I was a member of the AAAS plant ecology committee.
- I helped develop a *national conference* on the role of plant ecology in the environmental era.

"Public service—

- I advised the *state natural resources board* on land acquisition issues.
- I was a *consultant* to the Ramgo Oil and Gas Pipeline Company— for pay, by the way.
- I served on the Midland city *park commission.*
- I coordinated the department's revised state outreach program.
- I worked with school administrators, teachers, parents, and pupils on a *science curriculum.*
- I gave innumerable *public lectures*, particularly after my African trip.
- I appeared occasionally on University *radio and TV* station programs.
- I wrote a *popular brochure* on back-yard prairie restoration.

- I *testified* at a capital hearing on endangered plant species legislation.
- I prepared a *report* for the Midland Lake Protection Association on the long-term effects of agricultural runoff in the lake basin on lake eutrophication.
- I chaired an *on-site team* evaluating the Weyawega Technical School science department.

"That's what I recall at the moment. As you can see, a lot of what's called service is really a form of teaching or research. For example, that consulting I did for those oil and gas people led to a modest research grant, and that eutrophication paper became a teaching tool in one of my seminars.

"Remember, that's my track record for a decade . Give you any ideas, Bill? You take it from there—and take it easy, but without copping out."

You take it from there, too.

SOME SPECIAL SERVICE CONSIDERATIONS

FUZZY DEMARCATIONS

Because the lines among teaching, research, and service are neither always precise nor universal, it behooves you to find out just exactly what each term means on your campus.

For example, "teaching" usually implies instruction in credit courses to students taking the course for credit toward a degree. But what if the course is non-credit, although in a classroom setting with traditional scheduling and procedures? Is that teaching or public service? The answer may depend on whether the non-credit instruction is supervised and funded by an academic department or whether it is an activity under an outreach agency. Your institution may in fact never have faced the issue.

Again, "research" usually implies creating new knowledge whose quality can be judged by peers in a refereed publication. But what if the same research is disseminated to a nonacademic audience in a magazine article, popular monograph, or speech? Is that research or teaching or public service? The answer may depend on the mores of your unit of assignment.

For example, Midland University's College of Letters and Science defines the distinctions this way:

> Textbooks, reports, newsletters, circulars, semi-popular articles, and similar publications are normally considered evidence of teaching ability or public service and will be considered creative work or productive scholarship only when they present new ideas or incorporate original scholarly research.

On the other hand, if your assignment is as an extension specialist in a land-grant college of agriculture, you will probably be told that "extension activities should not be confused with service; they should be evaluated as teaching or research."

Some institutions list "Consulting Activities" as a separate and distinct category in their criteria for promotion; others lump consulting under "public service" or even occasionally under "research." Paid consulting may not even count as anything other than a private activity.

The private or individual service category presents problems of its own. It usually implies activities you undertake simply as a private individual, divorced from your professional expertise and not an outgrowth of your academic discipline, such as working with a local church, Little League, or political campaign. But what if you're an assistant professor of political science advising a candidate for public office? An assistant professor of education running for a district school board post? Or an assistant professor of limnology organizing a fishermen's group? Are those private initiatives or legitimate public service?

In the face of all this lack of "service" specificity, you'd better determine exactly what means what in your department at your institution. You may discover you're performing public services without even knowing it!

A SERVICE PECKING ORDER

As the saying goes, all forms of service may be equal but some are more equal than others. At a land-grant university, public service may somewhat outrank institutional service and professional service.

At a liberal arts college, institutional service may take precedence. In a professional school, professional service may gain the honors.

Within each category of service, there is often a pecking order. That's what we were referring to earlier when we spoke of "high visibility" assignments.

Under public service, membership on a federal panel will carry so much prestige that the institution may grant a full or partial leave of absence. Just so, a one-minute appearance on MacNeil/Lehrer or Ted Koppel's "Nightline" will count for more than a lecture series on the campus radio station.

Under institutional service, election to an all-campus committee usually carries more weight than membership on an appointed committee. If the responsibilities are extensive, the institution may reduce teaching loads and supply staff support. Duty on a divisional committee will usually count for more than duty on a departmental committee, although membership on a departmental search or promotion panel certainly is a talisman of collegial confidence.

Under professional service, service on the editorial board of a learned journal, membership on a professional standards panel, or contribution to a curriculum revision are more prized than routine work on a program committee. With luck, your department will supply travel funds when necessary.

In terms of "perks," however, probably nothing equals membership on a faculty intercollegiate athletics board, with the accruing free travel and tickets to conference events. Professors have been known to lobby for such an assignment!

At some institutions, bylaws require that some committees include assistant professors. Otherwise new faculty will pretty much have to take what chance doles out. But if you have any choice, it's good to know the pecking order.

CONFLICTS OF INTEREST

In the realm of your public service as an individual professor, performing activities that manifestly draw on your professional expertise as an outgrowth of your academic discipline, you are pretty free to speak your mind without appearing to speak for your institution. However, it's probably prudent to remind your audiences from time to time that you're expressing personal beliefs and not those of your campus. But if you should assume any kind of administrative role in which you might appear to speak for your institution, then you'd better review the situation.

For instance, for many years as a journalism professor teaching science writing, the senior author (ACS) on the side wrote a Sunday natural resource conservation column for the local daily, with little fear that his pronouncements would be deemed those of the university. Partly because of the visibility that the column afforded him, he got appointed director of a new university conservation education program, and what he then was writing in his newspaper column could easily become construed as representing university policy. To avoid any appearance of conflict of interest, he resigned his freelance post as Sunday columnist.

That may have been a drastic solution, but it was effective! Incidentally, in the case of making the most of a good opportunity, ACS— freed from that weekly deadline—repackaged selected columns into *Everybody's Ecology* (Barnes, 1971) which became one of the texts for the new inter-college course he was asked to develop and moderate on "Environmental Management Problems, Principles, and Policies."

This isn't to say, of course, that you have to be mute if you serve in any administrative position. Quite the contrary, you have a positive obligation to help interpret an institution's performance and aspirations to the public but in a voice that clearly distinguishes between personal conviction and official policy.

Fortunately, the chance of new assistant professors, taking on the mantle of a campus administrator is slim, but they nonetheless ought to be aware of lurking problems of conflicts in roles.

BIG BONUSES

Before you even think, "I didn't bargain for any of this service business," and start considering how to get out of "busy work" and "Mickey Mouse" service obligations, realize that each form of service can bring you a brawny bonus.

Public Service. Imagine these scenarios: The alumni association secretary is always hard up for reunion speakers. The director of admissions pleads for faculty participation in high school career days (a campus euphemism for recruiting trips). The downtown Rotary Club wants somebody to talk about something. An out-state civic group wants a forum leader. A municipal research bureau needs help. The dean of continuing education importunes for evening adult class instructors. Your own dean hears you'd be a fit expert at a legislative hearing in your subject area. The chancellor invites you along on a fund-raising soirée.

Before you get on your high horse and turn your back on all such requests with the excuse you're too tied up teaching and researching, think again. What some dismiss cavalierly as nothing but an institution's "cheap public relations" is actually part and parcel of that matrix of activities that go into generating public and private support for institutional wherewithal—and your salary.

What's more, your institution's administrators are keeping little black books with the names of faculty earning brownie points as "good university citizens." While your name in their books won't protect you against repercussions from inept performance in teaching and scholarship, it won't do any harm either—and may someday be just the difference between promotion and a pink slip.

Institutional Service. In the luck of the draw, you'll wind up pretty quickly assigned to a department committee of one kind or another, and as the junior member you'll likely be appointed secretary. Don't bridle; look on it as an opportunity. There's nobody like a committee recorder to make an impression, because with the chore often goes the requirement that you draft the ultimate committee report.

Keep your eye on that prize. Your trouble will lie in the fact that committee deliberations can be elaborate and extended, and hence that the final report be something less than clear and concise, yet complete. So don't even attempt to be a court reporter inscribing each and every entry in the conversation. Capture the essence of who moved what to which effect.

Committee Report Crafting. In drafting the report, apply the 30/3/30 formula. What's that?

Well, the first number (30) means that many readers will stay with you for only about 30 seconds or so, no matter how compelling you think the subject. What you don't get across in 30 seconds of perusal, you won't get across at all.

So your report title can't be simply a label, like "Annual Report of the Department Library Committee." The title must give the gist of your total message in a strong declarative statement, like "In a Period of Fiscal Austerity, Faculty Are Obliged to Exercise

Restraint in Requisitioning Fugitive Serials." That either satisfies or intrigues your 30-second readers.

For colleagues who spend just three minutes leafing through your report, distill your principal subpoints down to strong declarative statements and display them as bold lines throughout the document, like mini-chapter headings. Either that or consolidate them in a one-page preamble to the report as a whole (sometimes called an "executive summary").

Then, for any 30-minute readers, you can give the full treatment in condensed type.

You'll recognize there's nothing unique in the 30/3/30 formula. It's the basic pattern of newspaper makeup: headlines for scanners, lead paragraphs for leafers, longer copy for avid readers. And it's the basic format for a half-hour TV newscast: first you get the headlines, then the main stories, and then, one by one commercials.

The 30/3/30 technique carries a big plus. There's almost no limit to the amount of discourse a faculty committee will insist on including in its statement. Applying the formula will produce a cogent report and preserve peace in the bargain.

Provided, of course, your recording is accurate. There's no fury like a colleague who thinks he or she has been misquoted or, worse, left out of the transcript. Political pitfalls abound for the committee report writer who's careless.

If you want to add a real touch of institutional-service professionalism to your report, apply the doctrine of completed staff action: affix to the report a draft of the memo the department chair is to issue if he or she accepts the committee's recommendations.

Chairing A Committee. There's only one trouble with becoming recognized as a competent committee secretary: you get named to **head** a committee!

Take that in stride as well. Here's a tip: a lot resides on your timing.

Regularity is important, in order that your department colleagues can arrange their schedules accordingly. So your call should always be for the same day at the same time, at least during any one term.

What day? What time? Your choice will be dictated by the teaching schedules or other unavoidable commitments of fellow committee members. You certainly don't want to pick a day and/or time when one or more professors simply can't attend. With luck you'll have several options. (You have to throw your own needs into the equation, of course.)

Choosing the day of the week can be an interesting exercise, assuming you have a choice: in the fresh of a Monday? a TGIF finale? Your venue may require T, W, or R. Or the weight of departmental tradition may simply dictate day and time.

Chances are your choice of time will ordinarily be limited to early morning, noon, or late afternoon. Sunrise seances can be popular with some colleagues, a plague to others. Bag lunches can be an effective solution. Late-afternoon meetings can work if you don't let them drag on and on. A sure way to avoid tedium is to pass out an agenda in advance, along with a synopsis of past discussion.

The meeting of a committee you chair doesn't have to be dull and forbidding; it can actually be an eagerly anticipated collegial get-together. Picking a favorable day and time can contribute mightily.

Your reward? A favorable impression on your department colleagues—and an assignment to a campus committee! Here's a big payoff in institutional service: you get to mingle with the very faculty members, or their associates, who may ultimately be on your P&T assessment committee. There's nothing like being known, if only in a limited way, as somebody other than a listing in a telephone directory. On a more substantive level, extra-department contacts, as we've said earlier, can energize both the scope of your teaching and the depth of your research.

For more extended discussion of *Effective Committee Service,* you might want to consult a handbook by that title by Neil J. Smelser (Newbury Park CA: Sage, 1993).

Professional Service. "The department chairperson is expected to supplement the opinions of colleagues within the department by critical appraisals from distinguished scholars at other universities."

That's a typical directive from a divisional P&T committee to a department chair about how he or she can best "sell" the department's recommendation regarding your promotion potential.

Now if you want to live dangerously, you can rely on whatever prestige your byline on "X" number of research papers has generated.

But if you really want to get into the flow, you'll start attending meetings of the most appropriate learned societies or professional organizations in your field.

Yet just attending won't be quite enough. You've got to start finding your way around your calling. While rendering proper obeisance to the big wheels there, concentrate on getting acquainted with those in attendance of your own status. It's often best done, not in a seminar, but at the bar. You'll all agree the dinosaurs in power ought to be put out to pasture, that what's needed is fresh ideas, attitudes, and energy. You'll have your chance, in fairly short order. Meanwhile you're cultivating just the sort of liaisons you can pull out of the hat when later your department chair says, "To document your case for promotion, we need the opinions of scholars around the country who can attest to your contributions. We have our own sources, but whom would you like to suggest as references¿"

Cynics may call it "the buddy system," but don't knock it.

There can be an added bonus in playing the convention game—a family affair. While some learned societies meet in the stuffy confines of a DC Dupont Circle hotel, others assemble in campus dormitories off-season where parents sleep barracks-style and kids run rampant. To get there you perform a cross-country tour that can be as exhilarating for your family as it is enervating for you. No matter. You've made it to Valhalla—the convention.

Once there, regardless of the accoutrements, you can start making professional contributions and personal ties. It's a terrible thing to say, but 40 years or so from now, when you're a retired emeritus, you may look back on those early convention experiences as being almost more satisfying than anything that ever happened back home, what with forming fast friendships, conquering society politics, and challenging disciplinary thinking.

However, to be perfectly frank, we have to admit not everybody is as enthusiastic about conferences as are we. For example, this diatribe on the subject by Camille Paglia, associate professor of the humanities at the University of the Arts in Philadelphia, in the May 1991 issue of *Arion*:

> The Modern Language Association convention sessions . . . splinter
> the profession into political special-interest groups like Washington

PAC lobbyists; they encourage the midget form of the "talk," which is simply a vehicle for cozy relationships and networking . . . and cram the moneychangers into the Temple instead of driving them out.

Attendance at conferences must cease to be defined as professional activity. It should be seen for what it is: prestige-hunting and long-range job-seeking junkets, meat-rack mini-vacations. The phrase, "He or she is just a conference hopper," must enter the academic vocabulary.

I look for the day when conference-hopping leads to denial of employment or promotion on the grounds that it is neglect of professional duties to scholarship and the institution. Energies have to be reinvested at home. The reform of education will be achieved when we all stay put and cultivate our own gardens instead of gallivanting around the globe like migrating grackles. . . .

Excessive contact with other academics is toxic to scholarship. The best thing for scholars is contact with non-academics, with other ways of thinking and seeing the world. . . . Instead of schmoozing with other academics at conferences, faculty should be required to acquire a sense of the general audience.[6]

Paglia's meat axe draws some blood, but we believe you follow her dictum at your own risk.

As a matter of fact, any debate over in-person conferencing may be moot, given the sensational rise of networking via computer. It's quite possible that Internet communicating will take the place of a good many professional service in-the-face committee meetings but whether that will constitute progress remains to be seen.

A big question: when it comes to promotion, tenure, and new jobs, how much credit will faculty members get for professional activities on electronic networks? That query brought a range of responses in a recent network debate.

Network activities "count a lot when people are considering whom to ask to write articles for publications and to speak at conventions and workshops," said Mary B. Jensen, director of the law library at the University of South Dakota. "When you're asked to write or speak because of your activities on the computer networks, that definitely counts when it comes to promotion, tenure, and job hunting."

But computer network activities don't count at all, according to William J. Hunter, an associate professor of teacher education and supervision at the University of Calgary, who said "the answer is None. To date no one here has even posed the question."

Stand by for later returns.

A CASE HISTORY IN SYMBIOTIC SERVICE

Once upon a time—in 1951, to be exact—there was a young ex-GI Ph.D. candidate in the department of government at Harvard University. Seeking funds and visibility, under the sponsorship of his major professor (who happened also to be the director of the Harvard Summer School), the grad student dreamed up something called a Harvard International Summer Seminar and became its director, meanwhile pursuing his studies in international history.

With minimum launching finances, the youthful director personally selected seminar participants from among promising young applicants around the world—elected officials, civil servants, and journalists, principally. After a faltering start, he built up the program—actively soliciting ideas and participation among the power structure of the Harvard faculty, seeking grants from foundations, and inviting as guest seminar lecturers an array of luminaries of the time from Eleanor Roosevelt to David Riesman to Walter Reuther.

With cocktail parties and potluck suppers, the young man's wife added a social dimension to the seminar's curriculum in politics, economics, and the humanities.

Of the 600 foreign students who participated before the summer seminar came to a close in 1959, many went out to become heads of governments, foreign ministers, news media executives, and bankers. Even in the 1990s, the erstwhile seminar director was still calling on some of his former students in his current role as a private international consultant on foreign affairs.

It is quite possible, of course, that the person's innate brilliance would have vaulted him to positions of prominence in academe and Washington without his having been the epitome of the proactive public service academician as a young man, but, as his biographer[7] says, "he excelled at articulation." We've been talking, of course, about Henry Kissinger.

A COST-BENEFIT ANALYSIS

The service syndrome carries a figurative and literal dollars-and-cents dimension to be considered. Let's examine the cost-benefit analysis facing Bill Campion in his first year at Midland.

In the state capital of Carthage, an hour-plus drive from Midland down Highway 32, the in-service training director for the State Department of Natural Resources hears about Bill's new graduate course in "Biological Aspects of Environmental Impact Analysis" and asks Midland's Dean of Outreach and Continuing Education to arrange for Bill to offer a non-credit seminar on the same subject for Department employees one night a week for a quarter in the Department office building. Under Midland policy, such an assignment carries with it both public service brownie points and a modest stipend in addition to base salary. The time commitment would be immeasurable indeed but, on the other hand, the chore would provide Bill a valuable opportunity to get to know some key state professionals in his field, and feedback from the encounter could work into Bill's regular teaching and research. To get a feel for department practice in such situations, Bill consults the chair, who goes over the pros and cons with him but seems to tilt in favor of Bill taking the job. Bill does.

In mid-quarter, one of Bill's adult students recommends Bill to one of the largest land developers in the area, Inhoff & Sons. They need an inventory performed next summer of any rare or endangered species of plant life on a tract of farmland projected as a shopping center—for a fee, of course. The department chair advises Bill that such a routine exercise would hardly qualify as research on the part of a professor but suggests it would be ideal practical work for a qualified grad student. Bill proposed to Inhoff & Sons that he supervise the project as a public service, with one of his doctoral candidates doing the actual field work for a stipend. Inhoff & Sons is happy to accept the arrangement. So is the grad student!

Bill's department can pick up the tab for only one professional meeting a year per each faculty member. Bill commits those funds to attending the annual convention of the Ecological Society of America, the No. 1 learned society in his field. But the great interdisciplinary crossroads for environmental management scholars and professionals is the North American Wildlife and Natural Resources Conference, affectionately known in the trade simply as "The

North American." Bill feels that as an aspect of professional service he should attend and participate in the session on applied ecology course development, but since the upcoming meeting will be in Anchorage, Alaska, his pocketbook would take a significant hit. Bill's wife suggests they bite the bullet and combine the trip with a vacation stopover at Yellowstone National Park, where they can also visit a hot springs flora field research station.

Midland's Dean of Forestry and Environmental Studies asks the Dean of Letters and Science for Bill to join a program evaluation committee in preparation for a site visit by a society of American Foresters panel. The L&S dean in turn propositions Bill's department chair, who calls Bill in for a conference on the matter.

"Bill," she says, "this is a tough one. I hate to turn our dean down but I think you may be getting a little over-extended on this service business. Besides, I'm about to name you a member of our department's standing committee on grad student affairs. Let's tell our friend the forestry dean to handle his own problems in-house this time."

Bill has to agree. The cost of going against the advice of the chair exceeds in this case any benefits that might accrue from working with colleagues across campus, but he'll willingly serve on his department's grad student affairs committee.

You'll have your own cost-benefit analyses to perform as you experience the ins and outs of the service syndrome on your campus.

THE "OTHER-DIRECTED" PROFESSOR
Economics Professor Holley H. Ulbrich[8] states the case for a service-oriented faculty member this way:

> "True" academics are supposed to listen to an inner voice, set their own agendas, and disdain the noisy voice of the world requesting service, advice, direction, vision, application. . . . I am a *client-centered* academic. I like to use economics for practical, applied purposes, to solve problems or to help people to find new and better ways of addressing policy issues and practical problems. . . . I like to use my expertise in state and local public finance to solve problems of governments, leadership training programs, citizen groups, and other typical constituencies of a university. These "customers" want the objectivity, thoughtfulness, the teaching-based communication skills, and the breadth and depth of analytical ability and background that they can find only in a university

professor. The inner-directed approach can be costly to universities in external support, financial and otherwise. . . . The higher education community must create an environment in universities that fosters and encourages a variety of personality types with a diversity of skills to enter academia to address the needs of *all* our constituencies.

While Ulbrich was obviously addressing the dimension of public service particularly, her principle is equally adaptable to institutional and professional service. But, she adds, "service activities may not only carry little weight in salary, tenure, and promotion decisions; they are often actively discouraged at aspiring research universities, especially among junior faculty."

Check out the ground rules at your institution—and your own talents and proclivities. You and your campus may be more "other-directed" than you think.

CLOSE ENCOUNTERS OF THE FOURTH KIND

Along about now we can hear some of you saying, "All this teaching/research/service trilogy is well and good, but isn't my institution interested in the real me—my character?" Of course! But most don't say so in so many words.

Some do quite precisely, however:

FACULTY MEMBER PERSONAL CRITERIA:

(1)
displays those marks of character and personality which
ensure his/her contributing to the missions of the University,

(2)
maintains a respectful attitude toward
the religious beliefs of others,

(3)
observes respectfully the rule of law as the basis
of constitutional government, and the fundamental human
and political rights of others.

That from the "Essential Appointment and Promotion Criteria" of a midsize Midwest urban university (of church affiliation).

Such a statement is not an isolated expression. Speaking at a national higher education conference in New Orleans in mid-January 1994, the president of the Carnegie Foundation for the Advancement of Teaching, Ernest L. Boyer, said that faculty evaluations should focus on "the professional characteristics of the scholar—honesty, persistence, courage."

If you don't find that frame of reference in the documents of your institution, don't assume character doesn't count; it may be all the more stringent a requirement for being unstated—a basic assumption by one and all.

Certainly an unprincipled person won't last long in academe, particularly under the increasingly close scrutiny by critics of academia in the '90s—unless he or she is a super con-artist or crook.

The exceptions are just few enough to prove the rule.

You have to appreciate, of course, that not everybody shares our relatively platonic view of the state of academic ethical standards. A "dean" of higher education administrators, Clark Kerr,[9] president emeritus of the University of California, takes a dim view of a "new academic culture" that is playing fast and loose with "knowledge ethics."

In Kerr's good, old "traditional paradigm in academic life," most faculty members were "part of a particular academic community as the center of their lives, and they took their on-campus citizenship responsibilities very seriously." Now, he says, "today's faculty members have more outside allegiances to agencies that fund research, to outside employers, to friends around the nation in direct contact via the computer and fax machines. . . . Alma Mater is, for some faculty members, a plural personality."

He goes on: "The ethics of the cultivation of knowledge were in better condition before they became so subject to the enticements of money from the outside and to the intrusion of politics inside."

His solution: Promulgation of a professorial code of conduct similar to those that police the medical and legal professions. But he frankly doesn't see much hope of such ethical standards coming about because of the preference of the academic world to "practice evaluative neutrality about its own ethical values." So he fears that "the academic profession may, in fact, be disintegrating slowly in some aspects of its ethical conduct."

A somewhat jaundiced reviewer of this manuscript supplies a second-hand horror story in support of Kerr's jeremiad:

> There are some real-life counter-examples to your contention that character counts for something in climbing the academic ladder to tenure. A state university professor with large research grants used a hefty portion of the money for his personal extracurricular activities, including buying a house for his *mistress!* The university "investigated" and exonerated him; only after he was jailed as a felon by the state did the university (after considerable prodding) fire him. And what did his disciplinary community do? Blackball him? On the contrary, he moved on to another university, maintained his status in the research "community," and even received a national award from his peers for his service!

We have to admit you can probably dredge up examples of similar travesties in academe, but we continue to cling to the perhaps naive belief that character does count on our campuses. If, on the other hand, there is indeed a serious problem of academic ethics, you're going to have to decide whether you're going to be part of the problem or part of the solution.

A FINAL SERVICE CHECKLIST

At Midland University, "documentation of service activity can include but is not limited to":

- Evidence of participation on committees, including chairs held and dates of service (especially demanding committee assignments should be identified).
- Evidence of coordination of programs, seminars, symposia, workshops, etc.
- Description and appraisal of work as advisor to student organizations.
- Description and appraisal of contributions made to professional organizations, especially offices held, committee assignments, task forces, etc.

- Evidence of work as a consultant on disciplinary matters, on editorial boards, as a reviewer or referee for scholarly publication and/or funding agencies, and as a referee for faculty members under review at other universities.
- Recognitions and awards for service.
- Evidence of presentations before community organizations.
- Evidence and appraisal of professional contributions made to agencies, industry, and public service organizations.
- Publication of reports, guides, handbooks, newsletters, circulars, etc.

"But," as a Midland mentor cautions, "don't trivialize your service activities by including too much. I've seen some faculty folders that indiscriminately contain so much padding that the more noteworthy activities are buried."

NOTES

1. Donald J. Jarvis, *Junior Faculty Development* (New York: Modern Language Association of America, 1991).

2. Susan Rava, paper presentation, Third National Conference on Training and Employment of Graduate Teaching Assistants, University of Texas-Austin 8 Nov. 1991.

3. Sandra E. Elman and Sue Marx Smock, "A Continuing Conversation about Professional Service," *AAHE Bulletin* May 1992: 10-13.

4. Clay Schoenfeld, *The Outreach University* (Madison, WI: University of Wisconsin-Madison Office of Inter-College Programs, 1977) ii-iv.

5. Scott Jaschik, "Political Activists Working to Change Land-Grant Colleges," *The Chronicle of Higher Education* 20 Mar. 1991: A 1.

6. Camille Paglia, "Academe Has to Recover Its Spiritual Roots and Overthrow the Ossified Political Establishment of Invested Self-Interest," *The Chronicle of Higher Education* 8 May 1991: B1-2.

7. Walter Isaacson, *Kissinger* (New York: Simon and Schuster, 1992).

8. Holley H. Ulbrich, "Can We Make a Place for the Client-Centered Academic?" *Academe* May-June 1992: 15-16.

9. Clark Kerr, *Higher Education Cannot Escape History: Issues for the Twenty-First Century* (New York: State University New York Press, 1994).

10 A BOTTOM LINE: GETTING PUBLISHED

"The Payoff for Publication Leaders" read the title of a "Trendlines" report in *Change: The Magazine of Higher Learning*.[1]

Looking at the characteristics of faculty who are most prolific in journal publications, researchers at the Carnegie Foundation for the Advancement of Teaching identified some rather striking distinctions between productive scholars and all other faculty responding to a CFAT national survey.

Among other traits, publication leaders:

- Receive higher salaries and rate their compensation "excellent."
- More frequently have outside income from consulting.
- Garner financial support for their research from a range of sources.
- Display consistency over time in the rate of publication.
- More likely teach graduate courses and for fewer hours.
- Have a positive view of the academic stature and environment of their institution.
- Are satisfied with their choice of profession.

These same publication leaders don't shirk their other duties; out of a reported average 50-hour work week, they spend 20 hours on teaching preparation and in-class presentation, 15 on research, and the balance on service assignments and other unspecified activities.

How can faculty publish more? Studies by Professor Robert Boice of SUNY-Stony Brook reveal the following characteristics of productive scholars:

> 1. They ration time devoted to lecture preparation in order to write continuously during most weeks of a term, even the busiest; they don't "binge."
>
> 2. They openly seek advice about scholarly writing from colleagues and they demonstrate high self-esteem by sharing rough drafts with reviewers. In other words, they aren't afraid to seek help.
>
> 3. They reject the self-defeating claim that "there are too few pages in scholarly journals to publish the majority of silent academicians who have something worth communicating."
>
> 4. Above all, they recognize writing is not simply an avenue for self-expression, best accomplished in an attic, but is a sophisticated form of social discourse. Firmly fixed in the author's mind is a sense of a specific audience and of a particular medium for reaching that audience.[2]

IN THE BEGINNING WAS THE WORD

THE WHY

A professor is, literally, in Webster's words, "one who professes," that is, "one who openly declares his beliefs, sentiments, etc." So publishing is simply a hallmark of your profession. Not to publish in some form may seem a denial of your calling.

But by expanding the dimensions of knowledge, by fulfilling your responsibility to interpret, you do more than merely satisfy standards of the professoriate; you gain that tremendous sense of satisfaction that comes from reaching out and touching someone.

Quite apart from these noble ends, of course, there's the bottom-line fact that, in order to meet the requirements for promotion to tenure—in most educational environments—you must present for review by a designated authority the evidences of your productive scholarship in such form, of such quality, and in such quantity as your department and institution dictate.

THE WHAT

Manifestly, there are many forms of professing. With the exception of the arts and some professional schools, however, the universal academic coin of the realm for purposes of evaluating scholarship has been for centuries and continues to be the printed word (although computer data bases on floppy disks may be the coin of the future).

Again, there are many forms of the printed word. For purposes of this manual we're going to concentrate on the three broad forms professors most commonly use to disseminate the fruits of their scholarship:

- the standard research paper or professional book,
- the interpretive article, essay, or monograph,
- the textbook.

Each of these major forms has certain permutations. The orthodox research paper for a scholarly journal, for instance, is readily adaptable to a technical report for practitioners, or expandable to a monograph or book-length treatise. The interpretive article can be made to fit the periodical of a learned society or a semi-popular magazine, or expanded to a campus press or trade book. Textbook chapters can be submitted independently as scholarly or popular articles, or the whole book condensed as an monograph.

While all three forms have much in common from the viewpoint of communication principles, each is distinct enough in its intended audience, development, construction, and submission to warrant the separate treatment we'll give them in the next chapter.

THE WHERE

Since your goal is not merely to get published but to get promoted, *where* you publish is a crucial consideration, because in the groves of academe one printed word isn't equal to every other printed word in terms of inherent prestige.

In general, a sort of academic "Nielsen rating" for your publication, "wheres" will look something like this, in descending order:

- Refereed scholarly journal, the more prestigious the better.
- Refereed professional journal or book.
- Book chapter.
- Non-refereed semi-professional periodical or textbook.
- Conference proceedings, essay collection.
- Semi-technical general circulation magazine.
- General circulation magazine or newspaper.
- Radio or TV documentary.

There are many subtleties and exceptions to this pecking order, depending on your discipline, department, college, institution, and the expectations of colleagues.

For example, it's one of the anomalies of academic life that if you were to appear in *TV Guide*—a periodical among the most widely read and highest-paying, with one of the lowest rates of acceptance—it wouldn't count for nearly as much as if you were to appear in an obscure, esoteric journal that charged you composition costs—*unless* you're in a professional communication arts department at an institution that values public service highly.

In other words, humanities scholars in liberal arts colleges usually enjoy a smaller range of options than do practitioners in professional schools in public universities.

On the other hand, professors in four-year colleges are more apt to be applauded for publishing papers on disciplinary teaching methods than are professors in research institutes.

Again, solicited works can carry different values. Sometimes colleagues may rate them higher than unsolicited work, since they show you've established a reputation. Others may give less credit, since there's the possibility the solicitors may have outlined the papers or even quietly collaborated.

If all this "where" business seems grotesque, grin and bear it: it's the name of the game.

THE WHO

Whatever its form, wherever it appears, writing for publication starts with *you*. You pick the subject. You select the medium of publication. You provide the data or lend the point of view. Writing for publication is inevitably a direct expression—an extension—of you. So before you start researching and writing, look in a mirror. Yes, that's right. What do you see? What motivates you to publish? What are your publishing goals? What are your strengths and weaknesses as a scholar/writer? The more sharply and frankly you analyze yourself before you even try to set words to paper, the better the odds you'll get into print.

What are some qualities that mark a good publishing scholar?

Curiosity, about the realm of your subject matter, about your intended audience, about the breadth and depth of publication media;

Craftsmanship, putting one word after another with clarity or flair, as the case may be;

Conscience, a basic regard for truth and honesty;

Confidence, the will to keep going in the face of rejection slips. As Sinclair Lewis once said, "Be egotistic as the devil, but don't tell anybody about it. It's not the will to be great that's offensive, it's the telling of it."

Want some help in measuring yourself against these attributes? Try answering these questions as honestly as you can:

Do you have scholarly talent? Do you have a passion to profess? Will you work diligently at tailoring your writing to the demands of a particular publication? Can you take advice? Will you rest on initial laurels? Will you always research and write your very best?

Assuming you can give yourself at least a B+ in most regards, then you're ahead of the game. Now just watch the company you keep and whom you consult.

CHOOSING ROLE MODELS

If you feel you need help in scholarly writing for publication, choose your sources of advice *very* carefully.

Donald K. Jarvis recently surveyed a small sample (117 professors at eight institutions) about their scholarly writing habits.[3] His results were shocking. Here's how they answered these questions:

- *"How do you generate ideas?"* Only 7% said they "test out ideas as papers." (Maybe that's why a journal editor has said submissions are typically "hackneyed, hastily conceived, turgidly written, deficient in clarity and perception.")
- *"How do you plan and protect time for a project?"* Some 66% admitted they try to use "small blocks or fragments of time." (That could account for commentator George S. Fichter going on record to state that too often scholarly publications are "void of all the vigor and enthusiasm with which the scholars pursued their research.")
- *"What sort of resources do you usually need?"* Only 3% used "papers circulated to attract feedback from others." (Perhaps that explains a publisher writing in *Daedalus* about manuscripts with "a lack of grace and wit and lucid style.")
- *"What is your style of researching?"* Only 8% replied that they "try to collect the needed books to have on hand."
- *"How do you get your outline into publishable form?"* Only 7% said they "make an outline." (No wonder engineer John M. McCullough has commented on "the amount of disconnected discourse dispensed each year as research.")
- *"How do you select a publisher?"* Only 9% "send a letter of inquiry with outline or abstract."

You can do a lot better than all of that if you use as your mentor what follows in this chapter.

As Jarvis concludes in his *Junior Faculty Development* handbook, you must establish the habit of research-and-writing early if you ever expect to establish it.

In his utilitarian guide, *Professors as Writers*, author Robert Boice agrees that you can acquire sound work habits—setting and meeting reasonable goals for editing, rewriting, and submitting manuscripts—if you work at it.[4] Editors Mark Zanna and John M. Darley have much the same to say in the chapter on publishing in their *The Complete Academic*.[5]

So let's move ahead to a consideration of key common denominators in all written communication.

THE ECOLOGY OF YOUR MANUSCRIPT

A principal reason why some scholarly papers fail to communicate—and hence fail to get into print—is simply because their writers fail to invest a decent amount of time and talent in organizing their facts and expressing their thoughts.

Fortunately the professoriate is coming increasingly to accept responsibility for the effective interpretation of productive scholarship. As *Scientific Monthly* has observed, "There is a growing recognition that if philosophical and scientific ideas cannot be explained in plain language, it is due in plain terms to the ineptness of the writer."

One of the first concepts to recognize at the outset is that there is no such thing as good writing in an abstract sense. There is good writing for one occasion, good writing for a special purpose, good writing for a particular audience, good writing for a certain medium, and so on. The first task of any writer, then, is not to start *writing* but to start *thinking*—thinking clearly and objectively about the "ecology" of his or her manuscript, that is, about the relationship between the manuscript and its environment. For example, to answer the question, "How long should my article be?" you have to ask in turn, "What subject, for what purpose, in what journal, when?"

Look at it this way: Robert Louis Stevenson once said a writer is like a juggler trying to keep a bunch of balls in the air at once. What he meant was that you as a writer must be conscious of a number of "ecological factors" as you go about translating thoughts into words on paper.

SUBJECT

Given any writing chore, it's essential to reduce your message to a paragraph or two that represents the absolute core of what you want to communicate. Now is when it's a mistake to think in terms of global problems, projects, or programs. The pertinent question is whether your topic boils down to a nub that somebody wants or needs to know about.

During the many years that Manning Pattilla has been reviewing extended manuscripts, he's discovered that in each case he could usually summarize the essential facts in one or two pages, and that the best articles could be reduced to one paragraph. If the summary of your theme seems to require a large amount of paper, your lack of brevity may indicate either that you can't yet see clearly the essentials of your article, or that you are bogged down in muddy details, or that you are using verbiage to make up for lack of substance.

Distilling your message is very useful. You can transfer it directly to your completed manuscript—as the covering abstract, as a part of the introduction, or as the summary, depending on the requirements of your chosen medium. But the biggest value of your "nutshell statement" to you will be as a compass, lending a sense of direction to your total writing task.

AUDIENCE

Having decided in general what you want to say, another step is to come to grips with your audience. For whom exactly are you writing? Fellow scholars in your field? In related fields? Practitioners? Administrators? Students? Laypeople? The more sharply you can delimit your audience, the easier will be your task and the more effective your presentation.

It will help if you picture a specific individual, the better to conjure up the backgrounds, experiences, intellects, prejudices, and needs your intended readers will bring to a consideration of your paper. Associated Press reporters, for example, are told to "write for a milkman in Omaha"; *New Yorker* writers are reminded that the magazine is not for "a little old lady in Dubuque"; while contributors to *The Elementary School Journal* are advised that "our readers are exclusively K-6 teachers and principals."

Your primary aim, remember, is to be *understood* and not necessarily to be *appreciated*. When you begin to contrive how your ideas will be received, not with the most efficiency by the reader, but with the most advantage to yourself—it is precisely then that you will run the risk of becoming confusing. For this affliction the very best antidote is to select an intended reader and write for that one individual.

MEDIUM

Where do you intend to publish your paper? You should always choose a journal—even though tentatively—before you write your article, because no two journals are identical in their requirements. The ideal article is so constructed that it is suited for only **one** publication. Probably more scholars falter here than at any other stage in communicating. They persist in writing first and searching for a periodical afterward.

In analyzing why a religious publication had rejected her manuscript, a comparative literature professor thought perhaps it was because one of her quotes contained some four-letter words. She rewrote the article, cutting out the offensive terms, and sent it back to the editor. Once again the paper was returned. This time there was a message scribbled on the margin of the rejection slip: "We do not wish to appear irreverent, but if you cut the hell out of this manuscript we still wouldn't accept it."

It is the matching of manuscript to medium that is the essence of consistent publication. No other aspect of writing is so frustrating—and so intriguing. That is why we devote a coming segment of this chapter exclusively to the topic.

PURPOSE

Why are you writing your article? To report new facts or insights? To elucidate a complicated concept? To comment on current trends? To synthesize a number of findings? To propound a novel theory? To entertain? Your purpose will help dictate your audience and your means of reaching it.

Wilbur Schramm, pioneer mass communication scholar, reduced the communication phenomenon to four elements:

1. The individual with a message to transmit.

2. The individual for whom the message is intended.

3. The message itself.

4. Unifying experiences, backgrounds, or goals that enable a message to be coded and decoded efficiently and effectively.

Element four is crucial. By capitalizing on known common denominators, you can lend to your message those aspects of appeal, clarity, force, and tone that go a long way toward guaranteeing that your reader will willingly receive and accurately interpret your communication.

OCCASION

The "when" of article writing is another factor that causes some scholars to stumble. Rarely is it possible to make a manuscript do double duty effectively. The piece of work composed originally as a convention address will have to be retailored if it is to become a journal paper, assuming it was an apt speech in the first place. The seminar term paper or graduate thesis is seldom (if ever) in proper shape for publication. This doesn't mean, of course, that materials can't be put to different uses. They can. But considerable carpentering is invariably essential.

TYPE

There are various types or forms of writing. As we've said, we deal with three of the more common in this book. The exact format you choose will emerge from a consideration of the ecological factors we've just outlined— subject, audience, medium, purpose.

Incidentally, think of that list as forming a wheel, not a ladder. In other words, you don't have to start with a subject; you can enter at any spoke. In reconnoitering media, for example, you may identify a subject. An occasion may suggest an audience. And so on. Whatever your starting point, in constructing your manuscript you can profit from a firm grasp of that key communication strategy—fitting manuscript to medium.

FITTING MANUSCRIPT AND MEDIUM

"A house," said Frank Lloyd Wright, "should be a circumstance in nature, like a rock or tree." Had the dean of American architects been talking about writing for publication, he could not have defined any more aptly the principle of forming the manuscript to fit the medium. For that's all we mean, that each piece of writing be a natural circumstance in the publication in which it's contained.

How do you make that happen? You begin by selecting a promising subject.

CHOOSING A COMPELLING SUBJECT

The most likely source for subject ideas will naturally be your own discipline in general and your specialty in particular. On one topic or another you have a near-monopoly.

Sometimes an avocation may provide a fertile field for subject matter.

Actually, subject ideas are all around, if you make a practice of looking for them—your classrooms, laboratories, libraries, museums; journals, magazines, newspapers, radio, TV; conventions and symposia; memories, chance observations, personal contacts and colleagues; house and home; history; the calendar; even your true loves and pet peeves.

You're a scholar, of course, not a media reporter, so to any potential subject you're expected to bring a high level of expertise as a principal investigator, performing artist, practicing professional, interpreter with more than ordinary insight, commander of cogent argument, connoisseur of rhetoric, master of technical detail, or some other type of specialist.

Testing Your Idea. In picking a subject to work on, then, look first in that mirror again. Can **you** handle the project? Is your idea really within your grasp? Or is it outside the range of your experience, expertise, ability, or stature? Don't sell yourself short, by any means; but on the other hand, it's probably foolhardy to tackle a champagne project on a beer capacity.

Assuming you've picked a subject within your scope, put it to these tests:

- Is your idea **useful** for your intended readers, or is it merely a means of self-expression for you?
- Is it **salient**? Does it make a difference now?
- Is it **timely**? A fresh entrée or a warmed-over casserole?
- Is it **substantial**, based on well-documented data or inspired insights, or is it sophomoric?
- Does it contribute something **new** to the profession?

And now the most important question: Do you know a publication into which your subject will fit?

To answer that question, there's no substitute for a thorough and continuous study of your options.

What About Your Thesis? The first subject idea to put to these tests could very well be your thesis, about which you're rightfully proud.

What do you do with it?

One option, of course, is to evaluate it in terms of turning the whole thing into a book—with considerable tailoring, no doubt. If you honestly believe that approach has possibilities, adapt the tactics we outline in a forthcoming chapter on getting a textbook published.

A second option is to extract any experimental data as a research paper, adapting the tactics we outline in a forthcoming chapter on getting research findings published.

A third option is to convert one or more of the chapters into an interpretive article or essay, adapting the tactics we outline in a forthcoming chapter on getting that form of productive scholarship into print.

Let's face it: a fourth option is to forget it. It's no criticism of a thesis that it has no exploitative value. After all, it's served its purpose.

Assessing the "market value" of your thesis—as of any subject idea—demands a thorough command of intelligence about the publishing world, to which we now turn your attention.

RECONNOITERING THE PUBLICATION WORLD

Casting About. There's no better place to begin your search for suitable publication outlets than your department reference room with its selected shelvings. It may be your good fortune to find an annotated bibliography of periodicals in your particular discipline; for example, a comprehensive annotated list of over 300 international journals accepting articles in the field of education: *Publication Sources in Educational Leadership: A Compilation of Publication Outlets for the Creative Exchange of Information in Educational Administration and Supervision* (Lancaster PA: Technomic Publishing, 1991).

But don't stop with visiting your reference room; its resources may be limited, or your best bets may lie in journals in collateral fields. So branch out to the campus library. There you're practically sure to find some excellent reference aids:

- For scholarly journals, *Ulrich's International Periodicals Directory*, *Standard Periodicals Directory*, *Serials Directory*, and/or *MLA Directory of Periodicals*.
- For publishers of trade books and magazines, *Writer's Market*.
- For publishers of scholarly books and textbooks, *Literary Marketplace*.
- For news media, *Gale Directory of Publications and Broadcast Media* (formerly *N.W. Ayer's*), and *Editor & Publisher International Yearbook*.

Don't hesitate to ask your reference librarian for clues to other aids. For example, of signal help in finding out what current American general circulation magazines are carrying is the *Reader's Guide to Periodical Literature*, a monthly index (later bound in semi-annual volumes) of articles by author, title, date, and publication, categorized under topic headings based on Library of Congress nomenclature.

There's one catch: the LC and hence *RG* can be slow in adopting newer classification options. For example, when a new breed of environmental scholars went to *RG* in the mid-'60s, the only articles they could find under "Environmental Management" referred to heating and air conditioning. What they were looking for they could locate only under assorted forms of "Conservation"—water, soil, forest, and so on. Today, of course, environmentalism has its own multiple *RG* categories.

Fortunately, activist college librarians are creating new subject headings every month to keep up with the *zeitgeist*, and pressuring the Library of Congress to step up its cadence in reflecting changing times. In the past decade the LC has added over 400 new headings, from "Anti-smoking movement" to "*Glasnost*" and "Tex-Mex music." But you're apt to find *RG* headings still lagging behind avant-garde scholarship. So, hunt.

And don't forget about the young and hungry journals that have appeared since the latest bound directory was published. Fortunately, *The Chronicle of Higher Education* regularly carries a valuable listing of new scholarly periodicals as they emerge, with a succinct description of what each one is looking for in the way of manuscripts.

Journals in your discipline may also offer occasional summaries of projected collections of invited papers.

Although it isn't essential that you use it, a very comprehensive and efficient way to do bibliographic research today is via a computerized search—looking both for papers published in your subject area and for publications likely to carry a paper on your topic. Essentially, via modems, you have over 500 on-line indexes to choose from that can put you in touch with countless books, periodicals, essays, pamphlets, and statistics. Also, many research libraries have CD-ROM (compact disc read-only-memory) indexes available, which work much like on-line databases. Again, most of these technological databases use the same subject descriptors as those provided by the Library of Congress.

Another recent innovation in bibliographic research is *Current Contents* on diskette. This index allows you to review the table of contents of thousands of scholarly journals in minutes, screen a full description of any article, and print preferred materials or save them to a floppy disk.

For a complete discussion on using computerized databases, see Professor Joseph M. Moxley's chapter on that subject in his *Writing and Publishing for Academic Authors* (Lanham MD: University Press of America, 1992). Or discuss even more recent tools with your campus librarian.

Professors seeking to expand articles into specialized books should pay particular attention to the more than 70 university presses that serve scholarship in effective and imaginative ways. In the wake of changes in commercial publishing brought about by corporate mergers, campus press lists may assume increasing relevance through the growing practice of commissioning or contracting in advance to sign up promising and desirable authors. The University of Tennessee Press has recently published Professor Paul Parson's book, *Getting Published: The Acquisition Process at University Presses*.

However, campus press publishers themselves are by no means in agreement on how to proceed in an era clouded by financial and cultural upheaval. At a recent convention, some argued for going after the best scholars, seeking wider audiences outside academe, and publishing serious general interest books that commercial publishers overlook. Others saw such a diversion of resources as a threat to what's supposed to be the lifeblood of university presses, the scholarly monograph.

Yet all could coalesce in honoring the Johns Hopkins University Press for bringing out a book that 49 commercial presses had turned down and which then sold 100,000 copies in 1989 alone— *Staying Dry: A Practical Guide to Bladder Control*, by academicians Kathryn L. Burgio, K. Lynette Pearce, and Angelo J. Lucco. Of course it didn't hurt that Ann Landers endorsed the book in her syndicated newspaper column.[6]

Do you have such a "Golden Fluke Award" book in your repertoire?

Another excellent source of up-to-date information on the world of scholarly publishing is the bimonthly review of academic life, *Lingua franca*, which regularly carries an "Inside Publishing" column. For example, in a typical issue you could have learned what Duke University's *South Atlantic Quarterly* is up to; that the Princeton Series of Contemporary Poets is in limbo; that Basil Blackwell is expanding its journals division; that the University of Pittsburgh is working on a series of original-language critical editions of 120 20th-century literary works from 22 Latin American and Caribbean countries; that the University of Virginia was seeking manuscripts for a new series, "Knowledge: Disciplinarity and Beyond"—books that track the histories, rhetorics, methodologies, and "institutional topographics" of academic disciplines; that the Ecco Press is inaugurating a new series of book-length essays on artists; and how the formative field of film studies has editors and publishers in a quandary about how to proceed. All good information for the scholar seeking outlets.

Nobody seems to know exactly how many scholarly journals there are, but most estimates place the number published in the U.S. alone in the tens of thousands. The Institute for Scientific Information, a reference data bank in Philadelphia, tracks articles in 7,000 scholarly journals, including foreign publications—probably only about 25% of what's actually out there. The Modern Language Association's most recent *Directory of Periodicals* lists some 3,200 journals dealing with literature, linguistics, language, and folklore alone.

Then there are 5,000-plus general circulation periodicals and an estimated 500 book publishers as well for you to analyze—and consider.

Not only is the number of periodicals in circulation at one time known imprecisely, new journals and magazines are born seemingly every day, as disciplines expand and/or fractionate and as differentiated audiences arise. As we've said, *The Chronicle of Higher Education* carries a listing of new scholarly journals just about every week, and *Writer's Digest* keeps track of new (and deceased) general circulation magazines. It pays to keep abreast of such developments because young periodicals tend to be hungry for manuscripts. A University of Mississippi journalism professor even publishes an annual annotated bibliography—*Samir Husni's Guide to New Consumer Magazines.*

Keep your eye as well on developments in the field of electronic journals—periodicals that are distributed over computer networks. At present they're held in low repute by many academicians, but they could stimulate a major shift in the nature of scholarly communication.

The Jan. 26, 1994, issue of *The Chronicle of Higher Education* recorded a breakthrough in the world of electronic journals when it reported that the Online Journal of Current Clinical Trials, a "virtual journal" which appears only in electronic form *sans* hard copy, has been selected by the National Library of Medicine for inclusion in its *Index Medicus*, a monthly publication of citations from roughly 3,300 biochemical journals used widely by researchers and doctors—"an important achievement" for its "publisher," the American Association for the Advancement of Science. Said Patricia A. Morgan, AAAS publications director: "We now have a solid template for peer-reviewed electronic scholarly publishing." The AAAS has since decided to sell that journal to a private publishing house.

Along with the appearance of scholarly journals that exist only on computers and never in type, a number of print journals are being distributed via computer as well as by mail. For example, a faculty team at Johns Hopkins has developed an easy-to-use system for displaying full text and images from three journals published by the University's press[7].

What all the swooshing world of CD-ROM and Internet is going to mean to scholarly publishing is now only dimly seen. The Seattle *Times* for March 4, 1994, quoted a University of Washington librarian as saying that "electronic journals will push libraries and scholars to convert to bytes on the information superhighway." But the source went on to say that "some older faculty members shun electronic journals." And it remains to be determined which venue will become dominant, CD-ROM or Internet.

At this stage of the game, tenure-track assistant professors will have to play it by ear.

However, it's a cinch that "information technology will play a major role in the reshaping of higher education to meet the needs of the next century," University of Wisconsin-Madison Chancellor David Ward believes. For example:

> The rate of change in the knowledge base has accelerated so much that there are now multimedia forms of expression. . . . There will be some functionally specific ways in which different kinds of media are appropriate for different kinds of information. . . . It doesn't mean that the book disappears but that the book now will share the stage with a variety of ways in which we express, store, and present information.[8]

The assistant professor who remains information-technology illiterate will probably become an endangered species.

Zeroing In. Unless the screen you used was too fine, your casting about should net you upwards of a couple dozen publications that would find your subject compatible. From your years as a grad student, you're no doubt abundantly familiar with several of them. All you know about the others is what you read in an annotated directory of periodicals. In such a case the best way to get a line on what a journal is accepting is to consult its "Guidelines for Contributors," which habitually appears on the inside back cover. If none's there or elsewhere, don't hesitate to write for one.

Here's what you might get from a hypothetical journal:

Guidelines for Contributors
THE JOURNAL OF AUSTRALIAN STUDIES

Submit to: The Pacific Rim University Press, 164 West Coronado Avenue, La Jolla CA 01293.

Style Guide: University of Chicago Press, *A Manual of Style*, or consult the "Note to Contributors" on the masthead of any issue of *Journal*.

Type of MS: Accepts original typescript, double-spaced research papers, interpretive essays, technical reports, book reviews related to Australian history, culture, public issues, demographics, geography, trends. Particularly interested in aborigine studies, genealogy of today's leaders, impact of U.S. media, endemic gambling, Anzac traditions, environmental hazards, economic strategies. Usual length: 2,500-3,000 words, with a maximum of 4,000-5,000. Average of six articles per issue.

Mechanics: Submit original on white opaque paper (8½" x 11") plus three copies with a self-addressed stamped envelope and a covering letter. Author(s), give full name, rank, department, and university, or any other pertinent identifying information. No cost or pay for articles published. Covered reprints available at a cost varying according to length. Author(s) receive(s) two copies of *Journal* and six offsheets free.

Disposition: Receipt of MS acknowledged within a week if accompanied by a self-addressed postcard. Decision of Editorial Board in four to six months. Published approximately a year after acceptance. Rejected manuscripts are sometimes criticized for possible reconsideration.

Such a guideline gives you a pretty fair idea of what you might submit and how, but changing times and editors may have passed by a guideline the publishers haven't adjusted since it was set in type a decade ago. In any case, there's really no substitute for analyzing a half-dozen current issues of your journals of choice.

What do you look at? The table of contents; the masthead slogan; the cast of characters—editors, editorial board (anybody you know?), authors; departments; advertisements; and, of course, the articles themselves in some detail.

What do you look for? Range of subject matter; style, treatment, organization, length; evidence of audience type and level;

proclivities of the editors; mechanics—charts, graphs, tables, illustrations; title and citation format; in short, all the increments of intelligence that can help you answer the question, "How can I best fit my MS to this medium?"

Analyze your market with all the finesse you can muster, "reading between the lines," as Michael Seidman[9] puts it, because "editors, even within the same genre, have their own tastes and needs." For example, Bill Campion of Midland discovered distinct differences between two related magazines by analyzing issues of *National Geographic* on the one hand and *Scientific American* on the other. Both publications might cover the same story, as Seidman points out, but the voice of the former is much more informal. Most of its articles are first-person narratives, almost casual in nature. This doesn't mean solid information isn't there; it means that the approach is that of sitting down with the authors while they regale you with tales of their discoveries. In *Scientific American,* the articles are more scholarly in nature. Reading that magazine is like sitting in a campus lecture hall.

A manuscript tailored for one publication will obviously not be a fit the other. Frankly, it takes just as much skill writing for *National Geographic* as it does writing for *Scientific American,* but for Bill Campion, the academic pecking order dictates that an appearance in the latter will outweigh an appearance in the former. So it goes.

Picking a Target Publication. Sooner or later you've got to pick a publication of first choice. What should be your criteria?

Prospect: Which publication offers the most likelihood of interest in an article on your subject matter—submitted by you? No matter how compelling your topic or your treatment, some media simply deny their pages to other than "name" authors.

Prestige: In which publication will your byline return the most in the way of brownie points toward tenure? As we've pointed out, in every discipline and institution there's a pecking order.

Balancing these two perspectives is a crapshoot. A journal with a high rate of acceptance may be at the bottom of the pecking order, while one at the top probably has a scandalous rate of rejection. Everything else being equal, it probably makes sense to go for the gold initially and then accept tin later if necessary.

Tailoring to Fit. Now you're ready to tailor your MS to fit your journal of choice. What do you tailor? First, the subject. Then your treatment of it—general style, approach, details you include and details you exclude, length, title, beginning and ending, phraseology, attributions, rhetorical devices, data presentation, illustrations— in short, everything except your facts.

The simplest sort of example:

When biochemist Karl Paul Link first announced the synthesis of a new rat poison in the research notes of a journal of analytical chemistry, he titled his brief paper "3-(1-phenyl -2-acetylethyl)-4-hydrox-coumarin as Hemorrhagic Agent." A more elaborate succeeding article for *Chemical Industries* was titled "Warfarin: A New Anticoagulant as Rodenticide." Describing the discovery and its discoverer for a newsmagazine, a national science writer headlined his piece "Karl Paul Link: Pied Piper of the Test Tubes."

That, in a nutshell, is fitting manuscript to medium. We'll have more to say about this essential technique in the next chapter as we discuss the three principal forms of disseminating productive scholarship.

YOUR METHODS OF WORK

Stake Out a Territory. In animal species it's a congenital habit to delimit a territory to facilitate reproduction. Your needs are the same. Your office will do admirably, so long as you continue to maintain rigid office hours for students. And provided it's within reasonable commuting distance from your residence. If the latter doesn't apply, then carve out a sacrosanct niche at home—in the basement, in the attic, in a corner of the master bedroom—wherever. You simply must have a previously prepared position of retreat.

Earmark Time. "Oh, I write when the spirit moves me." Forget it. Unless you reserve a set time each day or so for applying the seat of your skirt or pants to the seat of your chair, you'll never do it. Known for his prolific writing, the senior author of this manual (ACS) was frequently asked by colleagues, "When in the world do you ever find the time?" His invariable answer: "What were you doing last Sunday morning at 5 a.m.?" A dawn patrol may not be your dish, but find one you can live with.

Line Up Your Tools. What tools you use will depend on your field—applicable references, manuals, dictionaries, thesauri, and so on. The one common tool today: a word processor/computer. Tablets and typewriters are as out as the kerosene lamp—unless, of course, your retreat is a cabin without electricity. Nothing has so revolutionized the mechanics of scholarship as word processing. In fact, some publishers may even require that you do the whole composing process for them: you send them floppy disks of your final version, done according to their specs, and they translate them right into page-proofs. Today a computer illiterate scholar is an anachronism.

Composing on a word processor or computer can present a hazard, however. Computer literate professors can become afflicted with what newspaper editors call "screenitis"—a tendency to polish whatever is visible on one screen and ignore overall coherence. The result can be a "clean" but disjointed article. As one journal editor has noted, "At the level of the individual paragraph, the writing can be very good, but there is no train of thought linking paragraphs together. Some authors will even repeat an early sentence later on in an article, as if they had never read the paper through as a whole."

An antidote: print out an entire draft of hard copy and edit that, to make sure you've connected the knee bones to the thigh bones.

With all its advantages, "there's one last thing you should know about your computer," veteran writer Art Spikol[10] says: "As miraculous as it is, it can't hold a candle to you. It can't think. It can't write. it can't imagine. It has no talent. If you want to entrust your word-counting to your computer, fine. But don't entrust your reputation to it. Because when you submit your manuscript, your computer will assume none of the responsibility, and get none of the credit . . . and none of the blame."

Have Your Theme Well in Hand. A broad topic doesn't make an effective paper or article. You've got to define sharply in your mind a particular aspect or theme or angle.

For example, let's say you're an American historian in a liberal arts college in Illinois. For a special February edition, the editor of *The Illinois Magazine of History* is soliciting contributions on "Abe Lincoln in Illinois." That's too broad, too unmanageable, too fuzzy a subject for a journal—for a book, maybe, but not for a journal. If you say, "I'll do a paper on Captain Abe Lincoln's brief career as a soldier in the Blackhawk War," now you're beginning to arrive at a subject with a handle, but you've still got some focusing to do. Let's say your topic will be how Abe was like many GIs before and since—a reluctant volunteer who spent more time fighting boredom than Indians and who looked back in later years on his days of soldiering with both loyalty and loathing. Now you've got a true theme.

Always distinguish between subject as generality and subject as specificity—and cling to the distinction. That's your lodestar as you work.

Another example of narrowing a topic:

Under the broad rubric of "black women," you could begin by picking one of such options as these:

- A specific place—New York City, for instance
- Person—Maya Angelou
- Time period—Depression
- Type—Politicians
- Aspect—Teenage mothers
- Relationship—Employment
- Event—Assassination of Martin Luther King, Jr.

But you haven't sharpened your thinking enough yet for an article. Now you want to mix and match to distill a true journal report. For instance:

- Civil rights cases involving black women during World War II.
- Black parent involvement in school desegregation efforts.
- Female black Olympic athletes.
- History of the National Council of Negro Women.
- Shirley Chisholm's influence on the feminist movement.[11]

Now, give your chosen topic a news peg or a seasonal slant and you're off and running.

Make an Outline. If you don't make an outline, the piles of notes you have scattered around on desk or bedspread will show up just as scattered in your manuscript. What form your outline takes is unimportant. It can be just a list of key sequential facts scribbled on a scrap of paper. Or it can be a fully developed affair, following all the niceties of an English composition class assignment. Use whatever form best serves you. You may need a detailed outline in order to ensure unity, coherence, and emphasis. Or you may find a more fragmentary outline permits you to write with more spontaneity. Whatever the form, make sure you have some sort of article "map" in hand or in mind before you set to work.

As one commentator recounts, "For what it's worth, I take notes, let it gel, then outline one day and write the next. If I let the outline sit too long, I lose the cohesion."

Get Away From It All. Well, you say, I've done extensive research, I've got a hideaway and writing time, I've lined up my tools, I have a theme well in mind, and an outline. Now do I write?

No. Get away from it all.

We're not kidding. Store your notes and take a break for mental digestion. You're too close to your subject. If you start writing now, you'll tie yourself in a Gordian knot. So let your ideas rest. Your unconscious mind will take over and contribute to your paper a logic and a flair that you can never achieve if you move directly from note-taking to writing.

In short, what we're saying is that all writing—even a laboratory report— is creative writing. "The light that never was, on sea or land" can shine on a research paper quite as much as on a poem.

But don't let your voluntary sabbatical run on and on. Procrastination is the enemy of productivity.

Field-Test. Now let's jump ahead to the stage where you have a first draft in hand. What do you do? Field-test.

First, a really tough job—look at your own work with an eye sufficiently jaundiced to spot your own flaws. There is perhaps no aspect of writing so difficult as objectively judging your own MS. You're so close to your work that you can't see it as others will see it. The trouble arises because you cannot recognize that what you have so well-rounded in your mind you have simply not conveyed completely and clearly on paper. Looking over a draft, you are all too prone to read into it what is not there for the reader who does not know what you know.

The remedy? Steel yourself and submit your draft for critique by valued colleagues with varied talents: someone familiar with your subject matter, someone expert in quantitative or qualitative research, someone representing your target audience, someone qualified as a connoisseur of the English language—and then sit back and take it.

Some comments will be so complimentary as to be worthless, some so savage as to be devastating. Pay particular attention to suggestions about what you say, less to quibbles about how you say it. And then revise accordingly.

A word of advice: think twice about using a friend, a relative, or a spouse as a critic. You want to improve a manuscript, not break up a relationship.

PUBLISHING AND PRODUCING

Sometime in the process of field-testing your MS, it will be well if you take a hard look at it from the mundane viewpoint of good old-fashioned grammar and sheer readability. Not that we don't think that after 20-some years of schooling you aren't skilled in the basics. It's just that scholars in any discipline can fall prey to some nagging habits.

SEVEN DEADLIES

So called because they can kill the soul of your writing:

The Verbose. The use of a whole phrase when a single word will do, the long word instead of a short one—displaying your vocabulary instead of trying to get an idea across. Example: "A recent study has shown that leaf reflectance of infrared light is dependent mainly on the nature of the cell wall/air space interface of the chlorophyll-containing spongy mesophile cells and, to a lesser extent, on the cytological features of other tissues within the leaf." If you think you have to indulge in such verbosity for the sake of scientific respectability, at least supply a translation for the uninitiated, like this: "Depending on their makeup, different plant and tree leaves reflect infrared light in different ways to produce different colors on infrared photos."

The Hackneyed. Certainly you want to avoid expressions that through overuse have lost all their freshness. Studying writing burdened with clichés and redundancies, three Marquette University scholars found 10 in one 500-word book review:

"stink. . . state-mandated . . . boost . . . watered-down . . . stamp of approval . . . flawed and inaccurate . . . accepted and widely used . . . vigorously opposed . . . complied with at any cost."

The Passive. "It was determined that. . . ." Why, oh why scholars can never say, "I discovered" or "We found," we simply don't know. Perhaps it's simply a dodge to escape responsibility, or an inculcated modesty. The debility shows up in other ways: "The reason he left college was that his health became impaired," instead of "Failing health compelled him to leave college."

The Convoluted or Run-on Sentence. At its best, such construction impedes understanding; at its worst, it can trap you into comical inaccuracies in word usage, as in these varied examples dredged up by Columbia University composition detectives:

> In 1992 it will be exactly five centuries from the date when it is said Italian mariners whom the decline of their own republics had put at the service of the world of adventure, one of the group being Christopher Columbus, seem to have discovered America while seeking for Spain a legendary passage to the Indies to offset the achievement of Portuguese discoverers who had carved their names in the history books of the westward expansion of European culture and Christianity unless to be sure the heathens had triumphed instead of succumbing to the pernicious diseases and firearms that were obviously manifest evidence of the spirit of God moving on the waters of the new open seas stretching from Occident to Orient interrupted only by new continents of immense natural resources that were to sustain the emergence of hitherto undreamed of civilizations.

> The Mormon Church has no doctrinal position on when life begins but takes a hard line against abortions performed for reasons other than to save the life of the mother or in cases of rape and incest after counseling with a bishop.

Accent on the Negative. In other words, addiction to tame, colorless, hesitant, noncommittal language. Example: "*The Taming of the Shrew* is rather weak in spots. Shakespeare does not portray Katharine as a very admirable character, nor does Bianca remain long in memory as an important character in Shakespeare's works." How much better to say, "The women in *The Taming of the Shrew* are unattractive: Katharine disagreeable, Bianca insignificant."

Dangling Modifiers. Among the most common, the participial phrase at the beginning of the sentence that doesn't refer to the grammatical subject: "A soldier of proved valor, residents entrusted him with the defense of the city" should be "A soldier of proved valor, he was entrusted with the defense of the city." "As a young and inexperienced assistant professor, the assignment appeared easy to me" should be "As a young and inexperienced assistant professor, I thought the assignment appeared easy." Violations of this rule can be ludicrous: "As a mother of five, with another on the way, her ironing board was always up." And a final example, from a recent news report:

> "Beatitude," a student art exhibit that uses religious images to support abortion rights, is at the center of a controversy at Grover Whelan Community College. Students charged the college had engaged in censorship when officials, in response to complaints from other students and politicians, covered the display with black paper. After being kept under wraps for a day, college officials reviewed their decision and ordered it to remain on display.

The Dreaded "This." Technically called a demonstrative pronoun with an indistinct antecedent, **this**, referring to the complete sense of a preceding sentence or clause, can't always carry the load and so may produce an imprecise statement: "Visiting dignitaries watched as the ground was broken for the new high-energy physics laboratory with a blowout safety wall. This is the first visible evidence of the university's plans for modernization and expansion." **This** doesn't make clear what the "first visible evidence" is. Correction: "Visiting dignitaries watched as the chancellor broke ground for the new high-energy physics laboratory with a blowout safety wall. The ceremony afforded the first visible evidence of the university's plans for modernization and expansion."

Traffic Control. If you've gotten into the habit of strewing punctuation marks around indiscriminately, reconsider that habit and think of them in terms of their value as ways to control the flow of your words for greater impact and readability. Here are some simple rules:

Use a comma before a conjunction introducing an independent clause:

> "The early records of the city have disappeared, so the story of the first years can no longer be reconstructed."

Use a semicolon to join independent clauses:

> "Smith's theories are compelling; they command attention."

Use a colon after an independent clause to introduce a list, an amplification, or an illustrative quotation:

> "Today's headlines remind you of a classic line: 'These are the times that try men's souls.'"

Use a dash to set off an abrupt break or interruption and to announce a long summary:

> "Violence—the kind you see on TV—is not honestly violent. Therein lies its harm."

We could go on and on about all of this (Is "this" indistinct here¿), but after all, this (Whoops, we did it again!) is not supposed to be a refresher course in grammar. Better that you buy, read, and put on your nightstand a little paperback, *The Elements of Style*, by William Strunk, Jr. and E.B. White. First printed in 1935, it's a little out of date now: for example, it frowns on the common fare of TV announcers, breaking sentences in two; and it contradicts several newer style books by saying that in a series of three or more terms with a single conjunction you use a comma after each term except the last. But it's still a classic guide to making your words count. As *The New York Times* says, "It's as timeless as a book can be in our age of volubility."

The Importance Of Writing Well. In an excellent paper by that title in a *University of Iowa Graduate Bulletin*, Ralph Frasca makes the telling point that "the quality of your thoughts is perceived to be only as good as your ability to express them."[12] That proviso should be tacked to your bulletin board.

Now let's quote along with Frasca from a master of sideline language, Bobby Knight: "All of us learn to write by the second grade, and then most of us go on to other things."

The acerbic Indiana University basketball coach was commenting on sports writers, but may as well have been referring to professors. Regardless of the field of study, all professors are called upon to write, and writing ability is simply assumed to be part of the intellectual repertoire they've mastered over the years. Yet publication editors complain vociferously and often about the turgid and garbled prose of their would-be contributors, Frasca says. It's an unspoken maxim in most periodical offices that editors are more likely to hold lucid, concise, and technically correct papers in higher esteem than those that are poorly constructed. (Just think of how you probably react to student term papers and essay exams.)

The clarity and technical precision of your writing inevitably influence editorial decisions, particularly in the case of scholarly journals:

"The paper that needs less work, less language repair, is more likely to get an acceptance," according to Don McComb, editor of *The Journal of Communication Inquiry*. "If you submit a poorly written manuscript, we just find we can't work with it, because unless we find a reviewer who will take up the challenge of trying to get it into shape, we'll send it back and tell you it needs to be revised because the language is a problem."

Although you may be tempted to discount writing skills in favor of your capacity to think and reason, it's by your ability to communicate that such attributes are most often judged, Frasca points out. You may have a brilliant mind, but the value placed on that mind will be considerably diminished if you demonstrate an incapacity to translate its contents into effective prose.

Writing is a public act to attract the attention of others, so it's just plain insulting to tax their time and effort with a tortuous, vague, and incompetent display of putting one word after another.

Mastering good writing isn't "busy work," a distraction from your other responsibilities. It's a powerful tool you as an assistant professor need to communicate the contents of your mind and to influence judgments made about it. It takes practice and conscientious dedication.

For a related spritely discussion of "Loose, Baggy Sentences" and other debilitating grammatical illnesses, see Claire Kehrwald Cook's chapter in *Writing and Publishing for Academic Authors,* edited by Professor Joseph M. Moxley (Lanham MD: University Press of America, 1992). It's worthy of Strunk and White.

PROFESSIONAL PROCEDURES
Preparing Your MS for Submission. And now let's jump ahead still further, to the stage when you're ready to prepare a final draft.

You've written enough themes, term papers, and theses to know in general what to do—type or print out double-spaced on 8½" x 11" single-sided numbered sheets of white bond (no crude dot matrix printing and no spreadsheets). Besides numbering each page of the MS, it's well to include as well your last name, in case manuscripts get mixed up on an editor's desk.

Cover your MS with a letter to the editor that makes clear your status. (A professional letterhead adds aplomb.) Add on separate sheets any charts, graphs, tables, or illustrations, properly captioned. Include a large, self-addressed stamped return envelope. Add cardboard stiffening. Mail first-class in a 9" x 12" envelope, addressed to the editor by name. As a courtesy you can enclose a couple of extra copies of your MS, but in an age when photocopy machines are ubiquitous, it's not absolutely necessary to do so.

Rules for submitting magazine articles or book proposals vary somewhat from this procedure; we'll take them up in sequence later.

Keeping Records. Writing for publication requires organization, notably that you keep a record on each MS: stage(s) in preparation, date of periodical, date of acknowledgment, date of rejection or acceptance. You can make notations on a 3" x 5" card; you can keep an elaborate journal; if you want to be dramatic you can post the data on a bulletin board in your office for all to see; or you can keep a discreet computer record. The format isn't important; keeping track is—if only to avoid the embarrassment of sending the same article to the same magazine twice.

Here's a "bookkeeping form" suggested by Professor William Moore of the University of Kentucky:

MS Title _____

First Draft _____

Final Copy _____

Expenses Incurred _____

Sent to _____

Date _____

Rejected Date _____

Accepted Date _____

Publication Date _____

Some Standard Rules. Don't (repeat, **do not**) send a manuscript simultaneously to more than one publication. (Exception: textbooks can be submitted to several publishers at once.) First of all, if properly tailored, your MS will fit only one periodical anyway; second, your submission is a tacit guarantee that you are offering uncontaminated goods. For example, if you submit a paper to the higher education journal *Change*, you'll get back a card saying, "It is our assumption that your manuscript has not been concurrently submitted to any other journal or magazine; if it is under consideration by another publisher, please let us know immediately." The clear implication—"Don't play dirty pool with us."

If you're a nervous type and want to make sure right away that your MS has been received, enclose a stamped, self-addressed postcard that says something like, "We have received your paper, *Surviving in the Urban Wilderness* and have it under consideration."

Once you get that card back, don't hound the editor. Particularly in the case of refereed journals, review can take months as your MS makes the rounds of busy fellow professors. If you think it's really time to check up on an article, wait another week. Then send off a friendly tracer letter on the long shot that your MS has actually gotten buried in somebody's in-basket.

Don't ever send off a MS without keeping a copy, either a hard copy or a floppy disk, properly sequestered.

Don't give up after one rejection. Retailor and resubmit to another likely journal. (After multiple rejections, of course, a strategic withdrawal may be prudent; put the MS in a bottom drawer until you can approach it with renewed vigor and a fresh perspective.)

Don't wait too long to start your next project. To be a consistently published scholar, there's no substitute for keeping manuscripts in the mail.

Practicing Public Relations. And now comes that halcyon day when your paper appears in print. Don't bury your light under a bushel. Distribute reprints among appropriate colleagues, both on and off your campus, particularly those who reviewed your MS. Send a copy to the campus information office; the professionals there can judge whether it has any news value. Some relatives and friends may also appreciate knowing of your accomplishment.

Then anticipate your paper being cited by other scholars. There's no greater satisfaction. (Unless, of course, it's reaping book royalties—or getting promoted to tenure.) And then move on to other publication projects.

As you accrue a list of citations to your work, keep a running list (preferably in your computer) so you don't have to hunt them all down when you need to produce them.

Words From The Wise. As a finale to this survey of scholarly writing and publishing, we quote from Professor Howard B. Altman of the University of Louisville, who draws on his experience as a prolific author, lecturer, and member of the editorial board of *Academic Leader.* Some of his suggestions are complementary of what we've been saying, some novel:

1. Realize that manuscript evaluators are influenced by (a) relevance to topic, (b) clarity of argument, and (c) persuasiveness of presentation and conclusions.
2. Conform to a journal's guidelines with respect to content and style.
3. Have colleagues whom you trust read your MS critically and give you constructive feedback.
4. If you're under the gun to publish, aim for a journal whose rejection rate is not too high.
5. It's often easier to appear in foreign journals.
6. Don't over-footnote; that's what separates term papers from published articles.
7. Make sure your information and insights are accurate and current.
8. Keep an eye on the length of your paper. Most journals won't deal with an MS over 20 pages or under 5.
9. Consider finding a co-author who will contribute skills and knowledge supplementary to your own.
10. If you're a novice, test out your writing by submitting to a local outlet before attempting a national journal.
11. If your submission gets rejected anywhere, try, try again.[13]

If you sense some of Altman's thoughts are at variance with what's gone before in this manual, it's a good time to appreciate there's no one way to get published.

Mark of Distinction. As you go about developing a writing-and-publishing *modus operandi* that's right for you, we believe you'll discover that reporting about scholarship can be as challenging and rewarding in its own way as scholarship itself— communicating with fellow scholars and mediating between specialists and laypersons.

A university president[14] once pointed out that "a dozen fields of thought are today congested with knowledge that the physical and social sciences have unearthed, and the whole tone and temper of American life can be lifted by putting this knowledge into general circulation. I raise the recruiting trumpet for the interpreter."

As you walk the road to tenure, you can join the growing ranks of scholars adept at both research and interpretation. "These intergrades in human taxonomy," ecologist Aldo Leopold[15] wrote of such scholars, "are perhaps more important than those which so perplex the mammalogists and ornithologists. Their skulls are not yet available to the museums, but even a layman can see that their brains are distinctive."

THE "BUSINESS" SIDE OF WRITING

LEGAL AND ETHICAL CONSTRAINTS

It's a free country, but for writers, not that free. It would take a book, and then some, to cover all the ins and outs of press law. All we'll do here is outline key aspects a scholar ought to be conscious of.

Copyright. Facts as such can't be copyrighted, only the specific expression or wording of information. However, since the intent of copyright law is clearly to protect the original writer, acknowledgments are always in order, even if you don't use exact quotations. (Besides, what better way to demonstrate your scholarly diligence?)

When and how you can use such materials depends on whether a source is "free." You can quote freely from a source said to be in the public domain: your own interviews, works on which the copyright has expired, public documents, giveaway materials.

It's best to assume that any printed material not clearly in the public domain is copyrighted material. You can still quote from such material provided you do three things:

1. acknowledge the source fully,

2. obtain permission of the copyright owner, and

3. adhere to the doctrine of "fair use." The last is a thorny issue. The rule of thumb is 300 words or less, but that has no standing in the courts.

Since the specter of plagiarism shadows every scholar, the best thing to do is to cite everything and get permission for every direct or indirect *extended* quote. To do so, record the following data as you take notes from printed material:

1. from a periodical or newspaper—writer, headline, name of publication, address of publisher, date, volume and issue number, page(s),

2. from a book—author(s), title, date of publication, name and address of publisher, date of copyright and name of copyright holder, page(s).

To get permission to use a quote, you write letters to the copyright owners. Each letter should indicate exactly how the material is to be used, the precise passage(s) to be quoted, the context it will be quoted in, and the bibliographical acknowledgment you propose to use.

If all this sounds like work, it is. But remember, the law that makes it necessary is the same law that should protect your own work from word thieves.

Usually you'll be granted permission to quote gratis, unless an author has some reason for not wishing to be associated with your work. If you and/or a publisher stand to make money from your project, then the copyright owner will probably want a piece of the pie. Writers of song lyrics are particularly voracious. You'll just have to decide how big a bite you can afford.

It's ordinarily your responsibility as a writer to get all necessary clearances and file them with the publisher. When an editor accepts your manuscript he or she wants to be assured the title is clear.

"Copyright permission: it's not just a good idea, it's the law—and higher education isn't above the law. If you're wondering if you need copyright permission on a particular work, chances are you do. Unless you're positive that the 'fair use' doctrine applies, it's best to obtain permission." That's the word from Dennis R. Black, attorney and editor of *Perspective*: *The Campus Legal Monthly*.

Libel. If you have a hand in publishing something that injures another identified individual, you may be subject to suit for libel. If it is something that would be highly offensive to a reasonable person, you may be subject in some states to a suit for invasion of privacy. To be sure, it's highly unlikely that an academician would be subject to such hazards, if only because the deep pockets of a publisher are the more lucrative target. But it has happened. When in doubt, consult an attorney.

Ethics. A more likely hazard for a scholar is the slippery slope of questionable data or of breathing implications into those data that simply aren't there. Even in academe, there are different strokes for different folks, as the saying goes. The best advice we can give is just this: in the final analysis you have to live with yourself. If you can honestly rationalize behavior that might be cause for professional concern, OK. But if you know in your heart that what you're doing is alien to the better angels of your nature, don't do it. As Hoagy Carmichael once said, "Don't ever play anything that ain't right."

We can't guarantee, of course, that if you follow the guidelines of this chapter and the next you'll publish far and wide. However, you certainly improve your chances when you can learn from the successes and the failures of colleagues who've spent time trodding the paths of publication.

NOTES

1. Carnegie Foundation for the Advancement of Teaching, "The Payoff for Publication Leaders," Change Mar.-Apr. 1991: 27-30.

2. Robert Boice, "Writing Blocks and Tacit Knowledge," *The Journal of Higher Education* Jan.-Feb. 1993: 19-54.

3. Donald K. Jarvis, *Junior Faculty Development* (New York: Modern Language Association of America, 1991).

4. Robert Boice, *Professors as Writers* (Stillwater, OK: New Forums, 1990).

5. Mark P. Zanna, and John M. Darley, eds., *The Complete Academic* (New York: Random House, 1986).

6. Ellen K. Coughlin, "U. Presses Ponder Their Fate," *The Chronicle of Higher Education* 10 July 1991: A5.

7. Thomas J. DeLoughry, "Journals *via* Computer," *The Chronicle of Higher Education* 9 Mar. 1994: A25.

8. David Ward, "Technology and the Changing Boundaries of Higher Education," *Educom Review* Jan.-Feb. 1994: 23-27.

9. Michael Seidman, "Study the Market!" *Writer's Digest* Jan. 1994: 39-41.

10. Art Spikol, "Who's in Charge?" *Writer's Digest* Oct. 1993: 63-4.

11. Tara Fulton, unpublished paper, Loyola-University of Chicago Library, 1991.

12. Ralph Frasca, "The Importance of Writing Well," *University of Iowa Graduate Journal*: 1-3.

13. Howard Altman, "Helping Faculty to Publish," *The Department Chair* Spring 1991: 1, 18-19.

14. Glenn Frank, quoted in Benjamin F. Gruenberg, *Science and the Public Mind* (New York: Harper, 1935).

15. Aldo Leopold, "The State of the Profession," *The Journal of Wildlife Management* Nov. 1940: 346.

11 BELL, CANDLE, AND BOOK

As we said in the previous chapter, we're going to concentrate here on three principal forms of scholarly writing: the standard research paper, the interpretive article or essay, and the textbook. Distinctions among the three, however, are bound to be fuzzy. For example, what we say about developing a textbook generally applies to building a technical book out of a research paper or a trade book out of an essay. And much of what we say about tailoring an essay applies about as well to constructing a research paper or a textbook for a particular editor or publisher. So interpret freely between the sections of this chapter.

What is more, any disciplinary preference for any of the three forms of scholarly writing may be more imagined than real. For example, while what we're calling the standard research paper is most at home in the sciences, humanities scholars on occasion may employ the format. Likewise, while the interpretive article or essay is the format of choice for humanities scholars, professors in the sciences and professional schools also use it commonly. The textbook format is obviously interdisciplinary.

THE STANDARD RESEARCH PAPER

Each form of discourse takes its signals from the requirements of a particular type of publication; the research paper, for example, from the scholarly journal. The researching professor and the scholarly journal are symbiotic; neither could live without the other. Scholars necessarily, then, learn all they can about learned periodicals.

UNDERSTANDING LEARNED JOURNALS

Learned journals have as their mission to disseminate the fruits of research and productive scholarship. Few of them make money, or at least not much. If they at least break even, they're content. They're "kept" by learned societies, by universities, by publishing houses, by editors laboring gratis, by librarians, by scholar-subscribers paying high subscription rates. Their survival hinges on keeping up with the times, by publishing the works of known savants, by somehow defeating rising publication and mailing costs. A common fear: that they'll be rendered irrelevant by scholars who "break" results of their research in the press before their papers appear. That's why some journals will yank a paper if it's been upstaged, and why scientists are increasingly timing their public announcements to the appearance of their papers in refereed journals.

The thing to remember is that learned journals need you just as much as you need them. Without a flow of publishable manuscripts their editors would be bereft. So be a good sport and meet their needs.

RECOGNIZING YOUR OPTIONS

Let's say you're a new-found friend of Bill Campion at Midland University—an assistant professor of educational psychology in the School of Education. Your research emphasis is child development, and you have some interesting data and theories to communicate. You're reconnoitering for scholarly journals in your field that seek "reports of original research, especially empirical studies making contributions to theory."

If you cast your net widely enough, you'll find a whole range of options:

- *Journal of Applied Psychology,*
- *Journal of Counseling Psychology,*
- *Journal of Educational Research,*
- *Journal of Experimental Education,*
- *Journal of Experimental Psychology,*
- *Journal of General Psychology,*
- *Journal of Social Psychology,*
- *Peabody Journal of Education,*
- *American Educational Research Journal,*
- *California Journal of Educational Research,*
- *Child Development,*
- *Educational and Psychological Measurement,*
- *Harvard Educational Review.*

And probably some others that haven't made it into the directories yet.

Which journal you pick as your initial target will depend on an astute analysis of how well the thrust of your subject meets the thrust of a particular journal, on a comparison of rejection rates, and on a frank recognition of that well-known pecking order.

THAT PECKING ORDER

Determining the ranking of journals has become important to scholars and those who evaluate their performance, because although all journals seem to be created equal, in fact some are more equal than others.

Three techniques stand out when it comes to ranking professional journals:

- the *reputational* approach, in which a panel of scholars votes subjectively on which journals in a particular field are the more prestigious;
- the *citation analysis* approach, in which librarians determine the number of times a journal's articles are cited or quoted elsewhere;
- and the *rejection rate* approach, in which the easier it is to get into a journal, the lower its "Nielsen rating."

Each method is relatively crude. It's probably an ecological fallacy that the quality of an article can be determined solely from the ranking of the journal in which it appears. In fact, at least one study suggests greater variation in the intrinsic quality of articles appearing within a given journal than among journals.

Sociologists Ralph A. Weisheit and Robert M. Regoli advise scholars to "rank journals in sets or clusters rather than by assigning artificially precise indicators of rank."[1]

Be that as it may, the important pecking order for you is the one employed by your evaluators, assuming you can figure it out with any certainty. When in doubt, ask your librarian for an assessment. Variety is also an important consideration. As one reviewer notes, "If all your articles appear in one journal, even in the most prestigious, people may suspect you have an 'in' there."

Regardless of your journal of choice, the organization of your paper will follow a stylized outline common to almost all research journals, similar to the outline you used in planning your work and in writing a research proposal.

ORGANIZING YOUR PAPER

A research paper can be based on either qualitative or quantitative paradigms. At least in the physical, biological, and social sciences, it will usually include the following components, more or less in this order:

Abstract. Say, a hundred words or so, in which you summarize clearly and concisely the whole of your paper, from A to Z. Don't just say what you did; say what it means.

Problem Statement. A theory to be tested, a practical issue to be resolved, a question to be answered.

Review of the Relevant Literature. Without going back to the Punic Wars, it's better here to err on the side of inclusion rather than exclusion, lest you inadvertently leave out just the reference a reviewer may be looking for.

Description of Your Research Methodology. This section should be precise and complete enough that another scholar could replicate your research without stumbling.

Report of Results. Hew to the facts objectively; let the chips fall where they may.

Discussion. A frank recognition that your results did not support your hypothesis may be just as valuable as a positive outcome. Speculation about *why* you got what you did and *how* to direct future investigation may be the most significant aspect of your paper.

Summary. For those readers who'll only read your summary, give them both barrels. Where you draw conclusions, support them with appropriate research methodology and documentation. You can indulge in recommendations and/or conjecture so long as you identify them as such.

ABOUT STYLE

Not so long ago, a classics professor had some fun in a point-of-view piece in *The Chronicle of Higher Education* under the title, "Semantics and Symbioses: How to Write an Article to Impress Your Peers." Among other recommendations, Marleen Boudreau Flory said:

1. In the title, try to hide the subject from the readers;

2. Lavish attention on your footnotes because all readers will read them, only a few the article itself;

3. When it comes to style, protect yourself by writing everything in the passive voice and by inventing new terminology nobody knows;

4. Keep before you at all times a mental picture of a board of review counting pages.

Flory was only half-kidding. Unfortunately it's true that some scholars "impose upon themselves a certain technical lingo as a mark of professional respectability." As *Scientific Monthly* has complained: "The specter haunts these scholars, not of a frustrated reader, but of a tart review accusing them of superficiality." As a matter of fact, the senior author of this manual once got back a manuscript with this notation: "This work is so interestingly written we are persuaded it is not sufficiently scholarly."

Schoenfeld changed all the active voice to passive voice, all the first and second person to third person, most of the monosyllables to polysyllables, and sent the MS to a sister journal—where it was happily accepted.

If you think this sort of advice is an aberration, here's more in the same vein:

Be very careful when choosing a title for your article. Promotion committees never read papers, but they do see titles. The more pedantic, the better; scholarly work isn't supposed to be interesting. I almost called my articles on dictionary usage in last year's *French Review* "Practicing Safe Lex," until I realized that promotion committees would see them. Of course, don't make the titles so pedantic that no journal will want to publish them.

Be sure to cite as many sources as possible. A long bibliography has come to represent thoroughness of research. It helps get articles published in the first place. Even colleagues who do not read your work may flip to the back of a reprint to look at the bibliography.

Avoid first-person articles or simple reports on how you do things [in the classroom]. Some colleagues do not even consider this research, no matter how useful it may be. . . . By comparing one's own program with what has been described in the literature, one can accomplish the same thing, but not make it look like memoirs. Thus, "TA Supervision in French at State University" becomes "Alternative Models for Supervision."

That's advice from Joel Walz of the French department at the University of Georgia, writing in the November 1991 *AAUSC Bulletin*.

It doesn't have to be that way. And indeed scholarly journals are increasingly asking you to break away from the straitjacket of scholasticism. So let your thoughts flow out naturally and simply, as if you were speaking to a colleague or leading a seminar. In other words, talk to your keyboard; and talk to say something, not to show off.

This approach will help you use straightforward English, with a minimum of gobbledygook, tortured construction, and Edwardian prose. Strive always for the phrase that most strikingly imparts meaning, even if it borders on the colloquial. Edward Schten, for example, lifted a scholarly article in *Public Administration Review* out of a scholarly rut by writing about "good guy" public servants vs. "bad guy" pressure groups. In a recent *Journal of Higher Education*, reporting on reasons for a national decline in the number of transfer students from community colleges upward, W. Norton Grubb said the answer was not a single stab in the back but a concatenation of a large number of causes—what he called "death by a thousand cuts." Observing the 500th anniversary of that fateful voyage of Columbus in 1492, historian David Gelman wrote, "Over the centuries, his reputation has tended to expand and deflate like some unruly Thanksgiving Day parade balloon." In the same vein, historian David Gates spoke to Columbus: "You started out with the best intentions. You were going to get rich *and* save the world. You didn't see any contradiction there. You were the first American."

It must be admitted, of course, that in some disciplines there may be a certain risk attached to sounding too "popular," particularly on the part of an assistant professor. If that's your situation, adjust accordingly.

ABOUT DATA PRESENTATION

In "The Science of Scientific Writing" in a recent *American Scientist*, Judith Swan of Princeton and George G. Gopen of Duke[2] offered some excellent advice on how to choose from a variety of formats in presenting your data:

- A list of data sets is easier to interpret than a line of data separated by semi-colons, especially when the data sets may also contain other symbols, such as equal signs (=) or Greek letters.
- Presenting the data sets in columnar form with clear column headings would be better.
- Numerous columns of data are best presented in tables.
- Data columns or tables should flow exactly as we read, with contextual material on the left in a pattern that produces an expectation of regularity, and clarifying or statistical information to the right, in order of greater and greater detail. It might be easier to think of it as "an outline lying down."

TAILORING TO FIT

In making an initial evaluation of how well you've married your research paper to the requirements of a particular journal, editors and reviewers are drawn inevitably to two inescapable components—your title and your citations.

The Title. While an editor may edit your title or change it all together, it's the mark of the pro to propose one as suitable as possible. And you should be able to do so accurately and with feeling, since learned journal formats, typography, and metier change very little from issue to issue. In structure, style, and even letter count, strive for an exact fit.

If your journal of choice prefers stark labels, use one, like "Weight Gain Investigations Revisited" for *American Journal of Clinical Nutrition*. For *Science News*, a paper on the same subject might be titled, with more flair, "Fat and Fiction: Calorie for calorie, the thin gain more—and other weighty findings."

In the same vein, writing for *American Heritage*, William L. Rivers titled a historical profile thus: "Thurlow Weed: Back Room Strategist." For a more scholarly journal he might have called it "A Study of the Influence of Thurlow Weed on the Election of John Quincy Adams."

What you don't include in your title can be just as diagnostic of its fit as what you put in, and vice versa. For example, take this title/subtitle in *Journalism Quarterly*:

> **The Press and NEPA: The Case of the Missing Agenda**
> With respect to "the most sweeping environmental law ever passed by a United States Congress," neither the daily press nor specialized periodicals played an agenda-setting role. Congress constructed its own social reality.

The author could use the terms "agenda-setting" and "social reality" freely because they're in the lexicon of every professor of mass communication, but the National Environmental Policy Act (NEPA) had to be explained as "the most sweeping . . . law."

A similar example: In the title of this manual, the terms "mentor" and "tenure" are apt, since their meaning is familiar on any campus; in a manual for another profession, you'd have to substitute alternate terms familiar to that audience.

Signature. The signature (byline) for journal articles is likewise all-important as a proof that a potential author has studied the journal in question and therefore is worthy of serious consideration: type style and location (beginning or end; left, right, or center) of author's name, academic affiliation, rank. There are dozens of combinations—yet only one for each journal.

Clean Copy. Misspelled words, triple letters, missing copy, repeated lines, grammatical errors, and so on can only suggest that the author takes neither his/her work nor the audience seriously. (And don't trust your computer's spelling and grammar checking programs to do it all. Even the best programs won't catch every sort of mistake.)

Citations. Next to—if not before—your title/abstract and signature, editors and reviewers will look at your footnotes/references/bibliography.

For one thing, they'll check to see how current your MS is. If your dates are all three years or more old, you're passé.

Then they'll look for names of authors known to be crucially pertinent to your subject matter (perhaps even their own). If you've ignored relevant papers, you're in trouble.

Finally they'll inspect the style of your references, because nothing is so diagnostic of the degree to which you've tailored your MS to the specifications of the journal in question. A miss is as good as a mile.

If you've seen one reference, you've seen 'em all? Guess again. There are more than two dozen formats in common use today, sometimes even within a single discipline—AGU, AAA, APSA, MLA, Chicago A, Chicago B, AIP, ASM, ANSI, CBE, LSA, GSA, ACS, APA, ASA, Cambridge, UP, AIBS, AMA, ICMJE, RAI, Praeger, SSSA, Turabian, Wiley.

For example, a so-called standard humanities footnote style (carried at the bottom of each printed page in a journal; in a book, at the end, chapter by chapter; in each case, preceded by a serial number superscript clued to a corresponding number at the appropriate place in the text):

> [9]Clay Schoenfeld, "Communicating Research Findings," in Robert J. Griffin *et al.*, *Interpreting Public Issues* (Ames: Iowa State University Press, 1991), p. 269.

Or a so-called standard hard sciences reference style (carried alphabetically at the end of the paper or book, with the date appearing after the cited author's name in the text):

> Schoenfeld, Clay 1991
> "Communicating research findings," in Griffin *et al.*, Interpreting Public Issues. Ames, Iowa: Iowa State University Press. 490 pp. 269.

A common variation, in which the cited references are listed alphabetically at the end of the paper or book and assigned a serial number, that number then appearing in association with the citation in the text:

> 21. SCHOENFELD, C., 1991, Communicating research findings, in Griffin *et al.*, Interpreting Public Issues (Iowa State University Press, Ames), 269.

Some journals may employ both footnotes and references, the former to indicate source of research funding and/or prior presentation at a conference, to acknowledge the assistance of any collaborators, and to pay the inevitable homage to a significant other "without whom the pursuit of my career would be dust and ashes." Other journals may call for a bibliography in which you include source materials not specifically cited.

And so on and on through picayune variations. The variations may seem slight to you, but they're significant in an editor's eyes.

Don't (repeat, **do not**) adopt any of these styles—or any other— unless it's the one in current use by the journal at which you're aiming. Which means, of course, that you've got to consult a current issue and/or its "instructions to contributors."

If you get rejected by your journal of choice and are readying your MS for an alternate submission, don't forget to adjust your reference format accordingly. Failure to do so will only suggest that your research may be as sloppy as your conformity to convention.

Fortunately, if you use a computer, there's at least one citation program that will do all the work for you, once you've entered information in the data file. Just call up the journal-specific style you want and press the proper keys. An Einstein or a Dewey never had it so good.

PERSPECTIVES

At least by implication, any research paper can well express basic tenets of scholarship. The essence of science is its trying, testing, and trying again. Viewed in this fashion, science becomes a determined, never-ending search in every nook and corner for knowledge of the way things really are and usually operate. The scientific method is a way of investigation which relies on rigorously exact testimony. The aim of research is objective verification. The techniques themselves are varied. And each project is always a gamble.

Let's allow those two previously quoted *American Scientist* authors the last word:

> Although scientific data, analysis, and concepts can be complex, their expression need not be incomprehensible. The goal of scientific discourse is, after all, communication. The intent of scientific writers, therefore, as with all writers, should be to produce clarity in communication without oversimplifying the issues.[3]

Although you may bridle at the straitjacket format of the conventional research paper, psychology professor Donald W. Fiske[4] recommends a "conformist, Milquetoast approach" in which you "stay with the conventions in terms of format, style, and citation" because "they have generated good research reporting, and editors and reviewers are comfortable with them. Save any iconoclasm for the classroom." That's sound advice in our book.

For a more expansive treatment of *Successful Publishing in Scholarly Journals,* see a new book by that title by Bruce A. Thyer of the University of Georgia, Athens (Thousand Oaks, CA: Sage, 1994).

THE INTERPRETIVE ARTICLE OR ESSAY

When she was a young Wesleyan University professor, Sheila Tobias decided "to do what a lot of scholars can't bring themselves to do—write about their work for a wider audience. Research is done and reports are written, but somehow I didn't feel the people were reading them. I asked myself, How do you get people to read things? I concluded the answer was, You use a narrative writing style." The result was a best seller, *Overcoming Math Anxiety*, and over 100 articles in periodicals from *Atlantic Monthly* and *Family Circle* to *Harvard Educational Review*.

"Those articles gave me an opportunity to reach more readers," she says. Now the College Board has published *Breaking the Science Barrier*, written in collaboration with her husband, Carl Tobias, a physics professor at the University of Arizona, based on an earlier report, *They're Not Dumb, They're Different: Stalking the Second Tier*, about students who did well in high school but then drop out of college chemistry "because they find it dull." Sheila Tobias is now a much-in-demand consultant for the Science Foundation Research Corporation.[5]

Tobias' work exemplifies the fascinating range of exposition types and publication opportunities covered by the article/essay rubric: a philosopher's sermonette, a humanist's familiar essay, a historian's interpretation, a sociologist's analysis, a biochemist's commentary, a lawyer's argumentation, a political scientist's point-of-view article, a publisher's editorial, a journalist's news feature, an engineer's manual, an outreach specialist's bulletin, a business professor's prediction, and so on.

These variations may differ in degree, but not in kind; so we can say some things in general about writing articles and essays for publication. In fact, in the sense that a book is simply an extended article or an articulated assembly of chapter-essays, this discourse applies to book writing as well. (However, we do devote a later separate unit to the special case of textbook writing.)

CATEGORIES OF ARTICLE/ESSAY OUTLETS

There are seven categories of periodicals you can contemplate as outlets for the fruits of productive scholarship in the form of the interpretive article or essay. In order of scholarly "prestige," they are:

I. The Scholarly Journal that does not carry reports of investigations in the form of the standard research paper but does carry statistical studies in discussion mode, as well as issue-oriented essays. Published by a learned society, a professional association, or a school/college/university. Refereed.

II. The Professional Journal interested primarily in the application of knowledge to practitioner problems and issues. Published by a professional association or a government agency. Usually refereed.

III. The Technical Journal carrying "how to" articles and provocative essays for the field. Published by a commercial house. Not refereed in the academic sense, but the editors are no pushovers.

IV. **The Semi-Scholarly Magazine** published commercially yet with very high standards of sophistication and exposition. Its sophisticated subscribers want the best in contemporary literature and commentary, particularly when the author's credentials contribute to the impact. Not refereed, but carries great prestige in most circles.

V. **The Consumer Magazine,** happy to translate syntheses of new research written in terms a layperson can understand and appealing to his or her need to know. Published by a commercial press. Not refereed in the academic sense, but professional editors put manuscripts through a fine screen.

VI. **The Extension/Outreach Bulletin** that translates the results of campus research and scholarship into utilitarian information for an institution's lay constituency. Can be edited, illustrated, published, and distributed by campus specialists, or contributed by the author to a citizen group or government agency. A valued activity for extension and professional school professors.

VII. **"Op Ed" Pages** appear in almost every large daily newspaper. They devote "op ed" (opinion-editorial) pages to essays on current cultural, political, and scientific issues. While some of these essays will be staff-written, newspaper editorial section editors are always on the lookout for penetrating discussions by guest columnists, particularly by reputable authors residing in the newspaper's circulation area. Here is a natural outlet in which faculty members can share their expertise with a wider audience and gain visibility. That's been the experience, for example, of Mary Kathryn Harrington[6] at Cal Poly State University.

RECOGNIZING YOUR OUTLET OPTIONS

Let's say you're again that assistant ed psych professor at Midland University. You've scored with a research paper in *The Journal of Educational Research*, and now you're casting about for other means of communicating your child development findings in the form of articles or essays. By diligent searching you can identify a surprising number of options in each of these seven categories (we'll list only three periodicals each here):

I. *Teachers College Record, Catholic Educational Review, Educational Theory*

II. *Journal of Teacher Education, National Elementary Principal, Phi Delta Kappan*

III. *Scholastic Teacher, Teaching/K-8, The Instructor*

IV. *Atlantic Monthly, Harper's Magazine, New York Times Sunday Magazine*

V. *Gifted Children Monthly, Parents Magazine, Teaching Families*

VI. *Home Education in State, School Activities for Elementary Teachers in State, Midland PTA Pre-School Childhood Education Guidelines*

VII. Midland and Carthage dailies.

UNDERSTANDING THOSE COMMERCIAL MEDIA

At the outset, you have to recognize that you're dealing here, not with a kept enterprise like a learned journal, but with a *business* whose primary mission is making a profit by selling a service, that service consisting largely of providing news, entertainment, self-help for readers. Only by helping a magazine or newspaper stay solvent and flourish can you expect to appear in its columns.

Second, the commercial print media bear a legal and ethical responsibility to perform in the *public interest*. By tradition and statute they are common carriers of uncensored information. Don't expect a magazine or newspaper to become a consistent, exclusive purveyor of your point of view.

Third, *time and space factors* are crucial. A MS that isn't timely or that runs on and on page after page has little chance of making it.

Fourth, each of the media is really a collection of media. A newspaper, for example, has a variety of sections or pages. So does the typical magazine. The more sharply you can tailor your article to the requirements of a particular *sub-medium,* the better. For instance, our ed psych professor aiming at *Better Homes and Gardens* would tailor his or her article for its "Health and Education" section.

Fifth, each representative of the commercial print media has *a particular character*. It may be a philosophical bent, a geographic focus, a topical emphasis, a concentration on a certain public, a technical specialty, and so on. Fitting MS to medium is at least as important here as in the case of the research paper.

Finally, while the commercial print media are well-staffed with professionals, their editors are nonetheless on a constant prowl for what the trade calls free-lance writers, particularly new talent. As *Time* said recently, "Free-lance writers are indispensable to American print media today." You can join them if you practice the art of writing articles and essays with the finesse and discretion befitting an academician. There are at least fourscore commercial print media of the caliber of *Atlantic Monthly, Christian Science Monitor, Harper's Magazine, National Geographic Magazine, The New Yorker,* and *Smithsonian Magazine* that qualify as quasi-intellectual journals worthy of a professor's talents.

Let's say Bill Campion at Midland University has an idea for a semi-popular article on how the federal Endangered Species Act has operated both to save rare species of plants and animals from extinction and on occasion to stifle economic development in some depressed areas of the country. For ideas on where he might place such an article, he turns to the "Nature, Conservation, and Ecology" section of *Writer's Market*. There, under the magazine *Natural History*, he finds this tip:

> We lean heavily toward writers who are scientists. We favor an ecological slant in most of our pieces, but we do not generally lobby for any causes, environmental or other. The writer should have a deep knowledge of his subject, then submit original ideas in query. Acceptance more likely if accompanied by high-quality photographs. . . . Buy 60 mss. a year. . . . Length: 2,000-4,000 words. Pay $750-$1,500 plus additional for photos. Buy one-time rights.

That sounds like a promising outlet for what Bill has in mind. *Environment, The Amicus Journal, National Wildlife,* and *Sierra* are other possibilities listed, but because Bill knows that *Natural History* has an excellent reputation among academics, he opts to make it his initial target.

THE SPECIAL CASE OF THE PEDAGOGICAL JOURNAL

Much of the dialogue about college and university teaching and learning takes place in the pages of some 50 disciplinary journals devoted in whole or in part to matters of pedagogy. Examples:

- Pedagogical periodicals on teaching that cover a family of fields; e.g., *Journal of College Science Teaching.*
- Discipline-specific periodicals where fewer than half of the articles are on college teaching; e.g., *Journal for Research in Mathematics Education.*
- Discipline-specific journals where more than half of the articles are on college teaching; e.g., Journal of Agricultural Education.
- Discipline-specific journals exclusively on postsecondary teaching; e.g. College Composition and Communication.

Often faculty view these pedagogical periodicals as weak siblings of the more prestigious research journals. Their circulation to college faculty is more limited, their caliber often less consistent, and their reputation as the repository of advancing pedagogical findings not well established. When asked about these journals on teaching, many faculty tend to say that publication in them "doesn't count" because writing about teaching isn't "legitimate scholarship."

It doesn't have to be that way. Penn State's Maryellen Weimer,[7] editor of the national newsletter The Teaching Professor, who has made a study of these journals, offers blunt suggestions on how professors might reform their own contributions and hence the journals themselves:

Feature more informed practice. Don't just tell "war stories"; build on the research in the field.

Be more outward-looking. Look to other disciplines, look to the larger movements in the higher education community, look to collective efforts.

Confront issues of recognition and reward. A wider array of authors could further the visibility and credibility of these publications.

Forge a significant scholarship of teaching. A paper on pedagogy can be as scholarly as a paper on pediatrics.

"The discourse about teaching that occurs in these periodicals would be larger and richer," says Weimer, "if it was a conversation more academics took seriously."

For a handy guide to "Periodicals Related to College Teaching," see IDEA Paper No. 28 in the January 1993 issue of *Exchange* put out by Professor William E. Cashin's Center for Faculty Evaluation and Development at Kansas State University.

ORGANIZING YOUR ARTICLE/ESSAY

While the article/essay typically can vary considerably in its construction, it invariably will show three principles of design:

Force. Unlike the research paper, in which you save the best for the last, in the article/essay you're under an obligation to state your text, clearly and concisely, high up in your piece; not necessarily in the first sentence, as in the classic newspaper lead paragraph, but certainly on the first page or so of your MS.

Then you add force to your text by making it an integral part of a headline/beginning/ending team.

For example, this opinion piece by economist Kevin L. Kearns in *The Chronicle of Higher Education*:

> **The Economic Orthodoxies Offered U.S. Students Won't Prepare Them to Work in World Markets**
>
> The American economy today is being radically transformed by the trade and foreign investment patterns established by the rise of Japan, the economic integration of Europe, and the deindustrialization of the United States.
>
> Yet, in spite of the massive changes under way, much of the academic community acts as though it's business as usual. Unfortunately, they're dead wrong. . . .
>
> We need our best academic minds to help formulate a new national economic policy now.

No beating around the bush there. Kearns tells us what it's all about right away, and concludes on a concordant note.[8]

Another example. Let's say, anticipating the calendar, you decide to do an article for *Change* on the upcoming 100th anniversary of the university extension movement (a.k.a. outreach). To lend color to your beginning you borrow a vignette from *Time* and go on from there:

University Extension Comes of Age

Down the wilderness trail from the Tahawus Club to North Creek in New York State's Adirondack Mountains a rattle-trap buckboard jolted through the night, skidding out of ruts, swaying past boulders and tree stumps, creaking and clattering through the silence of the forest. The night was black and misty. The horses were barely under control. The passenger sat tensed and hunched, eyes screwed up behind steel-rimmed spectacles, mouth clenched tight like a steel clamp beneath a prairie-dry mustache, his thoughts projected far out across a new century big with change. "Too fast?" the driver shouted. Theodore Roosevelt, Vice President of the U.S. and due before dawn to become President of the U.S., rattled back like a Gatling gun: "Go ahead. . . . Go on. . . . Go on!"

It was in the fungible soil of Theodore Roosevelt's "Go on" era that the university extension movement first took root 100 years ago, pledged to bringing American life and American learning into fruitful partnership. Today, as extension organizations across the country plan observances, university extension faces new problems and new possibilities. . . .

For setting before the American people an unfinished agenda there are many agencies—public and private, federal and local, commercial and educational. But, says Robert H. Atwell, President of the American Council on Education, "none is more objective than the university." None is better motivated than a university with an unswerving commitment to outreach. None is better equipped than a professional university extension organization.

It is university extension that again can say to America: "Go ahead. . . . Go on!"

More expansive than the first example, but the headline/lead/text/ending team are definitely in evidence, lending symmetry and force.

Focus. By focus we mean, somewhere high up in your article, maybe even right at the beginning, reduce your subject to a picture a reader can visualize and identify with—a representative person or situation.

If you're describing something like new trends in first-year orientation at large universities, for instance, use plenty of national data, of course, but also focus on the experiences of one student on one campus in one week.

Or like this:

Older Students Blend Into Campus Scene

The first semester of classes at Midland University is about to close. Dispersed through the crowded lecture halls, or hanging tightly to seats in seminars, are students with not-so-young faces, faces that mirror experience, receding hairlines, furrowed foreheads.

More and more, the returning adult student is becoming part of the American university campus scene.

Midland's Mary Williams is typical....

"The university must be a tributary to a larger society, not a sanctuary from it," says A. Bartlett Jerome, Midland President. He speaks for college presidents across the country.

Another example, a *Chronicle of Higher Education* story. Its text:

A small but growing number of colleges are devising programs for minority children who are still in elementary school.

The focus:

Most afternoons, school buses pull up to Beloit College's campus just before 4 o'clock and a passel of chattering youngsters tumbles out. . . . [9]

Note how we lent focus to this section on writing and publishing the interpretive article or essay by profiling at the outset a newsmaking practitioner of the art.

Framework. That outline you construct as a method of work—make it pop out at your readers. Lead them by the hand through your entire development so they never have to say, "Gee, I'm lost."

A simple device: make your main points abundantly clear—1, 2, 3—just as if you were highlighting a lecture on a blackboard. Or try the technique used by a sociologist in an article on the government's effect on families in a *U.S. News & World Report*. She introduced each principal sub-topic with questions, like this:

- Can two pay taxes as cheaply as one? Should Mom go to work?
- Is the big, happy family out of date?
- Are courts promoting family breakups?
- What happens to the children?
- Is welfare an anti-family program?
- Where will the extended family live?

No matter how clearly you think your framework shows through, don't leave its relationships to chance. In ways both obvious and obscure, supply your readers with abundant connectives that lead them surely from one section to the next; terms like "now let's," "as we've said," "you'll remember that." Always keep them oriented to the terrain of your article/essay—and the "them" includes the reviewing editors, of course.

The "framework" principle is particularly useful for the professional school or extension professor in his or her public service role as consultant to a citizen group or organization. Let's say you're an assistant professor of agricultural economics asked to develop a public information folder for an area Resource Conservation and Development program in three cooperating counties: Price, Rusk, and Taylor (Pri-Ru-Ta). Don't put out something that looks and reads like a campus committee report; in both structure and appearance, make it sing by building strong declarative topic statements and emphasizing them in boldface type, like so many headlines:

Conserving and Developing Resources for a Better Community:
YOUR PRI-RU-TA RC&D PROJECT

☐ Informed and balanced resource planning/actions result from the RC&D approach
☐ Pri-Ru-Ta past and present measures add up to future accomplishments
☐ Sustaining RC&D leadership is local
☐ Many cooperating agencies support local commitment with technical assistance

☐ The backbone of an RC&D project is the citizen-agency review process

☐ An approved proposal can become a completed RC&D program

☐ Completed programs encourage more proposals

If all your audience reads are the headlines, they'll at least get the gist of your message; with luck you'll intrigue them to dive into the body of the copy.

STYLE

If you felt yourself somewhat under wraps in writing a research paper, in writing an article you can indulge in the flavor of your writing, its spirit, your feeling for the quality of words. In short, let yourself go.

In crafting your prose, avoid the old-fashioned, the verbose, the hackneyed, the pontifical; in other words—let's face it—don't sound like a faculty report. Use colorful adjectives, emotional verbs, rhythm, change of pace, figures of speech that appeal to the senses. In other words, effective style is "the evidence of things not seen."

Examples:

Harvard President Abbott Lawrence Lowell waxing poetic in the early 1900s as he pictures his vision of America: "aglow with universities and colleges like a field with campfires of an army on the march."

Clark Kerr having fun with plebeian interests of the era in *The Uses of the University*:

> I once said in the 1950s as Chancellor at Berkeley that the great administrative problems of the day were sex for the students, athletics for the alumni, and parking for the faculty; but it could better be said now that the problems are, instead, athletics for the students who have gone "straight," sex for the professors with some of whom the counterculture still finds support, and parking for the alumni as they return for their refresher courses.

Fritz Machlup, writing in *The Chronicle of Higher Education* about "A Recipe for a Good Graduate Department," starts out with—what else?—a recipe:

> Recipes are most expediently given in the pragmatic style of the cookbook. Here is my recipe for a good graduate department:
>
> Take 12 juicy professors of different brands and ripeness and place them together with 50 preheated thoroughly selected students at different stages of preparation on the same floor of a building, around a fine collection of books and journals and well-equipped laboratories; stir them for five to six hours a day; allow them to boil over several times and keep them simmering near the boiling point. Most students will be well done after about four years.

But Machlup doesn't just drop his figure of speech there; he uses it as a framework for the balance of the article, introducing each section with a "recipe" reference:

> Now to the ingredients. Naturally I begin with good professors. ... The second ingredient is good students. ... The next ingredient is the book collection and the labs. ... Now for the last directive in my recipe.[10]

Professor Barbara Wright, discussing in a *Change* article how the best and the brightest students seem to be turned off these days from careers in college teaching, employs allusion to construct an appealing title: "A Thousand Points of Flight: Or Why We Need a Kinder, Gentler Academy and How to Get It."

In his book chapter, "Why Not Write for Commercial Publication?" Professor Ben Johnson—who is what he calls a "crossover writer," that is, one who is successful in both scholarly journals and consumer media—humorously depicts faculty qualms over writing for general readers:"[11]

> All right, I admit it.
>
> Besides, I never intended to keep it a secret anyway. And too many people now know about it. My family has known for some time. My friends, including my colleagues at the University, have known for the last couple of years. My department chair has spoken to me about it several times. Even the Dean mentioned it to me the other day as we stopped to chat for a moment between buildings. He said some students—"my"—students had mentioned it several times over the past few terms when they filled out their end-of-the-semester "Course Evaluation Forms" for the courses I was teaching. He said that he'd like to talk to me about it when I had a few minutes.
>
> I'm a crossover writer.

He might have quoted that other Ben who once observed, "Only a fool won't write for money."

PERSPECTIVES

Bring to every article/essay the five perspectives your readers will bring:

- Human interest—one living, breathing person in an article is worth a shelf of statistics.
- Significance—Your readers are asking, "What's in this for me?" Make sure they understand.
- Timeliness—the act of happening now, or at least just about now.
- Geography—if your subject is local, does it have national manifestations as well? Or, if you're writing about a national event, is there a local angle?
- History—Does your subject have a relevant past? A promising future? Fill your readers in.

TAILORING TO FIT: USING A QUERY

In tailoring an article, you have a big advantage over tailoring a research paper: it's professional practice that you send a prospective editor a query before submitting the MS itself, a query being a letter inviting an editor to assign you a particular writing job.

You write and mail a query when you're well in command of your subject matter and its treatment but before you invest in closure. So the query system saves you a good deal of time and effort, not to mention demonstrating your professional know-how.

What exactly does a query contain if it's to perform its sales mission? In brief, your query should summarize or suggest

- your subject,
- its appeals,
- any special lures an editor will find enticing,
- extras, such as photographs, and
- you—your general competence and particular qualifications.

In a nutshell, Peter Blockson[12] says, "A query letter *must* convince an editor of two things: that your topic is worth pursuing—and that you're the best writer for the job."

There's no set pattern for a query. Sit down at your keyboard and talk to an editor, exhibiting your grasp of his or her needs as well as your grasp of the English language.

Just because one editor turns down your query idea won't mean the idea has no merit; send it out again, retailored. Editors don't always know what they're doing. For example, once the editors of *Reader's Digest* received a query from a biologist proposing to do an article on "what DDT may do to the delicate balance of nature besides wiping out insect pests." The editors weren't interested. Years later, with the publication of *Silent Spring*, the name of author Rachel Carson became a household word—and *RD* would have snapped up anything she offered.

After you've received a favorable response to a query and prepared an article MS for submission, insert in your package a cover sheet recapitulating the sales pitch elements you used in the query, just as a reminder to the editor of the value of your MS.

WORDS TO THE WISE

We must be frank and point out again what you probably already recognize: except in some appointments in some disciplines, what appears valuable to the editor of a commercial periodical will not carry the same prestige in the eyes of your colleagues as the appearance of a research paper in a rigidly refereed journal. From campus situation to situation, the evaluative scale varies considerably, so you'll just have to learn to sense where and when to bet your chips to your best advantage in the publishing game.

SHAKESPEARE DID IT, TOO

Somewhere along in this discourse we can hear some of you saying, "Isn't it really beneath my dignity to write for a narrow, plebeian, modern medium? If I'm going to be an outstanding publishing scholar, don't I want to write for all time — like Shakespeare, for instance?"

All right, let's take a look at Shakespeare. Nobody questions his greatness. What made him great? The very same principle of fitting message and medium that we've been talking about.

Shakespeare was a man with both eyes firmly focused on the box office, since the major portion of his income came from gate receipts. His competition was the bear-baiting pit, and he was always concerned to meet it—with murders, duels, battles, wrestling matches, star-crossed lovers, suicides, ghosts, witches, clowns, songs, costume parades, explosions, thunderstorms, and plain and fancy eye-gouging. By writing for Elizabethan Everyman, he wrote for you and me today.

Take another example: Lincoln's Gettysburg Address. Examine the audience: a crowd of Pennsylvania farmers and shopkeepers out in the weather, stultified by a two-hour-and-a-half address by a renowned orator of the time, whose name today is known only to a few. What did Lincoln do? He talked directly to his grass-roots audience. He used everyday, albeit lilting, language. He kept to the subject at hand. He kept it short. So his words are more remembered than those of any other president.

No, tailoring a message to fit an audience or a publication is not some cheap trick for a supermarket rack. It's a time-tested rhetorical device right out of the copybooks of literary masters.

Or, as author W. Somerset Maugham once said: "The nature of the vehicle whereby the writer approaches his public is one of the conventions he has to accept, and on the whole he can do this without any violence to his own inclinations."

THE TEXTBOOK

Writing a textbook can be a marvelously creative experience, a tough-nosed business, and a gamble.

Let's touch briefly on each of these aspects before we dive into the nitty-gritty.

First, the absolute expression of professing is writing a text. Not only do you hone your teaching materials and techniques, but you disseminate your knowledge and insights to a wider public.

Second, publishing a textbook takes a lot of up-front money—not yours but the publisher's. Hence, publishing means selling, and selling means marketing, in all of which you'll be expected to play a pivotal role. So if you don't have a stomach for a certain level of entrepreneurship, forget about writing a textbook.

Third, even a good textbook can rate so-so reviews and meager adoptions. On the other hand, from a first-class mass-market textbook the financial returns can be staggering. Consider, too, that the academic rewards also can vary. In some departments on some campuses, the author of a successful textbook is positively venerated; in others, a 100,000-word textbook may not count for as much as a 2,000-word research paper.

Fourth, you have to face the fact that, especially in the more elite institutions, potential textbook authors find among their colleagues an undercurrent of disdain for college textbook writing, as education communications consultant James Lichtenberg remarked in the October 1992 issue of *Change*. As he went on, "Faculty mentors and department heads are reported to counsel against spending time on textbook authorship, portraying it as something of 'no academic value' that may even work against success in promotion and tenure."

In the same issue, Russell Edgerton, president of the American Association for Higher Education, proposed a solution: "Textbooks should be rigorously peer-reviewed. The appearance of a new textbook, like the appearance of a new theory or finding, should be a significant event—an occasion for professional discussion."

Perhaps any cloud hanging over textbook writing, Paul A. Smith[13] suggests, is that a college textbook is unique among scholarly writing in that it is:

- Unabashedly a commercial venture,
- Aimed at a very specific market, and
- Purposed to take on a competing textbook as well as fill some gap in existing literature.

In other words, it is at once a business gamble and an intellectual exercise.

If you're still into writing and publishing a textbook, there's a good way to warm up if you haven't done so already—revamp one of the courses you're teaching or, better yet, develop a new course.

GETTING INTO PRACTICE: THE DEVELOPMENT PROCESS

Ordinarily as a new assistant professor you'll be teaching courses as assigned by the chair, with or without consulting you.

It's not impossible, however, that sometime in the next six years you'll have an opportunity to develop and teach a course that you design—and no more pleasing and challenging a teaching assignment could come your way. Not that teaching a standard course can't be interesting and challenging; it can, of course, particularly if you're encouraged to use your own creativity and approach. And yet constructing your own course has an added appeal, just as would designing your own home over taking one on the market.

What's more, developing a new course is ideal practice for writing a new textbook; consider the similarity as you go along.

If you've been brought into a department specifically to open up a new line of inquiry or instruction, you can be thrown into course development right away. More likely, you'll have to identify and occupy a niche that doesn't overlap exceedingly with existing courses. Perhaps it can be initially in a summer session curriculum, where innovation is often a dean's priority.

In either case the procedure is similar. You'll have to surmount in all likelihood the hurdle of a course evaluation and review committee whose mission is to monitor campus course proliferation in the interests of fiscal control and faculty norms. In essence, you'll have to prove your proposal is eminently worthwhile in its own right without impinging on the territories of other professors and/or departments while matching the mission of your college.

That's exactly what you'll have to do to convince the publisher to take on your textbook development proposal.

In either case, jump ahead in your mind's eye to the day you'll meet the first class in your new course. Draft a document that spells out exactly what you expect your students to gain, do, and accomplish—sort of a course syllabus, in other words, albeit couched in language attuned to a faculty committee or an acquisitions editor.

As you compose the document, here are some of the questions you might ask yourself:

- What level of student am I aiming at?
- What sort of background do I expect them to bring to the course?
- What do I expect them to carry away?
- So, then, what will the course content be?
- What will be its (my) purpose?

- What will I pose as student objectives?
- What will be my method of instruction?
- What text(s) or readings will I require?
- What other materials, if any, will my students need?
- What will be my schedule of instruction?
- What measures of student attainment will I employ?
- Will this course be required or optional? For whom?
- Where will it fit into the department/college/university curriculum?
- What exactly are my credentials for proposing this course?
- If I had to distill the key teaching points for this course, what would they be?

Given your particular situation, no doubt other questions will occur to you. As you face them, keep in mind your audience—your students, above all else.

As you'll see later on in this section on textbook writing, all we're suggesting is that you tailor your concepts to your primary medium, the classroom, and then adapt them as needed to intermediate audiences. As a matter of fact, the more quickly you place yourself in a framework of textbook writing, the sooner your course plan will take on a sharp sense of direction. Besides, you may very well discover you'll have to write a text anyway, particularly now that the courts have blown the whistle on assembling pseudo-texts of photocopied materials.

To further sharpen your thinking, try drafting the handouts you'll use for one or more instructional units, or as a textbook chapter introduction. Here's a possible outline, aimed at your student audience:

UNIT NUMBER: UNIT TITLE

- Your materials
- Our purpose
- Our scope
- Your objective
- Reading assignment
- Lab/library assignment

- Study notes
- Written assignment
- Points to remember

Or something like that.

Developing a new course can be as much fun as it is challenging, and it's an ideal training exercise for the main event—writing a textbook.

You don't need to be a seasoned teacher before you attempt to write a text. Indeed, a certain synergism may develop if your maturation and your manuscript proceed together. For example, the senior author (ACS) started drafting his first journalism text when he was an instructor. The resulting publisher's contract became part of his P&T dossier. (Incidentally, after his *Effective Feature Writing* [New York: Harper & Row, 1960] was in circulation, a 1965 Drake University poll of journalism professors and newspaper editors, asked to name "the ten most valuable references" for budding writers, rated *EFW* eighth. First? Strunk and White's *The Elements of Style*. Tenth? *The Collected Works of William Shakespeare*.)

UNDERSTANDING THE TEXTBOOK WORLD

Today's a good time to be thinking about textbook writing. Challenged by skyrocketing production costs, competition from computer software, and demands for better teaching, many publishers, authors, and higher education officials together are examining ways to improve the quality and status of college textbooks.

Debra E. Blum quotes Richard Greenberg, president of the Wadsworth textbook publishing company: "Publishers don't want to spend much money, students don't want to pay so much money, and many professors want to get back to the basics of pedagogy. All this can add up to a new kind of textbook that deserves a renewed kind of respect."[14]

Two organizations have recently entered the field: the Publishers/Higher Education Roundtable, sponsored by the American Association for Higher Education, and the Textbook Authors Association.

You can profit from this heightened attention if you know the territory:

- As campuses re-examine their faculty reward systems, the acclaim attached to textbook writing can change with the venue. At research institutions, the heavy emphasis placed on productive scholarship tends to give textbook writing comparatively low status, but on a growing number of campuses writing a textbook adds to teaching credentials for merit raises and promotions. While significant introductory textbooks may not be coming out of frontline research universities now, that leaves the door open for professors at institutions that recognize the importance of restructuring the pedagogy of a discipline.
- The need for bigger up-front investments by publishing companies has forced editors to demand more marketing sense on the part of textbook writers. When there's so much money involved in production and promotion, publishers expect authors to be sharply attuned to audience needs and wants, not to self-gratification.
- Textbooks have to be well-adapted to classroom conditions, because they face growing competition in the campus marketplace from instructional software, desktop publishing, and emerging technologies like electronic books.
- But the industry is by no means fading. The higher education textbook market saw almost $2 billion in new-book sales in 1990, up slightly from the previous year. Members of the Textbook Authors Association earned an average of $15,000 in royalties from the sale of their books. (Don't count on that much!) At most colleges, the money that professors earn from textbooks is considered their own, but some institutions take a percentage.
- Publishing companies can expect to invest anywhere from $25,000 to more than $1 million in a college textbook before printing ever begins—advances to authors, payments to proofreaders and reviewers, book design, illustrations, supplements. On the press a book can cost anywhere from $1 to $10 to produce. It may take several years to see your manuscript through to distribution—working with editors, designers, illustrators, contributors; proofreading, rewriting,

obtaining permissions to quote. If there's a co-author in-volved, double the ante.

- The royalty rate for a college text ranges from 10% to 19% of the publisher's net receipts, equal to sales minus returns and discounts, or about 15% of the book's list price. Some costs may come out of that percentage up front: advances, artwork, copyright permissions, indexing. It's up to the author to negotiate the best contract possible. It's usually desirable to retain a knowledgeable agent or at least seek advice from an experienced colleague.

- Some textbook publishers invest a great deal of skill and resources in marketing. Others simply seem to shoot a lot of arrows into the air in the fond hope that when they fall to earth they'll hit adopting professors. A sound rule of thumb is to assume that what marketing strategies and actions you don't personally provide won't get done—and then be pleasantly surprised when the company knows what it's supposed to be doing. At a minimum, purchase extra books, autograph them, and send them to likely prospects around the country. You can be your own best sales rep.

Blum quotes M.L. Reedy, executive director of the Textbook Authors Association, professor emeritus at Purdue University, and author of mathematics texts: "It's time to give textbooks the respect they deserve as important instructional tools in the class-room. Writing a textbook is a big task, but a rewarding one. You're helping students to learn, and may even put a little money in your pocket—and adding to your CV."

THE TEXTBOOK DEVELOPMENT/WRITING PROCESS

Know Your Course Requirements. So you're unhappy with the textbook options for one of your courses. What exactly is the matter with them, from your viewpoint? Their pedantic or sopho-moric style? Their surfeit or lack of substance? In what ways would your approach, your supplementary materials, your teaching points be better?

Know Your Market. Is the course you're zeroing in on unique to your campus, or is it pretty much universal? Is it a catalog artifact or does it have a future?

Know Yourself. Are you on top of your concept? Can you really handle the whole project? Do you have the time to spare from teaching, research, service, other writing, family, friends, recreation? How about logistical support? Should you seek a collaborator to share the work and broaden the market?

Draw Up a Brief Synopsis. Those are all tough questions. If they sound like many of those posed earlier in regard to a research paper or article, you're right. The players and their lines are basically the same; it's only the setting that is different.

So what do you do now? Well, remember how your first step in writing a paper or article was to reduce your subject to a nub? Do the same thing now, only in a more expansive form.

When your textbook appears, its jacket or back cover will carry a summary/sales pitch. Sooner or later your publisher will ask you to draft one. *Write it now.* Nothing will so rivet your mind to the task at hand; nothing will so keep you on track through months of labor. You may alter it later, of course, but don't postpone putting down at least an initial draft.

To illustrate, here's what the trade calls "the blurb" for Robert Kelly's two-volume introductory American history text, *The Shaping of the American Past:*

> The first textbook to be built around the "New Political History," *The Shaping of The American Past* by Robert Kelley, noted comparative historian, reveals how the great controversies which have shaken each era in the past are explained not simply by the conflict of economic interests and the struggle of political ideologies, but the ranging of ethnic group against ethnic group, the members of one religious faith against those of another, even life style against life style. Exploring these cultural roots makes the story come alive, for we learn to see in the past the same volcanic energies at work which have made our own time so tumultuous.
>
> The main stream of Volume I deals with the classic themes in American history: the founding of settlement and the sweep of population across the continent; the evolution of the society, its ways of life and its institutions; the great events and crises through which the

nation passed, from the Revolution through Reconstruction. Volume II narrates such themes as the rise of America as a world power; the growing complexity of its society through industrialization, urbanization, and immigration; the rise of a powerful national government, from Theodore Roosevelt to the modern presidencies. Especially close attention is paid to the years from 1960.

The Shaping of The American Past is an engaging book to read. A new synthesis, based on the latest scholarship, it bears the stamp of single authorship, continuity of interpretation, and coherence in structure.[15]

If modesty deters you from injecting adjectival superlatives, OK; Madison Avenue word merchants will insert them for you. But don't leave it to them to capture the essence of your text. You need that crutch now as a strong prop to lean on while you navigate the avenues and side-streets of MS construction.

THE PROSPECTUS STAGE

After you've expanded a good deal on your synopsis with plenty of perspiration and paper, you're ready to write a prospectus (a fancy name for a fancy query).

Publishers tend to think of textbooks as resolutions of six primary issues: content, elements, approach, market, competition, and author. To sell your textbook idea to a potential publisher, you must clearly delineate how you propose to resolve each of these issues.

Content. A draft table of contents will best suggest to the publisher your resolution of content. At a minimum you'll need a list of chapters with a two- or three-sentence explanation of what you propose to cover in each one. Better yet would be that list accompanied by full-scale section titles and subheads.

Approach. Your prospectus will also describe to a publisher your approach. A history textbook, for example, may take a social approach, an economic approach, a political approach. A mathematics text may involve a rigorous approach, an applied approach, a conceptual approach. A biology text may be built around a cellular approach, an organismal approach, an ecological approach. Your publisher will want to know your ideological and pedagogical leanings; in other words, your approach. Naturally you'll want to explain why your approach is appropriate, timely, significant, different.

Sample chapters are not essential to sell your idea but there's nothing like one or two to demonstrate your scintillating style and your command of those variables. What's more, sample chapters demonstrate that you can do more than generate good ideas; you can actually carry them out. A cautious publisher is always more inclined to explore your potential when he or she has at hand a sample of the goods. (N.B.: A sample chapter need not be Chapter 1—often the hardest to write.)

Elements. By "elements" a publisher means primarily the pedagogical features you intend to infuse into the exposition. Describe these compellingly in your prospectus. Different academic fields are accustomed to different standard features: in mathematics, elements comprise examples, exercises, and definition and theorem boxes; in business, elements comprise principles, problems, and cases; and so on. But the standard features, while customary and required, must not be your only features. Features are often the "handles" the publisher uses to promote a book.

Subtle content differences among texts, while important to teachers, are usually too technical for sales reps to discern or promote. Features, on the other hand, are grist for the rep's mill. Quite simply, the extent to which you and your publisher devise superlative features may well be the extent to which your book is a sales success—not just because these features probably make your book a better learning tool, but because they excite the sales force charged with exciting the market. (If all this sounds hardboiled, we told you so.) Historical notes, interviews, group activities, sidebar highlights, summary grids, challenging problems, photo essays, marginal notes—these and many other element options can constitute innovative, unique features that will set your book apart, pique a publisher's interest, and stimulate adoptions.

For example, a potent selling point in the prospectus for *Interpreting Public Issues* was the authors' promise that all examples of news analysis and case studies of in-depth reporting would be taken, not from the likes of *The New York Times* or *The Washington Post*, but from representative small-city dailies around the country, where fresh mass communication grads habitually find their first jobs. As the publisher told the authors, "Stick to this concept. It's a good drawing card because it's a fresh twist to the requisite examples and because it's meaningful and useful to students. Fresh and useful is a winning combination in any market."

Market. If you've picked a likely publisher, the acquisitions editor probably will have a pretty good idea about market potential, but he or she will still want to know your assessment. Describe in your prospectus the course your book will fit. Is it taught at two-year or four-year colleges or both? Ivy League or state universities or both? Is it a first-year, advanced, major, or service course? How big is the market? That is, about how many students across the country take the course each year?

If your market is a niche, that is, if your book can serve only a limited yet well-defined segment of the overall course market, say so. Nothing is more disheartening to a publisher than spending developmental money on your idea only to find it fits but a market niche. There's nothing wrong with writing a market-niche book; publishers sponsor them all the time, but they want to know the score up front.

Describe, too, trends in the market with which your idea is in tune. If the professional association in your field recently promulgated new curriculum recommendations, tell the publisher how your text meshes exactly with those stipulations. If an undercurrent of change is welling up in your field, tell the publisher how your text will give her or him a jump on competitors.

The more market savvy you display, the better you demonstrate your grasp of the whole undertaking.

Competition. Pick at least three texts widely used for the course your book will serve. Outline in your prospectus their generally accepted strengths and weaknesses. It's not wise to ignore or refute their strong points. Acknowledge them, but minimize them by suggesting unequivocally how the strengths of your book go one better. It's not wise either to spend paragraph after paragraph hammering away on—usually exaggerating—your competitors' weaknesses. Illustrate them, to be sure, but do so by contrasting those weaknesses with your superior advantages.

The Author (That's You!). A publisher who is ready to seriously consider your proposal needs reassurance of your reputation and your capacity to work hard. In a single page of your prospectus, outline your achievements and standing in your field. Don't lay it on with a trowel, but don't be overly shy either. A publisher wants to hear about **you.**

In your prospectus convince a publisher that you have the time, resolve, and stamina to handle a major writing task. Many first-edition texts take at least two years to write and rewrite, and another year to produce. Publishers will appreciate hearing that you might arrange a light teaching load or, better, a sabbatical. They'll want to know, too, whether you have access to word-processing equipment. If you're able and willing actually to compose on a computer, many publishers will be delighted at the prospect and will take your MS from a diskette, reducing the likelihood of typos.

AND SO TO MARKET

When do you send off your prospectus? After you're confident you can deliver on all its promises but before you go much further. Oh sure, it's possible to complete your MS before you test the waters, but that's really foolhardy. An interested publisher will likely have a good deal constructively to say about your plan, so wait for feedback before you plunge far ahead. Be prepared, though, to send a chapter or two in short order to a publisher who nibbles at your bait and wants to see more.

And now here's a big switch. Unlike the ethic governing the submission of research papers and interpretive articles, which limits you to approaching one publication at a time, in selling your textbook idea you can approach any number of publishers simultaneously—provided you are reasonably up-front about it. That's because fully evaluating a prospectus can be so time-consuming that if you submit to publishers one at a time, several years could pass before the right publisher gets a turn to see your brainchild. Publishers recognize this, so they expect you to canvass the field. A dynamite prospectus can prompt several favorable responses at about the same time, which puts you in the driver's seat.

Choosing Prospective Publishers. To whom do you send your prospectus? To publishers specializing, or at least dabbling, in your field. Who are they? Here's where we're almost tempted to say, "If you don't know, then maybe you're not ready for the writing task." To jog your market savvy, peruse the shelves of your department reference room, the campus library stacks, ads in professional journals, directories of text publishers, the sample texts that come to you.

Cruise the display concourse at your association convention. Talk to the publishers' reps there or when they come to your office to sell you their wares. (Some may even—oh, happy day!—proposition you to write a text for them.) In fact, some publishers require a sales rep's recommendation.

Be on the lookout both for the old established houses that carry great repute in your field, and for young and hungry houses eager to build their lists. If any colleagues have had publishing experience, pump them for tips about editorial support, marketing energy, royalty rates, and so on.

Of course, your savvy can deteriorate as publishing house control, interests, and personnel change mercurially these days. So yesterday's expert can be passé tomorrow.

Rather than submit your prospectus blind to a publishing house, Laurie Lindop[16] recommends that you address it to a specific editorial assistant by name. Her reasoning goes like this:

> Right now there's somebody in a publishing house just waiting to discover you and your manuscript—somebody who wants to lobby the editorial board on your behalf and see your book propelled onto the pages of an upcoming catalog. That somebody is an editorial assistant, and she's just waiting to push your book to the top . . . to prove she's got what it takes to become a full-fledged editor. . . .
>
> You can find the right assistant by making a list of books similar to your own or in a closely related field; the assistants who worked on those books are your target group. You can get their names simply by calling the editorial departments of publishing houses directly.

Because editorial assistantships are entry-level positions, the person you're seeking may have gone up or out, in which case use the name of his or her replacement.

Packaging Your Prospectus. Cover your prospectus with a personal letter on professional stationery in which you adapt your handy-dandy synopsis to its marketing mission. With well-chosen words, sell your sizzle as well as your steak. Mail unfolded first-class, addressed to the key editor by name. (It's worth a phone call to get it.)

Now What? While you're waiting for publishers to react, there are a couple of useful things you can do, besides betting on a positive outcome by working on another chapter or two.

FIELD TEST. Why not use your classes as a sample market to field-test your product? Take that sample chapter and either stake your students to free copies or get a local copy shop to act as publisher. Before you do, copyright. That's easy. Get the simple application form from the Copyright Office, Library of Congress, Washington DC 20559. Fill it out and return with a copy of your MS and the $10 fee. On your MS indicate "© 199_ by author."

After exposing your students to your draft chapter as supplementary reading, generate some feedback through questionnaires, focus groups, or even a pop quiz. But take any results under advisement; it's professors who adopt texts, students just buy and use them.

ANTICIPATE DEMANDS. Even the most sanguine publisher is going to lean on you for help in marketing your text, so start now to compile the lists of names and addresses he or she will want: experts you know directly or indirectly who might give you the sort of favorable capsule review a publisher likes to put on book jackets and in ads; colleagues you know directly or indirectly around the country who teach a course for which your text might be most appropriate; professional organizations in the field; journal editors you know directly or indirectly who might be inclined to give you a boost; ditto for newspaper book page editors, potential writers of your foreword, and so on.

KEEP YOUR EYES OPEN. Read those same journals and newspapers regularly for breaking news and commentary that can lend timeliness and significance to your MS. (You'll want to do the same after your text comes out, looking ahead to a second edition!)

KEEP RECORDS. Start keeping detailed records of all the legitimate expenses you incur in producing your textbook. They're deductible against royalty income. There are whole books on this subject; for example: *Tax Guide for College Teachers and Other College Personnel* (College Park MD: Academic Information Service), published annually.

KEEP YOUR NOSE CLEAN. Don't get so ensnared in your textbook project that you neglect what the comptroller is paying you for—teaching, research, service—or what your family and friends expect in the way of time and attention.

Signing That Contract. Assuming that glorious day arrives when you have a textbook contract in hand, break out the party hats—and consult a knowledgeable lawyer who can guide you through the fine print and help assess the rewards and constraints.

One textbook author/commentator lists such points as these to negotiate:

- How about a large advance as evidence of the publisher's commitment?
- How about a grant-in-aid to help defray expenses?
- Who pays for permissions?
- Who pays for artwork/photos?
- Is there a non-competition clause restricting your association with another publisher?
- Who will you work with after the acquisitions editor?
- Who makes the ultimate decisions on substance and style?
- How many complimentary copies do you receive?
- Who pays for any last-minute changes in page proofs?
- Can royalty payments be spread out over X years to escape heavy taxes in any one year?
- Is the publisher on the hook for a second edition?

Once you sign on the dotted line, add "under contract" to your CV!

"Come Blow Your Horn!" That's the title of an article by Robert Scott in the March 1994 issue of *Writer's Market,* the "bible" of trade and textbook writers. "In this day and age, promotion is crucial to any book's success," Scott says, and "the first rule for publishing success is that the best person to promote your book is you."

For example, using his own recent experiences and those of colleagues around the country, in 1991 the senior author (ACS) drafted a "text" titled *RETIREMENT 901: A Comprehensive Seminar for Senior Faculty and Staff.* With a publisher's contract in hand, he then set about developing journal and magazine articles based on the forthcoming book, each one tailored to a particular publication.

The result was, coincident with the publication of the book, the appearance of five different articles in five different publications read by academics, each one carrying a reference to *Retirement 901*—subtle yet sure "horn-blowing":

- "Answering the Big Question: When Should I Retire?", *AAHE Bulletin,* April 1992;
- "Retired Faculty: Sharing the Wealth," *Academe,* Sep./Oct. 1992;
- "Phasing Out to Relieve Retirement Shock," *The Department Chair,* Fall 1992;
- "The Phased Retirement as a Staff Development Strategy," *The Journal of Staff, Program, & Organization Development,* Winter 1992; and
- "The Retirees Are Coming—Or Are They?", *CUPA Journal,* Fall 1993.

Partially as a result of the promotion, *Retirement 901* (Madison, WI: Magna Publications, 1992) has done well in the marketplace. At this stage in his career, ACS doesn't need those citations for a CV, but the book royalties are welcome! Any publisher will welcome—indeed, expect—your participation in helping call attention to any book.

OBITER DICTUM

In developing this section on textbook writing and publishing, we relied significantly on a professional independent developer of textbooks for major publishing houses, Laurie Golson of Lake Bluff IL.
Her closure to you:

> Almost any teacher can write a textbook. But it takes vision to write a good one. And by 'good' I don't mean 'big selling.' No matter what its sales outcome, a textbook that honestly reflects the vision of a determined author is a good textbook. If you're the author of such a textbook, you can be proud of its quality.

For a more extended discussion of *Getting Your Book Published,* see Christine S. Smedley, Mitchell Allen, and Associates (Newbury Park CA: Sage, 1993).

THE ANTHOLOGY ABERRATION

So far in this section, we've been talking about the textbook as a custom-authored project. But what if your project is an anthology—an assembly of articles by other authors, together with your interlocutory comments? Time was when you could simply assemble a "coursepack" of photocopied materials, but in several celebrated decisions the courts have lowered the boom on the unauthorized photocopying of copyrighted materials for classroom use. Now comes electronic publishing to the rescue.

Through a new process known as electronic digital custom publishing (EDCP), computers empower professors to assemble texts on short order from a wide range of information sources. The process works like this: A publisher builds a computerized data bank of all its textbooks and periodicals. From that menu displayed on your work station, you can select chapters or parts of chapters from anything in the database. To that array you can add authorized current clippings and your own narrative or notes. Download to a high-speed printer, print out, bind—and you have any number of copies of an EDCP text in remarkable turnaround time and at a competitive cost per student. A half-dozen major college text publishers offer the service.

Although EDCP does solve the onerous problem of obtaining permission to reproduce copyrighted materials, it has the obvious drawback of being limited largely to what's available from one particular publishing house. But several plans are afoot for data banks representing multiple publishers. Stay tuned.

But what if you want to edit a conventional anthology, with all that concept implies in terms of searching out the holders of copyrights and gaining written permission for use? You now have three principal intermediaries who will do the work for you—for a modest fee: National Association of College Stores Copyright and Custom Publishing Support Services, Association of American Publishers PUBNET Permissions Network, and Copyright Clearance Center Academic Permissions Service.

Or, if you prefer to do the work yourself, there are a number of publications to help you, such as R.R. Bowker's series of directories of books-in-print, books-out-of-print, publishers, periodicals, and so on.

PRINCIPLES OF CONSISTENT PUBLICATION

As you know, when you come up for tenure your productive scholarship will be evaluated not only in terms of your performance to date but equally in terms of your promise in years to come. P&T committees take a dim view of one- or two-shot authors. Again, when you're up for promotion to full professor, the story will be the same. So the sooner you outline and begin a long-range publication plan as an intimate aspect of a lifelong career in academe, the surer your footing will become.

Fortunately there are a number of effective strategies you can employ to get maximum publication mileage out of every hour you spend on your scholarly pursuits.

To illustrate these strategies, the authors of this manual will share with you here some of their varied real-life experiences.

By way of background, Clay Schoenfeld (ACS) has a 40-year career in university administration, in a professional school, and in the social sciences. Hence his publication record spans far more time than you have as a candidate for associate professor, but that record can well suggest the options you can already begin to choose and adapt in building a formidable dossier. Robert Magnan (RM), on the other hand, is a relatively recent veteran of the publish-or-perish wars in the humanities, so the strategies he employed, beginning even as a graduate student, are directly relevant to your needs.

At any rate, we think you can draw some useful tips from what has worked for us—and for many others.

PRESENTING PAPERS

A typical convention of a learned or professional society will be built around a series of sessions or panels on current topics selected by the program committee, which in turn will make an advance announcement of the subject matter in demand. Cast as wide a net as you can for these announcements. A paper you're working on but which isn't yet ready to submit for publication may be just what a session chair is looking for. Usually you'll be asked to submit an abstract and a CV for review. Give it your best shot. Perhaps a senior colleague can also help arrange that you be invited to make a presentation. Jump at the opportunity.

Now here's a valuable tip: *Give them something to take home*. In other words, don't go with just notes or a fragmentary script; go with manifold copies of a complete, albeit draft, MS—complete with title, author, institutional affiliation, address, phone number, and the name, date, and place of the conference. Indicate at the top of every page something like "Draft" or "Not for publication." Pass it out or make it available at the close of your presentation, so as not to distract attention from your talk itself.

That handout is not only a great business card for potential contacts; it constitutes a type of published (that is, "made public") work, so you can add it right away to your dossier and CV.

You don't have to wait, of course, for a session or panel topic announcement to show up. If you have a paper in its final stages, why not suggest to a society program chair a session topic custom-made for your subject matter? (This approach naturally requires lead-time.)

Does presentation of a draft paper at a professional conference jeopardize its eventual acceptance by a learned journal? Not usually. Journal editors are gun-shy only of research results made known to the mass media in advance of peer review. But when you submit the paper you'll want to acknowledge its prior presentation in a footnote.

One pitfall in presenting papers: P&T committees may assign different values to different sorts of presentations, as we've said before. For example, the value of a solicited work may be problematic. Sometimes colleagues rate it higher than unsolicited work, since it shows that you've established a reputation. Others give less credit, since it's only nominally refereed, and since there's the nagging suspicion the solicitors strongly encouraged, maybe helped, even collaborated. By and large, though, any sort of presentation is better than none.

NETWORKING

In the world of productive scholarship, quite as much as in most callings, contacts are the name of the game. As at that first learned society meeting, make contacts—and keep in touch. It may take time and energy to build and maintain a utilitarian network, but there are considerable benefits.

Write letters now and then to members of your dissertation committee, updating them on your activities. Correspond with fellow grad students who are now out there in areas related to yours. When you attend those conferences, take the initiative to meet kindred scholars, both new and established.

Keeping in touch doesn't have to be tedious. Keep a log—another use for your computer—of your professional activities, research interests, related contacts (with a summary of their activities and interests), presentations, publications, and so on. (You should be doing this anyway, as you've learned, to maintain a record for your annual reviews and your P&T dossier.) Periodically, perhaps when you're feeling temporarily burned out, write a few "update letters," customizing your "brag sheet" with personal chitchat and questions about what your colleagues are up to. A few hours from time to time can keep you active in your network. Don't ignore phone or electronic mail options, either.

You can live well on the fruits of your professional grapevine. For example, RM kept in touch with several of his professors who had a professional stake in his progress as an alumnus. When one of them got involved in compiling a book about the literary representation of aging, he invited his former student to write a chapter. A few years later the same professor asked RM to translate an essay for a collection. Even later, another of his former professors, in the throes of organizing a conference session, suggested that RM submit a proposal, which she accepted.

In some examples to come, you'll see evidence of an ACS network in high gear.

The moral: If you want to be a shining star, it helps to be part of a constellation.

CAPITALIZING ON CALENDAR, CONTACTS

Editors of learned journals and professional magazines alike pay attention to anniversaries in their fields as a means of breathing currency into their publications. So it's a good practice to anticipate their needs.

Knowing that April 21, 1978, would mark the 30th anniversary of the tragic early death of ecologist/author Aldo Leopold, ACS proposed to compose a personal tribute to the man with whom he'd had contacts as a student.

To pre-empt space in an appropriate publication, ACS wrote a letter of query to Les Line, editor of *Audubon Magazine*—dated a year and a half in advance of the anniversary. Impressed with the evidence of thinking ahead, Line asked to see a 5,000-word MS. The resulting article, "Aldo Leopold Remembered," came out in the April 1978 issue.

Timing is important; contacts are helpful.

MULTIPLE PAPERS FROM ONE IDEA

ACS had illustrated the Leopold MS with original color transparencies depicting scenes highlighted in Leopold's best-selling Sand County Almanac. When Line rejected them as "not up to par," ACS wrote extended captions for each one and placed the result, "Our Leopold Legacy," in a 1979 *Wisconsin Sportsman*.

That's a simple illustration of how to milk as much as possible out of a single data set. For examples of more bountiful means of developing multiple papers from one idea, read on.

The passage of the federal Wilderness Act of 1964, reserving millions of American acres "where the earth and its community of life are untrammeled by man, where man himself is a visitor who does not remain," reserved as well a fruitful field of research for scholars in a dozen disciplines. By 1974 their studies cried out for analysis, consolidation, and application, so a trio of social scientists in USDA Forest Service research stations allied with universities set out to develop the first book-length treatise devoted exclusively to the philosophical, biological, social, and political dimensions of wilderness management.

For the chapter on wildlife management in wilderness, one of the three, John Hendee, enlisted the assistance of ACS, then an adjunct member of a department of wildlife ecology faculty. (Building on a chance acquaintance at a professional conference when they were both neophytes a score of years before, Hendee and ACS had become professional collaborators and personal friends. Hendee became Dean of the College of Forestry, Wildlife, and Range Sciences at the University of Idaho.) Their first draft resulted in "Wilderness Management for Wildlife: Philosophy, Objectives, Guidelines," a paper published in the 1976 *Transactions of the North American Wildlife and Natural Resources Conference*.

After the eventuating chapter on "Wildlife in Wilderness" in *Wilderness Management* came out in 1977, the two co-authors realized they had compiled enough material for a separate book, so they found a publisher for *Wildlife Management in Wilderness* in 1978. Over the next 18 months, spin-off reports and articles included: "Who's Minding the Wilderness Store?" in *The Journal of Soil and Water Conservation*, "Wilderness and Wildlife" in *National Wildlife*, "Managing Wildlife in Forest Wilderness" in *American Forests*, "Wildlife Management in Park Wilderness" in *National Parks and Conservation Magazine*, "Let's Keep Wilderness Wild" in *Outdoor Life*, and "Wilderness Wildlife Management Conflicts" in *Western Wildlands*. Matching their credentials to the standards of the various publications, the co-authors alternated as senior author.

The moral: Without pandering to popularization, it's perfectly possible to get multiple respectable mileage out of a single set of data, while more broadly disseminating your message to peers and public alike. You'll note also that the time-span for this exercise was well within the constraints imposed on tenure candidates.

Another example:

Growing out of their part-time roles in university administration, ACS and colleague Theodore Shannon were importuned by the Center for Applied Research in Education to write an introductory text, *University Extension*, as part of a series for graduate students in higher education administration. Their deadline: six months. They met it. The co-authors then realized that some of their chapters, properly focused and condensed, had the makings of journal articles. The result: "Whither Goest the CES?" in *Journal of Cooperative Extension*, "Factors Critical to Extension Success" in *The NUEA Spectator*, "The Professor and University Extension" in *The Journal of Higher Education*, "University Extension and Public Relations" in *College and University Journal*, "Emerging Patterns in University General Extension" in *The Educational Record*, "Evaluating University Extension" in *Adult Education*, "Azimuths for University Adult Education" in *Adult Leadership*, and "Extension's Continuing Education Model" in *The Journal of Alternative Higher Education*. Each paper, of course, indicated the source, and the textbook publishers were delighted with the free advertising!

The time-span for this exercise: two years.

Generating multiple papers from one central theme must, obviously, be guided by integrity, not just finesse. Each paper must represent a *substantial,* independent contribution in its own right, not just a cosmetic change in phrasing. Further, each target journal must be viewed by both its editors and its readers as being noncompetitive with all other publications in substance, style, thrust, and audience.

Violate these strictures and you'll merit a charge like this one from Sharon Boots, managing editor of *Analytical Chemistry*:

> This publish-or-perish business is getting out of hand.... I regularly receive papers that have been submitted elsewhere under different titles or with only minor changes.... I call it "salami science." People slice up their research results into "least publishable units" so they can get several papers out of work that rightfully merits one.

Engage in one or two escapades like that and your name is mud in the profession, and rightfully so.

SPLITTING YOUR DATA

In the late 1970s, anticipating the upcoming 10th anniversary of Earth Day in April 1980, ACS posed a question: "Was E-Day a passing fad or is the environmental movement a permanent fixture on the American landscape?" With the aid of his academic, media, and environmental networks, he began to assemble data and opinions from:

1. Twenty former undergraduate E-Day leaders on 15 representative campuses.

2. A dozen of the original young staff members of Environmental Action, the E-Day headquarters organization in Washington DC.

3. Another dozen former environmental activists, now relatively high up in the Washington environmental establishment.

4. "Big name" leaders of veteran and new environmental societies.

5. Student environmental clubs active on 22 campuses.

6. Environmental reporters for 40 daily U.S. newspapers, and editors of 27 old and new magazines carrying environmental materials.

7. Directors of 60 environmental studies programs in colleges and universities.

8. A dozen eminent opinion leaders in the U.S., Canada, Britain, and Germany.

9. Heads of member schools in the Association for Education in Journalism.

10. An extensive literature search.

Once all the disparate data were in hand, he put together a tome. He should have known better. It was long on length, short on focus—and "bounced" from three journals. Whereupon ACS took the obvious remedial action: he split his data, did considerably more research and cogitation, sought some collaborators, and developed a number of discrete papers tailored to the demands of various editors.

The results: these publications prepared in the time-span 1978-1982:

> **From Sources 1, 2, and 3:** "Student Eco-Activists Revisited: Long-Term Correlates of Earth Day," in *The Journal of Voluntary Action Research;* "Earth Day Leaders Revisited: Where Are They Now?" in *Environment.*
>
> **From Source 6:** "Ecological Conscience in the Newsroom," in *Journalism Quarterly;* "Assessing the Environmental Reportage of the Daily Press," in *The Environmental Professional.*
>
> **From Sources 3, 4, 5, and 8:** "Environmentalism: Fad or Fixture After 10 Years?" in *American Forests;* "Environmentalism: Over the Hill or Coming of Age?" in *Not Man Apart.*
>
> **From Source 7:** *Environmental Education in Action: Case Studies of Environmental Studies Programs in Colleges and Universities,* ERIC/SMEAC, The Ohio State University.
>
> **From Sources 6 and 10:** "American Magazines and the Environmental Movement: Symbiotic Relationship, 1966-1975," in *Journalism Quarterly; "Media Roles in a Social Movement: An Ideology Diffusion Model,"* in *Journal of Communication;* "Pitfalls and Possibilities in Environmental

Communication: A Review of the Research Literature," in *Environmental Education and Information*.

From Sources 6, 8, and 10: "Constructing a Social Problem: The Press and the Environment," in *Social Problems;* "The Press and NEPA: The Case of the Missing Agenda," in *Journalism Quarterly*.

From Sources 6, 7, and 9: "Environmental Communication Programs Come of Age," in *Journalism Educator;* "Environmental Impact: University Programs in Journalism," in *The Journal of Environmental Education*.

From Sources 4, 6, 7, 8, and 9: "Educating the Public: The Media and the Environment," in *The Environmentalist;* "Environmental Communication as Education," in *Facets and Faces of Environmental Education*, New Jersey School of Conservation.

All of these were in print between 1979 and 1983.

We trust you'll recognize the *programmatic* nature of this research/publication record—variations on a central theme. But, as you might imagine, not everyone in academia will agree with the "multiplier" approach. For example, this from a reviewer:

> I would never recommend that a new assistant professor spend time preparing different versions of the same data set for different outlets and levels of readers. He or she should use the same time more wisely working on more submissions to scholarly journals. Only full professors seem to have the luxury of trying to reach wider audiences!

A moral: While splitting your data can be a very effective strategy, it's no short cut. Along with it goes research, compilation, submission, rejection, submission, rejection, remedial work, submission again.

Obviously there are professional hazards to be assiduously avoided if you propose to split your data. To quote Camille Paglia:

> The publish-or-perish tyranny has led the profession to become obsessed with quantity over quality. . . . Burger King now rules the campus. . . . Right now, young academics are caught in a bind that pits scholarly integrity against economic self-interest, particularly if they are responsible for children. . . . Rushing people into print right after grad school just leads to portentous fakery, which nobody reads anyhow.

Maynard Mack was already saying in 1969 to my graduate seminar at Yale that "95% of what is published in any given year should be ritually burned." The pressure on shaky novices to sound important and authoritative makes for guano mountains of dull rubbish.[17]

We're not recommending any such frantic proliferation, of course.

SAILING ON CROSS-CURRENTS

A prime strategy for generating multiple papers calls for practicing peripheral vision by bringing into your sights conferences and journals not directly in your discipline but not unrelated to your scholarly interests.

When RM was a graduate student in medieval French literature, the subject of his dissertation was "Aspects of Senescence in the Work of Eustache Deschamps," a lesser-known 14th-century writer. In diligently scanning department bulletin boards, he found out about a conference organized around the theme, "The Meanings of Old Age," sponsored by the Missouri Gerontology Institute. Drawing on his research, RM prepared a paper and made a presentation on medieval attitudes toward aging and sexuality.

The conference exposed RM as well to other work being done on the literary representation of aging—valuable data for his Ph.D. thesis. The Institute published his paper in its conference proceedings and Hunter College published an abstract in its newsletter. RM had found an academic cross-current, sailed along on a minimum of time and energy—and added to his CV a presentation, a published paper, and a citation.

At another conference RM found posted on a bulletin board some information about *Ars Lyrica*, a journal dedicated to the relationships of words and music through the ages. Several poems by his medieval Frenchman not germane to RM's dissertation provided material for a presentation at a subsequent conference— and forthcoming publication in *Ars Lyrica*.

When he found a proposal for a conference session on images of the apocalypse in medieval literature, and for another session on the *Book of Psalms* in medieval literature, RM considered what Deschamps had written in those two veins and prepared two presentations for the conference. In doing so, he gained entry into circles of scholars interested in tangential religious matters.

So don't wear blinders that obscure all but the publishing outlets in your little corner of the world. Are there associations or journals outside your specific area that might be interested in some aspect of your work? Is there a conference topic that touches your interests in some way? As you read articles and books in furthering your research, note references to unfamiliar journals and association publications. When you scan bulletin boards, consider whether you have anything to offer conferences or essay collections outside your usual preview.

There's a quadruple bonus to "working the neighborhood": presentations and papers outside your primary focus provide wider recognition of your scholarship, an opportunity for contacts off your beaten path, and proof for your colleagues that you aren't a one-trick pony.

A frequent P&T committee question: "Is the candidate continuing to develop beyond the thrust of his or her Ph.D. thesis?" Presentations, publications, and reference scholars in diverse areas can provide cogent evidence of scholarly development—especially valuable at an institution where the ultimate P&T committee is all-campus and multidisciplinary.

ORGANIZING A CONFERENCE/PROCEEDINGS

"One of the most exhilarating experiences of my academic life," writes Lagretta T. Lenker,[18] "has been developing a single idea into a funded grant proposal, then into an award-winning conference, and finally into a scholarly book."

You don't have to wait for a fitting symposium announcement to show up on a bulletin board; you can use your network to plant and water a seed. While organizing a custom conference is always possible, it's much easier to project a session that rides piggy-back on an annual convention.

To help stimulate research and policy formulation at that point where the wildlife sciences and the social sciences impinge, John Hendee and ACS formed a network of kindred scholars around the country—a People/Natural Resources Research Consortium. Then they persuaded the program chair of the 38th North American Wildlife and Natural Resources Conference to schedule two technical sessions in the genre. The resulting papers were published in the Conference *Proceedings* under the general title "Human Behavior Aspects of Wildlife Management."

When a concurrent new North American Wildlife Policy concluded that "our most neglected and crucial research needs are those concerning human social behavior," Hendee and ACS drew on the assembled papers and others to edit what in effect was an interim text for resource management grad students, *Human Dimensions in Wildlife Programs: Reports of Recent Investigations*, published by the Washington, DC Wildlife Management Institute.

If you think that only scholars with track records can organize a conference and/or edit a collection of papers, think again.

Beginning when he was a graduate student, RM used his research on Eustache Deschamps, that 14th-century French writer, as the basis for several presentations at the annual International Congress on Medieval Studies—one in 1982, one in 1985, and two in 1987. Because Deschamps is considered a minor figure, RM labored in relative obscurity. But his presentations nonetheless caught the attention of a few other young scholars interested in Deschamps. One of them then decided to organize a conference for which RM prepared a presentation. The other raised the possibility of founding a Deschamps society. (All it takes is a letterhead.)

Although organizing an entire conference involves a lot of work—especially if you aren't well-known—and may lack some P&T clout, it may be worth your while, as we've said, to propose sessions in conjunction with an established conference and/or to create a special-interest network of scholars in your particular area. There is indeed strength in numbers. Sessions can lead to opportunities to publish a collection of articles (perhaps with you as the editor). A society offers you a chance of serving as an officer, in addition to prominence as a founding member.

Remain ever vigilant for the knock of opportunity. A few years ago a colleague of RM was asked to help organize a symposium session. Although she was busy, she recognized that the activity would put her in contact with some major figures in her field, so she grabbed the opportunity. The benefits of networking and session inception are well worth the investment in time and energy.

FOUNDING A JOURNAL

As scholars open up ever more discrete fields of research, new journals multiply at a tremendous rate. It's not so difficult as you might think to participate in founding one.

In the early 1960s, before the term "environmental" had entered the higher ed lexicon, scattered cadres of scholars and their graduate students in an array of disciplines were beginning to try to identify the scope and depth of what would become, if not a new field, at least a redefined field of investigation and instruction. At the time, however, editors of existing journals, unaware of the coming wave, were uniform in their rejection of manuscripts with an environmental cast, not recognizing that sometimes a topic can be so prescient and important that research methodology and conclusions are secondary.

Frustrated by their consistent inability to break into print, those cadres of professors simply created their own custom journals, using a variety of backers with venture capital.

For example, botanists started *The Ecologist;* nuclear scientists, *Environment;* sanitarians, *Environment Action Bulletin;* psychologists, *Environment and Behavior;* lawyers, *Environmental Affairs;* urban and regional planners, *Environmental Comment;* engineers, *Environmental Science and Technology;* mass communicators and educators, *The Journal of Environmental Education;* librarians, *Environmental Abstracts;* and so on.

By 1974 a directory of journals open to environmental papers listed 27 that had not existed 10 years before. Some were to disappear when established journals began to welcome environmental submissions; others today are among "most cited" publications.

The moral is clear: if you're at the growing edge of an as yet unconsolidated field, identify fellow pioneers, locate an angel, and start your own journal.

Let's use the inception of *The Journal of Environmental Education* as a case study in how to go about it:

The *JEE* was actually the brainchild of two University of Wisconsin-Madison grad students, Keith Stamm in agricultural journalism (now professor of mass communication, University of Washington) and Robert Roth in curriculum and instruction (now acting dean, School of Natural Resources, Ohio State University).

They sold the concept to ACS, who then undertook to follow these procedures recommended by a publisher of multiple journals:

1. Draft an initial prospectus to use in lining up an editorial board well dispersed in terms of geography, discipline, and institution.

2. Prepare a "for instance" first-issue table of contents, plus a sample paper.

3. Make a thorough analysis of the width and depth of potential subscribers.

4. Prepare a first-year budget, preferably starting out with a quarterly.

5. Now put together the same type of detailed proposal you use to market a textbook idea.

6. Send the proposal to likely sources of funding. Your graduate school may maintain a kitty of funds as start-up money to encourage new journals. So may your campus press. Your learned or professional society may help. Then there are commercial publishing houses that make it their business to support a stable of journals exploring frontiers of scholarship, from Heldref Publications in Washington, DC to Sage Publications in Beverly Hills, CA.

In the case of the *JEE*, a local "angel" appeared in the form of the president of Dembar Educational Research Services, Inc., a Madison WI publisher of educational research journals and monographs. With a $5,000 stake and a well-conceived subscription campaign, the *JEE* came out in fall 1969 and broke even by the end of its first year.

Today the *JEE* is *the* journal in its multidisciplinary field, now a Heldref publication, a 3,000-plus circulation.

Incidentally, selecting outstanding papers from early journal issues, the editors put together two collections published in hard cover by Dembar: *Outlines of Environmental Education* and *Interpreting Environmental Issues. JEE* personnel also participated in energizing the North American Association for Environmental Education, which recently saluted ACS for "tireless, dedicated, creative service."

(What some of its members really meant was, "We made tenure, thanks to the outlet you provided for our research papers that didn't fit anywhere else.")

A final word: Your first couple of issues are your "show windows," your very best advertisements. Invest plenty of time and attention on them. Go for quality rather than quantity. Better to start out printing 32 top-notch pages than 64 second-rate. If you begin accepting almost every MS that comes in over the transom, you'll quickly gain a reputation as an "easy mark" and you'll have a tough time ever raising your pecking order rating.

As an alternative, in advance openly solicit contributions from "name" people in the field. It's the rare scholar or practitioner who won't have a conference paper in a drawer, ready to go. The first issues of the *JEE* were so distinguished it took some time to get up to that speed again. In the meantime, the *JEE* was collecting citations in other journals and compliments from readers—establishing its prestige quickly.

It must be admitted, of course, that *The Journal of Environmental Education* caught a wave, its inception coinciding by a few months with the arrival of the National Environmental Protection Act, the Environmental Protection Agency, the National Environmental Education Act, and Earth Day. You might not be so lucky.

On the other hand, waves come along all the time. In 1994, two young assistant professors at the University of Georgia decided to test the waters for a new journal devoted to black feminist thought. Layli Phillips, a pscyhologist, and Barbara McCaskill, a literary critic, posted an announcement for *The Womanist* on several discussion groups on the Internet.

"We were overwhelmed by the response," Phillips said. In just two weeks, almost 100 scholars from fields as diverse as literature and biology, volunteered to write for the publication. Librarians wanted to subscribe; so did women's studies and African American studies programs.

The inaugural issue came out in June 1994, with University of Georgia support. The founding editors are already contemplating an annual volume of the best scholarly articles.[19]

One reviewer remonstrates: "This is all absolute *craziness*— that an assistant professor found a journal. Even if he or she can find the time, it will be viewed as a 'vanity press.'"

As a possible response, we ask you to recall that "Case History of Symbiotic Service" in an earlier chapter, narrating the experience of a young Harvard Ph.D. candidate by the name of Henry Kissinger in conceiving and directing an International Summer Seminar. To add illumination to the seminar, Kissinger launched a quarterly journal, *Confluences,* devoted to disquisitions on foreign affairs. In his capacity as editor, the grad student dealt with a galaxy of distinguished contributors, many of whom were seminar presenters, thus adding luster both to the seminar and to the director's stature. As his biographer notes, "His eagerness to impress important people was matched only by his ability to do so."

Some, indeed, must have accused Kissinger of "vanity," but it didn't seem to impede his meteoric career at Harvard, in Washington, and on to a Nobel Peace Prize.

CO-AUTHORING, COLLABORATING

As you've seen, sharing your time and talent can open up publishing opportunities to you that would otherwise be denied, as well as professional and personal relationships. By hitching your wagon to a star, you can ride along on a mentor's reputation. Sometimes you've got to use a crutch before you can walk alone. Of course, it's not unknown that a junior professor can wind up doing a senior's work. So just make sure that you're not a beast of burden—and divorce yourself once you get a feel for the road.

To what extent should you share authorship on publications, and how will academic decision-makers evaluate your multiple-author research papers?

Professors Alan E. Bayer and John C. Smart present quantitative and qualitative evidence to suggest that:

- The practice has grown exponentially since World War II, until it represents the majority of work in many fields.
- The greatest degree of collaboration tends to occur in the "hard" sciences.
- Particularly in the humanities is there a markedly lower rate of collaborative scholarship.
- Collaborative scholarship can result in a better product, or at least in a higher rate of acceptance by more prestigious research journals.

- There seems to be a career path leading from single authorship to multiple authorship and back again.
- No uniformity exists among the disciplines with respect to who goes first, senior or junior author(s).
- A scholar who publishes almost exclusively as sole author may be negatively characterized as an uncooperative "loner" and one who does not adequately provide a mentor role for graduate students. Some evaluators, indeed, may view participation in co-authorship as a form of collegiality that should be rewarded.
- Those who publish principally as co-authors may be questioned for their ability to fulfill independently all the tasks expected of publishing professors. Collaboration can be costly for junior faculty, whose evaluators want to see at least some independent publications.

As you can see, you'll just have to feel your way in regard to the issue of multiple-author papers. There's no consensus out there.[20] The real question is, how will your review panel rate multiple-author papers versus single authorships? It's probably safe to say the latter will usually outweigh the former. So it's well to be judicious in investing in collaborative projects. On the other hand, dual authorship is better than none.

A computer-conferencing program could be a boon to joint authors of scholarly papers or texts. Apple Macintosh Group Technologies' "Aspects" lets as many as 16 people work together at their own computers, writing and editing the same document simultaneously. When one person makes a change, it appears immediately on all other computer screens.

What happens when two college professors from different disciplines, each with his own distinct writing style and personality, try to write a book together? The senior author (ACS) can testify the experience can strain professional relations and personal friendships for a time. But two professors at Metropolitan State University in Minneapolis, MN can testify that two heads can be better than one.[21]

Thomas B. Jones, history, and Chet Meyers, humanities, undertook to turn the proceedings of a teaching workshop into a fulllength book of practical tips on how to move from conventional lectures to small groups, simulations, case studies, and cooperative student projects. In so doing, they discovered the process of collaboration didn't water down their combined intellectual effort; in fact, "collaborating on every chapter forced us to continually clarify what we wanted to say." The result was a well-received *Promoting Active Learning: Strategies for the College Classroom* (San Francisco: Jossey-Bass, 1993).

Yet the question still remains: how will review panels evaluate the respective roles of any collaborating authors?

Joseph M. Moxley[22] has a practical suggestion for surmounting any hazards in the collaborative paper of which you aren't the lead author. Ask the principal investigator to write a frank statement explaining your role, and then include that statement in your promotion-and-tenure portfolio.

Evelyn Ashton-Jones[23] believes the times may be tilting toward a more understanding attitude on the part of department executive committees toward collaborative scholarship:

> We're at a transition point where two contradictory systems are in conflict—the traditional evaluation/reward system based on the assumption of individual performance, and an emerging method of inquiry that requires the expertise and efforts of pairs and groups of people working together to produce knowledge. . . . Not to collaborate is to limit one's scholarly potential and productivity and to deny oneself and one's discipline the fruits of cooperative scholarly effort that can come about only as the joint venture of minds working together.

Until that philosophy becomes generally accepted, however, it's probably well for an assistant professor to accompany any jointly authored works with some of which he or she is the sole author.

MULTIPLIERS

"Why don't you tell your readers how to title talks and articles to make them look different on a CV and to appear scholarly?" one reviewer suggests.

OK. Examples:

When the senior author (ACS) was asked to update his research on 1970 Earth Day leaders for a 1990 North American Association of Environmental Education panel presentation, he spoke from notes on the subject of "Those Original E-Day Leaders: Where Are They Now?" Turning the material into a submission to the *Journal of Voluntary Action Research,* he titled the paper "Long-Term Correlates of Volunteerism: Eco-Activists Revisited."

In reverse, when he was asked to update his 1981 research monograph, *The Environmental Information and Education Ecosystem,* for a 1992 conference on the public relations of environmental management, he again spoke from notes on "The Environmental Management/Mass Communication Mix."

In other words, tailor your title to the occasion at hand, and you'll automatically have varied entries for your CV—some scholarly, some more colloquial.

WHAT ABOUT AGENTS?

Should you aim at appearing frequently in consumer publications or via trade books, the question naturally arises, "Will an agent help?"

To answer the question, we have to distinguish between two broad types of writers and between two broad types of agents. One type of writer is the beginner. The other type is one who has begun to become established with a book or two or at least a half-dozen major articles in print. One type of agent is the literary agent who offers manuscripts to prospective buyers, bargains as to price, and negotiates contracts. In case of a sale, the agent retains a 10% or so commission and pays the balance to the author. The other type of agent is the professional critic who reviews the author's work and helps him or her improve it for the market. For this help the agent charges a reading and criticism fee.

Now here are the facts of life: the novice has only one choice of agent, the professional critic. With the rarest of exceptions, the literary agent simply won't invest time in a beginner. The established author, on the other hand, will be welcomed by an agent and can find such services invaluable.

In other words, you have to fight your way upward to the point where you almost don't need an agent before a good one will take you on and be of great help as liaison between you and publishers. In the meantime, you may find a reputable professional critic who will offer you honest criticism for a fee without picking your pocket.

How do you find an agent or critic? Ask around among colleagues, publishers' reps, and the like, or consult *Guide to Literary Agents* (Cincinnati: Writer's Digest Books, 1994).

At the peak of his career as a freelance writer for popular and semi-popular publications, the senior author (ACS) retained a literary agent who opened up publisher doors that might otherwise have not been in his ken, but of course it's unheard of to use an agent as a go-between with editors of scholarly publications.

MARK TWAIN SAID IT

To give birth to an idea—to discover a great thought, an intellectual nugget, right under the dust of a field that many a brain plow has gone over before. To find a new planet, to invent a new hinge, to find the way to make lightning carry your messages. To be the first—that is the idea. To do something, say something, see something, before anybody else—these are the things that confer a pleasure compared with which all other pleasures are tame and commonplace, other ecstasies cheap and trivial.

That was in 1869, in *Innocents Abroad*. Today he might well add, "But it doesn't count unless you publish."

NOTES

1. Ralph E. Weisheit and Robert M. Regoli, "Ranking Journals," *Scholarly Publishing* July 1984: 312-335.

2. Judith Swan and George G. Gopen, "The Science of Scientific Writing," *American Scientist* Nov.-Dec. 1990: 550-558.

3. Swan and Gopen 550-558.

4. Donald W. Fiske, "Strategies for Planning and Revising Research Reports," *Writing and Publishing for Academic Authors*, ed. Joseph M. Moxley (Lanham, MD: University Press of America, 1992).

5. Beverly T. Watkins, "An Outsider Pierces Veil of 'Math Anxiety' and 'Science Avoidance,' " *The Chronicle of Higher Education* 17 Apr. 1991: A 13.

6. Mary Kathryn Harrington, "Faculty Writing: Redirection and Renewal," *Innovative Higher Education* Winter 1991: 187-197.

7. Maryellen Weimer, "The Disciplinary Journals of Pedagogy," *Change* Nov.-Dec. 1993: 44-51.

8. Kevin L. Kearns, "The Economic Orthodoxies Offered U.S. Students Won't Prepare Them to Work in World Markets," *The Chronicle of Higher Education* 27 Mar. 1991: B1-3.

9. Denise K. Magner, "Using Latin and History, Beloit College Aims to Instill Desire for Higher Education in Low Income Children" *The Chronicle of Higher Education* 27 Mar. 1991: A31-32.

10. Fritz Machlup, "Recipe for a Good Graduate Department," quoted in Robert J. Griffin *et al.*, *Interpreting Public Issues* (Ames: Iowa State University Press, 1991): 126.

11. "Why Not Write for Commercial Publication?" *Writing and Publishing for Academic Authors,* ed. Joseph M. Moxley, (Lanham, MD: University Press of America, 1992).

12. Peter Blockson, "Queries That Work!" *Writer's Digest* Oct. 1993: 24-28.

13. Paul A. Smith, "Art and Agendas of Writing a Successful Book Proposal," *Writing and Publishing for Academic Authors,* ed. Joseph M. Moxley, (Lanham, MD: University Press of America, 1992.)

14. Debra E. Blum, "Authors, Publishers Seek to Raise Quality and Status of the College Textbook," *The Chronicle of Higher Education* 31 July 1991: A11-12.

15. Robert Kelly, *The Shaping of the American Past* (Englewood Cliffs, NJ: Prentice-Hall, 1975).

16. Laurie Lindop, "The Best Friend You Never Knew You Had: The Editorial Assistant," *Writer's Digest* Dec. 1993: 40-42.

17. Camille Paglia, "Academe Has to Recover Its Spiritual Roots and Overthrow the Ossified Political Establishment of Invested Self-Interest," *The Chronicle of Higher Education* 8 May 1991: B1-2.

18. Lagretta T. Lenker, "From Proposal to Print: Publishing Papers from Academic Conferences in Book Form," *Writing and Publishing for Academic Authors* ed. Joseph M. Moxley, (Lanham, MD: University Press of America, 1992).

19. Karen J. Winkler, "The Rise of Black Feminist Thought," *The Chronicle of Higher Education* 30 Mar. 1994: A12.

20. Alan E. Bayer and John C. Smart, "Career Publication Patterns and Collaborative Research Styles in American Academic Science," *The Journal of Higher Education* Nov.-Dec. 1991: 613-636.

21. Thomas B. Jones and Chet Meyers, "Collaborative Faculty Writing," *AAHE Bulletin* Feb. 1994: 7-9.

22. Joseph M. Moxley, *Publish, Don't Perish* (Westport, CN: Praeger, 1992).

23. Evelyn Ashton-Jones, "Coauthoring for Scholarly Publication," *Writing and Publishing for Academic Authors* ed. Joseph M. Moxley (Lanham, MD: University Press of America, 1992).

12 PRESENTING YOUR CREDENTIALS FOR THE ULTIMATE DECISION

Now comes the final race: surmounting the hurdles in the all-bets-off steeplechase to tenure. No matter what the odds the campus bookies have quoted, you can still win or lose, depending on how you traverse the final course.

Initially we had titled this chapter "Packaging the Product for Sale," but our reviewers thought that a little too "commercial," so we changed it. Yet that first-draft heading may actually be more accurate. While no assistant professor makes tenure on marketing strategies alone, you certainly could miss the mark if you don't package your wares properly.

The substance and style in which your department frames your P&T portfolio can indeed represent either a compelling consumer-oriented "package" or a humdrum CV short on documentation and conviction. Like it or not, at this stage of the game you're a "product"—not a living, breathing human being but an entity your reviewers can assess only from a bundle of inanimate papers. And you're certainly up "for sale" to various echelons of judges as either a hot item or a dud.

But never fear. We're about to lead you over and through the fences, ponds, and sand traps of that steeplechase finale to tenure.

CONTINUOUS PREPARATION

Your warm-up for the final starting gun you obviously should have begun and continued from the moment you reported to the campus course:

- Constantly refreshing your CV.
- Cataloging annual faculty activity reports.
- Amassing and distributing a supply of your published papers and citations.
- Preserving copies of your better sets of student evaluations.
- Preparing excerpts of published reviews and/or citations of your work, with sources indicated. (Your files may have a published citations index.)
- Accomplishing in good heart your varied responsibilities for varied echelons.
- Responding to requests from the campus instructional development office for copies of your most imaginative syllabi.
- Energizing new departures in disciplinary research and synthesis.
- Performing institutional service chores with a will and a way.
- Making yourself available to the campus outreach dean.
- Befriending colleagues, students, and staff alike.
- Listening carefully to suggestions from periodic review panels.
- Picking likely role models.
- Assimilating the realities of pragmatic career politics.
- Applying appropriate suggestions from the previous chapters in this manual in order to help you join a community of professors making themselves as useful as possible.

- Striving, all in all, to merit an evaluation on the order of that once bestowed by a London newspaper on a young MP named Winston Churchill: "A portentous amalgam of genius and plod."

There's a continual opportunity as well to practice a little discreet personal public relations:

- Cultivate key contacts.
- Supply the campus news service with items.
- Contribute to news note pages of professional journals.
- Circulate offprints of research papers and citations.
- Distribute reports of any committees you've chaired.
- Respond to queries from local news media.
- Present to strategic colleagues autographed copies of any books or monographs you've authored or co-authored.
- Apprise the chair of any awards or grants.
- In general, make yourself as visible as valuable.

Personal PR can be overdone, of course, but without it you may become just a name and your record just another personnel file.

In the final analysis, of course, the best public relations is not publicity but performance. And it is here that you can profit from one of history's great performers: "I am easily satisfied—with the very best."[1]

PICKING A MODEL

Despite their former association with the University of Wisconsin-Madison, the authors make no apologies in suggesting that you might well use as a model for preparing and presenting your own promotion-to-tenure documents the instructions provided by that institution to assistant professors and their department chairs in similar circumstances.

In its stature as an institution, in its faculty quality-control mechanism, and in the completeness and clarity of its *Form of Recommendations for Appointment or Promotion to a Tenured Position* (in this case, in its faculty division of the social studies), UW-Madison can serve admirably as a model.

THE INSTITUTION

When the first national ranking of institutions of higher education was assayed in 1906, 15 made the list. In rank order: Harvard, Columbia, Chicago, Cornell, Johns Hopkins, California-Berkeley, Yale, Michigan, MIT, Wisconsin-Madison, Pennsylvania, Stanford, Princeton, Minnesota, and Ohio State. Of those original 15, nine have remained consistently in the top 10. In alphabetical order: Cal-Berkeley, Chicago, Harvard, Michigan, MIT, Princeton, Stanford, UW-Madison, and Yale—by any standard, a remarkable record of sustained academic achievement.

Clark Kerr, Emeritus President of the University of California, wrote in the May/June 1991 *Change* that all but one of those nine institutions enjoy some form of geographic, economic, or cultural endowment. The one university to rise above what Kerr calls its "natural level" is Madison: "Madison rose and stays above both its general geographical location and the economic resources of its state—a great historic feat of self-levitation."

So, they must do a great many things right at UW-Madison. One is the university's faculty quality-control mechanism, under which every single assistant professor up for tenure—regardless of his or her department, school, college, interdisciplinary home, gender, race, creed, color, previous condition of servitude, or the clout of a dean—must run the gauntlet of one of four faculty-elected all-university divisional executive committees (biological sciences, humanities, physical sciences, and social studies) before the recommendation can go forward to the top administration. In its wisdom, the administration can conceivably do some more screening before sending an annual list on to the Regents. (A school or college dean can overrule a divisional committee, but only at his or her own risk.) Very few other institutions have such a daunting system of faculty self-governance, evaluation, and credentialing. Hence the standards and forms used in recommendations for promotion to tenure at Madison carry a certain quiet credential of their own.

Nor is it insignificant that for more than a decade the chief executive officers of America's three largest and most influential higher education associations have been UW-Madison staff products: Robert Atwell of ACE, Robert Clodius of NASULGC, and Allan Ostar of AASCU.

THE COMMITTEE CHAIR

Few people in academia today are so familiar with the multivariate ethos of the American professorate as John A. Ross. Scholar of the theory and practice of mass communication, with an emphasis on the role of the media in public environmental policy formulation, Ross is only recently retired as professor and former chair of the department of agricultural journalism, College of Agricultural and Life Sciences, University of Wisconsin-Madison. His former advisees today are staffing news media, government bureaus, conservation organizations, and college faculties around the country.

In addition, Ross served as assistant to the dean, associate director of the Institute of Environmental Studies, executive director of PROFS (the faculty PAC), member of the executive committee of the University faculty senate, and chair of the social sciences divisional committee.

It was as divisional committee chair that Ross revised and polished the University's "Statement of Criteria and Evidence for Recommendations Regarding Tenure" and devised a new "Form of Recommendation for Appointment or Promotion to a Tenure Position"—all to reflect more aptly the diverse qualifications and expectations that can characterize faculty in a "multiversity."

As Ross confides:

> It wasn't too difficult to work out the criteria, but it certainly was not easy during my three years on the committee to deal with specific cases . . . . But then I realized that you can, on a case-by-case basis, judge quality work. Rigor is rigor! To assume otherwise is not fair.
>
> It seems to me the key is to have people in the quality-control structure who understand and appreciate the varied responsibilities to which faculty members in a trivium-oriented institution can be assigned. Not all professors understand, and you'll never finish the job of internal education. But I'm convinced you can recruit good people and promote them, even in a climate of a very high, single standard of academic excellence.

The Ross sense of the fitness of things academic and his feeling for the quality of words inform and inspire the UW-Madison P&T form that follows.

STATEMENT OF CRITERIA AND EVIDENCE FOR RECOMMENDATIONS REGARDING TENURE

FACULTY DIVISION OF THE SOCIAL STUDIES UNIVERSITY OF WISCONSIN-MADISON

September 1992

The Executive Committee's criteria for appointment to tenure are intended to preserve and enhance the university's excellence and its function in developing the human intellect. Tenure contributes to this objective by giving a strong measure of security and protection to faculty members; it frees them to teach, inquire, create, publish, and serve with less concern for the immediate popularity or acceptability of their efforts than would be the case if termination of employment were a continual possibility. The granting of tenure is a long-term commitment of university and state resources which requires the proof of excellence in past performance and a forecast that an individual faculty member's intellectual vitality and future performance will continue to be of high quality for many years to come. There is no entitlement to tenure based upon a record that is merely competent and satisfactory.

The university, in considering a candidate's future contributions to the educational function, should accord major significance to all evidence of scholarly excellence and productivity. Scholarly excellence and productivity are measured by the quality of (1) research and scholarly publications; (2) teaching and the development of teaching material; and (3) service to the university, the public, and the profession. Research, teaching, and service collectively encompass the diversity of activities essential for all faculty, including those with extension responsibilities in integrated departments and professional schools, and others with specialized missions. The standards to be applied in judging research, teaching, and service, and the role of faculty with budgeted extension responsibilities, are elaborated below.

I. Research

The candidate should have demonstrated the ability to conduct research that reflects original scholarship and makes a contribution to knowledge. Competence may be demonstrated by the ability in one or more of the following categories:

- to conduct research with appropriate methodological technique and rigor;
- to conceptualize and theorize in an original way, with logical and mathematical formulation as appropriate;
- to synthesize, criticize, and clarify extant knowledge and research;
- to innovate in the collection or analysis of empirical data; or
- to relate research to the solution of practical problems of individuals, groups, organizations, or societies.

In evaluating the record of candidates with extension responsibilities, the evidence must show that the candidate's work has significantly contributed to the translation and dissemination of the results of scholarly inquiry in his or her discipline for the benefit of society, and that this work has extended the knowledge base of the university to the citizens of the state.

Evidence of research performance and of a candidate's standing in a discipline includes

- scholarly books, monographs, chapters, bulletins, etc.;
- articles published or accepted for publication in scholarly or professional journals;

- extension publications and exemplary materials;
- reviews and other evaluations of the candidate's publications and manuscripts;
- citation of the work, if particularly frequent or laudatory;
- research awards, grants, and proposals;
- evaluations by authorities, especially those from other major universities, in the candidate's field of specialization; and
- papers read at professional meetings, invited lectures at other universities and learned societies, invitations to participate in professional meetings, editorial positions with major professional journals, testimony before governmental committees, and professional honors, awards and consultations.

II. Teaching

Evaluation of teaching ability and performance must take into account the wide range of approaches to teaching within the university. Besides the variations attributable to individual personality and style, there are distinctions among types of teaching situations both on and off campus. These include lectures, discussion sections, seminars, institutes, workshops, media presentations, laboratory instruction, in-service training, media courses, correspondence courses, individual tutorials, advising and consulting, and consultative exchanges with client groups by extension faculty. No candidate is expected to be equally proficient in all teaching situations; proficiency must be demonstrated in those teaching situations most appropriate to the candidate's teaching mission and responsibilities.

Evidence used to evaluate teaching ability and performance includes:

- surveys of student opinion;
- assessment by colleagues based on direct observation;

- course outlines, bibliographies, scripts, program development, exams given, and other teaching materials;
- assessment by teaching assistants, workshop participants, trainees;
- the record of student advising, consultations, and research supervision;
- development of new courses and teaching materials; and
- client and peer evaluations of extension program presentations. A balanced judgment of teaching ability must rely on more than one kind of evidence.

III. Service

Service activities fall into three general categories: public, university, and professional. All service activities must be adequately documented.

Public. Faculty members participate in various ways in carrying out the university's obligation to serve the state and the public. Public service may include membership on committees and boards, preparation of publications, articles and reprints for the public, testifying at public hearings, speaking to or consulting with public bodies, and participating in or organizing workshops and conferences. Participation in activities in one's capacity as a citizen outside the university is not ordinarily considered. Public service activity shall be evaluated according to the level of skill and success in communicating and applying the knowledge of one's field of professional competence.

The Executive Committee recognizes that public service is a major, and for many a primary, duty for faculty with extension responsibilities. The documentation in such cases must clearly demonstrate either how the candidate is meeting the extension program needs of the public through the teaching, coordination, and evaluation of outreach programs or how the candidate's work may have aided in shaping public policy. Evidence should be presented showing that a candidate with extension responsibilities has been able to identify program needs, develop and teach programs to address those needs, use new and existing information in program development, skillfully deliver programs to the public, and evaluate those programs.

The Executive Committee requires specific, reliable evidence of productivity, quality, and creativity in public service and outreach activities. Such evidence includes a description of the activities, the nature of the problems and the public served, the objectives sought, the methods employed, and the results achieved.

University. The effective operation of the university requires a high degree of faculty participation and, at times, intensive activity in faculty government, departmental and university committees, administrative roles, advisory functions, and similar tasks. All faculty must share in this task, but the Executive Committee recognizes that a heavier burden may and should fall on the shoulders of more senior (and already tenured) faculty members.

Professional. Service to one's profession or academic discipline may occur at local, state, national or international levels. Appropriate activities include service as an officer; member of a board, committee, or task force of a professional group; on-site visits; reviewing research proposals or manuscripts; and organizing and participating in professional and technical meetings such as training institutes, workshops, conferences, and continuing professional education.

IV. Weighing the Evidence

A recommendation for promotion or appointment with tenure should identify the candidate's relative balance of responsibilities and accomplishments in research, teaching, and service. Demonstrated excellence in at least two of these areas is normally required. Occasionally a tenure recommendation may be generated for a candidate, other than one who has primarily extension responsibilities, whose efforts and abilities are not well balanced among research, teaching, and service. Such recommendations are welcomed where the candidate is clearly exceptional in either teaching or research, not inadequate in the other, and where the overall balance within the candidate's department will not be adversely affected. Where a recommendation is made primarily on an exceptional record in either research or teaching, the evidence must show clearly that the candidate is one of the very best in his or her field, and that the candidate's contributions should extend beyond the university; there should be evidence that the candidate has contributed creatively to teaching in the field. Unusual rapport with students is important, but not by itself sufficient to support a case for tenure based primarily on teaching. Significant public service contributions may strengthen a case for tenure but, except in the case of faculty with budgeted extension/outreach responsibilities, cannot be the primary basis for a tenure recommendation.

A tenure recommendation may be made on the basis of significant outreach activities for a candidate with primarily extension/outreach responsibilities. In such cases the evidence must show that the candidate is recognized both within and outside the university in his or her field, and has made significant contributions to outreach through an appropriate balance of teaching, research, and public service. The Executive Committee recognizes that translation and dissemination of research results through teaching and service are the most important responsibilities of a faculty member with primarily extension responsibilities.

If a tenure recommendation is based on administrative service as the major activity of the candidate at the present time, or where tenure is sought for an administrative appointment from the outside, evidence of excellence in either teaching or research (with adequacy in the other) must also be presented to demonstrate the candidate's ability to fill a teaching and/or research function when his or her administrative activities come to an end.

FORMAT OF RECOMMENDATIONS
FOR APPOINTMENT OR PROMOTION
TO A TENURED POSITION

Tenure appointments are governed by Chapter 4, "The Faculty Divisions," and Chapter 7, "Faculty Appointments," of the *Faculty Policies and Procedures*; the procedures of the relevant school or college; and the attached "Statement of Criteria and Evidence for Recommendations regarding Tenure, Division of the Social Studies."

If the candidate's proposed tenure appointment is to be divided among several departments, each department's executive committee must make an affirmative recommendation (see Ch. 7.02 of *Faculty Policies and Procedures*). In such circumstances, the chair of the department that is principal sponsor of the recommendation is responsible for preparation of the supporting material described below.

Each recommendation for appointment or promotion to a tenured position must include:

I. A letter of transmittal from the appropriate dean or a statement indicating that the dean has given approval for requesting the advice of the Divisional Committee.

II. A covering letter from the chair of the sponsoring department. The letter should include:

A. A statement indicating the nature of the proposed appointment including the percent of time devoted to extension activities, if applicable. If past and/or proposed appointments are divided among several departments, indicate the nature of the arrangement and the fraction of appointment in each department.

B. The number of eligible voters in the departmental executive committee during the semester of the tenure decision and the exact vote, including absences or abstentions. (If appropriate, explanation of absences or abstentions should be given.) In the case of divided appointments, the Divisional Committee requires a letter from the chair of each department providing the information for that executive committee.

C. The number of years of probationary service the candidate will have completed at the end of the current academic year.

D. A departmental evaluation of the candidate's *research, teaching,* and *service,* which should include factual and judgmental statements about each area. The evaluation should address the candidate's blend of research, teaching, service attainments, and anticipated contributions to the future development of the department, as well as the tenure standards applied in comparable departments elsewhere. It should review the factors entering into the department's judgment in relation to the Divisional Committee's "Statement of Criteria." The use of superlatives without analysis of the work is not helpful.

In the case of divided appointments, provide a summary of the contribution of the candidate to the relevant other departments. If the recommendation is to be made on the basis of an exceptional case, extensive documentation and justification are expected.

III. *Curriculum Vitae* with entries corresponding to the list below:
- Name;
- Formal Education;
- Title of Thesis;
- Positions Held (list chronologically, with no time period unaccounted for);
- Special Honors and Awards;
- Research and Publications: proper bibliographical form should be followed, *listing the names of coauthors in sequence as published,* and paging. Names of journals should be given in full. These groupings may be useful: books and monographs;

research and other scholarly papers; minor publications and book reviews. *Those that are peer reviewed should be indicated by an asterisk.* Publications not based on work performed as an assistant professor at UW-Madison should be identified. Extension publications should also be separately identified. Number each publication in the vita and identify each publication submitted with that number. (Use small self-stick tags for marking each publication with its number.)

- Research and Publications in Progress;
- Research Support (source, dates, and amount);
- Teaching (principal areas and experience);
- Service (public, university, and professional).

IV. Documentation of Research Output. The Divisional Committee requires:

A. Two copies of each of the candidate's significant professional publications. (These will be returned to the department.)

The chair of the department should also select two research publications that are considered most representative of the candidate's work and forward **twenty copies** of each for distribution to the entire Divisional Committee. For extension candidates, one of these documents should be illustrative of typical extension documents meant for use by the unit's clients.

B. For coauthored publications give the full reference, including the names of all coauthors and an indication of what role the candidate has played in the research and writing. Each candidate is to be asked to estimate his or her contributions in percentage terms to any jointly authored publication, including the following data: (a) percent contribution to conceptualization; (b) percent contribution to methodology and data analysis and (c) percent contribution to writing.

C. For publications that are peer reviewed, the department chair should provide an evaluation of the quality and standing of the publication outlet. For nonrefereed publications, evaluation of the work's research and scholarly merit should be solicited from recognized authorities in the field. Please also distinguish peer-reviewed articles from non-peer reviewed pieces clearly on the candidate's curriculum vitae. When possible please include the acceptance rate of the various journals. This information may be available from the Memorial Library reference department if you do not have ready access to it. For extension publications, also indicate for each publication outlet any specialized nonacademic audiences for which it is designed and its influence on public policy and welfare.

D. Evidence of acceptance for publications "in press" or "accepted for publication."

E. As evidence of the candidate's stature in the field, letters of evaluation from distinguished scholars should be solicited by the departmental executive committee. At least five letters of evaluation of the scholarly activities must be provided by authorities in the candidate's own field, including at least four letters from outside the University of Wisconsin-Madison. In most cases more than eight (8) letters is excessive. Extension candidates should also include letters from recognized extension leaders and professional experts in the candidate's field. Peer and client evaluations are also to be included. Provide a sample copy of the letter sent to distinguished scholars that requests their evaluation; the letter should include a request for general comments about the candidate's several contributions and request to explain how the evaluator knows the candidate. A list of all persons solicited for letters should be provided, indicating their affiliation and their stature in the field. A statement should also be included in the document acknowledging that *all* letters received have been submitted; if not, the reasons should be specified. The chair should identify any relationship (major professor, previous colleague, etc.) the evaluator may have with the candidate. In general, letters from people not closely associated with the candidate are given more weight by the committee.

F. Each candidate is to prepare a succinct statement on his or her future research and teaching plans, say, over the next five years. This should not be more than three pages.

V. Documentation of Teaching. The Divisional Committee requires:

A. A chronology covering all of the candidate's teaching experience at the University of Wisconsin-Madison, and other teaching to the extent possible. Teaching at other institutions must be chronicled and course evaluations provided. For classroom teaching, list each course by course number and title, and indicate its enrollment and whether undergraduate or graduate. For other teaching situations, off campus or nontraditional, be specific about the type of situation, duration, level, and audience or participants. This chronology should include a list of graduate students supervised.

B. Evidence of the candidate's general abilities as a teacher. *Assessment of teaching performance requires several kinds of evidence.* Most evidence of teaching performance can be placed in one of the following six categories:

1. Surveys of student opinion. Such surveys are most useful if they have been prepared by departments for general and anonymous administration, using carefully selected questions that have proven useful in the particular teaching situation. *Comparative information for*

other faculty and similar courses or teaching situations is necessary.

When the mean values for student evaluations are provided to document an individual's teaching, please provide the standard deviations as well. In every case, include information comparing the candidate's evaluations to those of others in the same department. If such comparative information is not available, please so indicate. Student evaluations are useful. Peer reviews, if available, may also be submitted together with other materials such as course syllabi. Contextual factors the department has found important (size of class, difficulties of material, preparation of students, etc.) should be noted.

2. Assessment by workshop participants, trainees, teaching assistants, or others. Such evidence should summarize systematically, rather than simply quoting a few laudatory comments.

3. Assessment by colleagues.

4. Course outlines, bibliographies, scripts, and other teaching materials. Selected examples should be accompanied by an evaluation by colleagues or other experts.

5. Record of student advising, consultations, and research supervision. Some candidates for promotion to tenure, and most candidates for appointment to tenure, will have a record of such service as major professor to graduate students. The subsequent performance of these students and advisees may provide useful evidence of the capabilities of a candidate.

6. Development of courses, programs, and teaching materials. Special consideration should be given to documentation of attempts

at new or improved teaching methods and materials, and to evaluation of their effectiveness.

C. For extension candidates, description of up to three significant extension programs in which the candidate made a major contribution. Use the following format:

1. Identify the problem, the clientele, and the needs assessment procedure.

2. Outline the objectives.

3. Provide details on the method of instruction and delivery, innovative teaching methods, materials, aids or approaches, and client evaluation of the program's effectiveness.

4. Document the significance of the program and its relevance to the social problems in the state and nation, and its potential or demonstrated impact on public policy and welfare.

VI. Documentation of Service.

To be relevant in tenure decisions, service activities must clearly involve a high level of skill in communicating and applying the knowledge of one's professional competence. Documentation of service should highlight individual efforts that are especially significant. The discussion should identify the nature of the tasks performed and the particular responsibilities of the candidate. When service is a major aspect of a candidate's responsibilities, letters should be solicited from authorities in the field evaluating the impact of the service and its importance to the university.

Evidence of public service may include:

A. Consultations to the community and significant advisory work with government, business, or industry.

B. Outreach program planning and development.

C. Membership on committees and boards.

D. Public lectures and presentations.

E. Participation in radio, television, and ETN programs.

F. Service in official positions of public organizations or agencies.

G. Publications for nonprofessionals.

H. Testifying at public hearings.

I. Preparation of reports.

J. On-site visits.

K. The development of exemplary materials.

Evidence of university service may include:

A. Major committee assignments in the department or the university.

B. Chair or associate chair of a department or dean or associate dean of a school or college.

C. Coordinator of statewide outreach programs.

D. Special administrative assignments in a department, college, or university.

Evidence of professional service may include:

A. Membership on state, regional, or national review panels, study sections, councils, etc.

B. Membership on editorial boards of professional journals or other reviewing or editing activities.

C. Office of national or international scientific, professional, and educational organizations.

D. Leadership in the development of continuing professional education for personnel in the field.

VII. Presentation of the Case.

No useful purpose is served by the receipt of complex and expensively packaged tenure materials. The following specific suggestions are to be followed in assembling tenure proposals.

A. Number all pages of the document in consecutive order. Copy documents on both sides of the page, where possible, for handling ease.

B. Include a table of contents.

C. A simple metal clamp may be used to contain the document.

D. Plastic dividers with tabs are unnecessary. A colored sheet of paper with a heading identifying each section is sufficient.

E. Do *not* use "Accopress" or 3-ring binders or any other bulky cover.

F. Do not use expandable "accordion" files except when necessary to contain publications.

G. When publications or other materials (such as manuals, tapes, or irreplaceable items) are sent in limited number for reviewers, please list these items on a separate sheet for special handling.

H. Prepare *20 copies* of the tenure document (including 2 selected publications).

I. Copies must be submitted at least *three weeks before* the divisional committee meeting.

J. Questions about tenure documentation should be directed to the divisional committee office.

K. If documentation is incomplete, delays in committee review may ensue.

A ROSS OBITER DICTUM:
Ross states:

> Regarding the presentation to a divisional committee at Madison, under Faculty Rules and Regulations it is the responsibility of a departmental executive committee to prepare the documents and make the case for promotion to tenure. In practice, obviously, the candidate does a lot of the work.
>
> However, in my experience, the strongest presentations are the ones where a subcommittee of the department executive committee does the homework to make the case. The most impressive cases I reviewed, assuming academic competence, were the ones where there was a *synthesis* of the candidate's work within the context of its importance to the field. In other words, the best proposals were interpretations of the science, with 'generalizations.' This is precisely what we try to teach science writers.

A WORD OF CAUTION

It probably isn't necessary to tell you this, but we'll do it anyway: the promotion-to-tenure form we've exposed you to is a "for instance" only. Even though it's employed by one of the more distinguished institutions of higher education in the country, it's not to be followed slavishly in any cases other than in the social studies at UW-Madison.

For example, your institution may have its own recommended form, which you should definitely follow. Lacking such guidance, remember that UW-Madison is a "multiversity," so its policies and procedures—and resulting forms—are not exactly applicable at a teaching-oriented college, a graduate research institute, or an out-reach-bent urban university. Remember, too, that the specimen form is that of the divisional committee of the social studies. Although the forms used by the divisions of the humanities, the biological sciences, and the physical sciences at UW-Madison do not differ in kind, they do differ in some degree.

Nonetheless, we think it worthwhile that you examine the UW-Madison form. If nothing else, it seems to establish certain parameters of scope and evidence. And it certainly is explicit in terms of mechanical instructions—which again may or may not be relevant to your situation. (For instance, your P&T committee may be impressed by a portfolio tied up in ribbons, so to speak.)

The bottom line: the UW-Madison P&T form is at least a starting point you and your department chair can use to spark discussions and detective work on how to best present you as a compelling candidate for tenure.

At the moment, no topic is more important in your life!

LOOKING AHEAD TO TENURE

You propose to join a great and noble American reality and an even more challenging American dream—higher education.

THE UNREALIZED POTENTIAL

But American higher education has not yet realized its potential, in the view of Alexander W. Astin,[2] professor of higher education and director of the Higher Education Research Institute at the University of California, Los Angeles.

The problem, Astin says, is that three powerful and interrelated values—materialism, individualism, and competitiveness—have come to dominate America's major institutions—including higher education. As a result, he holds, flawed measures of campus excellence have come to replace the measure that really ought to count—ability to develop the talents of students to the fullest.

Astin is not without hope for the future, however. He sees three sources of great potential for change. First, the great diversity of the American "system" of higher education. Second, its inherent creativity and capacity for critical analysis. And third, remarkable institutional autonomy.

With regard to the last factor in particular, most colleges and universities retain almost complete control over those decisions and policies that matter most:

- *whom* to admit and on what basis;
- *what* to teach them and how to teach it;
- what *rules and requirements* will govern student conduct;
- how to *test and certify* students;
- *whom* to hire and the criteria for hiring, tenuring, and promoting them;
- the *manner* in which faculty treat each other as professional colleagues; and
- to what *ends* faculty devote their discretionary time.

What is so striking about that list of autonomous responsibilities and privileges is that, without exception, they are *faculty* prerogatives, not those of administrators, trustees, or lay bodies. So, if higher education is to participate in helping create Astin's society that is "less materialistic, fearful, and competitive, and more generous, trusting, and cooperative," it will be faculty who will pull it off—and that includes junior faculty who have just made tenure as well as senior professors.

THE FUTURE, UNIVERSITIES, AND YOU

- Are our institutions doing enough to surmount the tensions that affect our ability to maintain a growing, competitive economy while providing adequate security and opportunity for all citizens?

- Are they contributing sufficiently to help society enjoy efficient corporate management, technological progress, competent government, effective public schools, a sustainable environment, and the conquest of poverty with its attendant afflictions of crime, drug abuse, alcoholism, and illiteracy?
- Are our institutions of higher education doing enough to build in their students, faculty, and administrators a stronger sense of civic responsibility, ethical awareness, and concern for the interests of others?

If you agree that the answer to those questions, posed by Harvard Emeritus President Derek Bok in his *Universities and the Future of America*,[3] is at least a qualified "No," then you and your colleagues have your work cut out for you.

Tenure, remember, is not so much a reward for past performance as it is a wager that a past record is clear promise of greater distinction. As a land-grant dean once advised his college P&T committee:

"In granting tenure, institutions should be like bankers lending money—they should require collateral. The collateral should be the most precisely measured potentiality possible."

REALITIES AND MYTHS

Richard M. Millard, longtime academic leader and author of *Today's Myths and Tomorrow's Realities*,[4] says higher education faculty face four key challenges—**realities:**

1. Meet changing conditions,
2. Provide contexts that make possible life-span learning,
3. Meet social requirements of adequate advanced education for minorities and the economically disadvantaged and,
4. Help the country meet increasing challenges of international competitiveness.

To accomplish these goals, to face realities, Millard holds there are seven key areas in which it's imperative that academicians modify certain key assumptions—**myths:**

1. The academy's "sacred cows"—the normative character of the past, the nature of college students, the peripheral role of older students, and the focus on "the university" as the primary vehicle for higher education.
2. "Turf wars"—emphasis on institutional autonomy, and opposition to state-level coordination and planning.
3. Curriculum—confining and even arbitrary traditions about the relationship between the arts and sciences and professional and occupational education.
4. Quality—how really to measure it, and what does and does not undermine it.
5. Access—the role of remedial education.
6. The information society—the explosive development of educational technology as a "threat" to the sanctity of the classroom, job security, and quality control of long-distance learning.
7. Relationships between business and industry and the academy—the concern that such liaisons will dilute institutional integrity.

Whether you think Millard's realities and myths are perennial or transient, enervating or inspiring, real or imaginary, worth confronting or disposable, they'll be on your agenda for discussion as a tenured professor in any venue. At least your academic life won't be dull—unless you make it so.

A NEW ACADEMIC REVOLUTION?

After spending a year observing the higher education scene from the vantage point of the American Association for Higher Education's offices in Washington DC, Jon Wergin[5] returned to his post in educational studies at Virginia Commonwealth University for the 1993-94 academic year convinced "that we are in the middle of an academic revolution in this country and that we will probably see more change to the academy in the next 10 years than we have in the last 50."

Among the changes Wergin predicts are these:
- Accelerated changes in student demographics, leading to an era of "a new student majority"—students who are older, more ethnically diverse, part-time, and place-bound.

- Computers have already changed the way we live, and they will begin to change how we work inside the classroom, affecting the dynamics of teaching in positive ways.
- We will more frequently be using the "classroom" only in its most figurative sense, conducting "classes" in which the students may be dispersed by many miles.
- We will be working more as teams. Individual faculty members might contribute their talents and interests to the goals of the group. The view of the faculty member as the "Lone Ranger of the Academy" will have gone the way of Mr. Chips.
- Our scholarly priorities will have shifted in response to a more expanded and inclusive definition of scholarship that will be evident in the research we do.
- The boundaries between the academy and the community will slowly dissolve as we redefine our "outreach" missions.

If only *some* of Wergin's predictions come true, anybody looking ahead to tenure is in for some exciting times.

LADDER TO TENURE—2010

One of the "revolutions" you may be contemplating is one in which you seek to reform some of the rungs in the academic ladder you're climbing to tenure. You aren't alone.

At a recent National Science Foundation[6] colloquium on "America's Academic Future," a panel of young college and university tenure-track professors, looking to year 2010 and beyond, envisioned these characteristics of a faculty support mechanism "during the critical years to tenure:"

1. An environment supportive of individual faculty interests and abilities.

2. Physical and fiscal infrastructure providing adequate support for both quality research and instruction.

3. Students viewing their faculty as having jobs that are fun and rewarding.

4. Senior faculty viewing junior faculty development as a primary responsibility.

5. Tenure, promotion, and related reward criteria applied with more regard to an individual's contributions to an institution's overall academic mission.

6. All aspects of scholarship in teaching, research, and service truly recognized.

7. The status of teaching elevated.

8. Young persons entering the professorate because they want to inspire all students to higher achievements.

With luck, the ladder to tenure you're climbing exhibits many of those qualities. If not, once tenured you can be part of the solution.

MARCHING BREAST FORWARD

We don't know of a better way to wrap up this manual than to send you off with a paraphrase of Stanford professor of public service John W. Gardner's address at Stanford's 100th commencement ceremonies in June 1991:

> If and when you settle into a tenured career, you cannot write off the danger of complacency, boredom, growing rigidity, imprisonment in your own comfortable habits and opinions.
>
> If you are conscious of the danger of going to seed, you can take countervailing measures:
>
> Keep your curiosity, your sense of wonder. Discover new things. Care. Risk. Reach out.
>
> The test will be whether in confusion and clash of interests, distracting conflicts, and cross-purposes, temptations to self-indulgence and self-exoneration, you have the strength of purpose, the guts, the conviction, the spiritual staying power to build a future worthy of your past.

And, in case your struggle for tenure left wounds—to you and to others—heed this paraphrase of a Winston Churchill benediction:

> We must turn our backs on past traumas. We cannot afford to drag forward across the years the tensions which have sprung from the injuries of the past.

The story is told about Marshall Lyautey just after he assumed control of French territories in North Africa. Surveying the barren sweep of the veldt around him, he turned to his aide and said, "We must plant trees."

"But sir," the aide responded, "in this climate it will take a hundred years for a tree to grow to full height."

"In that case," Lyautey replied, "we have no time to waste. We must begin this afternoon."

NOTES

1. Winston Churchill, quoted in Richard Hough, *Winston and Clementine* (New York: Bantam Books, 1990): 113.

2. Alexander W. Astin, "The Unrealized Potential of American Higher Education," *Innovative Higher Education* Winter 1992: 95-114.

3 . Derek Bok, *Universities and the Future of America* (Durham, NC: Duke University Press, 1990): 3.

4. Richard M. Millard, *Today's Myths and Tomorrow's Realities: Overcoming Obstacles to Academic Leadership in the 21st Century* (San Francisco: Jossey-Bass, 1991): 6-8.

5. Jon W. Wergin, "A New Academic Revolution," *VCU Teaching* Winter 1993-94: 6-7.

6. National Science Foundation, *A Report of the Presidential Young Investigator Colloquium on U.S. Engineering, Mathematics, and Science Education* (Washington, DC: 1993).

APPENDIX A: WHAT DO I DO IF I DON'T MAKE TENURE?

TO BE READ ONLY IF YOU DON'T RECEIVE TENURE

Theoretically, nobody should ever run a full six-year obstacle course and then involuntarily fail to make tenure. A whole series of events should transpire to prevent such a thing:

- The candidate's Ph.D. regimen should have been sufficiently rigorous to provide ideal training for an assistant professorship.
- A search and screen committee should have accomplished its task so thoroughly that the chosen candidate was a sure bet for tenure.
- Department, campus, and domestic support systems were in place and functioning effectively.

- The candidate herself or himself quickly grasped and strove to meet institutional expectations in regard to teaching, research, and service.
- Individual mentors and collective review committees offered constructive suggestions—or clear warnings.
- In either case, the messages were sufficiently precise that the candidate need have no doubts about a likely course of events.
- In response, the candidate either voluntarily picked up the cadence to ensure a favorable final evaluation or opted to seek success elsewhere.
- P&T panels were of one mind about the caliber of candidate desired and the fit of the candidate in question.

In an ideal world, assistant professors would rarely fail to make tenure. But this isn't an ideal world, so you should consider your options.

FOUR ALTERNATIVES

What if *you* don't win the big prize? That's a tough question—one that's probably darkened your bright hopes on occasion.

First of all, it's not the end of the world. Remember that. Life goes on.

Keep calm. Above all, avoid saying or doing anything that you might later regret. Sure, it's only human to feel disappointed, even rejected or maybe betrayed, and to strike out, to lose your cool.

So just try to relax. Maybe get away somewhere, if only for a weekend, to let loose. The tenure process is usually very stressful—even when the candidate succeeds. Then collect your thoughts and feelings and plan your next step.

If you don't make tenure, you have basically four options:

- Try, try again.
- Check out legal avenues.
- Pull out the most recent job list and a good map.
- Build a career in another profession.

The decision depends on your situation in the department and division, your CV, your personal circumstances, and your state of mind.

OPTION 1: TAKE ANOTHER SHOT
This is your most likely option:

  (a) if you went up for tenure before your clock ran out,

  (b) if there's no tenure-or-out ultimatum in your department or division,

  (c) if you were turned down by your colleagues in the department in a close vote,

  (d) if vacancies are about to occur in the department, or

  (e) if the negative decision came at the dean's level, especially if for financial reasons.

Consider fiscal trends and the job market as well. Some higher education experts predicted a few years ago that the mid-'90s would be a time of faculty shortages. But by early 1994 the situation for new Ph.D.s had dimmed considerably:

> The optimism generated by those forecasts has disappeared . . . .Instead of a mushrooming demand, doctoral recipients are finding a shortage of tenure-track openings and a glut of candidates. The market has been bad for several years ... and no one seems to have a grip on when—or if—it will improve.[1]

With the current confusion and the increasing budget cutbacks in academia, institutions are filling instructional gaps with part-timers. Also, the end of mandatory retirement could mean fewer openings, as colleges and universities are less able now to afford golden parachutes to persuade older faculty to retire.

Given the emerging and predicted trends, it might pay to keep abreast of developments at your institution, noting any difficulties in recruiting and retaining faculty in your area. If you decide to take another shot at tenure, understand that your chances may not improve within the year, but that you should push as hard as ever nonetheless: if you miss out again, at least your CV will make you more attractive elsewhere, when you compete against the growing numbers of new Ph.D.s.

Meet with your mentor and/or advisory committee to discuss the reasons why you didn't receive tenure. If it's a question of presentations and publications, then you know what you have to do and how much time you have to do it. (So get going already!) If the decision was financial, keep working—and cross your fingers for an improvement in the fiscal environment your next time up. But if you lost out because of your teaching or service, differences of personality and/or politics, or similar problems, face it: it's unlikely that you can improve your chances at tenure within a year.

You might also consider switching from the tenure track to a parallel line, such as academic staff.

One of the junior author's former colleagues, who joined the faculty of a small, private institution, was recently denied tenure. Unable to continue along the tenure track, she moved into a quasi-permanent academic staff teaching position. It may well have been a case of *felix culpa*, since she's now able to devote her energy to teaching, free of any expectations to "publish or perish."

Another colleague went through a similar shift. After her negative tenure vote, she was appointed to head the campus center responsible for training teaching assistants, where she can now pursue her primary interest—teaching—and work on a textbook with a major publisher.

OPTION 2: FILE AN APPEAL

If you feel that you were unjustly denied tenure, whether through some technicality or misunderstanding or because of discrimination (yes, even in the enlightened '90s!), then you may seek justice through prescribed channels. Since these differ from institution to institution, find documentation on the appropriate procedures and consult with your mentor or other ally.

If your blackball occurred at the all-campus level, it's possible that the decision could be overturned through the intercession of a distressed department chair and a feisty dean.

If a straightforward appeal, a grievance, or similar action is out of the question, you might want to invest in outside legal counsel. There are some precedents for obtaining remedial compensation through court decisions or out-of-court settlements. Although almost all tenure lawsuits have been "lost causes," according to one attorney in higher education, some courts have lately shown less reluctance to get involved in academic matters and less reverence for campus personnel procedures.

Procedural Matters. With those points in mind, review the following legal decisions:

- In *Davis v. Oregon State University*, 591 F.2d. 493 (9th Cir. 1978), a written tenure policy carried more weight than a chair's oral promise that the plaintiff would receive tenure "as a matter of course." The disappointed faculty member lost out.
- In *McLendon v. Morton*, 249 S.E. 2d 919 (W. Va. 1978), a West Virginia court ruled a professor denied tenure had been deprived of a "property interest" and minimal due process rights. It held that institutions must give faculty members notice and an opportunity for a hearing before the final decision to deny tenure.
- In *LaVerne v. University of Texas System*, 611 F.Supp. 66 (S.D. Tex. 1985), the court ruled that if a university has published procedures governing tenure, a professor can't base a claim to tenure outside those procedures. The moral: know the rules—and don't count on making it outside those rules.
- In *Levi v. University of Texas*, 840 F.2d 277 (5th Cir. 1988), the court allowed a university to deny tenure because the professor's grading policies were deemed too lenient. Although grading policies weren't considered in the tenure decisions of other faculty, the court ruled that there was a rational link between the grading policy and the legitimate goal of maintaining a certain level of instructional quality. Remember: academic freedom protects you—but there are limits.

Since the key to a successful lawsuit is in obtaining evidence, the 1990 U.S. Supreme Court ruling in *University of Pennsylvania v. Equal Employment Opportunity Commission*, 110 S.Ct. 577, is a landmark decision. Declaring that Title VII of the Civil Rights Act applies to higher education, the Court opened faculty review files for a professor who claimed discrimination in her negative tenure decision.

This decision affirmed the decisions rendered in a series of tenure cases, including *In Re Dinnan*, 661 F.2d 426 (11th Cir. 1981), *EEOC v. University of Notre Dame du Lac*, 715 F.2d 331 (7th Cir. 1983), *EEOC v. Franklin and Marshall*, 775 F.2d 110 (3rd Cir. 1985), and *Gray v. Board of Higher Education of City of New York*, 92 F.R.D. 87 (S.D.N.Y. 1981), *rev'd*, 692 F.2d 901 (2d Cir. 1982). As Justice Harry Blackmun expressed the Supreme Court decision:

> The costs associated with racial and sexual discrimination in institutions of higher learning are very substantial. Few would deny that ferreting out this kind of invidious discrimination is a great if not compelling governmental interest. . . . If there is a 'smoking gun' to be found that demonstrates discrimination in tenure decisions, it is likely to be tucked away in peer review files.

The ruling in *University of Pennsylvania v. EEOC* should allow faculty greater means to bring legal action under Title VII of the Civil Rights Act of 1964 and the Equal Pay Act (both passed in 1972), through the Equal Employment Opportunity Commission, and Title IX of the Education Amendments of 1972 (as amended in 1974, 1976, and 1987), through the Office for Civil Rights, U.S. Department of Education.

Cases of Discrimination. Between 1970 and 1984, federal courts considered 42 charges of discrimination in tenure decisions, according to George R. LaNoue and Barbara A. Lee, authors of *Academics in Court: The Consequences of Faculty Discrimination Litigation* (Ann Arbor: University of Michigan Press, 1987). From those cases LaNoue and Lee concluded:

> One can speculate that where academic plaintiffs have raised procedural/jurisdictional issues that were part of the mainstream of civil rights law, they have been relatively successful. But where they have raised claims that touched the distinctive nature of the academic personnel process, judges have been reluctant to intervene. (pp. 30-31)

That situation is changing. For an update on litigation in this area, you should consult *Tenure, Discrimination, and the Courts* (Ithaca NY: ILR Press, 1993), by Terry L. Leap, professor of management at Clemson University, and "Suing for Tenure: Legal and

Institutional Barriers," an article by Kathryn R. Swedlow in the Summer 1994 issue of *The Review of Litigation* (University of Texas School of Law). In recent years courts have seemed less and less reluctant to intervene in academic matters, particularly in light of increasing general criticism of practices and privileges in higher education.

Consider, for example, the highly publicized case of Ceil M. Pillsbury, an assistant professor of accounting at the University of Wisconsin-Milwaukee. When her department colleagues voted in December 1989 against granting her tenure, it hit her hard.

"I always believed that if a woman got the job done, everything would be just fine," she said in an interview three years later.[2] Discrimination? "I wouldn't have believed in a million years it could happen to me."

When it did, Pillsbury took the case to the U.S. District Court in Milwaukee in October 1991. And she came heavily armed with evidence: "I'm an accountant. Proper documentation is everything."

She also promoted her case by seeking publicity. She faxed regular updates to the media and she called reporters to notify them when the NBC TV news program *Street Stories* featured her case. She also was the focus of an an article in *Business Week,*[3] in addition to making *The Chronicle of Higher Education* and the Associated Press network regularly. While her legal fees came to $25,000, she spent about $61,000 in other expenses, including $7,000 on phone calls, $13,000 on postage, $3,000 to fax documents and reports, and $10,000 for photocopying.

The result? In January 1993 the University of Wisconsin System settled with Pillsbury, agreeing to pay her $40,000 in back pay and $86,000 in expenses and to allow her to seek tenure again at UW-Milwaukee or at the nearest System campus, UW-Parkside in Kenosha. The settlement also stipulated that Pillsbury would receive the pay of a tenured professor at UW-Milwaukee even if she were denied tenure a second time and worked at UW-Parkside or UW-Green Bay, where she taught after leaving UW-Milwaukee and where she was recommended for tenure.

But Pillsbury didn't just win a second chance. She caused a few other things to happen:

- After she testified at a state Joint Legislative Audit Committee hearing, the committee ordered an audit of UW-Milwaukee's affirmative action office.
- The University of Wisconsin-Milwaukee Faculty Appeals and Grievance Committee ruled that the denial of tenure had been discriminatory.
- Pillsbury received the suppport of a campus women's group and the faculty union.
- The governor signed a bill to let UW campuses appoint appeals committees to review faculty credentials and grant tenure if the department is found to have discriminated in denying it.
- The U.S. Labor Department investigated allegations of sex discrimination and found a campus-wide "pattern and practice" of sex discrimination.
- A state representative sponsored a bill to modify the state's Family and Medical Leave Act to cover female faculty on the tenure track. (Pillsbury was pregnant when she came up for tenure.)

Pillsbury called the outcome "a win-win settlement for everyone involved, for the UW System, for myself, for the women in the Wisconsin System, and especially for the taxpayers."[4]

Although she considered her fight for tenure "a horrible ordeal," she didn't regret her decision to fight. In an interview for a national newsletter, she offered some advice for female faculty who believe that they have been the victims of discrimination: decide if you are in a position, both financially and emotionally, to fight for your cause. "If you are, assume it is your duty to do so, your responsibility to yourself, your daughters, and to men too."[5]

She also advised faculty who take on an institution to "find out who cares on campus and get them involved." She noted, "I was persistent and went to every extreme. . . . I went to the press, and I created pressure from all different sources."

She learned something that helped her in her battle:

> The more days passed, the more calls I got from women who were similarly mistreated, the more I read and heard about statistics on

women, the more I realized that I had been oblivious to the real situation. It was a systemic, not an individual, situation.

Now that she's a tenured professor in the UW-Milwaukee School of Business, Pillsbury remains realistic about her battle with department colleagues. "I don't expect to be loved or even to be liked by everyone. I expect to be treated in a professional way, and they do."[6]

Professional Help. Like Pillsbury, you may not be alone in your tenure battle. For information and support you might turn to the American Association of University Professors (1012 14th St., NW, Suite 500, Washington, DC 20005; Ph: 202/737-5900). This association has long been fighting for academic freedom and fair treatment of faculty, chronicling the results in its bulletin, *Academe*.

There are also attorneys who specialize in academic battles. One recent advertisement in *The Chronicle of Higher Education* made the case bluntly:

ACADEMIA
It's supposed to be a haven for teaching and learning.
The job description doesn't include grievances.
Or arbitration. Or litigation.
The job description doesn't include fighting ...
for tenure
for promotion
against discrimination
against harassment
Most faculty grievances can be resolved informally.
Some lead to litigation.

The attorneys noted that they were formerly "university professors, deans, and institutional counsel," adding, *"They know academia is no haven."*

You may not need a specialized attorney, but you should be willing to do whatever it takes to win. A legal battle may be very expensive—even if not the $86,000 spent by Pillsbury—and the psychological costs can be staggering.

Warning. Involving the courts is a very difficult and chancy route. The odds are against you, since courts have traditionally tended to avoid intervening in "academic matters."

And even if you win, you'll probably lose. Faculty and the dean are unlikely to accept you as a colleague if you bring the court into their academic world. If you succeed in winning tenure the hard way, that's only the first half of the battle. You may feel great pressure to go elsewhere to continue your career—and probably without the benefit of letters of recommendation. And wherever you go, you'll bear the stigma of a "troublemaker."

Take the case of Marcia Lieberman. After losing her tenure discrimination suit against the University of Connecticut—*Lieberman v. Gant*, 474 F.Supp. 848 (D. Conn., 1979), *aff'd,* 630 F.2d 60 (2d Cir. 1980)—she was very disappointed and abandoned her attempt to obtain a full-time teaching position. The results of 10 years of litigation, with five judges, 23 attorneys, the Connecticut Women's Educational and Legal Fund, the AAUP, and dozens of faculty and administrators? Lieberman described herself as financially ruined, without a career, in poor health, and at risk of marital problems.

Then there are some faculty who win some sort of victory, like Pillsbury, or like Connie Rae Kunda, Mary Lou Kendrigan, Clare Dalton, Reginald Clark, Jenny Harrison, Joe Reese, and Cynthia J. Fisher.

Kunda was denied tenure at Muhlenberg College (PA) in 1974. Her case—*Kunda v. Muhlenberg College*, 463 F.Supp. 294 (E.D. Pa. 1978), *aff'd,* 621 F.2d 532 (3d Cir. 1980)—was finally resolved in 1980, as the courts awarded her "conditional tenure." Most of the faculty were pleased with the decision. Kunda continued along her career path, receiving her promotion to full professor in 1987.

Kendrigan, a social studies professor at Michigan State University, failed in 1983 to receive tenure. She sued the university in 1986 for sex discrimination, arguing that she and another woman were the only professors ever denied tenure in that department, where she was in 1983 the only female professor on the tenure track. Kendrigan, then teaching a few miles away at Lansing Community College, won her case in October 1991 and received a $400,000 award.[7]

Dalton was in the School of Law at Harvard until 1987, when the school denied her tenure. She took the matter to court, while she moved a few miles to Northeastern University, where she received tenure in 1989. Then, in September 1993, Harvard settled with Dalton, agreeing to donate $260,000 to her project to train law students as legal advocates at the Domestic Violence Institute. She noted, "One of the important things to me was that there was not a gag order, so the case is out there to support and inspire women."[8] She also learned a lesson in moving to Northeastern: "One of the things I understand much better now than when I went to Harvard in 1981 is that there is such a thing as institutional fit, and the truth is you're going to be professionally happier in a place whose values match your own."[9]

Clark was an assistant professor of education at the Claremont Graduate School (CA) who failed in his try for tenure. Although his colleagues in the education department voted 5 to 3 to recommend tenure, a campus review committee voted 4 to 1 to deny it. Clark, who is black, then sued the school for race discrimination, based on racist comments made in his presence and during discussions of his tenure candidacy. After a mistrial, in March 1990 a second jury awarded Clark $1 million in compensatory and punitive damages and $416,000 in legal fees. The California Court of Appeal upheld that verdict and award. The California Supreme Court voted 6 to 1 in July 1992 not to review the case. Clark noted at that time that the tenure decision had "totally transformed" his career, adding, "If I had not pursued this matter, my conscience would not have rested."[10]

Harrison, a mathematics professor at UC-Berkeley, went up for tenure in 1986 and failed by a vote of 19 to 12. Three years later she sued the university for sex discrimination. Her appeal cost at least $150,000 in legal expenses—some of it provided by more than 200 donations. In 1993 Berkeley and Harrison reached a settlement that granted her another review by a committee outside the math department, based on her updated credentials. The committee unanimously recommended tenure, which the chancellor approved. Several of her colleagues insisted that Harrison did not deserve tenure and they resented what they perceived as "shameless, intimidating lobbying" which resulted in the "imposition" of tenure from outside the department. The controversy went electronic, as members of the department debated the situation in e-mail messages. Harrison commented, "I guess I'm not surprised. I have claimed . . . that there was a hostile environment, and this just confirms it."[11]

Reese, an English professor at Spelman College, was denied tenure in 1991. He filed charges with the federal Equal Opportunity Employment Commission and a federal court, asking for $1 million. His claim: that the historically black college was guilty of reverse discrimination against him, a white professor. Spelman categorically denied the charges. A month later, Reese and Spelman agreed to settle out of court, on terms that were to remain confidential. A Spelman spokesperson stated, "While the parties remain in disagreement about the issues raised, both Professor Reese and Spelman are pleased that the dispute has ended amicably and without the expense and other burdens of continued litigation."[12]

Most recently, a biologist who sued Vassar College for illegally denying her tenure won her case in a federal court—a decision that legal experts called "a first for academe." Fisher was denied tenure in 1985 and left the college in 1986. She charged Vassar with sex and age discrimination. The dispute centered around an eight-year period when Fisher interrupted her career to raise her children. She returned to academia in 1974, then applied for tenure in 1985, when she was 53. "It was continually thrown in my face," Fisher said. "I was a very productive scientist and, no matter what I did, the last statement made about me was always that I had been out of the field for eight years. Minds were made up—she is a housewife and that's all she can do." Legal counsel for Vassar—which had admitted only women for over a century, until 1969—indicated that the college would appeal the ruling. Fisher said that the ruling "will give women the courage to fight for their rights and be evaluated on their credentials and not on stereotypes."[13]

What Constitutes Reasonable Cause? If you fail to receive tenure for reasons other than procedual violations or discrimination, you may find that the courts are unlikely to favor your cause. Two cases provide recent evidence of this judicial reluctance to intervene in academic matters.

Two sociology professors at Indiana University-Purdue University at Indianapolis, Kenneth D. Colburn Jr. and Robert M. Khoury, were denied tenure in 1987 for damaging the image of the sociology faculty through "written and verbal comments to people outside the department." They sued, alleging violations of their First Amendment rights to free speech. They lost their case in a U.S. District Court, then appealed the decision. In August 1992 the Seventh Circuit Court of Appeals ruled against them, finding that free speech protection applies only in matters of public concern, not in "internal personal disputes," even in a public institution. The ruling noted that "the fact that the issue could be 'interesting' to the community does not make it an issue of public concern."[14]

An associate law professor at the State University of New York at Buffalo, Jeffrey M. Blum, spoke out for the decriminalization of marijuana and against the UB "Statement on Intolerance" and criticized the law school curriculum. When UB officials warned him in April 1992 that he might not receive tenure because of his lack of scholarship, he withdrew his name from tenure consideration, then sued for reinstatement and $8 million. In July 1993 a U.S. District Court judge upheld a federal magistrate's report supporting the university.[15]

OPTION 3: SEARCH FOR GREENER PASTURES

Consider what you have to offer higher education. If you lost out on tenure because your scholarship wasn't up to departmental, divisional, or institutional expectations, check out your possibilities with another institution that places less emphasis on scholarship, especially if you're stronger in teaching and service. If, on the other hand, you've got impressive presentations and publications, but lower grades for teaching, or you don't fit into the political or social climate, maybe you can find a niche where scholarly productivity is the primary criterion.

Sure, it would be great if every new Ph.D. found the perfect job right away and then stayed there happily ever after. But we all know that life doesn't work that way. (Just ask all those "gypsy scholars" out there!) And remember: if there are faculty shortages as once predicted, higher education may become more of a "seller's market" by the late-'90s.

You may decide that it's worthwhile to enlarge or shift your area of specialization somewhat. Is there a glut of faculty in your field¿ Are branches developing¿ If you're alert to trends, you can add some new arrows to your quiver.

So, try to be open to seeking your fame and fortune in another venue. It's always difficult to pull up the stakes, fold the tents, say goodbye to friends and neighbors, and hit the road. It can be particularly difficult to move, of course, if you have a family with strong ties to the area. (Have you considered staying home with Option 4¿) But it's not unusual for faculty to move about within the academic world—and the best way is with a healthy optimism, a sense of adventure—and a portfolio of letters of recommendation, however temperate.

Over the last dozen years the junior author (RM) has collected stories of interesting faculty career paths. Several may serve as examples of good moves:

- D.T. was an assistant prof shared between a language department and the department of instructional development at a large state university. At tenure time, both departments voted in his favor, but neither pushed his case at a higher level, primarily because his chief interest was teaching and his dossier was long on presentations but short on publications. The university offered to move him to academic staff, but he preferred to take an academic staff position elsewhere, at a smaller, top-notch research institution. Several years later, he packed his bags once again, to move to a midsize university with an emphasis on teaching, where he soon became chair of the language department.

- A.C. landed a job at a prestigious, small public college, where she was assured that teaching was top priority. When the college shifted its emphasis toward more research and publication, she failed to receive tenure. She filed an appeal and shopped around. The college reversed its decision about the time she received an offer from a small, religious school, where she'd have an opportunity to work in a department with an innovative teaching program. She seized the opportunity to move to a better academic climate.

- J.P. failed to make tenure at a small, private, and prestigious college. Her husband, in the same department, decided to look elsewhere before he came up for tenure. J.P. expressed an interest in studying law, so they found a major university with an opening for him and a good law school for her. Several years later, he received tenure and she was beginning her second career, as an attorney.

Not every story will have a happy ending. But these faculty and others like them have taken their unfavorable tenure decisions positively, as an indication that they didn't really fit their environments. So they found opportunities to develop their potential and pursue their interests elsewhere, at more suitable institutions, among colleagues who appreciate what they have to offer higher education. It wasn't easy, but it was worth it.

OPTION 4: BUILD ANOTHER CAREER

It's not too late to change career directions. (Sometimes a negative tenure decision can be a blessing in disguise!) Just take some time to assess your talents and interests, using such instruments as the Strong-Campbell Interest Inventory and the Myers-Briggs Type Indicator. Then explore career possibilities along those lines.

If you've shown talent in research, you may want to try the corporate sector or the government, or to go into private consulting. If you enjoy teaching and are reasonably good at working with people, consider a career in training, social services (private or public), or personnel/human resources.

Some former faculty have fashioned distinguished ex-campus careers.

Consider Paul Wellstone, for example. He was once a political science prof at Carleton College. His department voted unanimously in 1974 against offering him tenure. Outside evaluators subsequently recommended that the decision be reversed. Although he finally received tenure, it wasn't enough, so he put his knowledge of political science into practice: he went on to represent Minnesota in the U.S. Senate.

Or take this case:

In 1967, a professor's son with a Trinity B.A., an Oxford M.A. in philosophy, and a Princeton Ph.D. in political science (thesis: "Beyond the Reach of Majorities: Closed Questions in the Open Society") landed a teaching position at Michigan State. After an unhappy year he moved on to the University of Toronto. The fit was no better there, so he spun off as a speechwriter and jack-of-all-trades for a U.S. Senator in Washington. Today you know him as Pulitzer Prize-winning *Newsweek*, ABC, book, and syndicated commentator George Will. Like Walter Lippmann before him, Will "chose the role of helping produce public sense in the community rather than pursuing truth in individual solitude in the academy."

But it isn't only in *Who's Who* that you find examples of faculty expatriates "making it on the outside." From his personal acquaintances, the senior author (ACS) can cite random instances of representative assistant professors who broke rank into successful professional careers:

- Gene Kroupa was an accomplished "numbers cruncher" who didn't hit it off with colleagues in a department of journalism. He's now president of Gene Kroupa and Associates, a market research and analysis firm in Madison WI.
- Earl Braly returned safely from the Korean Conflict to internecine warfare in an English department. Before he could be fatally wounded, he left for a long and lucrative hitch in public relations with various organizations in Washington DC.
- Richard Heilman never felt entirely at home in a department of wildlife management. He was recently retired as a senior biologist from the U.S. Fish and Wildlife Service.
- Carol Holmes got caught in an interdisciplinary environmental studies institute without a safe departmental haven of her own. She's now head of environmental education programs for a large metropolitan K-12 school system.
- Douglas Jones failed to make tenure in a school of mass communication. You may recognize his name: he's the freelance author of the celebrated book (and movie) *The Court Martial of George Armstrong Custer* and other self-illustrated novels of Army life in the Old West.
- Martha Jones-Van Dyke never felt comfortable as a token woman in an all-male department of electrical and computer engineering, a discomfort that translated into slow research progress. When Zenith recruited both her and her husband with great enthusiasm, she left the campus to become a data systems team chief.

Almost any senior faculty member can cite similar illustrations of the point that not making tenure doesn't have to be the end of the line. For other stories of life after tenure denial, a reader recommends In the Company of Scholars: The Struggle for the Soul of Higher Education, by Julius Getman, a law professor and former president of the American Association of University Professors (Austin: University of Texas Press, 1992).

CAREER-CHANGE GUIDES

There are plenty of career guides out there, including some specifically for people embarking on career changes:

Richard N. Bolles, *The Three Boxes of Life and How to Get Out of Them: An Introduction to Life/Work Planning*. Berkeley CA: Ten Speed Press, 1981.

Richard N. Bolles, *What Color Is Your Parachute?* (Berkeley CA: Ten Speed Press, 1989).

W. Todd Furniss, *Reshaping Faculty Careers* (Washington DC: American Council on Education, 1989).

Mary Morris Heiberger and Julia Miller Vick, *The Academic Job Search Handbook* (Philadelphia: University of Pennsylvania Press, 1992).

Carole Hyatt, *Shifting Gears: How to Master Career Change and Find the Work That's Right for You* (New York: Simon and Schuster, 1990).

Ronald L. Krannich, *The Educator's Guide to Alternative Jobs and Careers* (Woodbridge VA: Impact Publications, 1991).

Jean Russell Nave and Louise M. Nelson, *Mid-Career Crisis* (New York: Putnam, 1991).

K.P. Reilly and S.S. Murdich, *Teaching and Beyond: Nonacademic Programs for Ph.D.'s* (Albany: State University of New York Press, 1984).

You may even get some valuable advice and assistance from the career placement center on your campus. Take tests to determine your abilities and interests: you might be surprised at what you learn about yourself. Consult with "headhunters."

Pursue your education. Take courses in areas tangential or totally apart from your areas of specialization. Try workshops and short courses at a community college. Use your network of contacts: talk with colleagues, friends, relatives, and neighbors to explore possibilities. Be alert to ideas and interests that might develop into career opportunities.

Above all, keep an open mind and be confident in your education and abilities. Good luck!

NOTES

1. Denise K. Magner, "Job-Market Blues: Instead of the Anticipated Demand, New Ph.D.s Are Finding Few Openings," *The Chronicle of Higher Education* 27 Apr. 1994: A17.

2. Denise K. Magner, "Accounting Professor Is Unlikely Heroine in Battle Against Sex Bias at Wisconsin." *The Chronicle of Higher Education* 10 Feb. 1993: A15-A16, A18.

3. Lori Bongiorno, "Where Are All the Female B-School Profs?" *Business Week* 7 Dec. 1992: 40.

4. Michael C. Buelow, "UW Admits Tenure Mistake." *Wisconsin State Journal* 23 Jan. 1993: 1A-2A.

5. Mary Dee Wenniger, "Tenure Lawsuit: When to Fight, What to Expect, How to Win." *Women in Higher Education* Sept. 1993: 4.

6. Wenniger 4.

7. Courtney Leatherman, "Faculty Notes: Jury Awards Former Professor $400,000 in Sex-Bias Case," *The Chronicle of Higher Education* 14 Aug. 1991: A14.

8. Mary Dee Wenniger, "Bias Costs Harvard Law School $260,000." *Women in Higher Education* Nov. 1993: 9.

9. Courtney Leatherman, "Woman Who Took on Harvard Law School Over Tenure Denial Sees 'Vindication,' " *The Chronicle of Higher Education* 6 Oct. 1993: A19-A20.

10. Christopher Shea, "California Supreme Court Upholds Big Award in Tenure Bias Case." *The Chronicle of Higher Education* 5 Aug. 1992: A12.

11. Denise K. Magner, "Debate Over Woman's Tenure Continues at Berkeley." *The Chronicle of Higher Education* 20 Oct. 1993: A16.

12. Dennis Black, "Managing Faculty Means Litigation," *Perspective: The Campus Legal Monthly* June 1992: 5; *Academic Leader* Aug. 1992: 7.

13. Denise K. Magner, "Judge Says Vassar Discriminated Against Married Woman," *The Chronicle of Higher Education* 25 May 1994: A17.

14. "Shorts," *MEMO: to the president* (American Association of State Colleges and Universities) 25 Sept. 1992: 2; U.S. Court of Appeals, 7th Circuit, report no. 91-2866.

15. Donn Esmonde, "Making Noise at UB Can Get You Silenced; Just Ask Jeff Blum," *Buffalo (NY) News* 21 Oct. 1992; "UB Wins Ruling on Terminating Prof," *Buffalo (NY) News* 9 July 1993.

APPENDIX B: SUGGESTED READINGS

A DOZEN CLASSIC REFERENCES

Arnold, Matthew, "Literature and Science," in Robert H. Super, Ed., *The Complete Prose Works of Matthew Arnold*, Vol. 10 (Ann Arbor: University of Michigan Press, 1974; originally published 1884).

Brown, Elmer E., *The Origin of American State Universities* (Berkeley: University of California Press, 1903).

Butts, R. Freeman, *The College Charts Its Course* (New York: McGraw-Hill, 1939).

Flexner, Abraham, *Universities, American, English, German* (New York: Oxford University Press, 1930).

Jordan, David Starr, *The Trend of the American University* (Stanford CA: Stanford University Press, 1929).

Kelly, Fred J., *The American Arts College*; A Limited Survey (New York: Macmillan, 1925).

Meiklejohn, Alexander, *The Experimental College* (New York: Harper & Row, 1932).

Newman, John H., *The Idea of a University* (New York: Holt, Rinehart, & Winston, 1960; originally published 1852).

President's Commission on Higher Education, *Higher Education for American Democracy* (Washington DC: GPO, 1947).

Russell, John Dale, *American Universities and Colleges* (Washington DC: GPO, 1952).

Slosson, Edwin E., *Great American Universities* (New York: Macmillan, 1910).

Whitehead, A.N., *The Aims of Higher Education* (New York: Macmillan, 1929).

A SCORE OF INTERIM READINGS

Astin, Alexander W., *Four Critical Years* (San Francisco: Jossey-Bass, 1977).

Baldridge, J. Victor, *Power and Conflict in the University* (London: Wiley, 1971).

Baskin, Samuel, *Higher Education: Some Newer Developments* (New York: McGraw-Hill, 1965).

Bowen, Robert O., *The New Professors* (New York: Holt, Rinehart, & Winston, 1960).

Burch, Glen, *Challenge to the University: An Inquiry into the University's Responsibility for Adult Education* (Chicago: Center for the Study of Liberal Education for Adults, 1961).

Clapp, Margaret, Ed., *The Modern University* (Ithaca NY: Cornell University Press, 1950).

Eddy, Edward D., *Colleges for Our Land and Time: The Land Grant Idea in American Education* (New York: Harper, 1957).

Fowlkes, John Guy, Ed., *Higher Education for American Society* (Madison: University of Wisconsin Press, 1949).

Jencks, Christopher, and David Riesman, *The Academic Revolution* (New York: Anchor Books, 1968).

Kerr, Clark, *The Uses of the University* (New York: Harper & Row, 1966).

Miller, Richard I., *The Assessment of College Performance* (San Francisco: Jossey-Bass, 1979).

Millett, John D., *The Academic Community* (New York: McGraw-Hill, 1962).

National Association of State Universities and Land Grant Colleges, *Scope Report* (Washington DC, 1958).

Rudolph, Frederick, *The American College and University* (New York: Knopf, 1968).

Sanford, Nevitt, *The American College* (New York: John Wiley, 1962).

_____, *College and Character* (New York: John Wiley, 1964).

Schoenfeld, Clarence A., and Donald N. Zillman, *The American University in Summer* (Madison: University of Wisconsin Press, 1967).

Schoenfeld, Clarence A., *The University and Its Publics* (New York: Harper & Brothers, 1954).

Shannon, Theodore J., and Clarence A. Schoenfeld, *University Extension* (New York: Center for Applied Research in Education, 1965).

Veysey, Laurence R., *The Emergence of the American University* (Chicago: University of Chicago Press, 1965).

FOUR DOZEN CURRENT COMMENTARIES

Altbach, Philip G., and Robert O. Berdahl, Ed., *Higher Education in American Society* (Buffalo NY: Prometheus, 1987).

Anderson, Martin, *Imposters in the Temple* (New York: Simon & Schuster, 1992).

Bardo, John W., *Teaching? Research? Service?* (Washington DC: American Association of State Colleges and Universities, 1990).

Barzun, Jacques, *The Culture We Deserve* (Middletown CT: Wesleyan University Press, 1989).

_____, *The Forgotten Conditions of Teaching and Learning* (Chicago: University of Chicago Press, 1991)

Bennett, William J., *To Reclaim a Legacy: Report on the Humanities in Higher Education* (Washington DC: National Endowment for the Humanities, 1984).

Bloom, Allan, *The Closing of the American Mind* (New York: Simon and Schuster, 1987).

Boice, Robert, *The New Faculty Member* (San Francisco: Jossey-Bass, 1992).

Bok, Derek, *Higher Learning* (Cambridge MA: Harvard University Press, 1986).

_____, *Universities and the Future of America* (Durham NC: Duke University Press, 1990).

Bowen, Howard R., and Jack H. Schuster, *American Professors: A Resource at Risk* (New York: Oxford University Press, 1986).

Boyer, Ernest L., *Scholarship Reconsidered: Priorities of the Professoriate* (Princeton NJ: Carnegie Foundation for the Advancement of Teaching, 1991).

_____, *College: The Undergraduate Experience* (New York: Harper and Row, 1987).

Cahn, Steven, *Morality, Responsibility, and the University* (Philadelphia: Temple University Press, 1990).

Chubin, Daryl E., and Edward J. Hackett, *Peerless Science* (Albany: SUNY Press, 1990).

Clark, Burton R., *The Academic Life: Small Worlds, Different Worlds* (Lawrenceville NJ: Princeton University Press, 1987).

Clark, Mary E., and Sandra A. Wawrytko, *Rethinking the Curriculum* (New York: Greenwood Press, 1990).

Creswell, John W., et al., *The Academic Chairperson's Handbook* (Lincoln: University of Nebraska Press, 1990).

D'Souza, Dinesh, *Illiberal Education: The Politics of Race and Sex on Campus* (New York: Free Press, 1991).

Eaton, Judith S., *The Unfinished Agenda* (New York: John Wiley & Sons, 1990).

Diamond, Robert M., and Bronwyn E. Adam, Eds., *Recognizing Faculty Work,* New Directions for Higher Education No. 81 (San Francisco: Jossey-Bass, 1993).

Getman, Julius, *In the Company of Scholars* (Austin: University of Texas Press, 1992).

Gambino, Richard, *Racing with Catastrophe* (New York: Freedom House, 1990).

Gilley, J. Wade, *Thinking About Higher Education: The 1990s and Beyond* (New York: ACE/Macmillan, 1992).

Gmelch, Walter H., *Coping with Faculty Stress* (Newbury Park CA: Sage, 1993).

Harris-Jones, Peter, Ed., *Making Knowledge Count* (Montreal: McGill-Queen's University Press, 1991).

Huber, Richard M., *How Professors Play the Cat Guarding the Cream* (Fairfax VA: George Mason University Press, 1992).

Jarvis, Donald K., *Junior Faculty Development* (New York: The Modern Language Association, 1991).

Johnson, Paul, *Intellectuals* (New York: Harper & Row, 1990).

Kadish, Mortimer R., *Toward an Ethic of Higher Education* (Stanford CA: Stanford University Press, 1991).

Kuh, George D., and Elizabeth J. Whitt, *The Invisible Tapestry: Culture in American Colleges and Universities,* ASHE-ERIC Higher Education Report No. 1 (Washington DC: Association for the Study of Higher Education, 1988).

Levine, Arthur and associates, *Shaping Higher Education's Future: Demographic Realities and Opportunites, 1990-2000* (San Francisco: Jossey-Bass, 1989).

Millard, Richard M., *Today's Myths and Tomorrow's Realities* (San Francisco: Jossey-Bass, 1991).

Neumann, William F., *Persistence in the Community College*, Ph.D. Dissertation, Syracuse University, 1985 (Ann Arbor: University Microfilms).

Orem, Sue Don, and Deborah Brue, Eds., *Practical Programming in Continuing Professional Higher Education* (Washington DC: American Association for Adult Continuing Education, 1991).

Pascarella, Ernest T., and Patrick T. Terenzini, *How College Affects Students: Findings and Insights From Twenty Years of Research* (San Francisco: Jossey-Bass, 1991).

Riesman, David, *On Higher Education: The Academic Enterprise in an Era of Rising Student Consumerism* (San Francisco: Jossey-Bass, 1980).

Santovec, Mary Lou, Ed., *Building Diversity* (Madison WI: Magna Publications, 1990).

Schaefer, William D., *Education Without Compromise: From Chaos to Coherence in Higher Education* (San Francisco: Jossey-Bass, 1990).

Schuster, Jack H., and Daniel W. Wheeler & Associates, *Enhancing Faculty Careers: Strategies for Development and Renewal* (San Francisco: Jossey-Bass, 1990).

Shaw, Peter, *The War Against the Intellect: Episodes in the Decline of Discourse* (Iowa City: University of Iowa Press, 1989).

Slaughter, Sheila, *The Higher Learning and High Technology: Dynamics of Higher Education Policy Formation* (Albany: SUNY Press, 1990).

Smith, Page, *Killing the Spirit: Higher Education in America* (New York: Viking, 1990).

Sorcinelli, Mary Deane, and Ann E. Austin, Eds., *Developing New and Junior Faculty,* New Directions for Teaching and Learning No. 50 (San Francisco: Jossey-Bass, 1992).

Tinto, Vincent O., *Leaving College: Rethinking the Causes and Cures of Student Attrition* (Chicago: University of Chicago Press, 1987).

Westmeyer, Paul, *A History of American Higher Education* (Springfield IL: Charles C. THomaas, 1985).

Wilshire, Bruce, *The Moral Collapse of the University: Professionalism, Purity, and Alienation* (Albany: State University of New York Press, 1990).

Wright, Peter W. G., Ed. *Industry and Higher Education* (Bristol PA: Open University Press, 1990).

INDEX

ABOUT THE AUTHORS

A. CLAY SCHOENFELD (a.k.a. Clarence A., Clay) holds degrees from the University of Wisconsin-Madison and two Armed Forces colleges. He is a University of Wisconsin-Madison emeritus professor of journalism and mass communication, emeritus affiliate professor of wildlife ecology/environmental studies, and emeritus dean of inter-college programs/special students/summer sessions.

The founding executive editor of *The Journal of Environmental Education*, he is the author, co-author, or editor of 30 books and innumerable research papers and articles in the fields of higher education administration, wildlife conservation, and mass communication, his latest being *Interpreting Public Issues*, with others (Ames: Iowa State University Press, 1991), Retirement 901: A Comprehensive Seminar for Senior Faculty and Staff (Madison, WI: Magna Publications, 1992), and *Reaching Out: How Campus Leaders Can Communicate More Effectively With Their Constituencies*, with Linda Weimer and Jean Lang (Madison, WI: Magna Publication, 1995).

Past president of four higher education associations, Schoenfeld has taught from Arizona State to Alaska and continues to be a consultant to colleges and universities from Maine to Hawaii, as well as to state and federal natural resource management agencies. Before being retired as an Army colonel after rising from private, he served as Commandant of the Wisconsin USAR School and as Reserve Deputy Chief of Public Affairs in the Pentagon.

Schoenfeld is now Contributing Editor of Magna Publications' national monthly newsletter for deans and department chairs, *Academic Leader*.

ROBERT MAGNAN earned a B.A. in English (with teaching certificate) and an M.A. in French at Michigan State University, then a Ph.D. in French (minor: medieval studies) at Indiana University. He taught for 13 years at MSU, IU, and the University of Wisconsin-Madison, with short stints at the Université des Sciences Humaines (Strasbourg, France) and Beloit College (WI).

As a graduate student and faculty assistant, Magnan edited a graduate journal, presented papers at scholarly conferences, published articles in journals and books, translated articles and poetry for publication, collaborated in designing a multidisciplinary course, edited scholarly papers for colleagues, and helped develop language textbooks.

Magnan is currently Senior Editor at Magna Publications. In his work with Magna, he has edited *147 Practical Tips for Teaching Professors* (1989) and *First Steps to Excellence in College Teaching* (1990), and collaborated on *Classroom Communication: Collected Readings for Effective Discussion and Communication* (1989), *Teaching College: Collected Readings for the New Instructor* (1989), *Building Diversity: Recruitment and Retention in the '90s* (1990), *Charting Your Course: How to Prepare to Teach More Effectively*, *The Quality Professor: Implementing TQM in the Classroom*, and *Contemporary Theories of Education* (forthcoming).